First International Conference on Credit Analysis and Risk Management

luncheon keynote speech, Uday Rajan provided an analysis from his University of Michigan working paper that showed the importance of qualitative analysis of credit. On the other hand, at the dinner keynote speech that same day, Lawrence Mielnicki summarized some evidence at his bank (PNC) that subjective rankings of loans add only slightly to the power of statistical models of credit that rely on documented data.

Several panel sessions were devoted to methods of evaluating individual loans. For example, one lending officer provided some insights into the way the lending decision was made at her bank. She indicated the importance of evaluating the financial statements of potential commercial borrowers, but qualitative information is paramount in the lending decision. Asking the right questions of loan applicants and evaluating their responses are crucial in this process. Ratios, such as for debt service coverage and collateral, provide useful inputs into the subjective judgment on a loan applicant's ability to repay debts.

Austin Murphy utilized examples from his own text and supplement (2000, 2010) to explain how qualitative and quantitative data can be integrated in an integrated fundamental framework. Subjective evaluations of the future outlook for cash and coverage ratios are necessary in order to determine the risk of a debtor default. He asserted that the human mind has an incredible ability to analyze far more information than pure statistical models, which leave out many obscure factors that sometimes are only important in some circumstances. While recognizing the usefulness of mathematical models of credit, especially in terms of reducing the costs associated with human judgment, he recommended that human judgment should at least be applied to a sample of any loans that are made based strictly on mechanical credit scores or statistical relationships. Failure to do so can cause vital factors to be ignored that human common sense can easily pick up, such as with respect to statistical models resulting in continuing to issue approvals for NINJA (No Income and No Job or Assets) mortgages and no-doc loans (often called "liars loans" because there was no requirement to document the information on the loan application). He further proposed that asset-backed securities should gather and disclose lender qualitative ratings of the borrowers' 5 C's of credit (character, capacity, capital, collateral, and conditions) that may provide useful information to the final investors. He hypothesized that it would be optimal if lenders were given significant monetary motivation for the ex-post accuracy of such ratings in predicting defaults (and less incentives for just loan volume).

Patrick Sperti supplied an example of the way a commercial loan application is analyzed at his bank (Fifth Third Bank). Pro forma statements of cash flows are estimated based on an assumption of the loan being granted that provide an estimate of the cushion that exists to make debt service payments. Minimum guidelines for the debt coverage ratios are set for granting a loan request that vary by industry. Minimum collateral requirements also exist that depend on the type of asset being secured by a loan. Despite the minimums, there is also some flexibility in the actual lending decision. For instance, if a loan-to-collateral ratio is too low, a loan might still be granted if the coverage ratio is sufficiently in excess of a minimum and other factors are very positive.

Senthil Ramanth (Head of Credit Risk Analytics at Ace Cash Express) explained a model of how consumer credit is optimally evaluated. Using statistical associations between loan characteristics and subsequent defaults, a cutoff score can be computed that ensures the return on the loan covers the expected value of default losses. The credit losses must take into consideration both the probability of default (as estimated statistically) and the present value of any recovery in default net of collection costs. He also provided very interesting information on his own area of credit that is payday lending. Payday loans are extended to borrowers using their next payday as collateral. Despite the collateral, there are double-digit default rates because many borrowers don't come back to sign pay back the loan with their their paycheck. While these loans have a high double digit default rate, recoveries in default are also fairly high because failure to pay back dries up one of the borrowers' few sources of credit. While most of the borrowers have poor credit, over 90% of all borrowing applications are granted, as is justified given the very high effective interest rate on the loans (such as 15% over the pay period that might be just a week or two). That rate has to cover both expected default losses and the processing costs of making these typically very small loans. Credit approval is generally based on no prior default with the lender and some evidence of employment such as a pay stub, but there is generally no investigation of the borrower's general credit history.

Many conference sessions were devoted to estimating the probability of default, the payoff in default, or both. Most of the research papers presented relied on statistical or mathematical models, but there was extensive discussion of incorporating qualitative factors into the evaluation of credit. Besides the aforementioned research findings of Lawrence Mielnicki on this subject, a working paper by Lehman (2003) was cited that showed qualitative scores by loan officers were more important than hard data in estimating default losses at a commercial bank in Germany. A more extensive list of articles on the topic of the costs and benefits of qualitative credit analysis was provided in a paper presented by Dror

Parnes, who provided his own theoretical model's simulated results of such judgments.

Joseph Breeden and others provided examples of some of the existing hard data that has in the past been ignored by some lenders. For instance, the seasoning of loans is an important factor in determining default rates, with defaults tending to be lowest in the initial years after origination of a loan or bond. Higher returns are therefore earned early in the life of loans that may promote investment in risky new credits that actually have poor long-term risk-reward tradeoffs.[3]

Several sessions were also devoted to examining the effect of business cycles on defaults that showed credit portfolio risk and correlations vary at different points in those cycles. A few of the sessions also examined the riskiness of pooled debt securities like collateralized debt obligations (CDOs) that included an analysis of CDO-squareds, which are CDOs backed by CDOs by Erick Heitfield. In addition, one panel discussion was devoted to sovereign risk analysis that incorporated an explanation of an article by Altman and Rijken (2011), who empirically showed how aggregated Z scores for the corporate sector of a country can be used to anticipate the risk of default by the country itself on its own debts. Several of the articles presented at the conference that generated interesting discussions have either been published or accepted for publication.

For instance, one paper presented by Austin Murphy (2011) showed that the deregulation of credit default swaps (CDSs) was a major factor in causing the credit boom that led up to the 2008 crisis. In particular, without a requirement to disclose CDS positions and the risks associated with them, financial institutions were motivated to insure as many credits as possible in a process that effectively enabled them to leverage their shareholders' capital without limit, since neither investors nor regulators were fully aware of the risks. As these institutions competed for more short-term income through increasing sales of the CDSs, they began to accept ever lower premiums that then spilled over into dropping credit spreads. To enhance their competiveness in this market, they had an incentive to reduce the costs of evaluating the credits they guaranteed through the CDS sales by computerizing the entire process without costly qualitative analysis or even documentation of the information on loan applications that was input into the mechanical programs. Although there might be large future default losses on those guarantees, they would be largely incurred by uninformed liability-holders and government insurers of the undercapitalized institutions, and the institutions were able to earn

[3] An accounting change to increase the reserve for bad debts in the early life of new debt instruments might reduce incentives for overly zealous credit granting.

high premium income for their shareholders in any event, until the guaranteed debts defaulted. This sort of enormous pyramid scheme was concentrated in the residential mortgage market because it enabled refinancing any debts that couldn't be paid back with rising home equity collateral, which itself continued as long as the flow of credit into real estate continued to increase. To prevent such bubbles and the subsequent inevitable bursting of them with all its associated direct costs to taxpayers,[4] it was suggested that full disclosure of all CDS trading and positions be made available at all times for any institution participating in that market. Requiring capital and reserves to back CDS guarantees were also recommended.

Concluding Remarks

The First International Conference on Credit Analysis and Risk Management was an outstanding learning experience for all.[3] Some of the excellent research papers presented there are published in the Winter 2011 issue of the *Journal of Credit Risk* that was devoted to the conference.

A listing of all the sessions at the conference along with the panelists, presenters, and discussants is provided in Figure 1. While the conference supplied many important insights on credit analysis and risk management, more research into this vital field of finance is certainly merited.

A second conference is being planned for January 3-5, 2013 in Basel, Switzerland, where even more insights into debt markets may be obtained. For updated information on that second conference, please visit the website at http://www.oakland.edu/internationalcreditconference

---

[4] The costs to taxpayers of preventing the 2008 credit crisis from leading to a full financial collapse was explained to be trillions of dollars alone due to the U.S. federal government granting guarantees on enormous amounts of bad debts in order to rescue the financial system. The excess profits on investments that financial institutions were able to earn as a result of U.S. Federal Reserve subsidies to them in the form of cheap or zero-cost bailout financing consisting of trillions of dollars of loans also represents an additional cost, as it effectively transferred money available for open-market purchases in regulating the money supply directly to them, thereby benefitting their creditors and shareholders at the expense of the markets in general, just as did the Federal Reserve paying interest on the reserve balances of depository institutions starting in 2008. All that money might have much more optimally been used to help finance converting defaulting residential loans into shared-appreciation mortgages (SAMs) that would have allowed homeowners to continue to reside in their houses with substantially reduced payments (thereby minimizing the housing collapse and its negative effects on the economy that represent further enormous costs of the bubble).

Figure 1: Topics at the First International Conference on Credit Analysis and Risk Management

Opening Remarks on the History of Credit Analysis by Austin Murphy (Oakland University)
Teleconferenced presentation: CDS Pricing, Spreads, and Risk (Johanna Pleus, Swiss Institute for Banking and Finance)
Panel Discussion on *Credit Analysis of Individual Loans* (Lawrence Mielnicki, PNC and Austin Murphy, Oakland University)
Loan Pricing and Risk Management (Terry Benzschawel, Citibank) Swati Virmani
New Risk Analysis Tools in Accounting—a Modification of the Z-Score (Seong Cho, Oakland University) Fu Liang
Credit Risk in Shipping Finance (Thomas Schumacher, University of Hannover & Deloitte Consulting) Herbert Rijken
Analysis of New Corporate Bond Issues (Igor Kozhanov, University at Buffalo) Hong Qian
Institutional Investor Benefits from Securitization (Anit Deb, TU Darmstadt) Ranadeb Chaudhuri
Credit Rating Changes (Qin Wang, University of Michigan-Dearborn) Igor Kozhanov
The Effect of Allowing Unregulated Credit Default Swaps (Austin Murphy, Oakland University) Dror Parnes
Rating Outlook Review (Herbert Rijken, VU University) Julia Sawicki
Securitization Risk Measurement (Daniel Roesch, University of Hannover) Ranadeb Chaudhurii
Panel Discussion on Teaching Credit Analysis (Austin Murphy, O.U., Kimberly Plunkett, Comerica, Elena Popova, Kresge)
Panel discussion on *Commercial Credit Analysis* (Patrick Sperti, Fifth Third Bank and Lawrence Mielnicki, PNC)
Operating Lease and Credit Assessments (Rick Johnston, Purdue) Mohinder Parkash
Credit to Low Income Mortgagors (Michel Dietsch, University of Strasbourg) Andres Sagner
Practical Consumer Credit Risk Analytics (Senthil Ramanath, Ace Cash Express) Andres Sagner
Modeling Credit Risk (Indranarain Ramlall, University of Mauritius) Rajeev Singhal
Credit Analysis of Financial Statements (Yin Yu and Austin Murphy, Oakland University, Julia Sawicki, Dalhousie University)
Debt Liquidity Premiums (Steven Shin, Ping Chen, Morgan Stanley) Anit Deb

Sovereign Debt Analysis (Kevin Lucey, O'Keefe & Associates, Joe Callaghan, Oakland U., Herbert Rijken, VU University)
Does Modeling Framework Matter? (Yalin Gunduz, Deutsche Bundesbank) Dale Rosenthal
Lunch Keynote Speech: *Importance of Soft Analysis in Credit Evaluation* (Uday Rajan, University of Michigan)
Probability of Default Implied by the Market (Terry Benzschawel, Citibank) Swati Virmani
Implications of CDO Ratings for Originating Banks (Anit Deb, TU Darmstadt) Frank Lehrbass
Estimating Consumer Defaults (Andres Sagner, Central Bank of Chile) Yin Yu
Default Estimates on Low Risk Portfolios (Rung Roengpitya, Pratabjai Nilla-Or, Bank of Thailand) Seong Cho
Estimating Default with Soft Information (Dror Parnes, University of South Florida) Ellen Zhu
Estimating Systematic Risk (Liang Fu, Oakland University) Hong Qian
Analysis of Loss Given Default (Abdolreza Nazemi, University of Karlsruhe) Ellen Zhu
Credit Concentration (Chinmay Naralkar, Aditya Bisen, Goutam Sanyal, ICICI Bank) Rajeev Singhal
Relation between Defaults and Losses (Jon Frye, Federal Reserve Bank of Chicago) Terry Benzschawel
Estimating Mortgage Delinquincies (Qingqing Chen, Office of the Comptroller) Michel Deutsch
Dinner Keynote Speech: *Using Statistics to Analyze Credit* (Lawrence Mielnicki, PNC)
Examples of Statistical Analysis of the Credit Markets (Eric Heitfield, Federal Reserve, and Joseph Breeden, Strategic Analytics).
A Hedge Fund's Perspective on Debt Cycles (Jose Gonzalez-Heres, Morgan Stanley) Hong Qian
Risk Decomposition (Philipp Rindler, European Business School) Fatih Yegenoglu
Insurance Risk (Huong Dang, University of Canterbury) Swati Vermani
Debt Governance and Cost of Debt (Jason Wei, Federal Reserve Bank of New York) Swati Virmani
The Design and Validation of Economic Models (Michael Jacobs, U.S. Treasury) Donna Free
Measuring Credit Risk and Financial Reporting (Julia Sawicki, Dalhousie University)Mohinder Parkash

Earnings Smoothness and Cost of Debt (Ed Owens, University of Rochester) Jason Wei
Measuring Risk (Fatih Yegenoglu, Okan University) Philipp Rindler
Correlated Defaults (Dale Rosenthal, University of Chicago) Chen Qinqing
Credit Risk Management of a Commodity Sales Portfolio (Frank Lehrbass, GMX) Srdjan Stojanovic
Bankruptcy Risks and Costs (Ellen Zhu and Rajeev Singhal, Oakland University) Ed Owens
Portfolio Pricing and Risk Management (Srdjan Stojanovic, University of Cincinnati) Swati Virmani
Hedge Fund Risk Management (Joseph J. Gerakos, University of Chicago) Liang Fu

References

Altman, E. (1968): Financial ratios, discriminant analysis and the prediction of corporate bankruptcy, Journal of Finance, 23, 589-609.
Altman, E., Rijken, H. (2011): Assessing sovereign default risk, Journal of Corporate Finance 23 (Winter), 20-31.
Callaghan, J., Murphy, A., Qian, H. (forthcoming): The First International Conference on Credit Analysis and Risk Management, Cambridge Scholars Publishing: Cambridge.
Lehman, B. Is it worth the while? SSRN manuscript #410186 (2003).
Murphy, A. (2000): Scientific Investment Analysis, Quorum Books: Westport.
—. (2010): Scientific Investment Analysis: Supplement, SIA: Goodlettsville (Fifth Edition).
—. (2011): The effect of allowing unregulated credit default swaps, International Review of Applied Financial Issues and Policy (forthcoming).

CHAPTER ONE

HISTORY OF CREDIT ANALYSIS

AUSTIN MURPHY

The First International Conference on Credit Analysis and Risk Management opened with remarks from me on the History of Credit Analysis. In this brief overview, I explained that once upon a time credit analysis involved the 5 C's of Credit: Character, Capacity, Capital, Collateral, and Conditions. Different lenders put varying degrees of emphasis on the each, with American bankers tending to focus more on Capacity than Capital than continental European lenders for instance. However, it was generally agreed by all that Character was all important.

Although this basic method of credit analysis functioned effectively to channel funds to those most likely to repay the debts, it wasn't extraordinarily efficient as it relied heavily on the subjective judgment of expensive loan officers and credit analysts. As a result, the costs of borrowing that had to pass on these expenses to borrowers were high. Bank training programs in credit analysis, cash budgets indicating how and under what circumstances debts could be repaid, and the use of accounting ratios facilitated the process, but it remained labor intensive.

As computers began to spread across industry, automation of the credit evaluation process began, with Edward Altman's Z-Score published in the *Journal of Finance* in the 1960s being the most famous example. This ratio utilized statistical analysis of a few ratios to predict the risk of default with a particular score. Credit scoring had begun, and it advanced over the next few decades into very sophisticated models. Competition among lenders then allowed the costs of borrowing to fall to levels much closer to those of government paper.

Some lenders even started to utilize pure statistical models to make credit-granting decisions for smaller loans such as for credit cards, automobile loans, and mortgage credit. However, most lenders tended to realize that some qualitative analysis of the loans was still required, at least in audited samples. Most importantly, lenders holding portfolios of loans based strictly on computerized statistical programs could be manipulated into granting credit to riskier borrowers than the models implied from their limited number of parameters.

Securitizations of debts began shortly after the process of simplifying the analysis of credit with a few statistical parameters. The mortgage markets were first, but they themselves relied on documentation of character, capacity, capital, and collateral, including a bona-fide but somewhat subjective appraised value of the underlying real estate. Except in exceptional cases that required qualitative analysis, the loan-to-value ratio had to be below 80%, as lenders had found that in such cases the incentives of the borrowers had to find a way to pay back their loans were extremely high, given their equity investment in the house would be lost along with their home itself if they failed in their contractual amortized repayments of principal and interest.

The markets for securitized debts rose rapidly in subsequent decades, as most mortgages as well as many auto loans and credit cards were put into such pools for public investors to purchase in various packages. Both the enhanced liquidity of the pooled debts and the expedited evaluation procedures for analyzing them enabled the costs of borrowing to be significantly reduced even while lenders and investors enjoyed expanding profits with limited risks.

In 2000, however, the U.S. government was pressured by lobbyists in the banking industry to allow a form of credit insurance without any regulation, capital requirements, disclosure, or oversight. These guarantees of debts were called credit default swaps. There was no limit on how many such guarantees could be sold.

Many financial institutions took advantage of this deregulated environment to issue massive numbers of these credit default swaps in order to maximize their short-term profits from the income that could be received from them in the initial year(s) of loans when the probability of default tends to be much lower than in subsequent years. They employed highly sophisticated mathematical and statistical analysis of the credits to be guaranteed but there was little or no qualitative evaluation of the debts underlying the credit default swaps.

With many of these guarantors of debts being banks and insurance companies with the best credit ratings, and with no one knowing the extent of the risks that existed from the credit default swaps because of the complete lack of disclosure, lenders were motivated to make loans that satisfied the statistical programs of the final loan guarantors without any concern for the risks involved. In particular, the loans would be packaged in pools to be sold to other investors who were willing to buy the securitized products because of the guarantees of the credit default swaps and their Aaa ratings. Over $60 trillion of these credit default swaps were in existence by the year 2008, although no one knew the exact size because there was no disclosure.

In 2007-2008, however, defaults began to rise significantly on many of the debts, many of which were already being called "liar's loans" due to the lack of documentation needed to satisfy the sophisticated computer programs of the guarantors of the debts from the credit default swap issuers. Many "no-doc" loans were indeed made without a requirement to provide tax returns or other documented evidence of income or capital, nor without a requirement for a bona-fide appraisal of the underlying collateral of the loan. Loans were even made with the loan value being less than the collateral value to borrowers without documented income as the guarantors' statistical programs assumed they could be refinanced with rising values in the collateral that was typically residential real estate. Thus, NINJA loans, i.e., loans to borrowers with No Income and No Job or Assets were justified according to the sophisticated statistical analysis and therefore made because the computer programs enabled a guarantee to be provided on them.

As default rates on the NINJA and similar loans rose, the market prices of these debts began to fall, as investors started to lose confidence in the ability of the credit grantors to make payments to cover losses on the debts. Under the terms of the credit default swap contracts, more collateral had to be posted by the credit guarantors to cover the expected rise in payoffs that were implied by the falling market prices. A liquidity crisis ensued that caused market prices of debts to fall dramatically, thereby leading to further doubts about the ability of financial institutions to survive and cover their obligations, whose full extent was unknown. Only a massive bailout in excess of $20 trillion in lending, capital infusions, purchase of bad debts, and guarantees of credits by the U.S. government prevented a complete financial market collapse.

The moral of the story of course is to re-regulate the market for credit default swaps. Such regulation requires at the very minimum full disclosure of the extent of the exposure of any issuer on any day, so that markets can determine if any particular institution has taken on too much risk and therefore penalize it in a timely fashion via market prices themselves. Capital and reserves to cover losses should also be required for all such positions.

It would also seem to be useful if business schools across the world began to teach credit analysis to all their finance majors. The mistakes that led to the 2008 crisis would likely have been avoided if the leaders of the world's major financial institutions had a better understanding of the intricacies of credit analysis.

CHAPTER TWO

LUNCHEON KEYNOTE SPEAKER

The luncheon keynote speaker provided an enlightening and entertaining talk on the usefulness of qualitative judgments in the evaluation of credit. The slides attached to the Appendix of this chapter summarize the remarks well and need no further elaboration.

After the speech, the problem of incorporating qualitative judgments into the process of credit analysis was briefly discussed. One suggestion advanced by Austin Murphy was to have a significant portion of the variable income of lending officers be based on qualitative ratings they give to borrowing applicants. These ratings could be normalized statistically for any racial or gender bias on the part of the individual officer to ensure no discrimination. Such ratings would then be provided in the documentation that is available to investors in securitized products into which the loans might be sold. These kickbacks to lending officers would be shared with their lending institutions in order to provide incentives to the employers to hire and train good credit analysts.

Deductions from servicing income on securitized loans would also be taken from lending institutions with ratings by their officers that have proven to be poor indicators of default losses. Such deductions would provide further motivation to the lending institutions to replace lending officers who are poor evaluators of credit, as well as motivate them to have higher standards for hiring lending officers and training them in the art of credit analysis.

The various additional payments and deductions would be incorporated into the contractual cash flows involved in any securitization. To some extent, the variable payments and deductions would provide an offset to default losses on the pooled loans. In addition, since such payments would optimally replace a large portion of the commission income to lending officers and their employers, it should result in an increase in both information and loan quality without any net increase in costs.

Hard versus Soft Information

- Concepts are intuitive but imprecise.
    - "I cannot define an elephant, but I can recognize one when I see it."
- Hard information: easily obtainable, verifiable.
    - E.g., financial statements of a firm, tax returns of borrower.
    - We can write contracts on hard information.
- Soft information: more costly to obtain, not verifiable to a third party. (Stein, 2002).
    - "Trustworthiness" of borrower.
    - Professionalism, "Honesty".
    - What is the likelihood the borrower will default?
- More broadly, soft information may encompass information that is costly to verify, so remains unverified.

Benefits of Soft Information

- Is soft information valuable in credit evaluation? Of course.
- The world is populated by good and bad types of borrowers.
  - Hard information is sometimes not enough to distinguish between them.
- The role of capital markets is to allocate capital toward positive NPV projects.
- Unless all available information is used, capital may be misallocated.
  - Lower profits for lenders.
  - Overall loss of social welfare.

What Borrowers/Loans Are Most Affected?

- In what credit situations is soft information most important?
- Young and small firms.
  - High failure rate, no credit history, no reputation to maintain.
- Individuals with low wealth or assets.
  - No collateral to back debt.
- Large loans.
- That is, it is most important for the riskiest loans.

Why Does the Distinction Matter?

- Hard information is verifiable, so can be contracted upon.
  - Easier to provide a loan officer with incentives to acquire hard information.
- Incentives to acquire soft information affected by organizational design and market changes.
  - Soft information fragile, is easily "lost".
- Stein (2002): soft information lost in hierarchical/large firms.

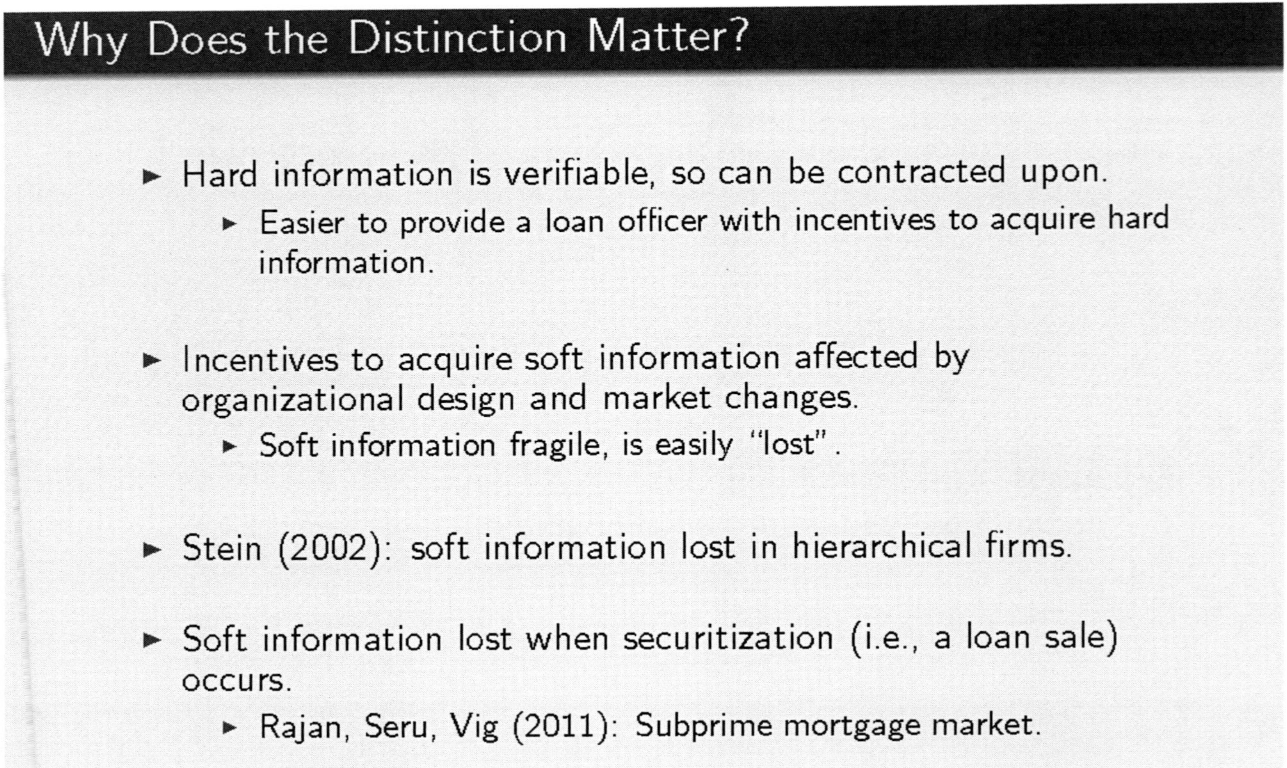
Why Does the Distinction Matter?
Hard information is verifiable, so can be contracted upon.
Easier to provide a loan officer with incentives to acquire hard information.
Incentives to acquire soft information affected by organizational design and market changes.
Soft information fragile, is easily "lost".
Stein (2002): soft information lost in hierarchical firms.
Soft information lost when securitization (i.e., a loan sale) occurs.
Rajan, Seru, Vig (2011): Subprime mortgage market.

Securitization and Distance

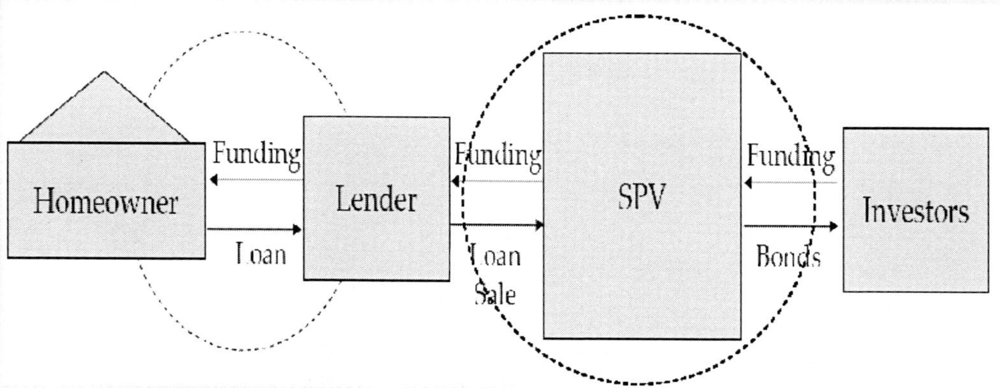

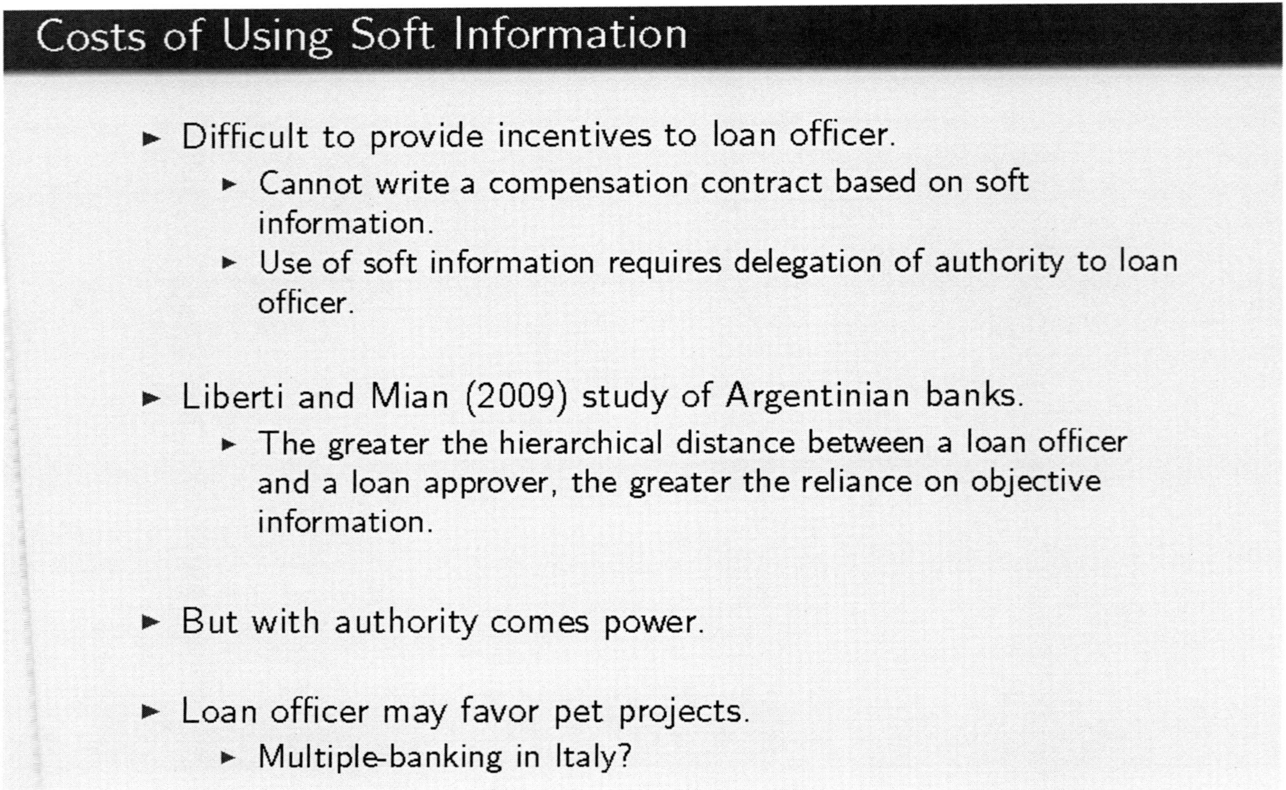
Costs of Using Soft Information
Difficult to provide incentives to loan officer.
Cannot write a compensation contract based on soft information.
Use of soft information requires delegation of authority to loan officer.
Liberti and Mian (2009) study of Argentinian banks.
The greater the hierarchical distance between a loan officer and a loan approver, the greater the reliance on objective information.
But with authority comes power.
Loan officer may favor pet projects.
Multiple-banking in Italy?

Soft Information or Bias?

- Lender may believe he has soft information, but may just be biased.
- Ravina (2008) study of prosper.com data.
- Beauty has value.
  - "Beautiful" borrowers pay 81 bp less on loans, more likely to get funded.
  - "Average" borrowers effectively pay 141 bp more on loans.
  - But beautiful borrowers default at higher rates.
- Black borrowers pay about 140 bp less than white borrowers, default at lower rates.
- Lenders more willing to lend to borrowers who are similar to themselves.

Identifying the Importance of Soft Information

- How can academics uncover the importance of soft information in credit evaluation?
- Difficulty: soft information, by definition, is unverifiable by a third party.
  - So often unobserved by an econometrician as well.
- Possible approaches to testing:
  1. Consider large versus small banks.
     Berger, Miller, Petersen, Rajan and Stein (2005).
  2. Consider dependence on hard information.
     Rajan, Seru and Vig (2011).
  3. Consider banks/firms which require loan officer to provide a quantitative assessment of soft information or overall quality.
     - Liberti and Mian (2009), Agarwal and Hauswald (2011): banks.
     - Einav, Jenkins, Levin (2009): Subprime auto loans.

Small Business Lending: Framework

- Framework comes from Berger and Udell (2002).
- Relationship lending especially important for small businesses.
  - Relationship lending depends heavily on soft information.
- Soft information collected by loan officer, hard to share with rest of management team.
  - Leads to agency problems between loan officer and bank.
- Small banks make more efficient use of soft information.
- Bank consolidation is therefore a matter of concern.

Small Business Lending: Tests

- Berger, Miller, Petersen, Rajan and Stein (2005).
- Large banks lend to larger firms.
- Large banks lend at a greater geographical distance.
- Borrowers from large banks have fewer face-to-face meetings with loan officer.
- Large banks enter shorter, less exclusive relationships.
- All findings are consistent with small banks being better able to manage soft information.

Technology and Soft Information contd.

- Petersen and Rajan: Changes in technology imply that distance is less important.
- Agarwal and Hauswald (2011): Distance still matters in collecting soft information.
- AH look at loan applications by small firms to single large bank.
- Regress

$$\ln(\text{PropScore}_i) = \beta_0 + \beta_1 \cdot XCI_i + \beta_2 \cdot XNRM_i + u_i.$$

- Residual u_i represents soft information.
    - Affects availability and pricing of credit in local area.

Illustration of Lucas Critique

- Securitization increases distance between borrower and investor.
  - Soft information difficult to transmit to investor.
  - Some verifiable information also may not be reported to investor.
- Incentive effect: Lender focuses on characteristics reported to investor (hard information).
  - Worse quality loans issued among borrowers with same observable characteristics.
  - Changes relationship between observable borrower/loan characteristics and default likelihood.
- Leads to a systematic failure of statistical default models: Defaults increase in set of borrowers for whom unreported information is valuable.
- Applies to any statistical model that uses observed variables without adjusting for ‘changed meaning’ of the variables.

Hypotheses

- Implications for both interest rates and defaults.
- Hypothesis 1: After securitization, r_i depends more intensively on X_i, the variables included in contract between lender and investor.
- Hypothesis 2: After securitization, r_i is a worse predictor of default.
- Hypothesis 3: After securitization, keeping fixed X_i, defaults increase in set of borrowers for whom excluded variables are more informative.
  - Low-documentation loans, borrowers with low FICO scores and high LTV ratios.

Intuition

- On each borrower i, lender chooses:
  (i) whether to make a loan. Let $A_i = 1$ if loan is made.
  (ii) interest rate on loan, r_i.

- Let $X_i =$ hard (verifiable) information reported to investor.
  $Z_i =$ other hard and soft information lender can obtain, not reported to investors.

- If lender retains loans, A_i, r_i depend on X_i, Z_i.

- Now suppose lender sells all loans to investors.
  - Price paid by investor on loan i depends only on r_i and X_i.
  - Costly for lender to collect Z_i, so it stops doing so.

- After securitization, A_i, r_i depend only on X_i.

Data

- Primary data set: Newly-issued securitized mortgage loans in the subprime sector.
  - As of December 2006: includes 7 million active loans.
    - Vendor estimate: covers 90% of securitized subprime market.
- Primary data set includes all variables reported by lender to investor.
  - Important variables: FICO score and Loan-to-Value (LTV) ratio.
- Secondary data set: loans issued by New Century Financial Corporation (NCFC).
  - 2nd largest subprime mortgage lender in 2006.

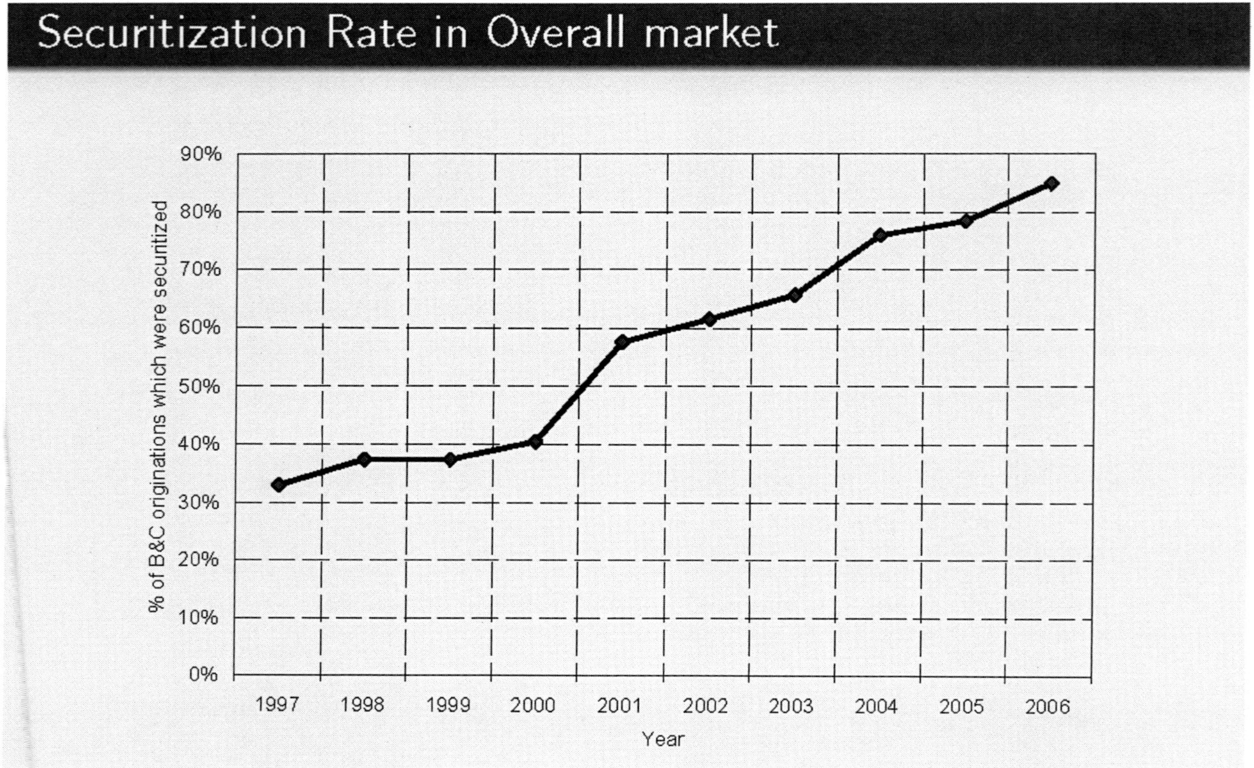
Securitization Rate in Overall market
% of B&C originations which were securitized
90%
80%
70%
60%
50%
40%
30%
20%
10%
0%
1997
1998
1999
2000
2001
2002
2003
2004
2005
2006
Year

Testing the Hypotheses

- In the aggregate, securitization in subprime mortgage sector increases sharply over time.
- We consider 1997–2000 to be a low securitization regime. 2001–2006 is a high securitization regime.
- The bulk of our tests examine changes in the data over time.
  - Some cross-sectional tests on defaults.
- Time series properties are important for a regulator. Difficult to predict changes in the time series.

Reliance on Reported Information

- Consider the following regression, run year-by-year:

$$r_i = \alpha + \beta_{FICO} \times FICO_i + \beta_{LTV} \times LTV_i + \epsilon_i.$$

- Examine R^2 of regression over time.

Evidence from Single Lender: NCFC

- Consider data from New Century Financial Corporation.
  - Large lender in subprime mortgage market.
  - Data set contains both retained and securitized loans.
- Contains information used by lender but not reported to investors.
- NCFC constructs internal rating measure ("Rating").
- R^2 of base model increases from 11% to 27% over time.
- Contribution of internal rating measure to R^2 falls over time.
  - Also, internal rating measure less important in Accept/Reject decision over time.

Defaults and Interest Rates

- Default $\equiv$ Delinquent for at least 90 days.
- For loan i issued at time t, define

$$\text{Actual Default}_{it} = \begin{cases} 1 & \text{if loan defaults within 24 months} \\ 0 & \text{otherwise.} \end{cases}$$

- Interest rate captures lender's assessment of riskiness of loan.
  - Lender considers borrower and property specific information.
  - Also accounts for lender's expectation about future economic conditions.
- Regress default event on interest rates, year-by-year, logit.

$$\text{Prob}(\text{Actual Default}_{it} = 1) = \Phi(\beta_0 + \beta_r r_{it}).$$

Underperformance of Default Models

- For 1997–2000 (low securitization regime), estimate

$$Pr(\text{Default}=1) = \Phi\begin{pmatrix} \beta_0 + \beta_{FICO} \times FICO + \beta_{LTV} \times LTV + \\ \beta_r \times r + \beta_{ARM} \times ARM + \\ \beta_{Pre} \times Prepenalty + \gamma^s \end{pmatrix}$$

- Interact all variables with low-documentation dummy I^{Low}.

Actual vs Predicted Defaults

- For each year 2001–2006, for each loan issued, compute a predicted default probability:

$$Pr(\widehat{\text{Default}}_{i,t+k} = 1) = \Phi(\widehat{\beta}_0 + \widehat{\beta}.X_{i,t+k} + \widehat{\gamma}^s)$$

- Prediction $\text{Error}_{i,t}$ = Actual $\text{Default}_{i,t}$ − Predicted $\text{Default}_{i,t}$.

- Predicted Default as of time loan is issued.
  - Actual defaults in next two years will depend on realized path of macro conditions, house prices, borrower-specific shocks.

- Absent a change in screening standards, the prediction errors should be uncorrelated with X variables, should average out to zero across up and down states of economy.

Mean Prediction Error

- Plot kernel density of prediction errors in each year.
  - Too much data to plot loan-by-loan.
  - Instead, average out errors across loans at each FICO score.
  - Call this "mean prediction error" at that FICO score.
- Plot the kernel density of the mean errors.
- Prediction errors are overwhelmingly positive.
  - Few observations below zero.

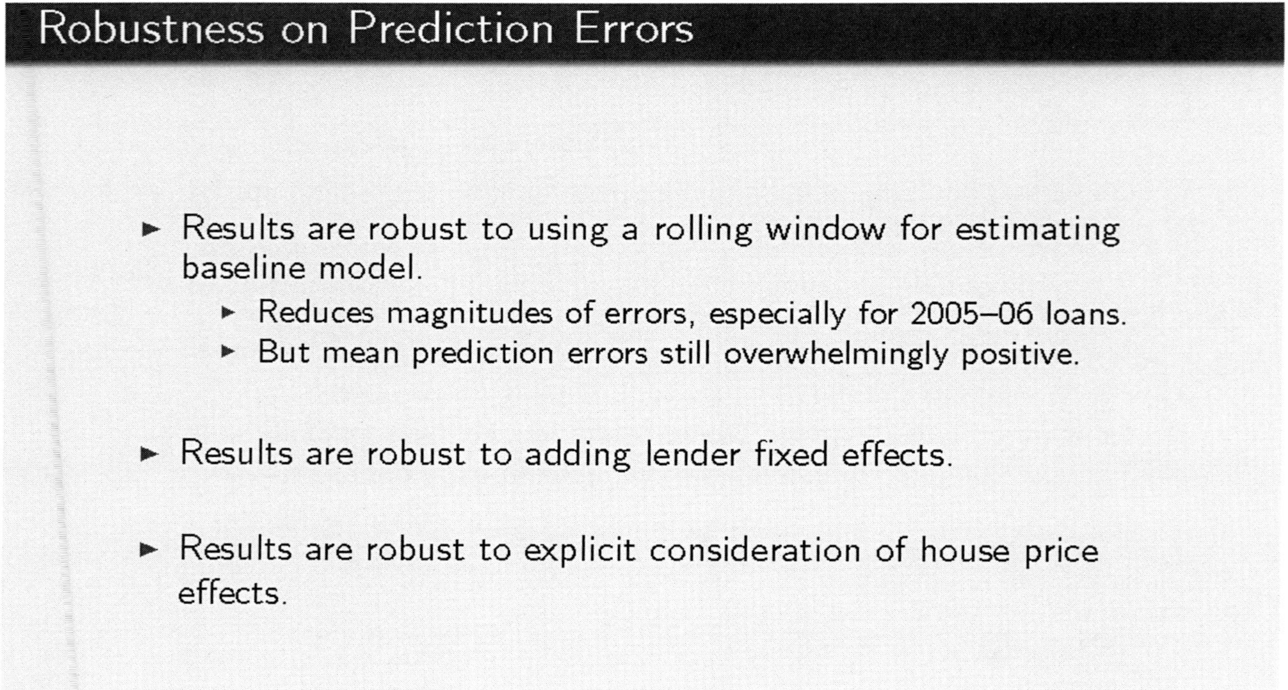
Robustness on Prediction Errors
Results are robust to using a rolling window for estimating baseline model.
Reduces magnitudes of errors, especially for 2005–06 loans.
But mean prediction errors still overwhelmingly positive.
Results are robust to adding lender fixed effects.
Results are robust to explicit consideration of house price effects.

Placebo Test

- Consider performance of model in low securitization regime.
  - Consider default predictions for 1999–2000 loans.
- Estimate model for 1997 and 1998 to make 1999 predictions. Estimate model for 1997–1999 to make 2000 predictions.
- No change in lender incentives over this period. Should deliver zero prediction errors on average.

Hard Information Variables Change

- Liquid market for a complicated security typically relies on a fundamental valuation model.
    - Construct and validate the model with previous data.

- Securitization leads to an incentive problem: Lender focuses on parameters reported to investors, ignores soft information.
    - Predictable change in quality of loans issued, based on information reported to investors.
    - Leads to systematic underprediction of default models as we move from low securitization regime to high securitization regime.

- Meaning of hard information variables (i.e., implications for default) changes across regimes.

- Findings caution against blind use of statistical default models to regulate market participants or value securities.

Conclusion

- Soft information in credit evaluation remains important.
- Technological changes have led to more efficient use of hard information.
  - Perhaps an over-reliance on hard information.
- Degree of delegation to loan officer depends on trade-off between incentives to collect soft information and agency costs.
- Hard information itself may change its meaning in response to market forces.

Bibliography

- The talk has been based on the following research papers.

- Agarwal, S. and R. Hauswald (2011), "Distance and Private Information in Lending," *Review of Financial Studies* 23 (7): 2757–2788.
- Berger, A., N. Miller, M. Petersen, R. Rajan and J. Stein (2005), "Does function follow organizational form? Evidence from the lending practices of large and small banks," *Journal of Financial Economics* 76 (2): 237–269.
- Berger, A. and G. Udell, "Small Business Credit Availability and Relationship Lending: The Importance of Bank Organisational Structure," *Economic Journal* 112 (477): F32–F53.

Bibliography, contd.

- Liberti, J. and A. Mian (2009), "Estimating the Effect of Hierarchies on Information Use," *Review of Financial Studies* 22 (10): 4057–4090.
- Rajan, U., A. Seru and V. Vig (2011), "The Failure of Models that Predict Failure: Distance, Incentives and Defaults," Working Paper, SSRN.
- Ravina, E. (2008), "Love & Loans: The Effect of Beauty and Personal Characteristics in Credit Markets," Working Paper, SSRN.
- Stein, J. (2002), "Information Production and Capital Allocation; Decentralized versus Hierarchical Firms," *Journal of Finance* 57 (5): 1891–1921.

CHAPTER THREE

SUMMARY OF 7/23/11 KEYNOTE SPEECH AT THE FIRST INTERNATIONAL CONFERENCE ON CREDIT ANALYSIS AND RISK MANAGEMENT

LAWRENCE MIELNICKI

There are many fine papers bound between the covers of this book. They are based on sound research conducted with academic rigor, replicable by other academics or practitioners, with fully disclosed results. This chapter, based on my keynote address at the first International Conference on Credit Analysis and Risk Management at Oakland University in July of 2011, represents the professional observations, opinions, and proprietary research gathered over the past 17 years at three financial institutions and a credit reporting agency. The results I will cite are not fully disclosed nor will they be replicable by the academic community as they were developed from proprietary data sources in perhaps that most rigorous of laboratories: the private sector.

For more than 100 years, banks had been making credit decisions to small businesses in pretty much the same way they made credit decisions to larger firms. A loan officer took an application that included some financial history; the prospects of the industry in which the company was engaged; the prospects of the company based on things like market position and the quality of the company management; and the gut feel of the officer. An assessment was made as to the collateral a prospective business borrow would pledge as well.

While credit scoring for small business has been around since the early 1990's, it's only in the last 10 years that improvements in data and adequate samples of both goods and bads have made it practical for use in driving the credit decisions at banks and other financial institutions. The early small business credit scores were developed and driven off of trade data that did not include much, if any, bank performance. Proprietary research conducted over the past 10 years at 3 major financial institutions leads me to believe that the state of the industry is such that credit scores can be used as the primary, and often sole, decision criteria to extend credit for the majority of borrowers to whom banks lend in their small business portfolios.

Before the creation of interstate banking most small businesses had few options for outside financing. Every small town and even some smaller cities had two or so commercial banks. Business owners banked at say,the First National Bank of Smallville or the Smallville Bank and Trust Company. The small business owner had his personal and business accounts with one of these fine institutions. He may have known the President or at least a Vice President. They played golf together. Their children may have gone to the same schools and their wives probably volunteered on the same committees (remembering this was the 1950's and 1960's). When he had need for working capital or a new piece of equipment, he saw people who he knew and who knew him. He provided the required financial statements which the bankers analyzed with regards to what the prospects of that business were and the quality of the business owner's managerial skills and morals. While the scenario presented above may represent an extreme, a version of this scenario existed in some form in most bank credit decisions. Perhaps the owner and the banker were not good friends but the banker could make inquiries, ask for references, or even drive by the plant to make some qualitative assessment of the creditworthiness of the potential borrower.

With the advent of interstate banking, smaller banks were acquired by larger ones reducing the number banks in the US. Economic theory tells us that the reduction in the number of banks reduced competition and the small business owners in my story should have had less access to capital at a higher cost. Actually the opposite happened. Before, the small business borrower really was limited to the few financial institutions in his town or county. Now, a small business borrower could access the financial resources of banks in the larger financial centers. Additionally, non-bank banks were now also interested in providing funding for the small business. Competition for the loan business of these smaller businesses increased and as it increased, prices dropped consistent with economic theory. Making smaller dollar loans to smaller businesses using methods and paradigms similar to that of large loans to larger businesses was not as profitable in the new environment.

The early credit scorecards for business, built on business trade data of the type historically found in databases such as Dun and Bradstreet, were valuable in reducing the cost of the credit decision for the very small dollar extensions of trade credit, especially when the receivable was due 10,15 or 30 days from the date of invoice. Bankers looked with skepticism on these tools due to the larger amounts borrowed and the longer repayment terms. Even when they were comfortable to start using these credit scores to help inform their decisions, business bankers felt they needed the comfort of the qualitative information of their banking ancestors. Attempts to improve the usefulness of these scorecards for bankers by inviting bankers to contribute application and performance data were not successful at first because the banks were reluctant to share data for fear that competitors could mine their best customers if their performance was reported.

Ten years ago, acknowledging that having historic information on potential customers would help banks make better credit decisions, a group of banks formed the not-for-profit Small Business Financial Exchange (SBFE). In joining the SBFE, banks agree to share information on performance of their customers but agree that the data will only be used for credit decisions and not for marketing purposes. Other credit bureaus have since formed similar bank-specific contributory databases with varying degrees of success. The availability of financial-specific performance has increased the predictability and accuracy of bank loan scorecard models.

There are papers in this book that examine the value of qualitative data in improving the credit risk decision for small business. It goes without saying (and the papers will prove to an academic standard) that qualitative credit data, like the kind our 1960's banker used, can be used to augment financial data in making sound credit decisions. The primary issue, in my opinion, is whether the marginal value gained greater than the marginal cost of acquiring and validating such data?

A number of years ago, I asked seasoned loan officers to rate their loan clients on the: quality of the industry; quality of the company in the industry; the quality of the management; and the experience of the management (not considering number of years since that could be more easily quantified) for loans ranging up to $5 million. The rating scale was 1 to 5 with 1 being the worst and 5 being the best. What I found was that in the eyes of the loan officers, none of their clients were below a 3 in any of the categories and most were 4 and 5. This was a large sample across multiple New England states. There might be an argument that the sample is censored since it represented approved applications for credit, however the officers were rating their entire book that included seasoned accounts. It is unreasonable to believe that years after an initial censoring (credit decision) that there was no degradation in the quality of the credits in the subjective eyes of the loan officers.

More recently while developing credit risk scorecards on data up to $3 million in exposure, an attempt to include policy (qualitative) variables. In the presence of good bureau behavior model performance, the policy variables, while statistically significant, provided marginal contribution to the ability to separate potentially good from potentially bad applications for credit. This analysis was not biased by a censored (approved) portfolio but included rejected applications whose subsequent performance was inferred by their credit behavior to other institutions. Additional evidence that objective data and a well fit model can be sufficient to make sound small business credit decisions.

More successful have been attempts to augment financial data with business and consumer credit bureau data in a model to predict risk. Moody's Riskcalc, a widely used model to risk rate privately held firms using acquired financial statement information, was successful at ranking risk. At the same time, a behavior scorecard designed primarily for the smaller credits was available. This scorecard uses business and consumer credit bureaus and internal bank performance data to rank risk. The behavior scorecard, per se was not as predictive in the higher dollar exposure ranges of the portfolio and similarly, Riskcalc, per se, was not as predictive in the lower dollar exposure ranges. Merging the two scores (either augmenting the financial data with the behavioral or augmenting the behavioral with the financial depending on your point of view) raised the predictability. The results are very promising and are summarized below:

Segment	Behavior KS	Risk Calc KS	Combined KS
Whole Portfolio	.339	.347	.430
$250 M to $500 M	.357	.229	.370
$500 M to $1 MM	.396	.495	.542
$1 MM to $3 MM	.311	.471	.496
$3 MM to $5 MM	.311	.360	.386

So we see that in the lower exposure end of the portfolio where the Behavior Score has more power as measured by the Kolmogorov-Smirnov (KS) statistic. In the middle exposure range of the portfolio the behavior score is able to augment the Riskcalc raising the predictability.

The history of making decisions to extend credit to small businesses started with a mix of quantitative (financial) and qualitative (character/ability to manage, etc.) in a time when it was likely that the banker knew or was in the proximity of where the credit decision was being made so this information was readily available. As interstate banking grew, more often than not the credit decision to smaller businesses was being made centrally and the qualitative information was more expensive and less reliable. As the quality of the data in business credit bureaus improved, the ability of bureau behavior models to predict credit behavior also improved for the smallest of the businesses and the smaller exposure loans. Banks, facing more competition for these customers and the concomitant reduction in margins need to make these decisions in a more productive way. This is especially true for the larger, more complex small businesses that require loans at large exposure levels. The combination of vendor financial models and the commercial bureau behavior models will give banks more confidence to make score-assisted loans to larger customers than ever before.

CHAPTER FOUR

COMMERCIAL CREDIT ANALYSIS

AUSTIN MURPHY

This panel discussion largely involved a lending officer for a large bank providing a case analysis of how a decision on a loan application to an individual commercial borrower is made. A spread sheet illustrating the projected cash flows and coverage of debt service payments was provided.

Specific minimum coverage ratios that vary across industry are required, as is sufficient collateral and capital. Nevertheless, qualitative adjustments are allowed, especially between ratios when one or more are weak. The time needed to make a lending decision was stated to be about aweek. However, that time interval included 3-4 days to have the IRS verify taxreturn data provided by the loan applicant.

There were many questions and much discussion from the dozens of session attendees. More research and teaching on this subject would clearly be useful.

CHAPTER FIVE

TEACHING AND LEARNING CREDIT ANALYSIS

AUSTIN MURPHY

In this panel discussion, a case example is provided of how to evaluate an individual corporate credit to a company with publicly available financial statements and other information. The same framework is utilized as for the "Analysis of Individual Loans" that kicked off the live conference, except that the procedures for evaluating the 5 C's of Credit for businesses are different than for individual people. The slides that were presented in the session are reproduced in the Appendix of this chapter for the case of an analysis of an investment in the debts of FEI Company on May 1, 2006, as is explained in more detail in the book *Scientific Investment Analysis* by Austin Murphy (first published by SIA Publishing in 2006).

Subsequently, other panelists, including a lending officer from a large commercial bank and an investment analyst with an institution with billions to invest, commented on how their own method of teaching and learning credit analysis involves more subjective judgment. Such analysis includes asking borrowing applicants the right questions to obtain necessary information. The more formal procedure shown in the Appendix to this chapter incorporates that information into the forecasting step, where the future outlook for the company's coverage ratio of its obligations and its cushion of cash to do so is evaluated. This step is well recognized to be very subjective, and asking the right questions can be very important in drawing the best possible conclusion on the outlook for a company's ability to make its payments on its debts.

In addition, there was some pointing out that the slides given in the Appendix didn't include many adjustments for off-balance-sheet items such as leases for which bank lending officers and credit analysts invariably adjust. Procedures for doing so was indicated to exist in the same referenced *Scientific Investment Analysis* on which the slides are based but were not included in the session material for clarity in presenting the basic material.

Also discussed was use of different coverage ratios, with bankers tending to use a ratio that includes principal as well as interest, whereas bond investors tend to look more at the Times-Interest-Earned (TIE). The widespread use of the latter stems from the fact that investors with access to the public credit markets tend to be able to obtain new credit to pay back principal as long as the interest on the older debts is paid. For smaller borrowers without access to public credit and possible junk financing, there is less assurance that mere coverage of interest payments will enable a firm to obtain new external funds to pay off principal coming due.

Teaching and Learning Credit Analysis

(the "easy" way)

Default Premium = D(1-L) / [1 – {D(1-L)}]
+ Systematic Premium = .05 x DebtBeta
Credit Risk Premium

D = Probability of Default
L = Expected Payoff in Default
DebtBeta = beta of debt (that can be approximated by the average beta of debts With a similar Default Premium)
5% = Estimated Risk Premium per unit of CAPM beta risk

Estimating the Probability of Default (D)

1. Compute average Times Interest Earned (TIE) in past and compare to average TIEs of other companies and their ratings to get a beginning rating
2. Evaluate if the trend in TIE was up or down, and adjust the credit rating up or down accordingly
3. Evaluate if the volatility in TIE is higher or lower than average, and adjust the credit rating up or down based on higher or lower volatility.
4. Determine if the outlook for the average and volatility of the TIE is going to get better or worse (and raise or lower the credit rating accordingly).
5. Do a cash budget to determine if there is above or below average liquidity to meet payment obligations (and adjust the credit rating accordingly up or down)

Table of Past Defaults, Losses, TIEs, and Betas

1 Credit Rating	2 Default Probability	3 Default Losses.	4 TIE	5 Beta
Aaa	0.10%	0.04%	16.1	0.03
Aa	0.15%	0.07%	11.1	0.09
A	0.23%	0.13%	6.3	0.18
Baa	0.50%	0.33%	4.1	0.27
Ba	1.95%	1.29%	2.3	0.36
B	2.83%	1.87%	1.2	0.45
Caa	3.96%	2.61%		0.54
Ca	10.00%	6.60%		0.57
C	>20.00%	>13.2%		0.60

Estimating the Payoff in Default (L)

1. Estimate what each of the asset categories might be worth in bankruptcy, using past averages as guidelines.
2. Take 5% or more out for bankruptcy costs
3. Pay off secured debt to the extent of the claim or the estimated value of the Collateral, whichever is less
4. Pay off unsecured creditors pro rata (i.e., divide remaining liquidation value by the total unsecured claims that can be computed as all liabilities less income tax liabilities and less any payoffs to secured debts in Step #3).
5. If there is any subordinated debt, transfer their dollar payoff in #4 to the creditors specified to be senior to them (often all interest-bearing debts) until The senior creditors are paid off in full. The subordinated creditors keep whatever is left (or nothing if the senior creditors can't be paid in full from this transfer)

Once D and L are computed, the Default Premium=D(1-L), and the beta is set equal to that of other companies with that Default Premium. After adding these Two to get the Credit Premium, adjustments to that premium can be made for embedded options like prepayment features.

For fixed rate debts, the resulting premium is added to the yield on Treasury debt of the same duration.

For variable rate debts, the premium is the extra yield above the base Treasury rate (or for loans based on Libor, etc., the premium is further adjusted by subtracting the LiborRate-TreasuryRate difference from the adjusted Premium).

Example with Credit Analysis of FEI Company on May 1, 2006

FEI TIE = -5.0 ('05), 3.4 ('04), = 1.9 ('03)

1. Compute Average TIE = 0.1 for FEI, so rating is Caa3 based on average TIE for Caa cos.
2. Evaluate Trend in TIE → no trend for FEI TIE (as up and down), so keep rating at Caa3
3. Volatility in TIE → high volatility (crosses many corresponding credit letter grades and even crosses the suicidal level of 1.0 in the most recent year), so lower to C
4. Outlook in TIE → big improvement in TIE seems likely in the future, with the backlog of new orders up substantially in the first quarter of 2006, with the announcement of a new product that will surpass that of the competition in power, and with industry demand likely to take off. The fact that the negative TIE in 2005 was largely caused by restructuring and write-offs that may be non-recurring and may increase operating profitability in the future even without the outlook for greatly improving demand after the large fall-off in sales In 2004 also contributes to a subjective forecast that the TIEs will increase significantly in the Future without any increase in volatlity, so increase the rating to B3.
5. Evaluate ability to pay bills with Cash budget → See Next Page for FEI; Conclusion: almost certain to be able to pay current Liabilities, so increase the rating to Ba3

Based on past history of default rates for Ba and B companies, the default rate for Ba3 companies is 2.20% per year

Net income before extraordinary items (Inc. St.)		$-78.158	
+Nonrecurring Write-off (Income Statement)		+25.352	
+Nonrecurring Write-Downs (St. of Cash Flows)		+9.631	= 6.408 + 3.223
+Nonrecurring Bond Offering Costs (St. of C.F.)		+1.108	
+Nonrecurring Loss (Inc. St. less 3-yr. average)		+4.900	= 8.5 - [(8.5+0.6+ 1.7)/3]
-Nonrecurring Gain		-0.797	
+Taxes (Income Statement)		+22.375	
=Expected Income before Tax		**-$15.589**	
+Dep. & Amort. (Statement of Cash Flows)		+24.276	= 15.023 + 9.253
=	**Expected Cash Flow before Tax**	**$8.687**	
+	Free Cash (Balance Sheet)	+215.226	= 59.177 + 156.049
+	0.8 x Receivables (Balance Sheet)	+78.700	= (0.8 x 98.330)
=	**Expected Operating Cash Reserves**	**$302.613**	
-	Current Liabilities or CL (Bal. Sheet)	-131.562	
+	Refinancing Accruals in CL (Bal. Sheet)	+58.100	= 9.2 + 5.2 + 43.7
+	Line of Credit (footnote 10)	+20.000	
=	**Expected Total Cash Reserves**	**$249.151**	

To Run out of Cash, need:

Reduction in Average Sales Price of	58.4%	= 249.151/427.229
Increase in Average Cost of Sales of	90.6%	= 249.151/275.406
Reduction in Unit Volume of	164.3%	= 249.151/(427.229-275.406

Asset	% Received	Total Value	Comment
Cash	100%	$20.10	Restricted, unlikely used prior to bankruptcy
+Receivables	90%	0	Probably sold prior to bankruptcy
+Inventories	20%	16.80	Specialized; quickly obsolete
+Deferred inc. tax	0%	0	Usable only if survive to earn taxable profits
+Other Current	10%	3.20	Questionable value in bankruptcy
+Net Property	30%	18	specialty/demo equipment
+LT Mkt Sec, Cash	90%	40.60	Mostly government bonds
+Goodwill	0%	0	
+Purchased Tech.	0%	0	Like goodwill and intangibles
+Deferred Tax	0%	0	
+Other 10%	4.50	Questionable value in bankruptcy	
=Total liquidation value		**$103.20**	
-Legal Fees (10%)		$10.32	Typical bankruptcy costs
=Net Liquidation Value		$92.88	
-Initial Payoff to Secured		$20.70	Credits secured by cash
=Proceeds to Unsecured		$72.18	
/Unsecured Claims		$332.008 = 131.562 -9.021 +225.000 +5.079 – 20.70	
Pro Rata Unsecured Payoff		22%	
X Present Value Factor		x.80	
Value at default		18% of unsecured claim	

Default Premium	= 2.20%(1-.18)	= 1.84%
Systematic Premium = 5%x.45		= 2.25%*
Credit Risk Premium required above T-bond		= 4.09%
+ Yield on T-bond of similar duration as FEI 0s23		= 5.23%
Required Yield on FEI debt w/o embedded options**		= 9.32%

*The default premium, measured as the probability of default multiplied by 1 minus the expected payoff on the date of default, is like a B3 bond, which tend to have CAPM betas of .45 (that are multiplied by a typical 5% risk Premium required on the market portfolio of all assets).
**Because the FEI 0s23 notes were convertible and putable, their required yield was actually far less (despite being callable), as determined exactly by SIA software that utilizes state-of-the-art option valuation methods that incorporate the inputs on credit risk of the probability of default and the expected payoff in default, as well as the relevant parameters on a debt's embedded options.

For a variable-rate loan to FEI based on the 3-month Treasury bill rate, the required spread on the loan would be 4.09%.

For a loan to FEI based on Libor, the spread required would be 4.09% minus LiborRate-TreasuryRate (so if Libor is 30 basis points above Treasury rates At the time of the loan, the spread would be 4.09%-0.30%=3.79% above Libor.).

CHAPTER SIX

ANALYSIS OF INDIVIDUAL LOANS

AUSTIN MURPHY

This panel discussion that kicked off the live conference focused on general procedures utilized to evaluate credit. It began with a theoretical overview of the basic model of credit analysis that essentially involves requiring a credit spread above risk-free government borrowing rates for the risks of a debt. Those risks include the risk of default, the risk of loss in case of default, the risk of systematic losses, the risks of embedded options, and liquidity risks. Because the conference was focused on credit analysis, and because many loans don't have embedded options like prepayment rights, those risks that can be analyzed with purely mathematical models weren't given priority in the discussions.

To provide a numeric content for the model, the panel opened with slides from me on a case example of an analysis of a fictitious loan application from a cartoon character George Jetson, who even had his own credit report. The importance of character as given in that report's history of his past payment delinquencies and bankruptcy makes a loan to him very risky, although it is concluded that sufficient collateral of value to George might make the loan a reasonable investment if the interest rate were high enough. An exact procedure is provided for determining that rate in the session slides that are reproduced in the Appendix to this chapter and that are based on a case problem in *Supplement to Scientific Investment Analysis* by Austin Murphy (first published in 2006 by SIA Publishing).

Subsequently, panelists commented on the costliness of such methods of evaluating smaller loans. The pros and cons of utilizing more computerized analysis was discussed.

Analysis of Individual Loans

Using the George Jetson Case

Estimating Credit Premiums Required

- Default Premium = D(1-L) / [1 – {D(1-L)}]
- + Systematic Premium = .05 x DebtBeta
- Credit Risk Premium

- D = Probability of Default
- L = Expected Payoff in Default
- DebtBeta = beta of debt (that can be approximated by the average beta of debts with a similar Deafult Premium)
- 5%=Estimated Risk Premium per unit of CAPM beta risk

Table of Past Defaults, Losses, TIEs, and Betas

1 Credit Rating	2 Default Probability	3 Default Losses.	4 TIE	5 Beta
Aaa	0.10%	0.04%	16.1	0.03
Aa	0.15%	0.07%	11.1	0.09
A	0.23%	0.13%	6.3	0.18
Baa	0.50%	0.33%	4.1	0.27
Ba	1.95%	1.29%	2.3	0.36
B	2.83%	1.87%	1.2	0.45
Caa	3.96%	2.61%		0.54
Ca	10.00%	6.60%		0.57
C	>20.00%	>13.2%		0.60

George's Loan Situation

- George Jetson is requesting a $10,000 1-year loan when the 1-year Treasury yield is 4.5%. The loan is not prepayable.
- Assuming a 3% transaction cost on the loan, what rate of return would you require?
- Assuming the loan could be packaged into a very liquid personal loan pool for an administrative and selling cost of 1%, what rate of return would you require?
- A cash budget for George Jetson revealed that he could save $9800 per year from his stable $50,000 in pretax salary. Besides the one automobile upon which there is currently a lien, he also owns two other cars, and the estimated wholesale value of those 3 cars is $10,000 total.

Analysis and Proposed Loan Terms

- The loan request exceeds the customer's expected savings from income and could probably not be paid back on time. However, Jetson could state that he could draw on his credit cards to pay back the differential.
- Because interest on the loan plus a substantial portion of the principal could be paid back in 1 year, this loan could potentially be restructured as a 1.5 to 2 year installment loan. Sufficient cash flow exists to pay off such a loan. In addition, monthly payments would help ensure that the savings from the monthly paycheck did actually get paid on the loan being made here.
- The customer has a very poor credit history that includes numerous delinquencies as well as court judgments and even a bankruptcy. The existing auto loan is even past due. The risk of default is high, unless proper controls are put on the individual to ensure that the forecasted savings are actually used to pay back the loan (and not spent or consumed instead).

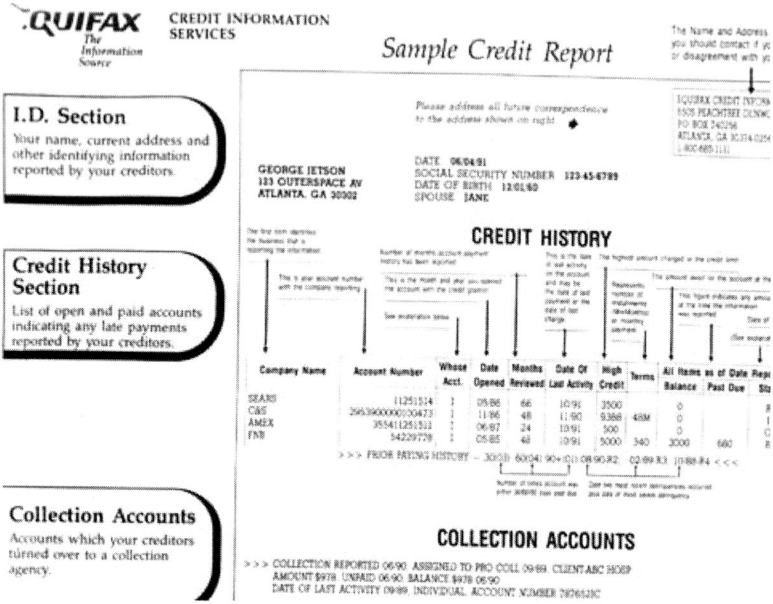

Proposed Loan Terms

- One possibility would be to refinance the auto loan, using all autos as collateral on a smaller $8000 loan (including $3000 to pay off the existing auto loan) that would be paid off in 12 monthly installments. The customer would have little incentive to default, because he would then lose his autos. However, given the individual's past history, even defaulting on secured loans before, as well as being delinquent, the probability of default remains high (at least 20%). In default, one would be able to get back perhaps half the value of the autos, or $5000 (net of the expenses of repossession).
- Therefore, the required return would be

	Risk-free rate	4.50%	
+	Default Premium	11.11%	= 0.2(0.5)/[1 -(0.2)(0.5)]
+	Systematic Premium	3.00%	= for C rated risk = (.05x.60)
+	<u>Transaction cost Premium</u>	<u>3%</u>	
=	**Required return**	**21.61%** (or 19.61% if loan can be securitized)	

CHAPTER SEVEN

TOWARD A BOTTOM-UP APPROACH TO ASSESSING SOVEREIGN DEFAULT RISK: AN UPDATE[1]

EDWARD I. ALTMAN AND HERBERT RIJKEN[2]

Abstract

We propose a totally new approach toward assessing sovereign risk by examining rigorously the health and aggregate default risk of a nation's private corporate sector. Models such as our new Z-Metrics™ approach can be utilized to measure the median probability of default of the non-financial sector cumulatively for five years, both as an absolute measure of corporate risk vulnerability and a relative measure compared to other sovereigns and to the market's assessment via the now liquid credit-default-swap market. Specifically, we measure the default probabilities of listed corporate entities in nine European countries, and the U.S.A., as of 2009 and 2010. These periods coincide with the significant rise in concern with sovereign default risk in the Euro country sphere. We conclude that our corporate health index of the private sector measured at periods prior to the explicit recognition by most credit professionals, not only gave an effective early warning indicator but provided a mostly appropriate hierarchy of relative sovereign risk. Policy officials should, we believe,

---

[1] This is an updated version of the article originally published in The Journal of Applied Corporate Finance, vol.23, No. 3, Winter, 2011.

[2] Edward Altman is the Max L. Heine Professor of Finance, NYU Stern School of Business, ealtman@stern.nyu.edu. Herbert Rijken is Professor of Finance, Vrije University, Amsterdam, the Netherlands, hrijken@feweb.vu.nl.The authors would like to thank Dan Balan and Matthew Watt of RiskMetrics Group, a subsidiary of MSCI, Inc., for computational assistance, and Brenda Kuehne of the NYU Salomon Center for her research assistance.

nurture, not penalize, the tax revenue paying and jobs generating private sector when considering austerity measures of distressed sovereigns.

During the past four years, bank executives, government officials, and many others have been sharply criticized for failing to anticipate the global financial crisis. The speed and depth of the market declines shocked the public. And no one seemed more surprised than the credit rating agencies that assess the default risk of sovereign governments as well as corporate issuers operating within their borders.

Although the developed world had suffered numerous recessions in the past 150 years, this most recent international crisis raised grave doubts about the ability of major banks and even sovereign governments to honor their obligations. Several large financial institutions in the U.S. and Europe required massive state assistance to remain solvent, and venerable banks like Lehman Brothers even went bankrupt. The cost to the U.S. and other sovereign governments of rescuing financial institutions believed to pose "systemic" risk was so great as to result in a dramatic increase in their own borrowings.

The general public in the U.S. and Europe found these events particularly troubling because they had assumed that elected officials and regulators were well-informed about financial risks and capable of limiting serious threats to their investments, savings, and pensions. High-ranking officials, central bankers, financial regulators, ratings agencies, and senior bank executives all seemed to fail to sense the looming financial danger.

This failure seemed even more puzzling because it occurred years after the widespread adoption of advanced risk management tools. Banks and portfolio managers had long been using quantitative risk management tools such as Value at Risk ("VaR"). And they should also have benefited from the additional information about credit risk made publicly available by the new market for credit default swaps ("CDS").

But, as financial market observers have pointed out, VaR calculations are no more reliable than the assumptions underlying them. Although such assumptions tend to be informed by statistical histories, critical variables such as price volatilities and correlations are far from constant and thus difficult to capture in a model. The market prices of options—or of CDS contracts, which have options "embedded" within them—can provide useful market estimates of volatility and risk. And economists have found that CDS prices on certain kinds of debt securities increase substantially before financial crises become full-blown. But because there is so little time between the sharp increase in CDS prices and the subsequent crisis, policy makers and financial managers typically have little opportunity to change course.[3]

Most popular tools for assessing sovereign risk are effectively forms of "top-down" analysis. For example, in evaluating particular sovereigns, most academic and professional analysts use macroeconomic indicators such as GDP growth, national debt-to-GDP ratios, and trade and budget deficits as gauges of a country's economic strength and well-being. But, as the recent Euro debt crisis has made clear, such "macro" approaches, while useful in some settings and circumstances, have clear limitations

In this paper, we present a totally new method for assessing sovereign risk, a type of "bottom-up" approach that focuses on the financial condition and profitability of an economy's private sector. The assumption underlying this approach is that the fundamental source of national wealth, and of the financial health of sovereigns, is the economic output and productivity of their companies. To the extent we are correct, such an approach could provide financial professionals and policy makers with a more effective means of anticipating financial trouble, thereby enabling them to understand the sources of problems before they become unmanageable.

In the pages that follow, we introduce Z-Metrics™, as a practical and effective tool for estimating sovereign risk. Developed in collaboration with the Risk Metrics Group, now a subsidiary of MSCI, Inc., Z-Metrics is a logical extension of the Altman Z-Score technique that was introduced in 1968 and has since achieved considerable scholarly and commercial success. Of course, no method is infallible, or represents the best fit for all circumstances. But by focusing on the financial health of private enterprises in different countries, our system promises at the very least to provide a valuable complement to, or reality check on, standard "macro" approaches.

But before we delve into the details of Z-Metrics, we start by briefly reviewing the record of financial crises to provide some historical perspective. Next we attempt to summarize the main findings of the extensive academic and practitioner literature on sovereign risk, particularly those studies designed to test the predictability of sovereign defaults and crises.

With that as background, we then present our new Z-Metrics system for estimating the probability of default for individual (non-financial) companies and show how that system might have been used to anticipate

---

[3] See, for example, Hekran Neziri's "Can Credit Default Swaps predict Financial Crises?" in the Spring 2009 *Journal of Applied Economic Sciences,* Volume IV/ Issue 1(7). Neziri found that CDS prices had real predictive power for equity markets, but that the lead time was generally on the order of one month.

many developments during the current EU debt crisis. In so doing, we make use of the most recent (2009 and 2010) publicly available corporate data for nine European countries, both to illustrate our model's promise for assessing sovereign risk and to identify scope of reforms that troubled governments must consider not only to qualify for bailouts and subsidies from other countries and international bodies, but to stimulate growth in their economies.

More specifically, we examine the effectiveness of calculating the median company five-year probability of default of the sovereign's non-financial corporate sector, both as an absolute measure of corporate risk vulnerability and a relative health index comparison among a number of European sovereigns, and including the U.S. as well. Our analysis shows that this health index, measured at periods prior to the explicit recognition of the crisis by market professionals, not only gave a distinct early warning of impending sovereign default in some cases, but also provided a sensible hierarchy of relative sovereign risk. We also show that, during the current European crisis, our measures not only compared favorably to standard sovereign risk measures, notably credit ratings, but performed well even when compared to the implied default rates built into market pricing indicators such as CDS spreads (while avoiding the well-known volatility of the latter).

Our aim here is not to present a "beauty contest" of different methods for assessing sovereign risk in which one method emerges as the clear winner. What we are suggesting is that a novel, bottom-up approach that emphasizes the financial condition and profitability of a nation's private sector can be effectively combined with standard analytical techniques and market pricing to better understand and predict sovereign health. And our analysis has one clear implication for policy makers: that the reforms now being contemplated should be designed, as far as possible, to preserve the efficiency and value of a nation's private enterprises.

Modern History Sovereign Crises

When thinking about the most recent financial crisis, it is important to keep in mind how common sovereign debt crises have been during the last 150 years—and how frequently such debacles have afflicted developed economies as well as emerging market countries. Figure 1 shows a partial list of financial crises (identified by the first year of the crisis) that have occurred in "advanced" countries. Overall, Latin America seems to have had more recent bond and loan defaults than any other region of the world (as can be seen in Figure 2). But if we had included a number of now developed Asian countries among the "advanced" countries, the period 1997-1999 period would be much more prominent.

Figure 1: Financial Crises, Advanced Countries 1870-2010

	Crisis events (first year)				
Austria	1893,	1989			
Brazil	1898,	1902,	1914,	1931,	1939
Canada	1873,	1906,	1923,	1983	
Czechoslovakia	1870,	1910,	1931,	2008	
China	1921,	1939			
Denmark	1877,	1885,	1902,	1907,	1921,
	1931,	1987			
DEU	1880,	1891,	1901,	1931,	2008
GBR	1890,	1974,	1984,	1991,	2007
Greece	1870,	1894,	1932,	2009	
Italy	1887,	1891,	1907,	1931,	1930,
	1935,	1990			
Japan	1942				
Netherlands	1897,	1921,	1939		
Norway	1899,	1921,	1931,	1988	
Russia	1918,	1998			
Spain	1920,	1924,	1931,	1978,	2008
Sweden	1876,	1897,	1907,	1922,	1931,
	1991				
USA	1873,	1884,	1893,	1907,	1929,
	1984,	2008			

Source: IMF Global Financial Stability Report (2010), Reinhart and Rogoff (2010), and various other sources, such as S&P's economic reports.

The clear lesson from Figures 1 and 2 is that sovereign economic conditions appear to spiral out of control with almost predictable regularity and then require massive debt restructurings and/or bailouts accompanied by painful austerity programs. Recent examples include several Latin American countries in the 1980s, Southeast Asian nations in the late 1990s, Russia in 1998, and Argentina in 2000. In most of those cases, major problems originating in individual countries not only imposed hardships on their own people and markets, but had major financial consequences well beyond their borders. We are seeing such effects now as financial problems in Greece and other southern European countries not only affect their neighbors, but threaten the very existence of the European Union.

Figure 2: Number of Sovereign "Defaults" 1824-2004

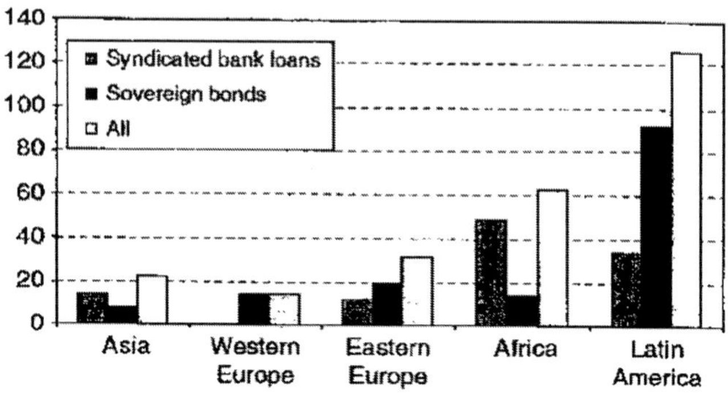

Source: Compilation by Ingo Walter, NYU Stern School of Business

Such financial crises have generally come as a surprise to most people, including even those specialists charged with rating the default risk of sovereigns and the enterprises operating in these suddenly threatened nations. For example, it was not long ago that Greek debt was investment grade, and Spain was rated Aaa as recently as June 2010.[4] And this pattern has been seen many times before. To cite just one more case, South Korea was viewed in 1996 as an "Asian Tiger" with a decade-long record of remarkable growth and an AA- rating. Within a year however, the country was downgraded to BB-, a "junk" rating, and the county's government avoided default only through a $50 billion bailout by the IMF. And it was not just the rating agencies that were fooled; most of the economists at the brokerage houses also failed to see the problems looming in Korea.

[4] On April 27, 2010, Standard & Poor's Ratings Services lowered its long- and short-term credit ratings on the Hellenic Republic (Greece) to non-investment grade BB+; and on June 14, 2010, Moody's downgraded Greece debt to Ba1 from A2 (4 notches), while Spain was still Aaa and Portugal was A1. Both of the latter were recently downgraded. S&P gave similar ratings.

What Do We Know about Predicting Sovereign Defaults?

There is a large and growing body of studies on the default probability of sovereigns, by practitioners as well as academics.[5] A large number of studies, starting with Frank and Cline's 1971 classic, have attempted to predict sovereign defaults or rescheduling using statistical classification and predicting methods like discriminant analysis as well as similar econometric techniques.[6] And in a more recent development, some credit analysts have begun using the "contingent claim" approach[7] to measure, analyze, and manage sovereign risk based on Robert Merton's classic "structural" approach (1974). But because of its heavy reliance on market indicators, this approach to predicting sovereign risk and credit spreads has the drawback of producing large—and potentially self-fulfilling—swings in assessed risk that are attributable solely to market volatility.

A number of recent studies have sought to identify global or regional common risk factors that largely determine the level of sovereign risk in the world, or in a region such as Europe. Some studies have shown that changes in both the risk factor of individual sovereigns and in a common time-varying global factor affect the market's repricing of sovereign risk.[8] Other studies, however, suggest that sovereign credit spreads are more related to global aggregate market indexes, including U.S. stock and high-yield bond market indexes, and global capital flows than to their own local economic measures.[9] Such evidence has been used to justify an approach

---

[5] One excellent primer on sovereign risk is Babbel's (1996) study, which includes an excellent annotated bibliography by S. Bertozzi on external debt capacity that describes many of these studies. Babbel lists 69 potentially helpful explanatory factors for assessing sovereign risk, all dealing with either economic, financial, political, or social variables. Except for the political and social variables, all others are macroeconomic data and this has been the standard until the last few years. Other work worth citing include two practitioner reports—Chambers (1997) and Beers et al (2002)—and two academic studies—Smith and Walter (2003), and Frenkel, Karmann and Scholtens (2004). Full citations of all studies can be found in References section at the end of the article.

[6] Including Grinols (1976), Sargen (1977), Feder and Just (1977), Feder, Just and Ross (1981), Cline (1983), Schmidt (1984), and Morgan (1986).

[7] Gray, Merton and Bodie (2006, 2007)

[8] See Baek, Bandopadhyaya and Chan (2005). Gerlach, Schulz and Wolff (2010) observe that aggregate risk factors drive banking and sovereign market risk spreads in the Euro area; and in a related finding, Sgherri and Zoli (2009) suggest that Euro area sovereign risk premium differentials tend to move together over time and are driven mainly by a common time-varying factor.

[9] See Longstaff, Pan, Pedersen and Singleton (2007).

to quantifying sovereign risk that uses the local stock market index as a proxy for the equity value of the country.[10] Finally, several very recent papers focus on the importance of macro variables such as debt service relative to tax receipts and the volatility of trade deficits in explaining sovereign risk premiums and spreads.[11]

A number of studies have also attempted to evaluate the effectiveness of published credit ratings in predicting defaults and expected losses, with most concluding that sovereign ratings, especially in emerging markets, provide an improved understanding of country risks for investment analytics.[12] Nevertheless, the recent EU debt crisis would appear to contradict such findings by taking place at a time when all the rating agencies and, it would seem, all available models for estimating sovereign risk indicated that Greece and Spain—and others now recognized as high-risk countries—were still classified as investment grade.[13] What's more, although most all of the studies cited above have been fairly optimistic about the ability of their concepts to provide early warnings of major financial problems, their findings have either been ignored or have proven ineffective in forecasting most economic and financial crises.

In addition to these studies, a handful or researchers have taken a somewhat different "bottom-up" approach by emphasizing the health of the private sectors supporting the sovereigns. For example, a 1998 World Bank study of the 1997 East Asian crisis[14] used the average Z-Score of

---

[10] See Oshino and Saruwatari (2005).

[11] These include Haugh, Ollivaud and Turner's (2009) discussion of debt service relative to tax receipts in the Euro area; Hilscher and Nobusch (2010) emphasis on the volatility of terms of trade; and Segoviano, Caceres and Guzzo's (2010) analysis of debt sustainability and the management of a sovereign's balance sheet.

[12] For example, Remolona, Scatigna and Wu (2008) reach this conclusion after using sovereign credit ratings and historical default rates provided by rating agencies to construct a measure of ratings implied expected loss.

[13] To be fair, S&P in a *Reuter's* article dated January 14, 2009 warned Greece, Spain and Ireland that their ratings could be downgraded further as economic conditions deteriorated. At that time, Greece was rated A1 by Moody's and A- by S&P. Interestingly, it was almost a full year later on December 22, 2009 that Greece was actually downgraded by Moody's to A2 (still highly rated), followed by further downgrades on April 23, 2010 (to A3) and finally to "junk" status (Ba1) on June 14, 2010. As noted earlier, S&P downgraded Greece to "junk" status about three months earlier.

[14] See Pomerleano (1998), which is based on a longer article by the author (1997). Taking a somewhat similar approach, many policy makers and theorists have recently focused on the so-called "shadow banking system." For example, Gennaioli, Martin and Rossi (2010) argued that the financial strength of governments depends on private financial markets and its ability to attract foreign

listed (non-financial) companies to assess the "financial fragility" of eight Asian countries and, for comparison purposes, three developed countries and Latin America. Surprising many observers, the average Z-Score for South Korea at the end of 1996 suggested that it was the most financially vulnerable Asian country, followed by Thailand, Japan, and Indonesia. As noted earlier, Korea's sovereign bond rating in 1996 was AA- (S&P). But within a year, Korea's rating dropped to BB-; and if not for the IMF bailout of $50 billion, the sovereign would almost certainly have defaulted on its external, non-local currency debt. A traditional macroeconomic measure like GDP growth would not have predicted such trouble since, at the end of 1996, South Korea had been growing at double-digit rates for nearly a decade.[15]

The Z-Metrics™ Approach[16]

In 2009, we partnered with RiskMetrics Group with the aim, at least initially, of creating a new and better way of assessing the credit risk of *companies*. The result was our new Z-Metrics approach. This methodology might be called a new generation of the original Z-Score model of 1968. Our objective was to develop up-to-date credit scoring and probability of default metrics for both large and small, public and private, enterprises on a global basis.

---

capital. They concluded that strong financial institutions not only attract more capital but their presence also helps encourage their governments to repay their debt. Chambers of S&P (1997) also mentions the idea of a "bottom-up" approach but not to the assessment of sovereign risk, but to a corporate issuer located in a particular country. He advocates first an evaluation of an issuer's underlying creditworthiness to arrive at its credit rating and then considers the economic, business and social environment in which the entity operates. These latter factors, such as the size and growth and the volatility of the economy, exchange rates, inflation, regulatory environment, taxation, infrastructure and labor market conditions are factored in on top of the micro variables to arrive at a final rating of the issuer.

[15] Afterwards, the World Bank and other economists such as Paul Krugman concluded that that crony capitalism and the associated implicit public guarantees for politically influential enterprises coupled with poor banking regulation were responsible for the crisis. The excesses of corporate leverage and permissive banking were addressed successfully in the case of Korea and its economy was effectively restructured after the bailout.

[16] For more details, see Altman, et al, 2010 "The Z-Metrics™ Methodology for Estimating Company Credit Ratings and Default Risk Probabilities," *RiskMetrics Group*, continuously updated, available from http://riskmetrics.com/Z-Metrics.

In building our models, we used multivariate logistic regressions and data from a large sample of both public and private U.S. and Canadian non-financial sector companies during the 20-year period 1989-2008.[17] We analyzed over 50 fundamental financial statement variables, including measures (with trends as well as point estimates) of solvency, leverage, size, profitability, interest coverage, liquidity, asset quality, investment, dividend payout, and financing results. In addition to such operating (or "fundamental") variables, we also included equity market price and return variables and their patterns of volatility. Such market variables have typically been used in the "structural distance-to-default measures" that are at the core of the KMV model[18] now owned by Moody's.

In addition to these firm-specific, or micro, variables, we also tested a number of macro-economic variables that are often used to estimate sovereign default probabilities, including GDP growth, unemployment, credit spreads, and inflation. Since most companies have a higher probability of default during periods of economic stress—for example, at the end of 2008—we wanted to use such macro variables to capture the heightened or lower probabilities associated with general economic conditions.[19]

The final model, which consists of 13 fundamental, market value, and macroeconomic variables, is used to produce a credit score for each public company. (And as discussed later, although our primary emphasis was on applying Z-Metrics to publicly traded companies, we also created a private firm model by using data from public companies and replacing market value with book value of equity.)

The next step was to use a logit specification of the model (described in the Appendix) that we used to convert the credit scores into probabilities of default (PDs) over both one-year and five-year horizons. The one-year model is based on data from financial statements and market data

---

[17] Our first model's original sample consisted of over 1,000 U.S. or Canadian non-financial firms that suffered a credit event and a control sample of thousands of firms that did not suffer a credit event, roughly a ratio of 1:15. After removing those firms with insufficient data, the credit event sample was reduced to 638 firms for our public firm sample and 802 observations for our private firm sample.

[18] Developed by Crosbie in 1998 and adapted for sovereigns by Gray in 2007.

[19] In all cases, we carefully examined the complete distribution of variable values, especially in the credit-event sample. This enabled us to devise transformations on the variables to either capture the nature of their distributions or to reduce the influence of outliers. These transformations included logarithmic functions, first differences and dummy variables if the trends or levels of the absolute measures were positive/negative.

approximately one year prior to the credit event, and the five-year model includes up to five annual financial statements prior to the event.

To test the predictive power of the model and the resulting PDs, we segregated all the companies in our sample into "cohorts" according to whether they experience "credit events" that include either formal default or bankruptcy (whichever comes first). All companies that experienced a credit event within either one year or five years were assigned to the "distressed" or "credit event" group (with all others assigned to the non-distressed group).

Our test results show considerable success in predicting defaults across the entire credit spectrum from the lowest to the highest default risk categories. Where possible, we compared our output with that of publicly available credit ratings and existing models. The so-called "accuracy ratio" measures how well our model predicts which companies do or do not go bankrupt on the basis of data available before bankruptcy. The objective can be framed in two ways: (1) maximizing correct predictions of defaulting and non-defaulting companies (which statisticians refer to as Type I accuracy) and (2) minimizing wrong predictions (Type II accuracy).

As can be seen in Figure 3, our results, which include tests on actual defaults during the period 1989-2009, show much higher Type I accuracy levels for the Z-Metrics model than for either the bond rating agencies or established models (including an older version of Z-Scores). At the same time, our tests show equivalent Type II accuracies at all cutoff levels of scores.[20]

Perhaps the most reliable test of credit scoring models is how well they predict critical events based on samples of companies that were not used to build the model, particularly if the events took place after the period during which the model was built (after 2008, in this case). With that in mind, we tested the model against actual bankruptcies occurring in 2009, or what we refer to as our "out-of-sample" data. As with the full test sample results shown in Figure 3, our Z-Metrics results for the "out of sample" bankruptcies of 2009 outperformed the agency ratings and the 1968 Z-score and 1995 Z"-score models using both one-year and five-year horizons.

---

[20] We assessed the stability of the Z-Metrics models by observing the accuracy ratios for our tests in the in-sample and out-of-sample periods and also by observing the size, signs and significance of the coefficients for individual variables. The accuracy ratios were very similar between the two sample periods and the coefficients and significance tests were extremely close.

Figure 3: Type I error for Agency ratings, Z"-score, and Z-Metrics agency equivalent (AE ratings (1989-2008): one year prediction horizon for publicly owned firms

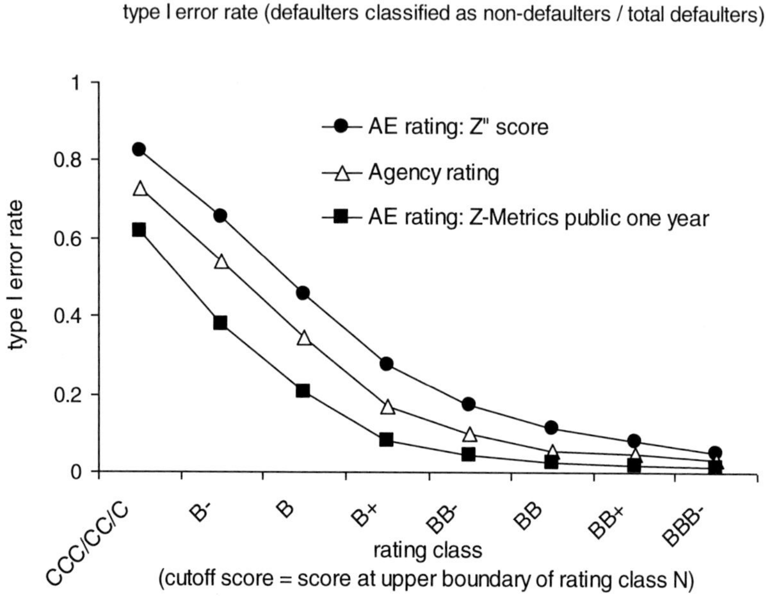

A "Bottom-Up" Approach for Sovereign Risk Assessment

Having established the predictive power of our updated Z-score methodology, our next step was to use that model (which, again, was created using large publicly traded U.S. companies) to evaluate the default risk of European companies. And after assuring ourselves that the model was transferable in that sense, we then attempted to assess the overall creditworthiness of sovereign governments by aggregating our Z-Metrics default probabilities for individual companies and then estimating both a median default probability and credit rating for different countries.

In conducting this experiment, we examined nine key European countries over three time periods, end of 2008, 2009 and 2010 (Figure 4) and again at the end of 2010 (Figure 5), when the crisis was well known. People clearly recognized the crisis and concern for the viability of the European Union in June 2010, when Greece's debt was downgraded to non-investment grade and both Spain and Portugal were also downgraded. Credit markets, particularly CDS markets, had already recognized the

Greek and Irish problems before June 2010. Market prices during the first half of 2010 reflected high implied probabilities of default for Greece and Ireland, but were considerably less pessimistic in 2009. By contrast, as can be seen in Figure 4, which shows our Z-Metric median PD estimates alongside sovereign CDS spreads over both periods,[21] our PD estimates were uniformly higher (more risky) in 2009 than early in 2010, even if the world was more focused on Europe's problems in the latter year. In this sense, our Z metrics PD might be viewed as providing a leading indicator of possible distress. It should be noted that the statistics in Figure 4 report only on the non-financial private sector, while those in Figure 5 include results from our banking credit risk model, as well.

For the first four months of 2010, our Z-Metrics' five-year PDs for European corporate default risk placed Greece (10.60%) and Portugal (9.36%) in the highest risk categories (ZC-ratings), followed by Italy (7.99%), Ireland (6.45%) and Spain (6.44%), all in the ZC category. Then came Germany and France (both about 5.5% - ZC+), with the U.K. (3.62%) and the Netherlands (3.33%) at the lowest risk levels (ZB– and ZB). The U.S.A. looked comparatively strong, at 3.93% (ZB-).

For the most part, these results are consistent with how traditional analysts now rank sovereign risks. Nevertheless, there were a few surprises. The U.K. had a fairly healthy private sector, and Germany and France were perhaps not as healthy as one might have thought. The U.K.'s relatively strong showing might have resulted from the fact that our risk measure at this time did not include financial sector firms, which comprised about 35% of the market values of listed U.K. corporates and were in poor financial condition. And several very large, healthy multinational entities in the U.K. index might have skewed results a bit. The CDS/5-year market's assessment of U.K. risk was harsher than that of our Z-Metrics index in 2010, with the median of the daily CDS spreads during the first four months implying a 6.52% probability of default, about double our Z-Metrics median level. Greece also had a much higher CDS implied PD at 24.10%, as compared to 10.60% for Z-Metrics. (And, of course, our choice of the *median* Z-Metrics PD is arbitrary, implying as it does that fully 50% of the listed companies have PDs higher than 10.60%.)

We also observed that several countries had relatively high standard deviations of Z-Metrics PDs, indicating a longer tail of very risky

---

[21] The median CDS spread is based on the daily observations in the six/four-month periods. The median Z-Metrics PD is based on the median company PDs each day and then we calculated the median for the period. The results are very similar to simply averaging the median PDs as of the beginning and ending of each sample period.

companies. These countries included Ireland, Greece and, surprisingly, Germany, based on 2010 data. So, while almost everyone considers Germany to be the benchmark-low risk country in Europe (for example, its 5-year CDS spread was just 2.67% in 2010, even lower than the Netherlands (2.83%), we are more cautious based on our broad measure of private sector corporate health.

2010 Results

Figure 5 shows the weighted-average median PDs for 11 (including now Sweden and Belgium) European countries and the U.S. as of the end of 2010. Note that we now are able to include PDs for the banking sectors (listed firms only) for these countries, an important addition, especially for countries like Greece, Ireland and the U.K. The results show the large difference between Greece (16.45%) and all the rest, but also that the "big-five PIIGS" stand out as the clear higher risk domains. Indeed, we feel that Italy could be the 'fulcrum" country to decide the ultimate fate of the Euro (see our "Insight" piece in the *Financial Times*, June 21, 2011).

CDS Implied PDs

Figure 6 shows the implied PDs for the "Big-Five" European high-risk countries from the start of 2009 to mid-July 2011, just after the European Union's comprehensive rescue plan was announced (July 21, 2011) for Greece and a contingent plan for other countries. Note that while the PDs, based on CDS spreads and assuming a 40% recovery rate, all came down from their highs, all still imply a considerable default risk.

2010 vs. 2009

As noted earlier from Figure 4, our PD estimates for 2009 were uniformly higher (more risky) than those for early 2010. One important reason for the higher PDs in 2009 is the significant impact of the stock market, which is a powerful variable in the Z-Metrics model—and in many other default probability models (notably, Moody's KMV). Recall that the stock markets were at very low levels at the end of 2008 and into the early months of 2009, while there was a major recovery later in 2009 and in early 2010.

Figure 4: Financial Health of the Corporate, Non-Financial Sector: Selected European Countries and U.S.A. in 2008-2010

Country	Listed Companies	*Z-Metrics PD Estimates: Five-Year Public Model* Y/E 2010 Median PD	Y/E 2009 Median PD	Y/E 2008 Median PD	Five-Year Implied PD *from CDS Spread** 2010	2009	2008
Netherlands	85	3.56%	3.33%	5.62%	2.03%	2.83%	6.06%
U.S.A.	2226	3.65%	3.93%	6.97%	3.79%	3.28%	4.47%
Sweden	245	3.71%	5.31%	6.74%	2.25%	4.60%	6.33%
Ireland	29	3.72%	6.45%	7.46%	41.44%	12.20%	17.00%
Belgium	69	3.85%	5.90%	5.89%	11.12%	4.58%	5.53%
U.K.	507	4.28%	3.62%	5.75%	4.73%	6.52%	8.13%
France	351	4.36%	5.51%	7.22%	4.51%	3.75%	4.05%
Germany	348	4.63%	5.54%	7.34%	2.50%	2.67%	3.66%
Italy	174	7.29%	7.99%	10.51%	9.16%	8.69%	11.20%
Spain	91	7.39%	6.44%	7.39%	14.80%	9.39%	8.07%
Portugal	33	10.67%	9.36%	12.07%	41.00%	10.90%	7.39%
Greece	93	15.28%	10.60%	11.57%	70.66%	24.10%	13.22%

*Assuming a 40% recovery rate (R); based on the median CDS spread (s). PD computed as $1\text{-}e^{(-5*s/(1-R))}$.

Sources: RiskMetrics Group (MSCI), Markit, Compustat.

Figure 5: Weighted Average Median Five-Year (PD) for Listed Non-Financial* and Banking Firms** (Europe and U.S.), 2010

	Non-Financial Firms		*Banking Firms*					
Country	PD (%)	Weight	PD (%)	Weight	Weighted Average (%)	Rank	CDS Spread PD (%)***	Rank
Netherlands	3.56	0.977	11.1	0.023	3.73	1	2.03	1
Sweden	3.71	0.984	17.3	0.016	3.93	2	2.25	2
Belgium	3.85	0.972	12.4	0.028	4.21	3	11.12	8
France	4.36	0.986	14.0	0.014	4.49	4	4.51	5
U.K.	4.28	0.977	15.5	0.023	4.54	5	4.73	6
Germany	4.63	0.983	13.1	0.017	4.77	6	2.50	3
U.S.A.	3.65	0.837	13.8	0.163	5.30	7	3.79	4
Spain	7.39	0.948	10.9	0.052	7.57	8	14.80	9
Italy	7.29	0.906	20.0	0.094	8.48	9	9.16	7
Ireland	3.72	0.906	77.6	0.094	10.65	10	41.44	11
Portugal	10.67	0.971	12.1	0.029	10.71	11	41.00	10
Greece	15.28	0.921	30.1	0.079	16.45	12	70.66	12

*Based on the Z-Metrics Probability Model. **Based on Altman-Rijken Model (Preliminary). ***PD based on the CDS Spread as of 4/26/11.

Figure 6: Five-Year Implied Probabilities of Default (PD)* from Capital Market CDS Spreads, Jan 2009 – Jul 22, 2011**

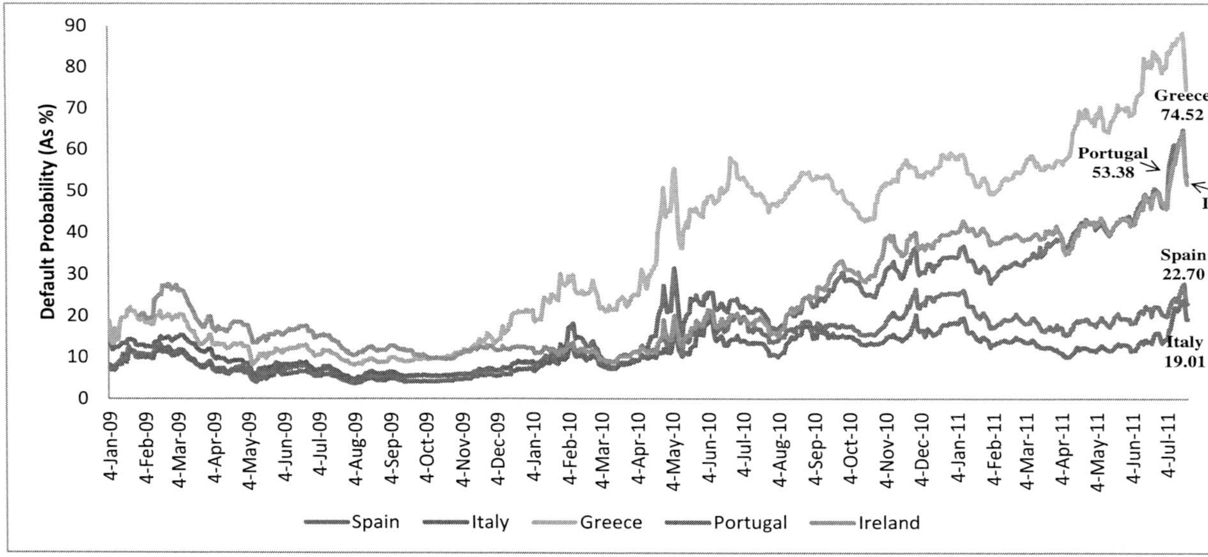

* Assumes 40% Recovery Rate. PD computed as $1\text{-}e^{(-5*s/(1-R))}$. ** On July 19, 2011, PDs for all countries peaked as follows: Greece 88.22, Portugal 64.74, Ireland 64.23, Spain 27.54, and Italy 23.74.
Sources: Bloomberg and NYU Salomon Center.

Figure 7 shows, for each of our nine European countries and the U.S., the percentage increases in median stock market index levels and sovereign PD levels between the first six months of 2009 and the first six months of 2010. As can be seen in the figure, most countries enjoyed increases of greater than 20%. Only Greece had a relatively low increase (5.5%), consistent with its modest improvement in its Z-Metrics PD (-8.4%). Figure 6 shows the percentage improvement (lower risk) in sovereigns' PDs in 2010, which are largely consistent with the increases in stock market index values. Note that Ireland stands out in that while its stock market index value increased by 26.2%, its corporate sector experienced only a modest improvement (-7.4%) in its Z-Metrics' median PD. This may be attributable to the earlier austerity measures taken in Ireland, as compared to those in other distressed European nations. But likely more important were changes in the many other variables in the Z-Metrics model that are not affected by stock prices, particularly the fundamental measures of corporate health.

Figure 7: Median Percentage Change in Various Country Stock Market Index Values and Z-Metrics' PDs Between the First Six Months of 2010 vs. 2009

Country	Index	Median Percent Change (2010 vs. 2009)*	Median Z-Metrics Percent Change (2010 vs. 2009)
France	CAC40	24.1%	-23.6%
Germany	DAX	31.8%	-24.5%
Greece	ASE	5.5%	- 8.4%
Ireland	ISEQ	26.2%	- 7.4%
Italy	FTSEMIB	18.2%	-24.0%
Netherlands	AEX	34.4%	- 25.3%
Portugal	PSI-20	17.8%	-22.4%
Spain	IBEX35	20.9%	-12.9%
UK	FTSE100	27.8%	-37.6%
USA	S&P500	31.9%	-43.6%

*Median of the various trading day stock index values and PDs, first six months of 2009 vs. First six months of 2010.

Sources: Z-Metrics Model calculations from RiskMetrics (MSCI) Group, Bloomberg for stock index values.

Comparing PD Results Based on Privately Owned vs. Publicly Owned Firm Models

As shown in Figures 4 and 5, the improvement (reduction) in Z-Metrics PDs for most countries in 2010—a period in which most EU sovereigns appeared to be getting riskier—looks attributable in large part to the stock market increases in almost all countries. But to the extent such increases could conceal a deterioration of a sovereign's credit condition, some credit analysts might prefer to have PD estimates that do not make use of stock market data.

With this in mind, we applied our private firm Z-Metrics model to evaluate the same nine European countries and the U.S. The private and public firm models are the same except for the substitution of equity book values (and volatility of book values) for market values. This adjustment is expected to remove the capital market influence from our credit risk measure.

Figure 8 summarizes the results of our public vs. private firm Z-Metrics models comparative PD (delta) results for 2010 and 2009. For eight of the ten countries, use of the private firm model showed smaller reductions in PDs when moving from 2009 to 2010 than use of the public model. Whereas the overall average improvement in PDs for the public firm model was a drop of 1.91 percentage points, the drop was 0.79% for our private firm model. These results are largely the effect of the positive stock market performance in late 2009 and into 2010. But improvements in general macro conditions, along with their effects on traditional corporate performance measures, also helped improve (reduce) the PDs. Moreover, in two of these eight countries—the U.K. and France—not only did the public firm model show an improved (lower) PD, but the private firm model's PD actually got worse (increased) in 2010 (as indicated by the positive delta in the last column of Figure 8).

Figure 8: Private Vs. Public Firm Model PDs in 2010 and 2099

	No. Listed Companies		Public-Firm Z-Metrics Model			Private-Firm Z-Metrics Model		
			PDs	PDs		PDs	PDs	
Country	*2010*	*2009*	*2010*	*2009*	*Delta**	*2010*	*2009*	*Delta**
Netherlands	61	60	3.33%	5.62%	-2.29%	5.25%	6.00%	-0.75%
U.K.	442	433	3.62%	5.75%	-2.13%	6.48%	5.97%	+0.49%
U.S.A.	2226	2171	3.93%	6.97%	-3.04%	4.28%	4.80%	-0.52%
France	297	294	5.51%	7.22%	-1.71%	7.33%	7.19%	+0.14%
Germany	289	286	5.54%	7.34%	-1.80%	6.29%	7.56%	-1.27%
Spain	82	78	6.44%	7.39%	-0.95%	8.06%	9.32%	-1.26%
Ireland	28	26	6.45%	7.46%	-1.01%	6.31%	6.36%	-0.05%
Italy	155	154	7.99%	10.51%	-2.52%	8.14%	9.07%	-0.89%
Portugal 30	30	9.36%	12.07%	-2.71%	8.73%	9.62%	-0.89%	
Greece	79	77	*10.60%*	*11.57%*	*-0.97%*	*11.03%*	*13.93%*	*-2.90%*
Average			6.28%	8.19%	-1.91%	7.19%	7.98%	-0.79%

*Negative sign means improved credit risk.
Sources: Figure 4 and Riskmetrics (MSCI).

Correlation of Sovereign PDs: Recent Evidence on Z-Metrics vs. Implied CDS PDs

As a final test of the predictive of our approach, we compared our Z-Metrics five-year median PDs for our sample of nine European countries (both on a contemporary basis and for 2009) with the PDs implied by CDS spreads in 2010. The contemporary PD correlation during the first third of 2010 was remarkably high, with an R^2 of 0.82. This was a period when it was becoming quite evident that certain European countries were in serious financial trouble and the likelihood of default was not trivial. But if we go back to the first half of 2009, the correlation drops to an R^2 of 0.36 (although it would be considerably higher, at 0.62, if we excluded the case of Ireland). Ireland's CDS implied PD was considerably higher in 2009 than 2010 (17.0% vs. 12.0%), while the Z-Metrics PD was relatively stable in the two years (7.5% and 6.5% respectively).[22] In 2010, whether we calculate the correlation with or without Ireland, the results are essentially the same (0.82 and 0.83).

Given the predictive success of Z-metrics in the tests already described, we were curious to find out whether it could be used to predict capital market (i.e., CDS) prices. So, we regressed our public firm model's 2009 Z-Metrics median, non-financial sector PDs against implied CDS PDs one year later in 2010. Admittedly, this sample was quite small (10 countries) and the analysis is for only a single time-series comparison (2009 vs. 2010). Nevertheless, these two years spanned a crucial and highly visible sovereign debt crisis, whereas the PDs implied by prior years' Z-Metrics and CDS showed remarkably little volatility.[23]

As can be seen in Figure 9, the correlation between our Z-Metrics PDs and those implied by CDS one year later proved to be remarkably strong, with an r of 0.69 and R^2 of 0.48. In sum, the corporate health index for our European countries (plus the U.S.) in 2009 explained roughly half of the variation in the CDS results one year later.[24]

---

[22] No doubt the CDS market was reacting quite strongly to the severe problems in the Irish banking sector in 2009, while Z-Metrics PDs were not impacted by the banks. This implies a potential strength of the CDS measure, although the lower CDS implied PD in early 2010 was not impressive in predicting the renewed problems of Irish banks and its economy in the fall of 2010.

[23] The last time an entire region and its many countries had a sovereign debt crisis was in Asia in 1997-1998. Unfortunately, CDS prices were not prominent and the CDS market was illiquid at that time.

[24] Several other non-linear structures (i.e., power and exponential functions) for our 2009 Z-Metrics vs. 2010 CDS implied PDs showed similar results. In all

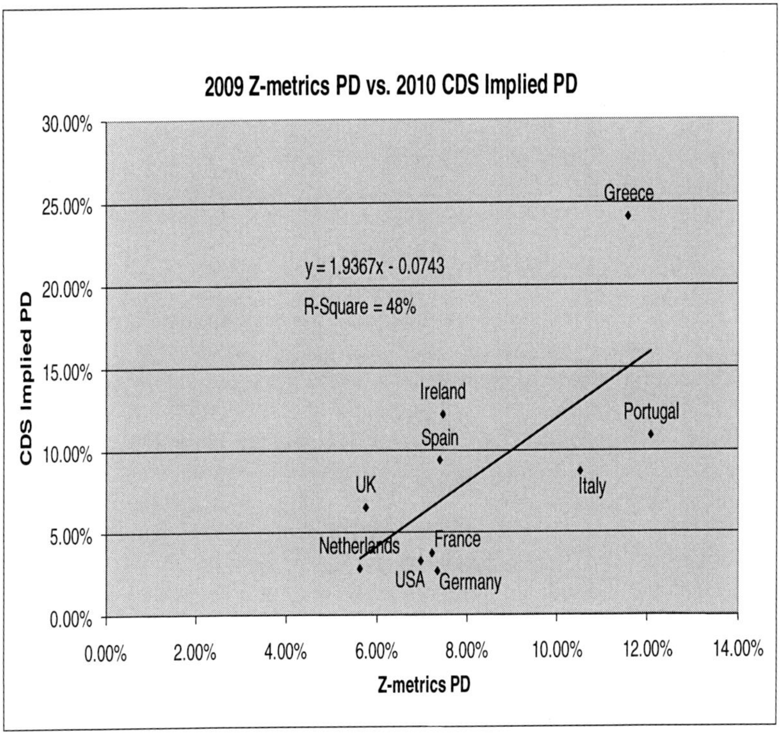

Figure 9.

A potential shortcoming of our approach is that we are limited in our private sector corporate health assessments to data from listed, publicly held firms. This is especially true for relatively small countries like Ireland (with just 28 listed companies), Portugal (with 30), Greece (79), Netherlands (61), and Spain (82). Since the private, non-listed segment is much larger in all of the countries, we are not clearly assessing the health of the vast majority of its firms and our sovereign health index measure is incomplete.[25]

---

cases, we are assuming a recovery rate of 40% on defaults in calculation of implied sovereign PDs.

[25] We suggest that complete firm financial statement repositories, such as those that usually are available in the sovereign's central bank be used to monitor the performance of the entire private sector.

But if the size of the listed firm population is clearly a limitation in our calculations, there does not seem to be a systematic bias in our results. To be sure, the very small listings in Ireland, Portugal, and Greece appear heavily correlated with their high PDs, but the country with the lowest PD (the Netherlands) also has a very small listed population. Another potentially important factor is that the listed population in countries like the U.K. and the Netherlands is represented quite heavily by multinational corporations that derive most of their income from outside their borders.[26]

Conclusion and Implications

As the price for bailing out distressed sovereigns, today's foreign creditors, especially the stronger European nations, are demanding a heavy dose of austerity. Several governments, including those of Greece, Ireland, Spain, Portugal, Italy, and the U.K., have already enacted some painful measures. Others, such as France and Hungary, have either resisted austerity measures or faced significant social unrest when austerity measures have been proposed. These measures typically involve substantial cuts in cash benefits paid to public workers, increases in retirement age, and other reduced infrastructure costs, as well as increased taxes for companies and individuals. The objective is to reduce deficits relative to GDP and enhance the sovereigns' ability to repay their foreign debt and balance their budgets.

While recognizing the necessity of requiring difficult changes for governments to qualify for bailouts and subsidies, we caution that such measures should be designed to inflict as little damage as possible on the health and productivity of the private enterprises that ultimately fund the sovereign. The goal should be to enable all private enterprises with clear going concern value to pay their bills, expand (or at least maintain) their workforces, and return value to their shareholders and creditors (while those businesses that show no promise of ever making a profit should be either reorganized or liquidated). For this reason, raising taxes and imposing other burdens on corporate entities is likely to weaken the long-run financial condition of sovereigns.

To better estimate sovereigns' risk of default, we propose that traditional measures of macroeconomic performance be combined with more modern techniques, such as the contingent claims analysis pioneered by Robert Merton and the bottom-up approach presented in these pages.

[26] Results showing the percentage of "home grown" revenues for listed firms across our European country sample were inclusive, however, as to their influence on relative PDs.

Along with the intuitive appeal of such an approach and our encouraging empirical results, the probabilities of sovereign default provided by aggregating our Z-Metrics across a national economy can be seen, at the very least, as a useful complement to existing methods and market indicators—one that is not subject to government manipulation of publicly released statistics. Using our approach, the credit and regulatory communities could track the performance of publicly held companies and the economies in which they reside—and by making some adjustments, unlisted entities as well. And if sovereigns were also willing to provide independently audited statistics on a regular basis, so much the better.

Appendix: Logit Model Estimation of Default Probabilities

We estimated our credit scoring model based on a standard logit-regression functional form whereby:

$$CS_{i,t} = \alpha + \Sigma \mathrm{B}_j \mathrm{X}_{i,t} + \varepsilon_{i,t} \quad (1)$$

$CS_{i,t}$ = *Z–Metrics* credit score of company *i* at time *t*

B_j = variable parameters (or weights)

$X_{i,t}$ = set of fundamental, market based and macroeconomic variables for firm *i* quarter *t* observations.

$\varepsilon_{i,t}$ = error terms (assumed to be identically and independently distributed)

$CS_{i,t}$ is transformed into a probability of default by

$$PD_{i,t} = \frac{1}{1 + \exp\,(CS_{i,t})}$$

- We compare Z-Metrics results with issuer ratings. To ensure a fair comparison, credit scores are converted to agency equivalent (AE) ratings by ranking credit scores and by matching exactly the actual Agency rating distribution with the AE rating distribution at any point in time.

- We also compare our Z-Metrics results to the well established Altman Z"-score (1995) model.[27]

References

Abassi, B. and R. J. Taffler, 1982, "Country Risk: A Model of Economic Performance Related to Debt Servicing Capacity," WP #36, City University Business School, London.

Altman, E. I., 1968, "Financial Ratios Discriminant Analysis and the Prediction of Corporate Bankruptcy," Journal of Finance, v. 23, 4, September, 189.

Altman, E. I. and E. Hotchkiss, 2006, Corporate Financial Distress and Bankruptcy, 3rd edition, John Wiley & Sons, NY and NJ.

Altman, E. I., et. al., 2010, "The Z-Metrics™ Methodology for Estimating Company Credit Ratings and Default Risk Probabilities," RiskMetrics Group, NY, June, available from www.riskmetrics.com/Z-Metrics.

Babbel, D. F., 1996, "Insuring Sovereign Debt against Default," World Bank Discussion Papers, #328.

Baek, I. A. Bandopadhyaya and C. Du, 2005, "Determinants of Market-Assessed Sovereign Risk: Economic Fundamentals or Market Risk Appetite?" Journal of International Money and Finance, Vol. 24 (4), pp. 533-48.

Beers, D., M. Cavanaugh and O. Takahira, 2002, "Sovereign Credit Ratings: A Primer," Standard & Poor's Corp., NY, April.

Bertozi, S., 1996, "An Annotated Bibliography on External Debt Capacity," in D. Babbel's "Insuring Sovereign Debt Against Default," World Bank Discussion Papers #328.

Caouette, J., E. Altman, P. Narayanan and R. Nimmo, 2008, Managing Credit Risk, 2nd edition, John Wiley & Sons, NY.

---

[27] Altman's original Z-score model (1968) is well-known to practitioners and scholars alike. It was built, however, over 40 years ago and is primarily applicable to publicly-held manufacturing firms. A more generally applicable Z"-score variation was popularized later (Altman, Hartzell and Peck, 1995) as a means to assess the default risk of non-manufacturers as well as manufacturers, and was first applied to emerging market credits. Both models are discussed in Altman and Hotchkiss (2006) and will be compared in several tests to our new Z-Metrics model. Further, the Altman Z-score models do not translate easily into a probability of default rating system, as does the Z-Metrics system. Of course, entities that do not have access to the newer Z Metrics system can still use the classic Z-score frameworks, although accuracy levels will not be as high and firm PDs not as readily available.

Chambers, W.J., 1997, "Understanding Sovereign Risk," Credit Week, Standard & Poor's January 1.

Cline, W., 1983, "A Logit Model of Debt Restructuring, 1963-1982," Institute for International Economics, WP, June.

Feder, G. and R. E. Just, 1977, "A Study of Debt Servicing Capacity Applying Logit Analysis," Journal of Development Economics," 4 (1).

Feder, G. R. E. Just and K. Ross, 1981, "Projecting Debt Capacity of Developing Countries," Journal of Financial & Qualitative Analysis, 16 (5).

Flynn, D., 2009, "S&P Cuts Greek Debt Rating as Global Crisis Bites," Reuters, January 14.

Frank, C. R. and W. R. Cline, 1971, "Measurement of Debt Servicing Capacity: An Application of Discriminant Analysis," Journal of International Economics, 1.

Frenkel, M., A. Karmann and B. Scholtens, eds., 2004, "Sovereign Risk and Financial Crises," Heidelberg and New York, Springer, xii, 258.

Gennaioli, N., A. Martin and S. Rossi, 2010, "Sovereign Default, Domestic Banks and Financial Institutions," Working Paper, Imperial College, London, July.

Gerlach, S., A. Schultz and G. Wolff, 2010, "Banking and Sovereign Risk in the Euro Area," Deutsche Bundesbank, Research Centre, Discussion Paper Series 1: Economic Studies: 2010.

Gray, D. F., R. Merton and Z. Bodie, 2006, "A New Framework for Analyzing and Managing Macrofinancial Risk of an Economy," IMF Working Paper, October.

Gray, D. F., R. Merton and Z. Bodie, 2007, "Contingent Claims Approach to Measuring and Managing Sovereign Credit Risk," Journal of Investment Management, vol. 5, No. 4, p.1.

Grinols, E., 1976, "International Debt Rescheduling and Discrimination Using Financial Variables," U.S. Treasury Dept., Washington, D.C.

Haugh, D., P. Ollivaud and D. Turner, 2009, "What Drives Sovereign Risk Premiums?: An Analysis of Recent Evidence from the Euro Areas," OECD, Economics Department, Working Paper, 718.

Hilscher, J. and Y. Nosbusch, 2010, "Determinants of Sovereign Risk: Macroeconomic Fundamentals and the Pricing of Sovereign Debt," Review of Finance, Vol. 14 (2), pp. 235-62. IMF, 2010, "Global Financial Stability Report," Washington, D.C.

KMV Corporation, 1999, "Modeling Default Risk," KMV Corporation, R. Crosbie.

Krugman, P., 1989, "Financing vs. Forgiving a Debt Overhang: Some Analytical Notes," Journal of International Business Studies, 17.

Longstaff, F., J. Pan, L. Pedersen and K. Singleton, 2007, "How Sovereign is Sovereign Credit Risk?," National Bureau of Economic Research, Inc. , NBER Working Paper: 13658.

Merton, R. C., 1974, "On the Pricing of Corporate Debt: The Risk Structure of Interest Rates," Journal of Finance, 29, May, 449.

Neziri, H., 2009, "Can Credit Default Swaps predict Financial Crises?," Journal of Applied Economic Sciences, Volume IV/Issue 1(7)

Oshiro, N., Y. Saruwatari, 2005, "Quantification of Sovereign Risk: Using the Information in Equity Market Prices," Emerging Markets Review, Vol. 6 (4), pp. 346-62.

Pomerleano, M., 1998, "Corporate Finance Lessons from the East Asian Crisis," Viewpoint, The World Bank Group, Note #155, October.

—. 1999, "The East-Asia Crisis and Corporate Finance – The Untold Micro Study," Emerging Markets Quarterly.

Reinhart, M. and K. Rogoff, 2010, "This Time is Different," Princeton University Press, Princeton, NJ.

Remolona, E. M. Scatigna and E. Wu, 2008, "A Ratings-Based Approach to Measuring Sovereign Risk," International Journal of Finance and Economics, Vol. 13 (1), pp. 26-39.

Saini, K. and P. Bates, 1978, "Statistical Techniques for Determining Debt Servicing Capacity for Developing Countries: Analytical Review of the Literature and Further Empirical Results," Federal Reserve Bank of New York Research Paper, #7818.

Sargen, H., 1977, "Economics Indicators and Country Risk Appraisal," Federal Reserve Bank of San Francisco, Economic Review, Fall.

Schmidt, R., 1984, "Early Warning of Debt Rescheduling," Journal of Banking and Finance, 8.

Segoviano, B., A. Miguel, C. Caceres and V. Guzzo, 2010, "Sovereign Spreads: Global Risk Aversion, Contagion or Fundamentals?," IMF Working Paper: 10/120, p. 29.

Sgherri, S. and E. Zoli, 2009, "Euro Area Sovereign Risk During the Crisis," International Monetary Fund, IMF Working Papers: 09/222.

Smith, R. and I. Walter, 2003, Global Banking, Oxford University Press, London.

Trebesch, C., U. Das and M. Papaioannou, 2010, "Sovereign Default Risk and Private Sector Access to Capital in Emerging Markets," IMP Working Paper: October.

CHAPTER EIGHT

SOVEREIGN CREDIT RISK CHANGES AND DOMESTIC EQUITY RETURNS

JOSEPH CALLAGHAN AND KEVIN LUCEY[1]

Abstract

Recent turmoil in the financial sectors of many economies has brought pressure on the fiscal conditions of many countries, leading some countries (e.g. Ireland and Greece) into sovereign debt crises. Recent research has also examined the link between credit conditions in the private domestic sector of an economy to sovereign credit conditions. In this study we reverse the order and examine the impact of sovereign credit risk changes on domestic equity markets of those countries. Specifically we examine credit rating changes of OECD countries and relate them to market-adjusted equity returns in these countries. We find a significant positive association between market-adjusted equity index returns and sovereign credit rating changes of these countries. Moreover, we find significant negative market-adjusted equity index returns for sovereign credit downgrade events. These results suggest that factors affecting government fiscal conditions have a systematic impact on their domestic equity markets. The implication for credit analysis is that sovereign credit conditions need to be factored into the credit granting decision to companies trading on those domestic exchanges or conducting business in those domestic economies.

[1] Joseph Callaghan is Professor of Accounting, Oakland University, Rochester, MI. Kevin Lucey is Senior Associate, O'Keefe & Associates, Bloomfield Hills, MI.

Results

Our analysis found that sovereign debt rating downgrades resulted in a negative market-adjusted stock index return in the downgraded nation, and ratings increases resulted in a corresponding increase in the individual nation's market-adjusted stock index returns. Two measures were employed: 1) a simple average of ccmadjret and 2) the linear association between ccmadjret and the sovereign credit rating score change (β):

1) $\overline{ccmadjret} = \frac{\sum_{i=1}^{N} ccmadjret_i}{N}$

2) $ccmadjret_i = \alpha + \beta\,(\Delta Credit\ Score_i) + \varepsilon_i,$
$where\ \varepsilon_i \sim iid\ N(0, \sigma^2)$

More specifically, when analyzing only the 24 downgrade events, we find a significant average decrease in compounded market-adjusted returns of **-2.25%**, (p<.0001, one-tail). However, an OLS regression of these adjusted returns on the magnitude of the credit change yields the following results:

This regression results in an insignificant overall linear relationship and slope. When we examine the same results for the 26 upgrades, the average compounded market-adjusted return is barely negative (**-0.07%**) and insignificant. The regression results for upgrades (unreported here) are similarly insignificant overall with a near-zero slope. When all events are combined, the regression results are significant. Specifically we obtain the following results:

Thus, for every unit change in a sovereign's credit rating score there is a 2.39% change in the compounded market-adjusted returns of an equity index broadly reflecting the equity performance of the domestic equity market of the sovereign undergoing that credit rating change.

Conclusion and Suggestions

Collectively our results indicate that there is a positive association between compound market-adjusted returns in the domestic equity markets of sovereigns experiencing credit rating changes. The implication is that the performance in the private sector is affected by the monetary and fiscal policies of the public sector. When the sovereign experiences a change in its credit environment, its domestic economy is impacted. This impact affects businesses whose equity securities are traded on their domestic exchanges. The implication for credit analysis is that sovereign credit conditions need to be factored into the credit-granting decision to companies trading on those domestic exchanges or conducting business in those domestic economies.

This study may be improved by examining more countries and examining them over more time periods. Also, the interactive effects between public and private sectors might be fruitfully examined. That is, a more general model simultaneously relating public sector policies with private sector credit conditions might provide better insight into underlying credit conditions of both sectors.

References

Altman, Edward, Rijken, Herbert, 2011. Toward a bottom-up approach to assessing sovereign default risk. Journal of Applied Corporate Finance 23, 20 – 31.

Brooks, Robert, Faff, Robert, Hillier, Joseph, 2004. The national market impact of sovereign rating changes. Journal of Banking and Finance 28, 233 – 250.

Cantor, Richard, Packer, Frank, 1996. Determinants and impact of sovereign credit ratings. Federal Reserve Bank of New York Economic Policy Review October 1996, 37 – 53.

Cavaglia, Stefano, Brightman, Chris, Aked, Michael, 2000. On the increasing importance of industry factors: Implications for global portfolio management. Financial Analysts Journal 56, 41 – 54.

Coleman, Rozlyn, 1996. Confronting budget deficits. International Monetary Fund Economics Issues 3.

Estrada, Javier, Kritzman, Mark, Pages, Sébastien, 2006. Countries versus industries in emerging markets: A normative portfolio approach. The Journal of Investing 15, 19 – 28.

Ferreira, Miguel, Gama, Paulo, 2007. Does sovereign debt ratings news spill over to international stock markets? Journal of Banking & Finance 31, 3162 – 3182.

Huang, Jingzhi, Lu, Lei, 2009. Macro factors and volatility of Treasury bond returns. Working paper.

Ibbotson Stocks, Bonds, Bills, and Inflation Valuation Yearbook (2011). Morningstar, Inc.

Kaminsky, Graciela, Schmukler, Sergio, 2002. Emerging markets instability: Do sovereign ratings affect country risk and stock returns? World Bank Economic Review 16, 171 – 195.

Keenan, Sean, 2000. Historical default rates of corporate bond issuers, 1920 – 1999. Moody's Investors Service Special Comment.

Radelet, Steven, Sachs, Jeffrey, 1998. The onset of the East Asian financial crisis. Working paper 6680 NBER.

Reinhart, Carmen, 2002. Default, currency crises and sovereign credit ratings. Working paper 8738 NBER.

Torres, Gabriel, Zelter, Jill, 1998. Ratings securitizations above the sovereign ceiling. Fitch IBCA December 29, 1998 special report.

CHAPTER NINE

DYNAMICS OF THE DEFAULT FREQUENCY OF CONSUMER FIXED-PAYMENT CREDITS

RODRIGO ALFARO, DAVID PACHECO AND ANDRÉS SAGNER[1]

Credit risk is one of the most significant risks to the banking business (Crouchy *et al.*, 2005; Drehmann, 2009). Therefore, both academics and practitioners have developed statistical models to quantify it. While there is a wide range of models available, the core of Basel II framework is based on Vasicek (1991), which is an extension of the Merton (1974) model. The model considers that the asset value of a given firm or individual can be decomposed into two factors: systemic and idiosyncratic. In this context, the default occurs when the asset value is below a certain threshold, which is a function of both business-cycle variables and characteristics of the debtors. The key parameters of the model are the Long-Run Probability of Default (*LRPD*) and the Asset Correlation.

In this paper we estimate the parameters of the Vasicek (1991) model to evaluate changes in credit standards for loan applications during 2005-2009. For this purpose, we regress default frequency against macroeconomic variables and characteristics of the vintage under the assumption that the

---

[1] Rodrigo Alfaro and Andrés Sagner are from Central Bank of Chile. David Pacheco is from Superintendency of Banks and Financial Institutions. We appreciate the comments and suggestions of Roberto Álvarez, Daniel Calvo, Rodrigo Cifuentes, Kevin Cowan, José Miguel Cruz, Sergio Huerta, Patricio Jaramillo, Felipe Martínez, Jorge Niño, Luis Opazo, Alejandro Pena, Yin Yu, attendants to the International Conference on Credit Analysis and Risk Management at Oakland University, attendants to the Macro-prudential Policy Workshop at the Central Bank of Chile, and seminar attendants at the Financial Policy Division of the Central Bank of Chile. The views expressed in this paper do not necessarily reflect those of the Central Bank of Chile or the Chilean Superintendency of Banks and Financial Institutions.

Chilean economy experienced a complete business cycle during 2003-2009.

The empirical results show that *LRPD* is around 14.6% and 13.1% if we consider the number and the amount of defaulted credits, respectively. These estimates are consistent with the values reported by QIS 5 (BIS, 2006) for consumer loans[2]. Finally, counterfactual exercises suggest a relaxing of credit standards for loan applications during 2006- 2007.

1. The Vasicek Model: A Quick Overview

Vasicek's (1991) model assumes the existence of a latent variable representing the asset value of a firm or individual, which can be decomposed into two unobserved and mutually independent factors: systemic and idiosyncratic. In this setup, the impact coefficient of the systemic factor is related to the correlation between assets (Asset Correlation), and together with the Long-Run Probability of Default (*LRPD*). Those are the key elements of the model and its calibration is particularly important in determining capital requirements under Basel II.

The model considers that a credit default occurs when the latent variable falls below a given threshold, which we assume to be time-variant, i.e. the threshold is a function of macroeconomic variables and characteristics of the vintage. Consequently, the *LRPD* is defined as the unconditional probability that the latent variable is below the long-run value of the threshold.

Under the assumptions that loans are homogeneous and granular, and the systemic factor is normally distributed, the impact coefficients of the time-variant threshold can be estimated by OLS considering as the dependent variable a transformation of the default frequency through the inverse cumulative distribution function of the idiosyncratic factor[3]. Moreover, since the asset correlation parameter is proportional to the variance of the model, the former can be identified from the Root Mean Square Error (*RMSE*).

---

[2] The values are comparable to non-G10 countries and banks of similar size to those that operate in Chile.

[3] See Alfaro, Pacheco and Sagner (2011) for technical details on the estimation strategy used.

2. The Data

The database used in this paper contains monthly information from January 2003 to June 2010 of each new consumer fixed-payment loan (vintage) registered in the Chilean banking system, namely an identification number of the debtor, a dummy variable identifying whether the credit is a "subprime" loan, and the amount and maturity of the loan[4].

Figure 1. Default Frequency of Vintages and Macroeconomic Variables

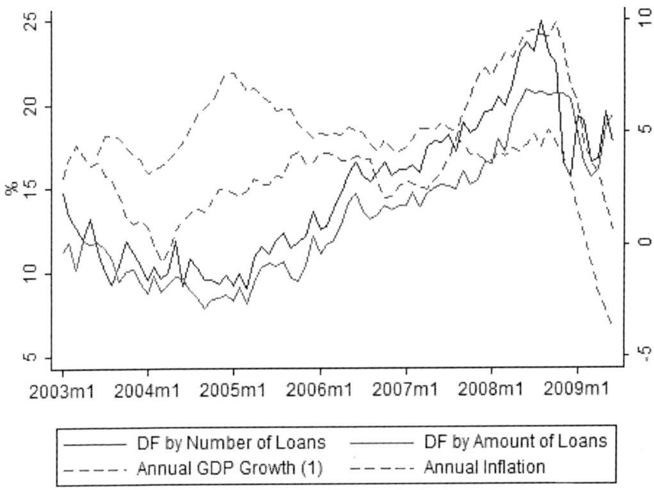

(1) 6 months moving average of the annual variation.
Source: Author's calculation based on information provided by SBIF.

The default frequency of new consumer credits generated in a given month at the banking system level is defined as the ratio between the number (amount) of non-performing loans registered over the next 12 months, and the number (amount) of total loans generated in the respective month[5]. As can be noted in Figure 1, both measures of the default frequency show a similar upward trend during the period 2003-2009.

[4] We concentrate our analysis in consumer fixed-payment credits, since according to SBIF reports, this type of loan accounted for almost 71% of the total amount of credits granted at the end of 2010. A "subprime" loan is a credit granted by consumer divisions of banks that have a higher risk.

[5] Since this measure of default is consolidated at the system level, it is higher than the default frequency obtained for any particular bank.

Moreover, the descriptive statistics of the series indicate that both distributions are quite similar (Table 1). This finding seems to confirm the assumption of homogeneity and granularity of new fixed-payment consumer loans at the banking system level.

Table 1. Descriptive Statistics of Default Frequency (%)

	By Number of Loans	By Amount of Loans
Mean	14.8	13.3
Std. Dev.	4.2	3.8
P10	9.6	8.7
P25	11.1	9.8
P50	14.7	12.5
P75	17.7	15.7
P90	20.4	20.1

3. Empirical Results

In our econometric estimations we consider four alternative versions of the dependent variable, derived from the two measures of the default frequency and the cumulative distribution function of the idiosyncratic factor, where we consider normal and logistic distributions.

Additionally, we consider two sets of regressors. The first set consists of macroeconomic variables such as: (i) annual GDP growth, which is expected to have a negative effect given that a positive economic growth would improve the income of debtors, and therefore the default probability would decrease[6]; and (ii) the annual inflation rate, for which a positive relationship is expected because an increment of this variable would result –via inflation tax– in a reduction in disposable income, thus deteriorating the ability to pay of debtors. The second set of regressors consists of variables that characterize the vintage: the proportion of "subprime" loans, average maturity and average loan amount.

---

[6] Although the literature suggests also the unemployment rate as a significant determinant of the default frequency, unreported estimates reveal a non-significant effect of this variable.

Table 2. Results for Vasicek Model and Default Frequency by Number of Credits (1) (2)

	(1)	*(2)*	*(3)*	*(4)*	*(5)*	*(6)*
Annual GDP growth		-1.7884	-1.6864		-0.0950	-0.0863
		(0.4392)	(0.3361)		(0.0263)	(0.0196)
Inflation rate		5.1074	4.5300		0.3031	0.2716
		(0.4255)	(0.3619)		(0.0266)	(0.0236)
Prop. subprime loans			0.6758			0.0346
			(0.1232)			(0.0075)
log(Avg. maturity)			-0.3390			-0.0192
			(0.1589)			(0.0086)
log(Avg. amount)			0.3410			0.0192
			(0.0866)			(0.0047)
Const.	-1.0632	-1.1871	-2.8521	0.5368	0.5290	0.4372
	(0.0205)	(0.0282)	(0.3285)	(0.0012)	(0.0017)	(0.0173)
LRPD	0.1439	0.1439	0.1439	0.1477	0.1477	0.1477
	(0.0046)	(0.0028)	(0.0022)	(0.0048)	(0.0028)	(0.0022)
Asset correlation	0.0318	0.0115	0.0071	0.0001	0.0000	0.0000
	(0.0053)	(0.0019)	(0.0011)	(0.0000)	(0.0000)	(0.0000)
RMSE	0.181	0.108	0.085	0.010	0.006	0.005
AIC	-44.19	-123.20	-158.11	-489.32	-572.46	-602.95
BIC	-41.83	-116.13	-143.97	-486.97	-565.39	-588.81

(1) Standard errors are in parentheses.
(2) Specifications 1 to 3 consider the Normal distribution for the idiosyncratic factor, while specifications 4 to 6 consider the Logistic distribution.

Table 3. Results for Vasicek Model and Default Frequency by Amount of Credits (1) (2)

	(1)	*(2)*	*(3)*	*(4)*	*(5)*	*(6)*
Annual GDP growth		-2.3988	-1.7576		-0.1266	-0.0861
		(0.4475)	(0.3793)		(0.0257)	(0.0199)
Inflation rate		4.9105	4.6134		0.2715	0.2570
		(0.3596)	(0.3343)		(0.0211)	(0.0192)
Prop. subprime loans			0.2451			0.0068
			(0.1176)			(0.0060)
log(Avg. maturity)			-0.5315			-0.0291
			(0.1610)			(0.0082)
log(Avg. amount)			0.3659			0.0199
			(0.0907)			(0.0046)
Const.	-1.1312	-1.2225	-2.2678	0.5331	0.5278	0.4740
	(0.0200)	(0.0312)	(0.2388)	(0.0011)	(0.0018)	(0.0115)
LRPD	0.1290	0.1290	0.1290	0.1326	0.1326	0.1326
	(0.0042)	(0.0022)	(0.0020)	(0.0043)	(0.0022)	(0.0020)
Asset correlation	0.0301	0.0086	0.0068	0.0001	0.0000	0.0000
	(0.0050)	(0.0014)	(0.0011)	(0.0000)	(0.0000)	(0.0000)
RMSE	0.176	0.093	0.083	0.010	0.005	0.004
AIC	-48.46	-146.42	-161.45	-503.60	-606.45	-620.89
BIC	-46.10	-139.35	-147.31	-501.24	-599.38	-606.75

(1) Standard errors are in parentheses.
(2) Specifications 1 to 3 consider the Normal distribution for the idiosyncratic factor, while specifications 4 to 6 consider the Logistic distribution.

The results in Tables 2 and 3 indicate that the estimated *LRPD* is around 14.4 to 14.6% and 12.9 to 13.3% when considering the number and amount of defaulted consumer fixed-payment loans, respectively[7]. We note that these results are in line with the 12% reported by QIS 5 (BIS, 2006) for countries with similar economic conditions[8], but we should remark that this number is small because it was not obtained at the system level, as was ours.

Regarding the asset correlation, the results give a wide range of values for this parameter (0% to 3%) because it is proportional to the *RMSE*, and therefore its magnitude depends largely on the model's fit. Notwithstanding, the asset correlation equal to 3% implicit in the model without exogenous variables (standard Vasicek's model) and both measures of the probability of default are in line with the values proposed by Basel II for those type of loans.

4. Counterfactual Analysis

The dynamics content in the characteristics of the vintage could be related to changes in the banks' credit standards. For example, from Tables 2 and 3 we see that the proportion of "subprime" loans tends to increase the probability of default. In order to quantify the effect of changes in credit standards on the default frequency, we forecast the latter variable for the period 2005-2009 considering that the characteristics of vintages remain on their average values observed in 2003-2004. That is, we generate a series of default frequency assuming no change in the characteristics of the vintage so that their dynamics are explained only by macroeconomic factors. Therefore, the difference between this series and the actual one can be attributable to changes in the credit standards of banks.

---

[7] The value obtained in the case of the logistic distribution is approximated by a logistic function because the parameter of the systemic factor is close to zero.

[8] Strictly speaking there is not a comparable figure given QIS 5 report average figures for a group of banks and countries. However, industry analysts recognize that 12% seems a reasonable value for default frequency on this type of loans.

Figure 2. Actual and Projected Default Frequencies

By Number of Loans

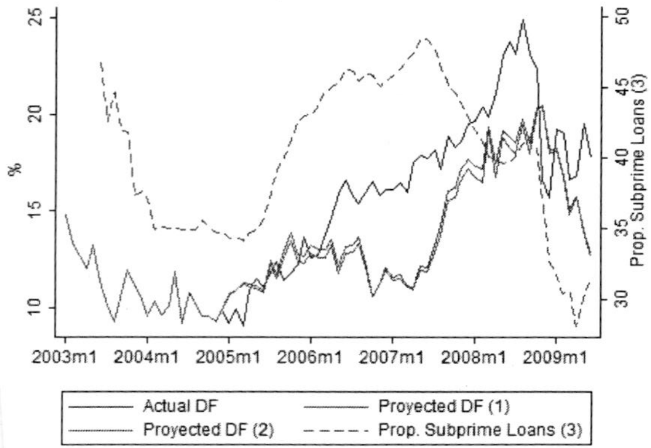

By Amount of Loans

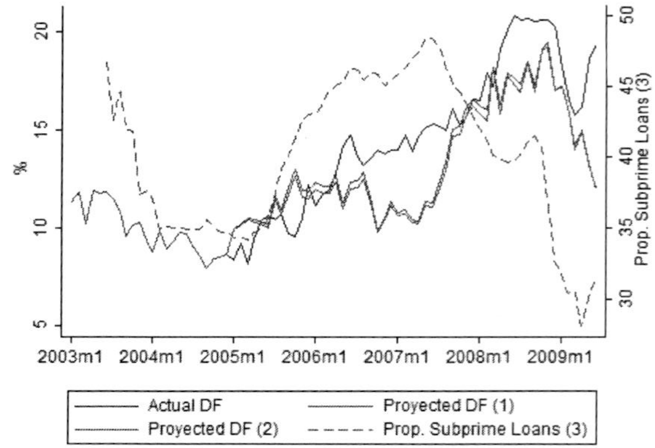

(1) Normal distribution function.

(2) Logistic distribution function.

(3) 6 months moving average.

Source: Author's calculation.

From Figure 2, we can note that between January 2005 and February 2006 the actual and predicted default frequencies moved similarly, indicating a period of no changes in the banks' credit standards. However, a gap appears in March 2006 and reaches a peak during the second quarter of 2007. This would be a period of relaxing of credit standards for loan applications. A crude indicator of this hypothesis is the dynamics of the proportion of subprime loans which also peaks during that period[9].

5. Conclusions

In this paper we estimate an extension of Vasicek's (1991) model for new consumer fixed-payment credits (vintage) of the Chilean banking system, allowing the threshold to be contingent to both macroeconomic factors and characteristics of debtors. Under the assumption that the economy experienced a complete business cycle during 2003-2009, and the homogeneity and granularity assumptions for the credit portfolio, the results indicate that the Long-Run Probability of Default (*LRPD*) is around 14.6% or 13.1% if the default frequency is measured by the number or the amount of credits, respectively. Finally, the counterfactual analysis suggests a relaxing on credit standards for loan applications during the period 2006-2007.

References

Alfaro, R., D. Pacheco and A. Sagner (2011). "Estimating the Dynamics of the Default Frequency of Consumer Fixed-Payment Credits," *Manuscript*, Central Bank of Chile.

BIS (2006). "Results of the Fifth Quantitative Impact Study (QIS 5)," Working Group on Overall Capital and Quantitative Impact Study of the Basel Committee on Banking Supervision, Bank for International Settlements.

Crouchy, M., D. Galai and R. Mark (2005). "The Use of Internal Models: Comparison of the New Basel Credit Proposal with Available Internal Models for Credit Risk," chapter 6 in *Capital Adequacy beyond Basel: Banking, Securities, and Insurance*, edited by H. Scott.

Drehmann, M. (2009). "Macroeconomic Stress Testing Banks: A Survey of Methodologies," in *Stress Testing the Banking System:*

[9] This period has also a favorable macroeconomic environment: an average GDP growth rate above 4.5% and low unemployment rates around 8.6%.

Methodologies and Applications, edited by M. Quagliariello, Cambridge University Press.

Merton, R. (1974). "On the Pricing of Corporate Debt: The Risk Structure of Interest Rates," *Journal of Finance* 29(2): 449-470.

Vasicek, O. (1991). "Probability of Loss on Loan Portfolio," White Paper, KMV Corporation.

CHAPTER TEN

MEASURING CREDIT RISK AND FINANCIAL REPORTING

JULIA SAWICKI[1]

Abstract

This session considers the measurement of credit risk from an accounting perspective. International and U.S. accounting standards currently require banks and other companies to report a wide range of financial instruments at fair values, a critical element of which is credit risk. Valuations based on observable prices determined in active, liquid markets are straightforward. However, many financial assets and liabilities do not trade actively requiring estimates based on inputs like credit rating, generic credit spreads, and / or other market inputs, assumptions and models. Numerous concerns about and criticisms of methods for estimating credit risk were exacerbated by the recent global financial crisis as market liquidity dried and use of model-based methodologies highlighted the difficulties in estimating fair values.

The motivation for this work is recognition among accounting scholars of a deficit in research into fair value measurement. The empirical studies tend to take fair values *as reported* and the field is generally lacking investigation into *how* they are determined. There are many shortcomings in the current accounting reporting framework. This session discusses issues, weaknesses, controversies and regulatory responses to the difficulties involved in measuring credit risk for financial reporting. We discuss practical and regulatory implications, citing empirical evidence, for the topics: procyclicality, measurement in illiquid and normal markets, implementation costs, and valuing liabilities for changes in own credit risk.

---

[1] The author is from Dalhousie University.

I. Introduction

The debate about the use of fair values in financial reporting rages on. At the extremes, it is seen as: evil, labelled as a direct cause of the recent financial crisis; saviour, the only way forward, the sole answer to fixing an accounting model that is broken. The issues are numerous and many of them not well understood. Inquiry, scientific investigation and evidence are emerging but the picture is far from clear. Many questions for investors, regulators, financial statement preparers, auditors, and ultimately the health of the financial system, remain.

This session deals with what is arguably the thorniest issue in the fair value controversy: the measurement of credit risk for financial assets and liabilities. We discuss several topics arising from the difficulty if measuring credit risk for fair value accounting (FVA). We begin by providing some background on accounting valuation, and the emergence of and justification for fair value measurement. Specific issues and concerns surrounding FVA include: procyclicality, measurement difficulties, implementation costs and the role of credit risk in measuring liabilities.

II. Background on Fair Value Accounting and the Incorporation Credit Risk

The traditional basis for accounting valuation has been historical cost. Although this achieves an objective, transaction-based measure, it is criticized for producing stale, backward-looking financial statements, far-removed from the current information relevant to investor decisions. This model has been adapted over recent times to increasingly reflect current values which arguably provide information more relevant to financial statement users. Standard setters are moving towards requiring that fair values are reported for all financial instruments.

The recent financial crisis brought the topic to center stage as an alleged major culprit in the near collapse of the financial system. Although it has been largely exonerated as a cause of the crisis, the debate about fair value accounting is intensifying as financial statement users, preparers, standard setters and regulators grapple with the increasing use of FVA and its complications.

Fair value is defined as: 'the price that would be received to sell an asset or paid to transfer a liability in an orderly transaction between market participants at the measurement date.[2] Fair value encompasses a variety of estimation approaches. Central to the measurement methodology is the fair value hierarchy which describes the valuation inputs. The three levels of the hierarchy span a continuum of objectivity, from: quoted prices on active markets (Level 1), to estimates based on observable inputs (Level 2), to estimates based on unobservable inputs (Level 3).

Incorporation of credit risk is critical to measuring fair value. The evaluation of credit risk considers factors such as netting arrangements, collateral, transaction structure and other contractual features. If the exposure is an asset position, counterparty risk is incorporated. A market participant perspective is emphasized, where the fair value reflects the credit risk impact on the price set by the market.

Two approaches to incorporating credit risk in fair value are described in the accounting standard (FAS 157). The first is a market approach where credit risk is impounded in the price and no explicit adjustment is required. Level 1 examples are: publicly listed equities, some public debt and exchange-traded derivatives. If market price inputs require adjustment for credit risk, credit default swap (CDS) rates and credit spreads can be used to adjust. Matrix pricing, where securities' relationship to other benchmark quoted securities is used to determine value, is consistent with the market approach.

The second method for incorporating credit risk in fair value is the income approach where future amounts are converted to a present (discounted) amount. Valuation techniques include net present value; option-pricing models, such as the Black-Scholes-Merton formula (a closed-form model) and a binomial (lattice) model. Credit risk is commonly incorporated in the discount rate, adding the CDS rate or bond spread to the risk free rate. Alternatively the CDS rate can be applied to the future cash flows, or used to calculate a credit risk adjustment based on implied risk of default.

The fundamental justification for the increasing use of fair values is decision making usefulness, termed 'relevance' in the literature. Proponents often appeal to transparency and argue that FVA captures economic reality in a useful way by reporting current values as opposed to historical costs. Several professional investor groups support fair value accounting for financial instruments arguing that it provides more accurate, timely, and comparable information to investors than alternative accounting

---

[2] Financial Accounting Standard 157 (FASB, 2006) and the IASB definition are similar.

approaches.[3] There is extensive empirical support for the relevance of fair value in the accounting literature.[4]

III. Issues, Controversy and Concerns

The accounting standard outlined above has come under intense scrutiny, prompted largely by its role in the financial crisis. A core element and an enormous challenge in applying the standard is the requirement to incorporate credit risk in the measurement. As standard setters expand its application[5] controversy and concern deepen.

Procyclicality

- Procyclical effects of FVA are complex, the evidence ambiguous. More work on the mechanisms of contagion is needed.
- If credit risk models do not appropriately incorporate the credit cycle and its effect on credit risk estimates in the model structure, overly optimistic (pessimistic) assessments in periods of expansion (contraction) may result.

Credit quality concerns during the recent credit crisis nearly reverberated into the collapse of the global financial system. In the early part of the crisis, critics pounced on fair value accounting as a major contributor to the pro-cyclicality of the financial system. FVA was seen as producing overstated of bank profits in the period leading up to the crisis and overstated losses during the crisis. This led to a "destruction of capital", followed by a vicious cycle of falling asset prices leading to accounting write-downs, which prompted asset sales to meet capital requirements exacerbating the fall in asset prices.[6]

---

[3] The CFA Institute, Center for Audit Quality, Consumer Federation of America, and Council of Institutional Investors expressed these views in a 2008 joint letter to the Securities and Exchange Commission.

[4] See Barth et al, (2001) and Landsman (2007) for reviews and empirical evidence. An important problem with most of these studies, however, is that the results hinge on the validity of the valuation model.

[5] Financial Accounting Standards Board (FASB, 2010) recently proposed that all financial instruments be measured at fair value. Currently, fair value measurement is optional for many assets and liabilities.

[6] The American Bankers Association (2008) argues that FVA caused excessive write-downs during the crisis.

Proponents of fair value accounting believe that it shows fluctuations of the market, but does not exacerbate cycles. They argue that fair value information provides early warnings to investors and regulators of changes in current market expectations when asset prices are declining and risk levels for financial institutions are increasing.

An extensive review by the SEC (2008) of the impact of fair value accounting on banks during the credit crisis concluded that fair value did not play a significant role in bank failures. Although several other analyses and empirical evidence suggest that fair value accounting did not play a major role in the financial crisis of 2008,[7] Laux and Leuz (2009) point out that the procyclical effects of FVA are complex, the evidence ambiguous and more work on the mechanisms of contagion is needed.

Furthering our understanding of the procycical effects of FVA requires specific consideration of the credit risk measurement models applied in estimating fair values. If model structure does not appropriately incorporate the credit cycle and its effect on estimates, overly optimistic (pessimistic) assessments in periods of expansion (contraction) may result. Allen and Saunders (2003) examine the treatment of cyclical factors in both academic and proprietary models. They conclude that systematic factors have been incorporated in models of default probability (PD), however this is not so for loss given default (LGD) and exposure at default (EAD). They also note that systematic correlation effects between these measures are not well understood.

Applying FVA in Illiquid Markets

- Difficulties in the selection of appropriate valuation inputs, reliability compromised by forced sales and a shift to model-based valuations.

Although not likely a cause of the crisis, accounting standards' weaknesses were exposed by the crisis, reducing the credibility of financial reporting. A report prepared by the Basel Committee on Banking Supervision (2008) discusses the valuation shortcomings exposed by the market turmoil. Banks faced many difficulties including: the selection of appropriate valuation inputs, determining reliability compromised by forced sales, over-reliance credit ratings to determine credit risk and a shift to model-based valuations.

Ball (2006) seems prescient in discussing reservations about fair value accounting. Firms tend to have positively correlated positions in

[7] See Laux and Leuz, 2010; Badertscher, et al, 2010; and Shaffer, 2010 for example.

commodities and financial instruments: ". . . they cannot all cash out simultaneously at the bid price, let alone at the ask. Fair value accounting has not yet been tested by a major financial crisis, when lenders in particular could discover that *fair value* means *fair weather value*." (italics added)

Measurement and Reliability

- Active markets do not exist for many assets and liabilities. Values based on models and estimates that are subjective; prone to error, bias and manipulation; and difficult to verify.
- Valuations are highly sensitive to model inputs.
- Market prices reflect numerous risks. Credit risk research has long grappled with the task of decomposing credit spreads

Even in stable, markets the measurement difficulties in applying fair value accounting are an important concern. For many assets and liabilities, active markets do not exist and fair values are based on models which use estimates that are subjective; prone to error, bias and manipulation; and difficult to verify.

PricewaterhouseCoopers (2008) provides examples of different methodologies for measuring credit risk illustrating how different inputs can result in significantly different outcomes. Practitioners and regulators express widespread concern over reliability and manipulation. Federal Reserve Board questioned the reliability and objectivity of fair values estimated using market credit spreads and internal model.[8] Nissam and Penman (2008) provide several press-reported comments by representatives of financial institutions and regulators where lack of comparability and reliability are often cited. Among these is the European Central Bank's (ECB) reference to the negative effects of the current state of the art in credit risk modelling on financial statement reliability,[9] noting the limited reliability of bank estimates of probabilities of default (PDs) for accounting purposes.

One of the problems with applying the FVA rules' requirement to include a credit risk adjustment is isolating the effect of credit risk in a transaction. The spread of the market interest rate for a particular instrument above the risk free rate is commonly taken as an indication of

[8] O'Brien, J., 2001, "The Use of Bank Internal Ratings Systems for Loan Fair Valuation", Board of Governors of the Federal Reserve System, Division of Research and Statistics, December.

[9] ECB Occasional Paper Series, No. 13, April 2004, *Fair Value Accounting and Financial Stability*, pages 7-9.

the credit risk. However, market prices incorporate several effects including collateral, liquidity and a time-varying price of risk. There is evidence that much of the spread is determined by factors other than default risk[10] with studies identifying taxes and liquidity as important determinants (Elton et al, 2001).

While empirical studies generally indicate that FVA provides relevant, reliable information, there is also evidence that value relevance depends upon measurement error and whether estimates are external or management determined. Will FVA continue to provide relevant, reliable information as it extends to a broader set of assets and liabilities, and under the new measurement and disclosure rules?

Costs / Complexity / Expertise

- Financial institutions face enormous challenges setting up systems that achieve consistency across accounting standards, counterparty risk measurement and performance measurement.
- Audit firms face expertise challenges in confirming valuations, requiring specialists trained in financial economics.

Fair value accounting is very costly and complex. Many argue that the benefits do not outweigh these costs (ABA 2006). Developing credit risk adjustments requires a deep understanding of market information, a command of the underlying credit risk theory, mathematical modeling and application of management judgment.

Audit opinions about valuation require knowledge about assumptions, input, and parameters of valuation models. Power (2010) sees fair value as a ' . . blueprint for redesigning the knowledge base of an entire profession' with implications for the need for external valuation expertise.

An example of the outsourcing of opinion is the relationship established between the International Valuation Standards Council (IVSC) and the International Accounting Standards Board (IASB) with a goal of providing guidance on the valuation of financial instruments. Interestingly, the IVSC is critical of the IASB's narrow, prescriptive approach with a limited range of possible valuation methods, arguing that the standards should set a principle and leave flexibility in the development of specific valuation methods (IVSC, 2009).

---

[10] Huang and Huang's (2002) tests of structural models and historical default probabilities attribute less than 25% of the credit spread to credit risk.

Critics readily point to the potential for manipulation under fair value accounting. Ironically, this is a primary advantage of FVA according to the SEC (2005) and supporters. In principle, the objectivity of marking-to-market disciplines managers who may have otherwise applied discretion in determining financial statement numbers. Gebhardt (2008) demonstrates earnings management opportunities for banks' loan loss provisioning under the current accounting for credit risk under a mixed-model (both historical cost and fair value).

Whereas fair value accounting in liquid markets limits the ability of managers to act opportunistically, marking-to-model increases opportunities for manipulation (Ball, 2006). The Federal Reserve Board Governor points to the potential for management bias (whether intentional or not) to result misstatements of earnings and equity, and sees a greater potential for misstated financial statements prepared using unreliable fair value estimates.

Aboody et al. (2006) find evidence that managers select model parameters to manage estimates of disclosed employee stock option fair values, raising the question of whether managers will act similarly when choosing models and parameters for value estimates of other financial instruments. Evidence of banks using discretion in fair value measurement to smooth earnings during the 2008 financial crisis is provided by Fiechter and Meyer (2011). Dechow et al. (2009) also report evidence that managers use the flexibility of FVA to smooth earnings in their study using income from securitization activities.[11]

IV. The Role of Credit Risk in Measuring Fair Value of Liabilities

The effect of accounting for changes in a firm's own credit risk is commonly referred to as 'counter-intuitive', but commentators are often much harsher in their criticism, moving to 'ridiculous' and more "... visceral response(s) to an intellectual issue."[12]

The rule requires that firms using fair value accounting mark both assets and liabilities to market. Asset fair values by definition provide the information that a financial statement user needs to assess the creditworthiness of an institution. Extending fair value measurement to liabilities is conceptually appealing and necessary to handle the effects of

[11] This is questioned by Barth and Taylor (2009) who acknowledge that, while Dechow et al.'s (2009) evidence is consistent with manipulation, the authors do not establish FVA as the source.

[12] Wayne Upton, ISAB project principal for the 2009 discussion paper, ww.cfo.com/article.cfm.13932186

hedging activities. While solid in principle, practical application produces effects that are unacceptable to many: deterioration (improvement) in a firm's credit rating increases (decreases) its net income.

Financial assets and liabilities which are written up or down to under FVA reflect changes in values which are driven by changes in expected cash flows and/or discount rate. As a firm's credit worthiness declines, the credit spread required by investors widens, thus increasing the discount rate and lowering the value of the instrument. Assuming a perfectly hedged situation, the higher discount rate applied to matched assets and liabilities would result in an equal decline in both asset and liability values and no effect on net income. The problem is that this symmetry does not hold in practice. Outside of the pure difficulty of being able to match hedging, many assets comprising firm value do not appear in the balance sheet (eg, reputation, real options). A change in a firm's reported asset values will thus be less than the change in liability values, giving rise to a balancing increase (decrease) in net income when the value of liabilities falls (rises) by more (less) than the value of assets.

There are other effects arising from changes in own credit risk, such as the transfer in wealth from debt holders to equity holders.[13] Barth et al. (2008) provide evidence this effect for firms with credit rating downgrades, and the IASB cites this effect as an argument for including credit risk in liability measurement.

Concern over increases in the net income due to deteriorating credit risk prompted the IASB to redeliberate. In October 2010, the standard setters announced a modification whereby a firm choosing to measure a liability at fair value should include effect due to changes in the entity's own credit risk in the Other Comprehensive Income section of the income statement, rather than as part of Net Income.

IV. Conclusion

This session provides a board overview of role of credit risk measurement for financial reporting purposes. We highlight several issues which are summarized as:

- A deficit in accounting knowledge about the determination of fair value and the incorporation of credit risk.

---

[13] As can be seen from the Merton (1974) contingent claims model of the firm, where equity holders hold a put option on the underlying value of the firm, written by the debt holders. Increasing the volatility of the assets (and or value of the assets) increases the value of the option.

- Expertise challenges for auditors verifying fair value with implications for outsourcing and readjustment of its knowledge base.
- Procyclical effects of FVA are complex, the evidence ambiguous and more work on the mechanisms of contagion is needed. Do models for measuring credit risk incorporate systematic effects?
- Valuations are highly sensitive to model inputs, estimates are subjective, prone to error, bias and manipulation, and difficult to verify.
- Costs and complexities faced by financial institutions setting up systems that are consistent across accounting standards, counterparty risk measurement and performance measurement.
- Opportunism and earnings management under marking-to-model.
- Accounting for own credit risk provides an example of an accounting treatment which is well-grounded in principle having undesirable effects in practice.

The road ahead is fraught with uncertainties and unintended consequences. This session is an initial step in identifying a path for investigation and understanding the where the path of fair value measurement may lead.

References

Aboody, D., Barth, M. and R. Kasznik. 2006. Do firms Understate Stock Option-Based Compensation Expense Disclosed under SFAS 123? *Review of Accounting Studies* 11, 1–33.

American Bankers Association. 2008. Letter to Robert Herz, Chairman of the Financial Accounting Standards Board. 13 November 2008.

Badertscher, B., Burks, J. and P. Easton. 2010. A Convenient Scapegoat: Fair Value Accounting by Commercial Banks during the Financial Crisis. SSRN: http://ssrn.com/abstract=1569673

Ball, R. 2006. International Financial Reporting Standards (IFRS): Pros and Cons for Investors. *Accounting & Business Research* 36, 5-27.

Barth M. and D. Taylor. 2010. In Defence of Fair Value: Weighing the Evidence on Earnings Management and Asset Securitizations. *Journal of Accounting and Economics*, 26-33.

Barth, M., W. Beaver, and W. Landsman, 2001. The Relevance Of The Value Relevance Literature for Accounting Standard Setting: Another View. *Journal of Accounting and Economics*, 31, 77-104.

Barth, M., Hodder, L. and S. Stubben. 2008. Fair Value Accounting for Liabilities and Own Credit Risk. *The Accounting Review*, 83 (3), 629-665.

Basel Committee on Banking Supervision. 2008. Supervisory Guidance for Assessing Banks' Financial Instruments Fair Value Practices. Consultative Document. November.

Dechow, P. and C. Shakespeare. 2009. Do Managers Use Securitization Volume and Fair Value Estimates to Hit Earnings Targets? *The Accounting Review, 84,* (1), 99–132.

Fiechter, P. and C. Meyer. 2011. Discretion in Fair Value Measurement of Banks during the 2008 Financial Crisis. Available at SSRN: http://ssrn.com/abstract=1522122

Elton, E., M. Gruber, Agrawal, D. and C. Mann. 2001. Explaining the Rate Spreads on Corporate Bonds. *Journal of Finance* 56, 247–277.

Financial Accounting Standards Board, 2008. Statement of Financial Accounting Standards no. 157: Fair Value Measurements. FASB, Stamford, CT.

Gebhardt, G. 2008. Accounting for Credit Risk: Are the Rules Setting the Right Incentives? *International Journal of Financial Services Management*, 3, 24 – 44.

Houweling, P., A.Mentink, and T. Vorst. 2002. Is Liquidity Reflected in Bond Yields? Evidence from the Euro Corporate Bond Market. Unpublished working paper, Erasmus University.

IASB Expert Advisory Panel. 2008. Measuring and Disclosing the Fair Value of Financial Instruments in Markets that Are No Longer Active. Draft document. September.

IVSC. 2009. IVSC Responds to IASB Fair Value Measurement Exposure Draft. 28 September. www.ivsc.org.

Landsman, W. 2007. Is Fair Value Accounting Information Relevant and Reliable? Evidence from Capital Market Research. *Accounting and Business Research Special Issue: International Accounting Policy Forum*: 19–30.

Laux, C. and C. Leuz. 2009. The Crisis of Fair-Value Accounting: Marking Sense of the Recent Debate. *Accounting, Organizations and Society* 34: 826-834.

Laux, C. and C. Leuz. 2010. Did Fair-Value Accounting Contribute to the Financial Crisis? *Journal of Economic Perspectives* 24: 93-118.

Merton, R.C. 1974. On the Pricing of Corporate Debt: The Risk Structure of Interest Rates. *Journal of Finance,*29, 449-470.

Nissam, D. and S. Penman. 2008. Principles for the Application of Fair Value Accounting. Working Paper. Center for Excellence in Accounting and Security Analysis, Columbia University.

Power, M. 2010. Fair Value Accounting, Financial Economics and The Transformation of Reliability. *Accounting and Business Research*, 40: 3, 197-210

Shaffer, S. 2010. Fair value accounting: Villain or innocent victim? Working paper, Federal Reserve Bank of Boston.

United States Securities and Exchange Commission, 2008. Report and recommendations pursuant to Section 133 of the Emergency Economic Stabilization Act of 2008: Study on mark-to-market accounting.

CHAPTER ELEVEN

APPROXIMATING DEFAULT PROBABILITIES WITH SOFT INFORMATION

DROR PARNES

Credit risk models traditionally concentrate on the quantitative characteristics of a borrower. These financial and accounting ratios are typically observable, verifiable, measurable, and programmable. Generally, these are the most desirable merits of credit scores and reduced-form credit schemes. In the past decade, however, we can observe a mounting interest among academics and practitioners in embedding soft qualitative data into credit methodologies. Numerous scholars have recommended the collection and deployment of subjective opinions and soft information by loan officers when assessing corporate creditworthiness.

Nevertheless, there are considerable challenges in building a soft information model. It is highly problematic to scrutinize and quantify soft qualitative data. Moreover, there are no accessible databases with relevant records on subjective views. Thus, it seems nearly impossible to empirically test such a theory. In addition, as described hereafter, there are several moral hazards of utilizing controversial soft data within credit risk evaluation techniques. Any future theory that embeds qualitative data must overcome these genuine hurdles.

To begin with, we must identify the boundaries of "soft information." Several scholars provide various definitions for this term. Rajan (1992) and Berger, Miller, Petersen, Rajan, and Stein (2005) define soft information as observations that cannot be credibly communicated from one agent to another. Petersen and Rajan (1994), Berger and Udell (1995), and Degryse and Cayseele (2000) suggest that soft information includes an assessment of the future prospects of the underlying borrower. These proprietary predictions are often compiled from informal interactions with the relevant customers, suppliers, competitors, and neighboring businesses. Camus and Godlewski (2005) identify the essential ingredients of soft information as follows: it is qualitative, it is forward looking, its collection is personal, and it contains subjective judgment, opinions, and perceptions. With slight deviation from prior studies, Liberti and Mian (2009) distinguish between subjective and soft information. The authors classify soft information as impossible to be codified, but subjective information as observations that can be categorized into grades. These grades, however, do not have a well-specified objective metric and hence cannot be objectively verified.

In light of these diverse classifications, I choose to define soft information as any qualitative relevant data about a borrower regardless of the means to obtain it. For example, my broad definition of soft information includes a private conversation with the firm's executives concerning future lines of business, but it also comprises a public press release on a projected layoff within the company. Both of these soft elements affect the borrower's creditworthiness. My wide definition of soft information further ignores whether the qualitative facts took place in the past or should occur in the future. For example, both an existing verdict on a major law suit against a firm and expected management turnover are included in the classification of soft information. Both of these qualitative events convey valuable information on the borrower's credit quality as well.

Next, to provide a sound motivation for the theory, I authenticate the vast use of soft information in practice. Many papers examine which financial institutions are more likely to utilize soft data and under which circumstances. Meyer (1998) demonstrates that relatively small firms, whose informational opacity precludes them access to public capital markets, often seek local community lenders. The geographic proximity allows the latter to obtain vital qualitative soft information while assessing corporate creditworthiness. Boot (2000) rationalizes that relationship lending is typically formed when banks develop special bonds with their clients, either by serving them over time or providing various financial products simultaneously. These personal ties allow loan officers to collect necessary soft information on the borrower.

According to Stein (2002), loan officers frequently receive informative yet non-contractible signals about future corporate projects to be financed and utilize this soft data to make informed credit decisions using their subjective judgment and personal experience. Berger, Kunt, Levine, and Haubrich (2003) conclude that large national banks tend to make hard-information-based transaction loans to larger, safer, and more transparent borrowers, while small regional financial institutions are likely to make more soft-information-based relationship loans to smaller, riskier, and more opaque borrowers.

Cole, Goldberg, and White (2004), Berger, Miller, Petersen, Rajan, and Stein (2005), Carter and McNulty (2005), and Berger and Udell (2006) find that large financial institutions typically have a comparative advantage in transactions lending that is based primarily on hard quantitative information, while small institutions are better able to execute relationship lending, which relies on soft qualitative facts. Hauswald and Marquez (2006) demonstrate that banks acquire proprietary soft information both to alleviate lending competition and to expand their market share. Inderst and Mueller (2008) incorporate soft information that influences a loan officer's credit decision while modeling the overall incentives to make new risky loans.

To further accentuate the unique contribution of my model I scan the literature and investigate whether the use of soft information is indeed beneficial when assessing the creditworthiness of borrowers. Lehmann (2003) empirically examines whether soft facts improve the forecast quality of bank internal credit ratings that are solely based on hard data. The author observes that the qualitative-information approach significantly and repeatedly outperforms the pure quantitative model. Grunert, Norden, and Weber (2005) provide strong evidence that the combined use of soft and hard information leads to more accurate predictions of future defaults than a single use of either of these components.

Norden and Weber (2010) explain that hard financial and accounting records are inherently backward looking, and they could be manipulated to optimize tax payments or dividends. On the other hand, soft qualitative information is ultimately stable, always available in real time for loan officers, and is forward looking, thus it adds to the predictive power of lenders. The authors find that taking into account subjective opinions in risk analysis can increase estimations' precision of borrowers' quality. Ergungor (2010) further declares that credit scores and other applicant sorting technologies solely based on hard information are expected to be less effective in low-income markets because of the lower quality of data and the higher risk involved in these particular loans.

Qualitative facts add vital aspects to credit assessment, but unfortunately, the collection and treatment of soft information convey two moral hazards and additional costs to lenders. The first moral hazard develops from *intentional* dishonest credit assessment. Krahnen and Weber (2001) advise against excessive use of subjective soft information, since this could lead to real difficulties in the detection of untruthful reporting. The authors assert that this may be a considerable problem when credit officers have an incentive to underestimate the credit risk of a particular loan. Nevertheless, the authors recommend against minimization of the discretionary decisions in the rating process because of their added value to the predictive strength.

Berger and Udell (2002, 2006) state that relationship lending based on subjective information could trigger agency problems within the lending financial institutions. These conflicts arise when the loan officer that has direct contact over time with the borrowing company is the sole repository of the soft information, which is not easily observed, verified, or transmitted to others. Nonetheless, the authors argue that small, closely held organizational structures with relatively few managerial layers are best at resolving these agency conflicts and managing soft data. Camus and Godlewski (2005) explain that as opposed to quantitative hard information, qualitative facts are problematic since they are non-verifiable and vulnerable to deliberate manipulations. The authors realize, however, that assessing the credit quality of borrowers with soft information is preferable than merely relying on quantitative facts, but it requires particular organizational modifications within the lending bank.

A second moral hazard evolves from *unintentional* biased credit appraisal. Berger and Udell (2004) detect robust deterioration in the ability of loan officers to assess creditworthiness of potential borrowers over the bank's lending cycle, which results in a general easing of credit standards. The authors explain that this phenomenon progresses partly due to a proportional increase in new credit officers that have never experienced a loan bust, and partly due to the atrophying skills of experienced officers as time passes since their last challenged loans.

Furthermore, the exploitation of soft information in credit assessment has a real price. Allen, DeLong, and Saunders (2004) explain that relationship lending based on soft information is expensive to establish and maintain. This problem is more pronounced among large banks, since these financial institutions have sufficient capital to make sizeable profitable loans, while spending time and effort to cultivate small accounts becomes an inefficient use of resources. As a result, Akhavein, Frame, and White (2005) show that an increasing number of large banks have begun to evaluate small business loan applications through credit scores, which rely on hard quantitative data rather than soft qualitative information and subjective views. Moreover, DeYoung, Glennon, and Nigro (2008) conclude that due to recent developments in information technologies, hard-information lending approaches could outperform soft-information relationship-based lending techniques in long-distance financial interactions and dispersed markets.

I cannot disregard these two moral hazards and the additional costs involved in collecting and utilizing soft information within credit evaluation methodologies. These are real evils that could deter banks from using subjective facts and might eventually harm the ability of lenders to assess the creditworthiness of borrowers. Thus, to better guide credit supervisors, in my article I search for an optimal range for the soft information-based endogenous model parameters.

In my study titled "Approximating Default Probabilities with Soft Information" I present a new structural model that approximates corporate creditworthiness with available soft information, qualitative data, and subjective opinions on managerial ability to overcome credit obstacles. I illustrate the proposed scheme by drawing empirical estimations from common credit scores and authenticate its advantages and disadvantages through ROC curve analyses. I further explore its economic added value through several lending simulations.

Overall, I have discovered that the proposed model performs exceptionally well throughout the area of high false positive rates, where loan officers misidentify a non-default as a default candidate and wrongly deny loans. This region is particularly profitable to lenders due to considerably higher lending rates for these doubtful loans. However, due to its inherent left censoring, the suggested scheme generally does not improve lending decisions in more lenient areas. I therefore recommend that loan officers utilize the theory primarily when existing credit scores, reduced-form schemes, or internal score-cards advise to decline loans. In addition, I suggest that loan officers exploit the present approach with great cautious; since the proposed model can be quite sensitive to some parameter estimations. On the other hand, I demonstrate that a vigilant deployment of the current model can considerably enhance lenders' profitability.

There are some important by-products to my analysis. While the key focus of the study is to offer a new theory that incorporates qualitative information into quantitative estimation of credit quality, I am able to gain valuable awareness of the link between changes in customary financial and accounting ratios and real credit adjustments, as well as managerial aptitude to take proactive steps to enhance corporate creditworthiness. I have realized that about 90% of all transformations in these financial quantities have genuine influence on the credit quality of firms. The remaining 10% are typically undisruptive due to counter economic forces. I further comprehend that managerial intervention is often limited in practice, and typically cannot offset more than 5% of the uncontrollable economic shocks.

References

Akhavein, Jalal D., Scott W. Frame, and Lawrence W. White, 2005, The diffusion of financial innovations: An examination of the adoption of small business credit scoring by large banking organizations, *Journal of Business* 78, 577-596.

Allen, Linda, Gayle DeLong, and Anthony Saunders, 2004, Issues in the credit risk modeling of retail markets, *Journal of Banking & Finance* 28, 727-752.

Berger, Allen N., and Gregory F. Udell, 1995, Relationship lending and lines of credit in small firm finance, *Journal of Business* 68, 351-382.

Berger, Allen N., and Gregory F. Udell, 2002, Small business credit availability and relationship lending: The importance of bank organizational structure, *The Economic Journal* 112, 32-53.

Berger, Allen N., and Gregory F. Udell, 2004, The institutional memory hypothesis and the procyclicality of bank lending behavior, *Journal of Financial Intermediation* 13, 458-495.

Berger, Allen N., and Gregory F. Udell, 2006, A more complete conceptual framework for SME finance, *Journal of Banking & Finance* 30, 2945-2966.

Berger, Allen N., Asli D. Kunt, Ross Levine, and Joseph G. Haubrich, 2003, Bank concentration and competition: An evolution in the making, *Journal of Money, Credit and Banking* 36, 433-451.

Berger, Allen N., Nathan H. Miller, Mitchell A. Petersen, Raghuram G. Rajan, and Jeremy C. Stein, 2005, Does function follow organizational form? Evidence from the lending practices of large and small banks, *Journal of Financial Economics* 76, 237-269.

Boot, Arnoud W.A., 2000, Relationship banking: What do we know? *Journal of Financial Intermediation* 9, 7-25.

Camus, Brigitte G., and Christphe J. Godlewski, 2005, Credit risk management in banks: Hard information, soft information and manipulation, Working Paper.

Carter, David A., and James E. McNulty, 2005, Deregulation, technological change, and the business-lending performance of large and small banks, *Journal of Banking & Finance* 29, 1113-1130.

Cole, Rebel A., Lawrence G. Goldberg, and Lawrence J. White, 2004, Cookie-cutter versus character: The micro structure of small-business lending by large and small banks, *Journal of Financial and Quantitative Analysis* 39, 227-252.

Degryse, Hans, and Patrick Van Cayseele, 2000. Relationship lending within a bank-based system: Evidence from European small business data, *Journal of Financial Intermediation* 9, 90-109.

DeYoung, Robert, Dennis Glennon, and Peter Nigro, 2008, Borrower-lender distance, credit scoring, and loan performance: Evidence from informational-opaque small business borrowers, *Journal of Financial Intermediation* 17, 113-143.

Ergungor, Ozgur E., 2010, Bank branch presence and access to credit in low- to moderate-income neighborhoods, *Journal of Money, Credit and Banking* 42, 1321-1349.

Grunert, Jens, Lars Norden, and Martin Weber, 2005, The role of non-financial factors in internal credit ratings, *Journal of Banking & Finance* 29, 509-531.

Hauswald, Robert, and Robert Marquez, 2006, Competition and strategic information acquisition in credit markets, *The Review of Financial Studies* 19, 967-1000.

Inderst, Roman, and Holger M. Mueller, 2008, Bank capital structure and credit decisions, *Journal of Financial Intermediation* 17, 295-314.

Krahnen, Jan Pieter, and Martin Weber, 2001, Generally accepted rating principles: A primer, *Journal of Banking & Finance* 25, 3-23.

Lehmann, Bina, 2003, Is it worth the while? The relevance of qualitative information in credit rating, Working Paper, University of Konstanz, Center of Finance and Econometrics.

Liberti, Jose M., and Atif R. Mian, 2009, Estimating the effect of hierarchies on information use, *The Review of Financial Studies* 22, 4057-4090.

Meyer, Laurence H., 1998, The present and future roles of banks in small business finance, *Journal of Banking & Finance* 22, 1109-1116.

Norden, Lars, and Martin Weber, 2010, Credit line usage, checking account activity, and default risk of bank borrowers, *The Review of Financial Studies* 23, 3665-3699.

Petersen, Mitchell A., and Raghuram G. Rajan, 1994, The benefits of lending relationships: Evidence from small business data, *The Journal of Finance* 49, 3-37.

Rajan, Raghuram G., 1992, Insiders and outsiders: the choice between informed and arm's-length debt, *The Journal of Finance* 47, 1367-1400.

Stein, Jeremy C., 2002, Information production and capital allocation: Decentralized vs. hierarchical firms, *The Journal of Finance* 57, 1891-1921.

CHAPTER TWELVE

PROPOSAL OF NEW HYBRID MODELS FOR PD ESTIMATES ON LOW DEFAULT PORTFOLIOS (LDPS), EMPIRICAL COMPARISONS AND REGULATORY POLICY IMPLICATIONS

RUNGPORN ROENGPITYA AND PRATABJAI NILLA-OR[1]

Introduction

One of the challenges facing both regulators and IRB-based banks regarding the estimation of IRB parameters lies in the area of probability of default (PD) estimation for low default portfolios (LDPs).[2] For regulators, the most important concern has to do with the underestimation of credit risk associated with LDPs as a result of data scarcity. The scarcity of default data leads to the difficulty in backtesting the PDs estimated from the risk models against the true historical default rates. For banks, the challenging task of LDP risk parameter estimation urges them to exclude these LDPs from the IRB calculation, though such treatment is not supported by the industry, as claimed in the joint industry working group discussion paper between the British Banker Association, London Investment Banking Association and International Swaps and Derivatives Association (BBA-LIBA-ISDA paper). Moreover, banks may choose to employ either the simple historical average approach or expert judgment to estimate the PDs instead, which can possibly progress to the underestimation of credit risk previously mentioned.

---

[1] The authors are from Supervision Group, Bank of Thailand.

[2] Although the general definition of LDPs varies very much across concerned parties, it can be loosely defined as portfolios with too limited default events to obtain a robust probability of default (PD) estimation according to the principles outline in the Basel II or internal risk management objectives.

There are a few theoretical approaches in estimating PDs for LDPs about which we will consider here: (1) the *most prudent* estimation by Pluto and Tasche (2006); (2) the *maximum likelihood approach* by Forrest (2005); (3) *CAP curve calibration* by Van Der Burgt (2007); and (4) the *margin of conservatism* by Benjamin, Cathcart and Ryan (2006).

This chapter elaborates on our *new hybrid models* as well as empirical tests of different theoretical approaches in estimating the PDs mentioned above. For the theoretical improvements to the existing theories, we discovered that the optimal k used to fit the exponential function to the actual CAP curve outlined in Van Der Burgt (2007) was very sensitive to the granularity of how one computed the cumulative number of borrowers and therefore we make a stance that the AR of the fitted curve should be between 40% − 80%, as seen in most best practices. Finally, we proposed three new hybrid models, merging two principles—Forrest (2005) and Pluto and Tasche (2006)—together.[3] Finally, our paper is the first of its kind to provide the PD estimate comparison between the *most prudent*, the *CAP curve calibration*, the *margin of conservatism*, and our *hybrid models*—on the virtual sovereign portfolio.

In this chapter, there are three separate sections dealing with different aspects of such estimation. The first section gives theoretical construction and empirical estimation of the new *hybrid model* class we proposed. The second section presents the proposal to cope with the possible underestimation of the PDs using the *CAP curve calibration.* We offer our policy recommendations regarding the PD estimation methods for LDPs in the last section.

1. The New *Hybrid Models*

Our new *hybrid models* rest upon the mix between the two existing approaches—the *most prudent* and the *maximum likelihood* approaches. The maximum likelihood approaches has the advantage of maximizing the likelihood of the PDs happening which is the concept that makes most sense but it is very calculation-intensive. To ease the computation burden, we employed the *most prudent method* instead of optimizing N dimensions for N-rating case. Our class of *hybrid models* can be thought of as easing away from the combination of PDs which produces the maximized likelihood in a systematic way (or in the *most prudent* way).

---

[3] As for the mathematical proofs of the necessary and sufficient conditions for the rank order property of the *most prudent* approach, we present them in our paper instead.

Theoretical construction

Let the likelihood function of N rating grades be defined as

$$\mathcal{L}(p_1, \dots p_N) = \mathcal{L}(p_1) \cdots \mathcal{L}(p_N), \tag{1}$$

where $p_1,\dots p_N$ are the PD estimates for each rating grade. Without loss of generality, let i=1 be the lowest risk grade and i=N be the highest risk grade. Equation (1) represents the general form of the likelihood function. Let $n_1,\dots n_N$ and $k_1,\dots,k_N$ be the total number of obligors and total number of defaults in each rating grade 1,…,N. For the case where *there is no asset correlation*, the likelihood can be written as

$$\begin{aligned}\mathcal{L}(p_1, \dots p_N) &= p_1^{k_1}(1-p_1)^{n_1-k_1} \cdots p_N^{k_1}(1-p_N)^{n_N-k_N} \\ &= \prod_{i=1}^{N} p_1^{k_i}(1-p_i)^{n_i-k_i} = \prod_{i=1}^{N} \mathcal{L}(p_i).\end{aligned} \tag{2}$$

For the case where *there is an asset correlation* ρ, the *expected* likelihood function is

$$E[\mathcal{L}(p_1, \dots p_N)] = \int_{-\infty}^{\infty} \prod_{i=1}^{N} \mathbb{N}\left(\frac{\mathbb{N}^{-1}(p_i)-\sqrt{\rho}y}{\sqrt{1-\rho}}\right)^{k_i} \left(1-\mathbb{N}\left(\frac{\mathbb{N}^{-1}(p_i)-\sqrt{\rho}y}{\sqrt{1-\rho}}\right)\right)^{n_i-k_i} \varphi(y)dy, \tag{3}$$

where $\varphi(y)$ is the standard normal density function, $\mathbb{N}$ and $\mathbb{N}^{-1}$ are the cumulative standard normal distribution and its inverse respectively, and y is the random variable distributed standard-normally. Equation (3) can be approximated by the summation with M intervals as

$$\begin{aligned}E[\mathcal{L}] &\approx \frac{1}{M}\sum_{j=1}^{M}\left[\prod_{i=1}^{N} \mathbb{N}\left(\frac{\mathbb{N}^{-1}(p_i)-\sqrt{\rho}\mathbb{N}^{-1}\left(\frac{j-0.5}{M}\right)}{\sqrt{1-\rho}}\right)^{k_i}\left(1-\mathbb{N}\left(\frac{\mathbb{N}^{-1}(p_i)-\sqrt{\rho}\mathbb{N}^{-1}\left(\frac{j-0.5}{M}\right)}{\sqrt{1-\rho}}\right)\right)^{n_i-k_i}\right] \\ &= \frac{1}{M}\sum_{j=1}^{M}\left[\prod_{i=1}^{N} \mathbb{P}(p_i, M_j)^{k_i}\left(1-\mathbb{P}(p_i, M_j)\right)^{n_i-k_i}\right],\end{aligned} \tag{4}$$

where $\mathbb{P}(p_i, M_j) = \mathbb{N}\left(\frac{\mathbb{N}^{-1}(p_i)-\sqrt{\rho}\mathbb{N}^{-1}\left(\frac{j-0.5}{M}\right)}{\sqrt{1-\rho}}\right)$.

The maximum likelihood concept requires us to maximize Equations (2) and (4) with respect to the PD of rating each rating grade i, p_i. In our *hybrid model* class, we employed the concept from Pluto and Tasche (2006)'s *most prudent approach* to solve for the PDs rather than finding the combination of PDs that maximizes the k-factor in the IRB formula like the original approach in Forrest (2005). Therefore, we define the likelihood function of the *collapse of rating grade i through N*, the highest risk grade, in a similar fashion as in the *most prudent* estimation as

$$\mathcal{L}(\vec{p}_i) = p_i^{k_i}(1-p_i)^{n_i-k_i}\cdots p_N^{k_N}(1-p_N)^{n_N-k_N} =$$
$$p^{k_i}(1-p)^{n_i-k_i}\cdots p^{k_N}(1-p)^{n_N-k_N}$$
$$= p^{\sum_{j=i}^{N}k_j}(1-p)^{\sum_{j=i}^{N}(n_j-k_j)}, \quad (5)$$

with $p_i = p_{i+1} = \ldots = p_i = p$ and merging the terms for the zero asset correlation case. For the case where there is an asset correlation,

$$E(\mathcal{L}(\vec{p}_i)) = \frac{1}{M}\sum_{j=1}^{M}\left[\prod_{i=1}^{N}\mathbb{P}(p_i,M_j)^{k_i}\left(1-\mathbb{P}(p_i,M_j)\right)^{n_i-k_i}\right]$$
$$= \frac{1}{M}\sum_{j=1}^{M}\left[\prod_{i=1}^{N}\mathbb{P}(p,M_j)^{\sum_{l=i}^{N}k_l}\left(1-\mathbb{P}(p,M_j)\right)^{\sum_{l=i}^{N}(n_l-k_l)}\right]. \quad (6)$$

With this setting, we proposed the *new class of hybrid models* for PD estimation of LDPs. Here, we propose one of the *hybrid models* here, the *hybrid MLE model*, while the other two models in the *hybrid* class can be found in Roengpitya, et al. (2011).

The Hybrid MLE Model

Let $\hat{\mathcal{L}} = e^{(-0.5\chi^2(1-CL,DF))} \cdot \mathcal{L}(\vec{p}_i^{\,MLE})$ where $\mathcal{L}(\vec{p}_i^{\,MLE})$ is the maximum likelihood value coming from replacing p with the observed default rate after collapsing the grades in Equation (5);[4] hence obtaining the maximum

---

[4] The likelihood function in Equation (3) is maximized where $p_i = \frac{k_i}{n_i}$, the observed default rate. This can be derived by differentiating Equation (3) with respect to p_i and setting it equal to zero.

likelihood possible and $CL \in [0,1]$ and *DF* are the confidence level and degree of freedom (set to 1) respectively after collapsing rating grades *i* to *N*. In a similar fashion, for the non-zero correlation case, let $E(\hat{\mathcal{L}}) = e^{\left(-0.5\chi^2(1-CL,DF)\right)} \cdot E\left(\mathcal{L}(\vec{p}_i^{\,MLE})\right)$ and the term $E\left(\mathcal{L}(\vec{p}_i^{\,MLE})\right)$ is the expected maximum likelihood in Equation (6), evaluated at the probability *p* that maximizes such equation. In the *hybrid MLE model*, the estimated PD for rating grade *i*, p_i^*, is the p_i^* that solves

$$p_i^* \; solves: \quad \mathcal{L}(\vec{p}_i) = p_i^{*\,\sum_{j=i}^{N} k_j} (1 - p_i^*)^{\sum_{j=i}^{N}(n_j - k_j)} = \hat{\mathcal{L}} \tag{7}$$

for the zero correlation case. If there is an asset correlation, it is the p_i^* that solves

$$p_i^* \; solves: E\left(\mathcal{L}(\vec{p}_i)\right) = \frac{1}{M}\sum_{j=1}^{M}\left[\prod_{i=1}^{N}\mathbb{P}(p_i^*, M_j)^{\sum_{l=i}^{N}k_l}\left(1 - \mathbb{P}(p_i^*, M_j)\right)^{\sum_{l=i}^{N}(n_l - k_l)}\right] = E(\hat{\mathcal{L}}). \tag{8}$$

Conservatism of the PD estimates from the *Hybrid MLE Model*

Proposition: If there exists the probability p_i^* obtained from the *hybrid MLE model* that makes Equations (7) and (8) hold with equality, then the estimated PD for rating grade *i*, p_i^*, will be **at least as conservative** as the PD estimated using the *most prudent* method of Pluto and Tasche (2006), p_i^{MP}, if the following conditions are met:

1. p_i^{MP} must satisfy $\dfrac{1-\gamma-\sum_{j=0}^{k(i+)-1}\binom{n(i+)}{j}p^j(1-p)^{n-j}}{\binom{n(i+)}{k(i+)}} \geq \hat{\mathcal{L}}$ or $\dfrac{1-\gamma-\sum_{j=0}^{k(i+)-1}\binom{n(i+)}{j}p^j(1-p)^{n-j}}{\binom{n(i+)}{k(i+)}} \geq E(\hat{\mathcal{L}})$ for the non-zero correlation case
2. both PDs must satisfy the condition $k_i \leq n_i \cdot p_i$ or the probability of default p_i must be greater than the observed default k_i/n_i for rating grade *i*. For the case where there is an asset correlation, both PDs must meet the condition, conditioning on M_j, $k_i \leq n_i \cdot \mathbb{P}(p_i, M_j)$.[5]

[5] This condition $k_i \leq n_i \cdot p_i$ is necessary for ensuring that an increase in *p* will lead to a decrease in $p^{k_i}(1-p)^{n_i - k_i}$ and vice versa, which is the condition necessary

where $k(i+) = \sum_{j=i}^{N} k_j$ and $k(i+) = \sum_{j=i}^{N} k_j$ denote the *cumulative* defaults and borrowers from the highest risk grade down to the rating grade *I* respectively. $1-\gamma$ is the confidence level defined to be in relation with the equation $1-\gamma = \sum_{i=0}^{k} \binom{n}{i} p^i (1-p)^{n-i}$ which reflects the binomial distribution assumption in the *most prudent* approach. $\hat{\mathcal{L}}$ and E($\hat{\mathcal{L}}$) are as defined in the previous section. $\binom{n}{i} = \frac{n!}{i!(n-i)!}$. The proof of this proposition can be found in Roengpitya, et al. (2011).

Rank Ordering Property of the PDs from the *Hybrid MLE Model*

Proposition: Without loss of generality, let there be *N* rating grades with rating grade *N* being the highest risk grade. Let n_i be the number of borrowers in an arbitrary better rating (lower risk) grade with k_i defaults and n_{i+1} be the number of borrowers in the next worse rating grade with k_{i+1} defaults. $E(p_i, n_i, k_i) = \frac{1}{M}\sum_{j=1}^{M}\left[\prod_{i=1}^{N} \mathbb{P}(p_i, M_j)^{k_i}\left(1-\mathbb{P}(p_i, M_j)\right)^{n_i-k_i}\right]$ is as defined in Equation (6) and define $\Delta = \frac{E(p_i, n_i+n_{i+1}, k_i+k_{i+1})}{E(p_i, n_i, k_i)\cdot E(p_i, n_{i+1}, k_{i+1})}$. The PD estimates stemming from the *hybrid MLE model* will retain the rank order, $p_i < p_{i+1}$, for a given confidence interval γ if the following condition is met.

For the zero-correlation case and non-zero correlation cases:

$$\frac{(p_i^*)^{k_{i+1}}(1-p_i^*)^{n_{i+1}-k_{i+1}}}{(p_{i+1}^*)^{k_{i+1}}(1-p_{i+1}^*)^{n_{i+1}-k_{i+1}}} = \frac{\mathcal{L}\left(\vec{p}_i^{\,MLE}\right)}{\mathcal{L}\left(\vec{p}_{i+1}^{\,MLE}\right)} \cdot \frac{1}{(p_i^*)^{k_i}(1-p_i^*)^{n_i-k_i}} > 1 \tag{9}$$

$$\frac{E(p_i^*, n_{i+1}, k_{i+1})}{E(p_i^*, n_{i+1}, k_{i+1})} = \frac{E\left(\mathcal{L}\left(\vec{p}_i^{\,MLE}\right)\right)}{E\left(\mathcal{L}\left(\vec{p}_{i+1}^{\,MLE}\right)\right)} \cdot \frac{1}{E(p_i^*, n_i, k_i)\Delta} > 1, \tag{10}$$

---

for the proposition to hold true. For the proof of this claim, please see Roengpitya, et al. (2011).

where $\mathcal{L}(\vec{p}_i^{\,MLE})$ and $E\left(\mathcal{L}(\vec{p}_i^{\,MLE})\right)$ are as defined in the previous section. The proof of this proposition can also be read in Roengpitya, et al. (2011).

A few notes on our *Hybrid Models*

On a final but very important note, since all the proposed models will have the PD estimates which deviate from the combinations of PDs that yield the maximum likelihood outcomes seen in Forrest (2005), there can be a case where

1. *the combination of PDs after our most prudent collapse yields the highest likelihood possible but this likelihood is less than* $\hat{\underline{\mathcal{L}}}$ *or* $E(\hat{\underline{\mathcal{L}}})$: we advise taking the PD value where the likelihood yields the highest possible value as the PD estimate for that rating grade; hereby calling these PDs constrained PDs
2. *the PD estimates have more than one values*: we recommend taking the most conservative value possible as the PD estimate for that rating grade

Empirical Analysis of the *Hybrid Models*

THE DATA USED FOR EMPIRICAL ANALYSIS

It is our choice to choose the sovereign borrowers to test the PD estimates from both the existing and our proposed models, as they are usually of low-default in nature as well as possessing sufficient data points to perform the empirical analysis. For the sovereign data, we used the S&P sovereign rating as of January 2009 to classify the rating of each country. The sovereign debt crisis data between 1975-2002 is from Savona and Vezzoli (2008) with the crisis episodes for the years 2003-2008 coming from *S&P Sovereign Ratings History* as of December 2009. The table containing information on sovereign debt crisis is presented in the appendix of Roengpitya, et al. (2011).

After identifying all the crisis episodes, we then created the population of countries to be included in our virtual portfolio. We used all of the countries having sovereign ratings as of January 2009. The list of countries and their January 2009 sovereign ratings as well as the table of the distribution of countries in our sample across S&P rating grades and the number of cumulative defaults[6] in each rating grade are presented in the appendix of Roengpitya, et al (2011). To better track the performance of countries before their default experience, we excluded the two countries with rating "D" from the sample. Therefore, there are 3,910 obligor-years and 66 defaults for the sovereign portfolio in the calculation.

There are two types of sovereign portfolio constructed by grouping the sovereign obligors into fewer ratings. The first type of the sovereign portfolio groups the S&P ratings into Ratings 1-6, using the Bank of Thailand's mapping of ECAIs for banks employing the standardized approach (SA). The other type of sovereign portfolio differentiates the S&P ratings into 7 different grades (which conveniently satisfy the internal rating-based (IRB) requirement), using the SA mapping and then adjusting so that the observed default rates between rating grades rank-order more smoothly. Table 1 below presents both types of grouping for the sovereign portfolio.

Table 1: Information of Both Sovereign Portfolio Types

Portfolio Type 1: Grouping by SA Rating Guideline

SA Grade	S&P Ratings	Ob-years	Defaults	ODR	Cum Ob-years	Cum Defaults	Cum ODR
1	AA-, AA, AA+, AAA	1020	0	0%	3910	66	1.688%
2	A-, A, A+	646	2	0.310%	2890	66	2.284%
3	BBB-, BBB, BBB+	578	9	1.557%	2244	64	2.852%
4	BB-, BB, BB+	748	28	3.743%	1666	55	3.301%
5	B-, B, B+	884	26	2.941%	918	27	2.941%
6	CCC+ or below	34	1	2.941%	34	1	2.941%

Portfolio Type 2: Grouping by SA Rating Guideline With Adjustments

Modified Grade	S&P Ratings	Ob-years	Defaults	ODR	Cum Ob-years	Cum Defaults	Cum ODR
1	AA-, AA, AA+, AAA	1020	0	0%	3910	66	1.688%
2	A, A+	510	1	0.196%	2890	66	2.284%
3	A-	136	1	0.735%	2380	65	2.731%
4	BBB, BBB+	340	4	1.176%	2244	64	2.852%
5	BBB-	238	5	2.101%	1904	60	3.151%
6	BB, BB+	442	9	2.036%	1666	55	3.301%
7	BB- or below	1224	46	3.758%	1224	46	3.758%

This table presents the information on both types of sovereign low-default portfolios, using the S&P ratings as of January 2009.

Empirical Results

The results of using our *hybrid models* to estimate the PDs for the virtual sovereign portfolio using the correlation of 0%, 4% and 12% are shown in Table 2.

[6] The cumulative defaults are accumulated across the years 1975-2009 and across countries within the same rating grade. Therefore, it can be thought of as the accumulation across obligor-years.

When comparing the PD estimation using our *hybrid MLE model*, with the *most prudent approach*, we found that our PD estimates on the virtual sovereign portfolio were more conservative. In addition, when considering two other approaches—the *margin of conservatism* and the *CAP curve calibration*,[7] our PD estimates are also higher. The following Figure 1 shows the PD estimate comparison between the four approaches for the 75% confidence level and zero asset correlation. Details of other cases are in our paper.

In Roengpitya, et al. (2011), we also provided the necessary and sufficient conditions for the PD estimates of our *hybrid models* to be more conservative than the *most prudent approach*.

Table 2: Results of PD estimation using Hybrid MLE Method

6-Rating Grade							7-Rating Grade					
Asset correlation=0%												
Grade	50%	75%	90%	95%	99%	99.90%	Grade	50%	75%	90%	95%	99%	99.90%
1	1.83%	1.94%	2.05%	2.12%	2.27%	2.46%	1	1.83%	1.94%	2.05%	2.12%	2.27%	2.46%
2	2.48%	2.62%	2.77%	2.87%	3.07%	3.32%	2	2.48%	2.62%	2.77%	2.87%	3.07%	3.32%
3	3.10%	3.28%	3.47%	3.60%	3.85%	4.16%	3	2.96%	3.13%	3.32%	3.44%	3.68%	3.98%
4	3.61%	3.83%	4.07%	4.23%	4.55%	4.95%	4	3.10%	3.28%	3.47%	3.60%	3.85%	4.16%
5	3.33%	3.63%	3.95%	4.17%	4.55%	5.16%	5	3.43%	3.63%	3.85%	4.00%	4.29%	4.65%
6	5.33%	7.55%	10.32%	12.32%	16.73%	22.55%	6	3.61%	3.83%	4.07%	4.23%	4.55%	4.95%
							7	4.14%	4.42%	4.72%	4.92%	5.33%	5.83%
Asset correlation=4%												
Grade	50%	75%	90%	95%	99%	99.90%	Grade	50%	75%	90%	95%	99%	99.90%
1	2.57%	3.12%	3.96%	4.54%	6.13%	8.14%	1	2.57%	3.12%	3.96%	4.54%	6.13%	8.14%
2	3.40%	4.10%	5.13%	5.85%	7.77%	10.18%	2	3.40%	4.10%	5.13%	5.85%	7.77%	10.18%
3	4.17%	5.00%	6.20%	7.04%	9.24%	11.99%	3	4.01%	4.81%	5.98%	6.79%	8.93%	11.61%
4	4.78%	5.72%	7.05%	7.99%	10.40%	13.41%	4	4.17%	5.00%	6.20%	7.04%	9.24%	11.99%
5	4.34%	5.28%	6.54%	7.48%	9.79%	12.83%	5	4.57%	5.47%	6.76%	7.66%	10.01%	12.92%
6	5.84%	8.58%	12.15%	14.85%	20.95%	29.30%	6	4.78%	5.72%	7.05%	7.99%	10.40%	13.41%
							7	5.40%	6.45%	7.90%	8.95%	11.56%	14.84%
Asset correlation=12%												
Grade	50%	75%	90%	95%	99%	99.90%	Grade	50%	75%	90%	95%	99%	99.90%
1	3.83%	5.19%	7.52%	9.06%	13.96%	19.81%	1	3.83%	5.19%	7.52%	9.06%	13.96%	19.81%
2	4.91%	6.56%	9.33%	11.13%	16.73%	23.30%	2	4.91%	6.56%	9.33%	11.13%	16.73%	23.30%
3	5.89%	7.79%	10.92%	12.95%	19.09%	26.23%	3	5.69%	7.53%	10.59%	12.57%	18.61%	25.62%
4	6.65%	8.73%	12.11%	14.33%	20.85%	28.47%	4	5.89%	7.79%	10.92%	12.95%	19.09%	26.23%
5	6.11%	8.09%	11.26%	13.51%	19.81%	27.66%	5	6.40%	8.41%	11.72%	13.86%	20.26%	27.70%
6	7.16%	11.01%	16.27%	20.32%	29.81%	41.30%	6	6.65%	8.73%	12.11%	14.33%	20.85%	28.47%
							7	7.41%	9.67%	13.28%	15.69%	22.57%	30.66%

[7] For the *margin of conservatism* approach, we used the minimization of the root-mean-square error to first come up with the initial PD estimates for our sovereign portfolio before applying the margin of conservatism to obtain the final estimates.

Figure 1: PD Estimate comparison between existing methods

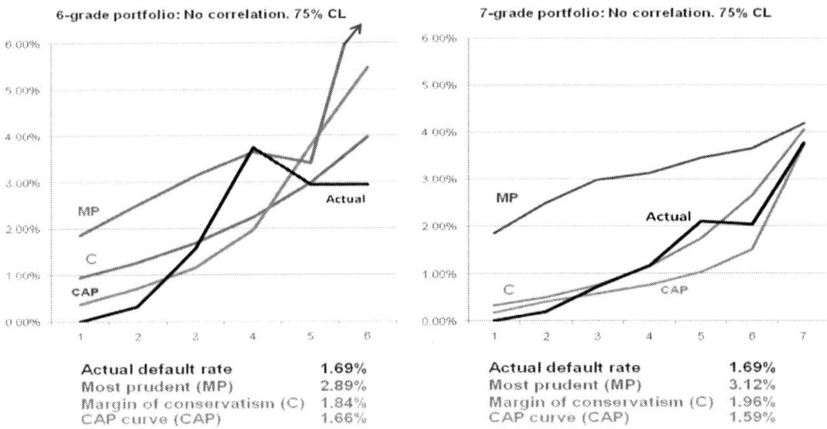

2. Caution in using the *Cap Curve Calibration* Method

In Van Der Burgt (2007), the author proposed an alternative approach for estimating PDs by calibrating the cumulative accuracy profile (CAP) curve which is used to assess the discriminatory power of the credit rating model. The model is simply a one-parameter (k) exponential function of cumulative defaults (y) and cumulative obligors (x).

$$y = f(x) = \frac{1-e^{-kx}}{1-e^{-k}} \tag{11}$$

To preserve the concavity of CAP curve, k should be a non-negative number. We determine the value k by minimizing the root mean square error;

$$RMSE = \min_k \sqrt{\frac{1}{N}\sum_{i=1}^{N}\left[y_i - \frac{1-e^{-kx_i}}{1-e^{-k}}\right]^2} \tag{12}$$

where i is the rating class i and N is the total number of rating grades. Given the estimated CAP curve and portfolio default rate, we can then derive the PD for each rating grade using the Falkenstein, et al. (2000)

methodology which is the multiplication of portfolio default rate $\langle D \rangle$ and the change of the CAP curve;

$$PD(R) = \langle D \rangle \frac{ke^{-kx}}{1-e^{-k}}. \tag{13}$$

One very important observation regarding RMSE minimization is that the value of k may be sensitive to the granularity of the rating grades. This can become problematic when the modeler has to make a choice between fitting the curve using raw ordinal scores of borrowers or using less-refined rating grades, as the optimal k obtained from each case will be different, leading to different estimates of the PDs as shown in Figure 2.

Figure 2. Illustration of different granularity for Cap Curve Calibration

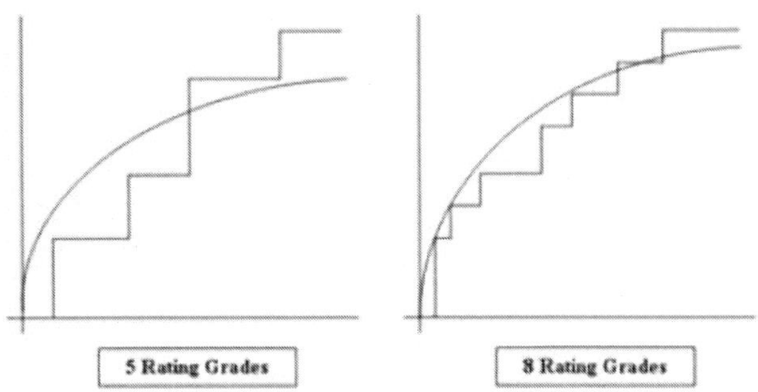

Our work then proves that an increase in the granularity of the rating grades does not guarantee an increase in k. We showed that it depended solely on the difference between the fitted curve and the actual value of $y_i - \frac{1-e^{-kx_i}}{1-e^{-k}}$ at each minimization point (for each rating grade). Hence, to make sure that the PD estimation is valid and appropriate for our portfolio, the stability of portfolio distribution through time should be checked. If the distribution changes significantly, the review of PD calibration is required.

The empirical study based on the same sovereign portfolio in the last section for the 6-rating case is summarized in Table 3.

It can be seen that the estimated PD in each grade is quite in line with the observed default rate. However, the estimated PD for rating 4 in the 6-

grade case seems to have underestimated the actual default. This verifies our proposition elaborated before; so a big change in the number of obligors in some grades can yield significantly poor PD estimates in those grades.

In other words, since the granularity of x can affect the optimal k, the next question to ask is how the change in the optimal k coming from the change in x can affect the PD estimates. Based on our mathematical proof, we concluded that an increase in k would not guarantee an increase in PD estimates. In fact, it depends on the critical cumulative obligor $\hat{x}$ deriving from the formula $(1-k^{*}\hat{x}) = e^{-k}(1-k^{*}\hat{x}+k^{*})$. To be precise, for each rating grade, if the number of cumulative obligors is less than $\hat{x}$, an increase in k would increase the estimated PD and vice versa.

Table 3: Results of Cap PD estimation for sovereign portfolio

SA Grade	Obligor-years	Defaults	Cum Ob-years	Cum Defaults	ODR	CAP PD
1	1020	0	100.00%	100.00%	0.000%	0.361%
2	646	2	73.91%	100.00%	0.310%	0.704%
3	578	9	57.39%	96.97%	1.557%	1.152%
4	748	28	42.61%	83.33%	3.743%	1.963%
5	884	26	23.48%	40.91%	2.941%	3.782%
6	34	1	0.87%	1.52%	2.941%	5.469%
Average					1.688%	1.659%
Estimated k						3.1426

From Table 3, if we try to increase the PD estimate for the 4th rating grade by relaxing the optimal k condition, i.e. increasing k in order to increase PD, we have to check whether it violates our critical cumulative obligor level, $\hat{x}$, or not. Given the estimated k of 3.1426, we got $\hat{x}$ equal to 27.31%. So an increase in k can severely lower the estimated PD for rating grade 4.

Table 4: Results of Cap PD estimation when increasing K

SA Grade	ODR	CAP PD k=2	CAP PD k*=3.1426	CAP PD k=4
1	0.000%	0.686%	0.361%	0.212%
2	0.310%	1.050%	0.704%	0.498%
3	1.557%	1.436%	1.152%	0.931%
4	3.743%	2.016%	1.963%	1.834%
5	2.941%	3.061%	3.782%	4.226%
6	2.941%	3.871%	5.469%	6.759%
Average	1.688%	1.676%	1.659%	1.640%

However, if we reduce k to 2, even though the PD of the 4th rating grade increase it might not be appropriated because this will reduce the implied predictive power of the credit rating. To illustrate, we used the accuracy ratio (AR) to validate the power of the credit rating which is, as in Van Der Burgt (2007), approximated by $AUC = \int_0^1 \left(\frac{1-e^{-kx}}{1-e^{-k}}\right) dx = \frac{1}{1-e^{-k}} - \frac{1}{k}$. Hence, $AR = 2\left[\frac{1}{1-e^{-k}} - \frac{1}{k}\right]$. As a result, when we reduce k from 3.14 26 to 2, AR will decrease from 45.38% to 31.31%, which is quite low comparing to any practical non-retail portfolio AR which ranges from 40 − 80%. In other words, the value k which does not lie within 2.67 − 10, in our opinion, should not be used.

To summarize, in employing the CAP curve method, one needs to think about the tradeoff between two aspects. On one hand, there is the accuracy of the estimated PD coming from both the curvature and the level of the fitted CAP curve. The curvature of the curve relies on the value of k, which can be adjusted to increase the accuracy as previously discussed. The level of the fitted curve represents how well the average estimated PD reflects the central tendency of the portfolio, denoted as $\langle D \rangle$ in the PD estimation formula. The adjustment on the value of $\langle D \rangle$ will lead to the shift of the fitted CAP curve, not the curvature. On the other hand, there is the issue regarding the AR of the fitted CAP curve previously mentioned. If this tradeoff does not yield a fruitful outcome, it can be the case that the existing rating methodology may not be effective enough and there is a need to fully review the rating methodology, such as factors used in rating model, the credibility of risk factors, etc., instead of trying to manipulate k, $\langle D \rangle$ or AR values.

3. Regulatory implications on LDP PD estimation

Our proposed hybrid models provide additional methods in estimating the PD for LDPs. The advantages of our methods are that they utilize the maximum likelihood concept but with a much easier computational process and that they possess the ability to yield the PD estimates despite the zero default case, like the original maximum likelihood principle. In addition, the principle incorporates the asset correlation into the PD estimates; hence making the estimates more conservative. As shown previously, the PD estimates from our models are comparable to the most prudent, if not more.

Nevertheless, the *hybrid* models still have the similar rank-order problem as in the most prudent. Therefore, if the financial institutions choose to employ our hybrid method for their LDP portfolios, they need to be aware of the possible rank-order problem from our hybrid model as well. In addition, financial entities need to judge for themselves how the PD estimates from our hybrid models perform when compared to their long-term historical default rates and should be cautious of any underestimation, especially on the low-risk grades. Our suggestion for regulators is that our models generally are most beneficial to less quantitatively resourceful financial institutions.

Regarding the use of the *CAP curve calibration* method, there can be a case where the different granularity used to fit the exponential function to the actual CAP curve can lead to different estimates of k and consequently the PDs. If the fitting leads to an increase in the optimal k, k^*, then there is an increase in the PD estimates of higher risk obligors and a decrease in PD estimates for the lower risk obligors. Given these conditions, the accuracy ratio (AR) of the fitted curve should be higher for a higher optimal k^*.

Therefore, when it comes to validating whether the financial institutions who choose the CAP curve method have set an appropriate granularity (for example using raw scores versus score bands) in fitting the function to the actual CAP curve, regulators need to consider both the optimal level of k^*obtained, the PD estimates as compared to the historical default rates, and the accuracy ratio. To prevent the underfitting or overfitting of the

CAP curve from differences in the granularity levels, we recommend that the accuracy ratio of the fitted CAP curve should be between 40% and 80%, as targeted by the best practice standard.

Conclusion

The issue of PD estimates for low-default portfolios (LDPs) has been a challenge to financial institutions and regulators alike, both in terms of coming up with appropriate PD estimates with sufficient conservatism and in terms of validating the estimates. Therefore, both financial institutions and regulators should be aware of the consequence of employing these methods for PD estimations and should be able to identify incidences where the

PD estimates may be too low to cover the default risk. In all, these theories are the existing estimation tools, which should be used in conjunction with other prudent qualitative judgments in order to ensure that the risk will not be underestimated for this specific type of borrowers.

References

Benjamin, Nathanael, Alan Cathcart and Kevin Ryan. (2006) "Low Default Portfolios: A Proposal for Conservative Estimation of Default Probabilities." Financial Services Authority.

Falkenstein, E., Boral, A., and Carty, L. (2000). RiskCalc for private companies: Moody's default model: rating methodology. Moody's Investor Service

Forrest, Alan. (2005) "Likelihood Approaches to Low Default Portfolios." Working Paper. Dunfermline Building Society

Pluto, Katja and Dirk Tasche. (2006) "Estimating Probabilities of Default for Low Default Portfolios." The Basel II Risk Parameters: Estimation, Validation and Stress Testing. Springer Publishing. pp. 79-103.

Roengpitya, Rungporn, Nilla-or, Pratabjai and Yodmuangcharoen, Pongsan. (2011) "Proposal of New Hybrid Models for PD Estimates on Low Default Portfolios (LDPs), Empirical Comparisons and Regulatory Policy Implications." Working paper.

Savona, R., Vezzoli, M. (2008) "Multidimensional Distance to Collapse Point and Sovereign Default Prediction" Carefin Working Paper, n. 12/08, Milano.

Van der Burgt, Marco J. (2007) "Calibrating Low-Default Portfolios using the Cumulative Accuracy Profile." The Journal of Risk Model Validation. Vol. 1, No. 4, pp. 17-33.

CHAPTER THIRTEEN

OFF-BALANCE SHEET LEASES AND CREDIT RISK

JENNIFER ALTAMURO, RICK JOHNSTON, SHAIL PANDIT AND HAIWEN (HELEN) ZHANG

Introduction

Since revelations about Enron's off-balance sheet entities, the financial world has taken a heightened interest in off-balance items. A common form of off-balance sheet financing is operating leases. A lease is a contract where the lessor conveys the right to use property or equipment to a lessee. Currently, accounting rules for leases in the United States distinguish between capital and operating leases. The rules attempt to differentiate leases which are more like financed purchases (capital leases) versus simply rentals (operating leases). Since capital leases are economically similar to financed asset purchases, the balance sheet reflects an asset and a liability related to the lease. In contrast, with an operating lease, no asset or liability appears – hence the term off-balance sheet financing. However, future operating lease payments are disclosed in the notes to the financial statements.

The use of leases has grown significantly over time and the majority seems to be operating leases. Critics argue that the bright line tests specified to differentiate leases result in economically similar transactions being accounted for differently, and provide firms with the opportunities to structure their lease agreements to get the desired accounting.[1] For example, one of the lease classification tests is based on a comparison of the present value of the lease payments relative to the fair value of the asset at the time of lease inception. A lease with a ratio of 90.1% is a capital lease, a lease with 89.9% is an operating lease – it is hard to argue

[1] SFAS 13 enumerates four tests to qualify a lease as a capital lease.

that these two differ economically, yet the accounting would be very different. To rectify this issue, accounting standard setters are proposing to change the rules. The fair value of the rights (asset) and obligations (liability) of a lease would be recorded at inception.

For managers to exert effort to structure lease contracts to achieve operating lease accounting suggests that managers believe some market friction exists and there is a benefit to operating lease accounting treatment. Whether investors and creditors accurately assess the risk implications of off-balance sheet financing activities has been a recent concern for regulators. Early studies provide evidence that creditors tend to ignore operating lease information when setting bond risk premiums and debt covenant restrictions. However, operating leases would have been less frequent and not as economically significant during those years. We explore how financial institutions and credit rating agencies evaluate credit risk associated with operating leases.

We also examine whether differential lease characteristics impact the incorporation of operating lease information in credit assessment. Credit rating agencies and banks can obtain additional information from company management, and could evaluate a lease transaction based on its economic characteristics. Thus, it is possible that banks and rating agencies condition their decision to capitalize operating leases on individual contract terms rather than mechanically capitalizing all operating leases. In a competitive lending market, clients may demand such consideration to the extent that it affects lending rates. It is not clear that rating agencies face the same competitive pressure. On the other hand, due to processing costs, it is possible that banks and rating agencies choose to assess all operating leases in the same manner, regardless of their economic characteristics. Since we do not have access to operating lease contracts, we instead explore operating leases in the retail and wholesale industry. We conjecture that most of those leases relate to store space. On the spectrum of risk and reward transfer, store leases are closer to rentals or "true leases" than in-substance asset purchases and financing since such leases are likely only a small percentage of the economic life of the building.[2] We therefore expect banks would be less likely to consider operating leases of retail firms in setting loan spreads since those leases are more likely both economically and legally "true" leases.

---

[2] We estimated the average number of years that retail assets are under lease. Based on some assumptions, we find that the average remaining lease term in the retail industry is approximately 8 years, well below the traditional depreciable life of building assets (25-45 years).

Our tests examine the incremental explanatory power of the capitalization of operating leases on syndicated bank loan spreads and S&P credit ratings. Loan spreads are defined as the deal-level average of the difference between the facility interest rate and LIBOR. Credit ratings are from S&P. We apply the S&P credit rating model since the variables differentiate credit risk. In the loan analysis we also include controls for loan characteristics. Specifically, we compare the adjusted R-squared of two regressions of loan spreads and credit ratings on the explanatory S&P financial variables. The first regression includes variables based on amounts reported in the published financial statements, while the second regression includes ratios calculated from reported figures adjusted for operating leases, essentially treating all operating leases like capital leases. The lease adjustments follow S&P's methodology for doing so. The sample period is 2000 through 2005 and includes 2,535 loan deals, including 1,372 with S&P credit ratings and 1,163 without. Banks and Finance companies are heavily underrepresented; Retail is overrepresented.

Findings

The mean *loan spread*, the dependent variable for the rated and non-rated sub-samples are 170 and 241 basis points, respectively. The independent variables include two interest coverage variables, one based on EBIT and the other based on EBITDA. When adjusted for operating leases, the interest coverage ratios decline. While earnings increase from the removal of rent expense (operating lease payments), and decrease due to implicit depreciation associated with the "capitalized" operating lease asset, the net effect on the interest coverage ratio is a decline related to the imputed interest from the operating leases included in the denominator. There are two cash flow ratios, funds from operations relative to debt and free operating cash flow relative to debt. The capitalization of operating leases leads to an increase in debt, causing a decline in the adjusted cash flow ratios. *Leverage* is measured as debt relative to debt and equity. *Leverage* increases due to the adjustment for operating leases. Similarly, *Return on Capital*, where capital includes debt, shows a decline for rated firms but no change for unrated firms after adjusting for operating lease capitalization. The average firm size, which is measured as the natural log of sales, is 7.9 in the rated sub-sample but smaller in the unrated sub-sample (5.6). Unrated firms are smaller users of operating leases on an absolute basis.

Contrasting the credit rated and the unrated sub-samples, we find that the unrated firms have lower leverage, higher coverage ratios and lower returns on capital, on average. Interest coverage and *loan spreads* are negatively correlated while *leverage* and *loan spreads* are positively correlated. More importantly, we find that the adjusted variables of interest – interest coverage, cash flow, *leverage* and *return on capital* – all have higher correlations with *loan spreads* than do the unadjusted variables.

Summary statistics of loan characteristics for the rated sub-sample are as follows: 60 percent of the loans are secured; the mean and median *credit rating* is a 10, which is BB+ or the top of the junk rating category. The loan amount represents, on average, approximately 14 percent of assets. The average maturity is 45 months. Thirty percent of the sample loans are term loans, the others are revolving loans. The loans contain 3.7 covenants on average. Average *credit spread*, which is calculated as the interest rate difference between AAA and BBB rated bonds, is 96 basis points. The unrated loans are more likely to be secured and are generally a larger percentage of assets.

In the presence of a credit rating, adjusting the ratios for operating leases does not appear to increase the explanatory power of the model. For unrated firms adjusted financial ratios add to the explanatory power of the model. The results suggest banks consider operating leases when setting loan spreads either directly in the case of unrated firms, or indirectly through the use of a credit rating in the case of rated firms. Our credit rating analysis always shows improvement in the explanatory power of the adjusted ratio regression model.

The sub-sample of retail/wholesale firms has a median of operating lease minimum lease payments in present value terms of approximately 15 percent of firm assets, reflecting the heavy use of operating leases by retailers. We find a decline in adjusted R-squared when the operating lease adjusted financial ratios are applied, in contrast to the earlier results where we found that bank loan spreads were better explained by adjusted financial ratios, thus suggesting that banks do not adjust for operating leases in the retail industry. In contrast, for credit ratings there is a large improvement in the explanatory power when ratios are adjusted for operating leases.

Combined, these results support our conjecture that there are cross-sectional differences in how banks assess the economics of operating leases for the purpose of determining loan spreads but this is not the case for Standard & Poor's credit ratings.

Conclusions

Regulators have raised concerns about the increasing use of off-balance sheet financing, including operating leases. They worry there is a risk that such arrangements will not be considered appropriately by a user of financial statements. There is sparse evidence on how sophisticated financial statement users incorporate the impact of operating leases in their credit risk assessment. We study 2,535 syndicated bank loans of companies that also use operating leases and find two distinct results. Banks appear to either rely on credit ratings which reflect the capitalization of operating leases or they adjust themselves. Further, we find that "true" leases may be less important in assessing credit risk. Specifically, operating leases in the retail industry appear to be treated like rentals rather than financed purchases for credit assessment.

Our evidence supports the value of information intermediaries, in this case rating agencies, who study and quantify the effect of off-balance sheet items, thus providing a service to both direct and indirect customers. However, since their capitalization process is mechanical and the underlying economics may differ across leases, the rating's information value may be diminished. In contrast, banks appear to be more discriminating in assessing the underlying characteristics of the lease in their loan pricing decisions, perhaps due to the competitive nature of the lending market.

Under current lease accounting rules a reader of financial statements is concerned that leases which are economically like a financed purchase do not appear on the balance sheet. This is of particular concern because managers may have negotiated the lease terms to get that result. To correct for this a reader can "capitalize" all the operating leases and adjust the balance sheet. However, to the extent that firms have economically different operating leases, correcting the original error may create another. At best, the reader has the two possible extremes – least conservative (as reported) and most conservative (as adjusted) – and the knowledge that the truth lies somewhere in between. The proposed new accounting rules may move us closer to the most conservative case from the current least conservative case.

CHAPTER FOURTEEN

MARKET-IMPLIED DEFAULT PROBABILITIES

TERRY BENZSCHAWEL[1]

Abstract

Default probabilities (PDs) for risky obligors are derived from market spreads and spread volatilities calibrated to normative PDs from credit models and agency ratings. The method is based on observations that (1) credit spreads, on average, are linear functions of spread volatility, both overall and as functions of rating categories; and that (2) investors require the same level of spread compensation per unit of spread volatility regardless of its source. Formalization of the market-implied PD method assumes that an obligor's spread value consists of two parts: compensation for default and compensation for credit spread volatility. Difficulties in estimating default probabilities from market data are described followed by an analysis of the credit risk premium. Finally, market-implied PDs are used to assess risk and relative value of global sovereign issuers of external debt.

1. Introduction

A fundamental aspect of credit analysis is estimating borrowers' probabilities of default (PDs). Although there is room for legal disagreement about what constitutes default on a financial asset, there is general agreement that it includes three types of credit event (Moody's, 2010). These are:

1. A missed or delayed payment of interest and/or principal;

[1] The author is from Citi Institutional Clients Group, New York, NY, USA. Email: terry.l.benzschawel@citi.com

2. Bankruptcy, administration, legal receivership, or other legal block to the timely payment of interest and/or principal; or
3. A distressed exchange whereby the issuer offers debt holders a security that amounts to a diminished financial obligation and the exchange has the apparent purpose of helping the borrower avoid default.

Accurate assessment of obligors' default risk is a critical component of the bank lending businesses. However, default modeling is becoming increasingly important in the context of the current regulatory environment and for modern credit trading and prime brokerage businesses. For example, the Basel accords (U.S. Treasury, 2007) offer regulatory capital advantages for financial firms using the Advanced Internal Models Based approach to calculate firms' PDs. In the past, credit trading businesses often ignored actual default probabilities, focusing instead on risk-neutral defaults. But with growing awareness of potential default-related loss from trading partners, banks now take credit reserves against mark-to-market gains. Also, financial firms often have prime brokerage businesses that provide margin secured by default-risky assets, requiring accurate assessment of their PDs. All these applications require a non-controversial, yet accurate, assessment of expected default probabilities.

Various approaches to modeling credit risk exist including fundamental analysis, agency ratings, statistical models, reduced form models, structural models and hybrids. Each has proved useful for some applications, yet none has proved entirely satisfactory for estimating actual default probabilities. A combination of recent theoretical work by Bonn (2000) and empirical work presented below has suggested a potential new approach to development of a market-based measure of firms' default risk. That method, representing an amalgamation of the capital asset pricing model (CAPM), statistical and structural credit models, and risk-neutral pricing is the subject of this paper.

2. Measuring the Credit Risk Premium

Given the demand for a market-based PD measure, "Why has computing accurate estimates of PDs proved so difficult?" Even though default rates vary over the credit cycle, so do credit spreads. Perhaps, by examining the relationship between credit spreads and default rates, one could make reasonable inferences as to default probabilities from knowledge of the current values of credit spreads. Then applying this knowledge to individual credits, one could determine what a given difference in spread means for probability of default. Although reasonable, implying default rates from credit spreads has not proved to be reliable. The left panel of Figure 1 displays annual average high yield default rates with credit spreads against the comparable default rates during each period shown at the right. Although overall spread levels and defaults are highly correlated (R^2=0.78), that relationship is not strong enough to be satisfactory for accurate prediction, particularly for individual firms. For example, the dashed lines in the figure show how large errors can be; in 2003, the average spread was 961bp, but the default rate was only 5.2% as opposed to the 9.1% prediction.[2]

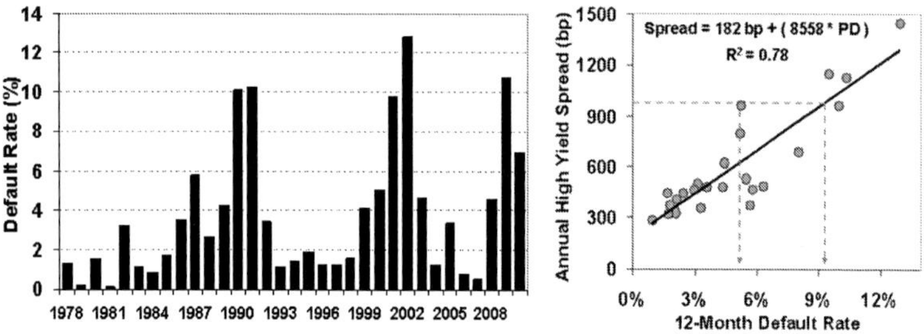

Figure 1. Left: Annual high yield default rates. Right: Annual average high yield credit spreads and annual default rates, 1986-2009.

A major difficulty in inferring PDs from bond prices is that bond spreads contain a risk premium that is not related to default, per se. That is, it is possible to decompose a spread into components due to default and a risk premium such that $s = s_d + s_\lambda$, where s_d is the compensation for default and s_λ is the credit risk premium. For a bond of duration *T*, we can approximate the spread compensation for default, s_d, as:

$$s_d = -\frac{1}{T}\ln\left[1-(p_T * LGD)\right] \quad , \qquad (1)$$

where *LGD* is *loss-given-default* or *1-R*, where *R* is the recovery value in default. The value of s_d can be thought of as the amount of spread necessary to break even with a similar investment in Treasuries given expected default and recovery for the risky bond. Also, since $s = s_d + s_\lambda$,

[2] Lagging the spread data only decreased the predictive power of the spread-default relation in Figure 1 (R^2 for one-year shift = 0.13).

if we use the credit spreads along with estimates of default probabilities we can solve for the risk premium, defined as s_λ , using the following relation:

$$s = s_\lambda - \left\{ \frac{1}{T} \ln\left[1 - \left(p_T * LGD\right)\right] \right\} \quad . \tag{2}$$

Equations 1 and 2 can be derived directly from the price-yield relationship and a derivation can be found in Choudhry (2006).

Figure 2 shows average monthly credit spreads by rating category for agency ratings from triple-A to triple-C, the calculated spread compensation for default using Equation 1, and the residual non-default spread implied by Equation 2. For these calculations, we used historical spreads from corporate bonds in Citi's Broad Investment Grade (BIG) and High Yield Indexes (Citigroup, 2011), a value of *T=4.5*, roughly the average duration of the bonds in question, and *R=40%* of face value. Notice that for all rating categories the break-even compensation for default is a small fraction of the overall spread compensation. In fact, nearly all of the spread for investment-grade bonds (ratings >= triple-B-minus) are due to the credit risk premium, rather than default. For high yield, default plays a greater relative role, but the average risk premium can be as large as 700bp.

S&P Credit Rating	4.5 Year Implied PD	Average Spread (bp)	Spread Due to Default (bp)	Non-Default Spread (bp)
AAA	0.3%	70	1	69
AA+	0.3%	87	4	82
AA	0.4%	88	5	83
AA-	0.5%	104	6	98
A+	0.6%	113	8	105
A	0.7%	122	9	112
A-	0.9%	137	11	126
BBB+	1.0%	160	14	146
BBB	1.3%	178	17	161
BBB-	1.6%	223	21	201
BB+	1.9%	326	25	301
BB	2.3%	366	30	336
BB-	2.7%	383	36	347
B+	3.8%	438	51	386
B	5.7%	511	77	433
B-	8.2%	588	113	476
CCC+	11.8%	891	164	727

Figure 2. Average credit risk premiums (non-default spreads) by credit rating category (1994-2010).

The credit risk premium varies over time. For example, the left panel of Figure 3 shows monthly values of 4.5 year duration U.S. Treasury bond yields and corresponding average investment-grade bond yields since 1994.[3] The dashed line is the addition to the Treasury yields of estimated yield compensation for default obtained using average PDs for the bonds from Sobehart and Keenan's (2002) HPD credit model.[4] The right plot shows the credit risk premium as the difference between the corporate bond yield curve and the U.S. Treasury plus compensation for default yields.

Figure 3 shows that the average investment-grade risk premium is about 125bp, very close to the average investment-grade credit spread over that period. However, the risk premium varies considerably around that value, having been below 50bp during high liquidity periods of the mid-1990s and mid-2000s. During the recent credit/liquidity crisis, that risk premium was roughly 650bp, but has returned to near-average levels by 2010.

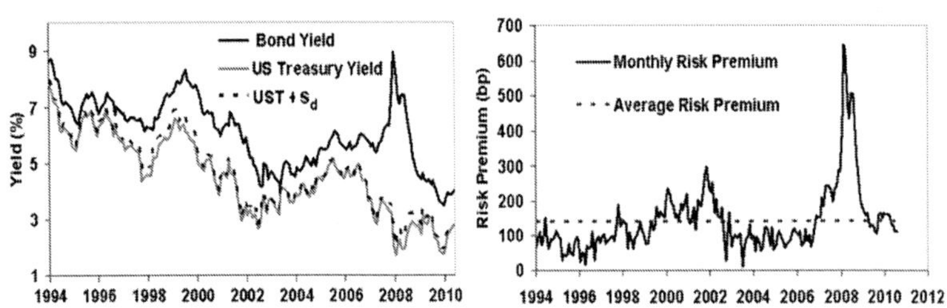

Figure 3. Left: Treasury yields, Treasury yield plus compensation for default, and corporate bond yields; Right: The credit risk premium, 1994 -2010.

To examine the dependence of the credit risk premium on the volatility of credit spreads, we calculated average monthly spreads and average five-year trailing spread volatilities by rating category from 1994 to mid-2010. That analysis, presented in

[3] The bond yields are those from the corporate bonds in Citi's Broad Investment Grade (BIG) Index.

[4] HPD stands for *Hybrid Probability of Default* as the model is a combination of a structural Merton-type model and a statistical, Altman (1968) type model.

Figure 4 revealed several facts useful for our development of market-based PD estimates:

- Logarithms of averages of 5-year rolling spread volatilities are linearly related to rating categories (open symbols in left panel);
- Ratios of spread volatilities are roughly 1/3 of average credit spreads for all rating categories (gray circles in left panel);
- The variability of the volatility-to-spread ratios is also constant across rating categories (triangles in left panel);
- Average five-year trailing spreads are linear functions of their five-year volatilities (middle panel); and
- Logarithms of average spreads by rating category after correction for median PDs from Sobehart and Keenan's HPD model using Equation 1 (right panel) are linear functions of log spread volatility.

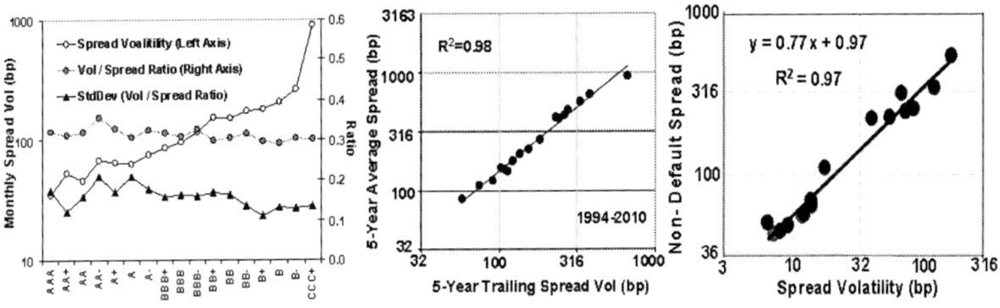

Figure 4. Left: Averages of rolling 5-year averages of spread volatilities by rating; Middle: Average 5-year trailing spreads versus 5-year trailing spread volatilities; Right: Non-default credit spreads by rating versus spread volatility for June 2010.

The results in Figure 4 suggest that, on average, the market charges the same amount of spread per unit of volatility regardless of whether it comes from a high quality credit or a risky one. If so, we can use Equation 2 along with a model for PDs that is correct, at least on average, to determine the current charge for volatility as in the right panel of Figure 4.

3. Market-Implied PDs

The proposed method for generating market-implied PDs is based on the observations that (1) an investor will require spread compensation for missed cash flows due to default; (2) that credit spreads, on average, are linear functions of spread volatility; and (3) that investors require the same level of spread compensation per unit of spread volatility for all credits.

Specifically, the method assumes that an obligor's credit spread consists of two parts: compensation for default and compensation for credit spread volatility. That is, a rational investor in a risky credit would never take less than the amount required to break even with a U.S. Treasury of similar duration. However, in addition, investors experience fluctuations in the market values of risky assets and must also receive compensation for that. The Capital Asset Pricing Model [5] specifies that the amount of compensation required should be directly related to the volatility taken on by the investor, thereby supporting our hypothesis that s_λ in Equation 2, for all credits at a given time can be expressed as:

$$s_\lambda = \lambda_t \sigma \ , \qquad (3)$$

where s_λ is the spread compensation over and above that for default and σ is its volatility. Using Equation 3, we can rewrite Equation 2 as:

$$s = \lambda\sigma - \left\{ \frac{1}{T} \ln\left[1 - \left(p_T * LGD\right)\right] \right\} . \qquad (4)$$

Although Equation 2 provides a framework for interpreting the relationship between credit spreads, default, recovery, and spread volatility, estimating p_T remains challenging, even when one has bond spreads and volatilities and can assume a reasonable value for *LGD* (e.g., *1-RV = 60%)*. This is because Equation 2 requires an estimate of the current market price of risk at time *t*, λ_t. The steps in the method are summarized below and described in detail in the remainder of this section. The method consists of:

- Assigning provisional PDs to commercial and industrial firms using the HPD model;
- Using PDs from HPD and firms' term structures of credit spreads, convert firms' bond spreads of arbitrary maturities to their one-year equivalent spreads;
- Subtract the one-year spread compensation for default obtained using Equation 1 from the total spread where *T=1* and *LGD=60%* and plot non-default spreads as a function of spread volatility;

---

[5]The implication is that the "Sharpe ratio" is the same for all credits. See Sharpe (2000).

- Fit a line of slope 1.0 to firms' log non-default spreads versus log spread volatilities (i.e., a constant Sharpe ratio line); the y-intercept of that line is the risk premium, λ_t ;
- For all firms, log spreads are plotted against log spread volatilities, including those without model PDs, and a line is fit through the ensemble of data points;
- For each point, adjust the spread and volatility along the shortest vector to the best fit line and use those adjusted values along with the λ_t, an assumed *LGD=60%*, and Equation 4 to determine firms' market-implied PDs;
- For any firm with a tradable bond and assuming an *LGD=60%,* infer a one-year spread from the term structure of credit spreads and calculate a market-implied PD using the spread-volatility adjustment described above along with Equation 4.

The left panel of Figure 5 illustrates the first step in the calibration process which consists of separating the spread compensation for default from the entire credit spread. The non-default spread is required along with the spread volatility to estimate the credit risk premium, λ_t. Although conceptually simple, some model is needed to estimate values of p_T. Recall the hypothesis that the current risk premium is a constant charge per unit of volatility, regardless of its source. If so, it might be possible to estimate the current risk premium from a source of PDs that need only be correct on average.

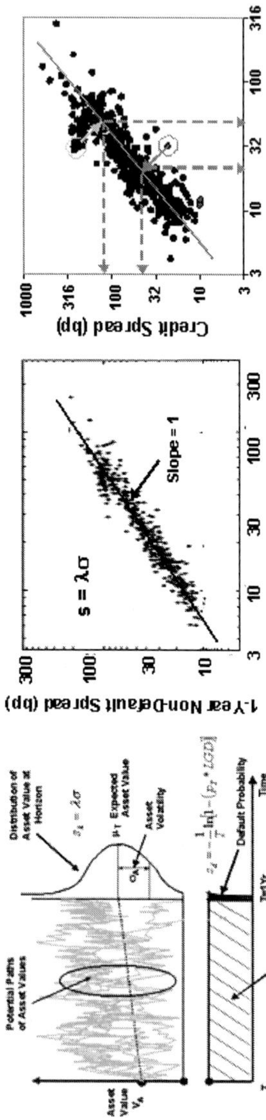

Figure 5. Stages in determining the market price of risk for computing market-implied PDs; Left: Separating spread compensation for default from the spread compensation for volatility. Middle: Estimating the current value of the risk premium, λ_t; Right: Plot of log spreads versus log spread volatility and adjustment of spreads and volatilities to fall on constant Sharpe-ratio line.

4. Using Model-Based PDs to Estimate the Credit Risk Premium, λ_t

Using historical average PDs from the rating agencies to estimate the risk premium proved problematic. First, as shown in the left panel of Figure 6, agency default rates by rating categories vary logarithmically, such that mean default rates are not good estimates of central tendency. Also, frequency distributions of annual default rates for several rating categories in Figure 6 demonstrate that the mean PD is a poor estimate of the PD for any rating category in any given year. Finally, as shown in the left panel of Figure 1, default probabilities are dependent on the economic cycle. Rating category median spreads might be used to establish monthly norms, but this is problematic because median values for PDs would remain constant across the credit cycle. Also, as shown in Figure 6, median PDs are zero for triple-B-minus credits and this is also true for all investment-grade credit categories.

For these reasons we used PDs from Sobehart and Keenan's HPD model to calculate non-default spreads for use in estimating daily credit risk premiums. Although structural and hybrid methods for estimating PDs have problems (see Keenan, Sobehart and Benzschawel, 2003), those were not critical limitations as regards estimating the credit risk premium. That is, while individual PDs from the model may be suspect, we assume that PDs over a large sample of firms will be correct on average.

If our hypothesis regarding a single volatility-dependent risk premium is correct, estimates the non-default spread compensation should be directly related to spread volatility. (Note: the right panel of Figure 4 has already demonstrated this for June 2010.) For our initial test, we used monthly median credit spreads by rating category from 1994 through mid-2010, but also needed estimates of default probabilities for each of those rating categories. Median non-default credit spreads by rating category were determined for each month from 1995 until mid-2010 using average historical PDs from published by Moody's or PDs from Citi's HPD model. Then, for each rating category in a given month, we used Equation 1 to calculate spread compensation for default and subtracted that spread from the median credit spread to leave the *non-default credit spread.*

Figure 6. Left: Five-year default rates by rating category on log (left) and linear (right) axes. Middle and Right: Distributions of annual default rates for Baa3- and B2-rated credits, respectively.

The left panel of Figure 7 displays values of R^2 for monthly fits of logarithms of non-default spreads to spread volatilities over our 16-year sample period. Two sets of R^2 series are shown; the gray curve in Figure 7 shows values of R^2 for fits generated using Moody's historical five-year average PDs by rating category. Clearly, the overall fit is poor; R^2s for non-default spreads and volatilities are very good during periods of high defaults (e.g., 2000-2002 and 2008-2009), but are extremely poor during periods of low defaults. However, median five-year default rates by rating category from the HPD model (black curve) worked very well as nearly all R^2 values are greater than 90% and most are over 95%. In fact, although overall default rates vary greatly over the credit cycle, median PDs change very little as reflected in the small influence of credit cycle on our fit of non-default spreads and spread volatilities. Clearly, what is important is not the HPD model, per se, but having a method for estimating median PDs for firms in each rating category that vary with the credit cycle, something not currently available from the rating agencies.

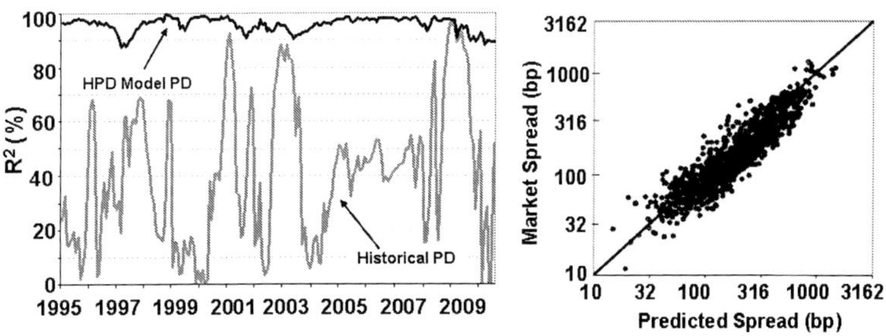

Figure 7. Left: Monthly R^2 for fit of log non-default spread versus log volatility by rating category, 1995-2010. Right: Actual and predicted spreads for May 28, 2010.

At least on aggregate data, median PDs from HPD are useful for estimating the credit risk premium and non-default credit spreads are linearly related to their spread volatilities. The method was used to estimate PDs from daily spread data at the individual bond level. To do this for any given day t, the credit risk premium λ_t is determined using that day's median spreads and PDs by rating category in accordance with the method used to generate the data in the left panel of Figure 7. Having λ_t, along with each bond's duration, T, and their p_T estimate from the model, we can use their trailing spread volatility to estimate an expected spread. We can then compare that spread with the observed spread on that day, s_t.

The right panel of Figure 7 displays market spreads for bonds from Citi's investment-grade and high yield Indexes on May 28, 2010 versus their predicted spreads from Equation 4. Because the universe of bonds has durations ranging from one- to 30-years, the volatilities used as inputs to Equation 4 were adjusted by the square root of T (i.e., their durations) relative to the 4.5 years used to calculate the risk premium, λ_t.. Model predictions falling on the solid line, the positive diagonal, are in perfect agreement with market spreads. Although the points in Figure 7 can be described well by a straight line, it appears that predicted spreads might be slightly higher than their corresponding market spreads.

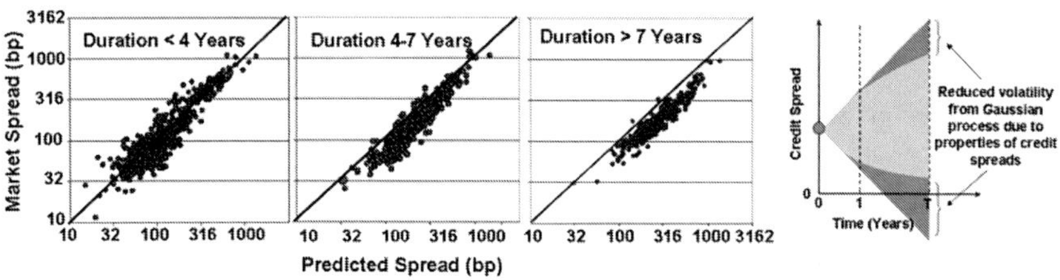

Figure 8. Three Left Panels: Actual and predicted spreads for May 28, 2010 segregated by duration. Right: Gaussian spread volatility envelope (darker area) and reduced volatility envelope (lighter area) due to limitations on credit spreads.

The reason for the consistent over estimation of credit spreads became apparent from examination of errors as a function of duration. For example, Figure 8 displays the same data as in the right panel of Figure 7, except segregated by duration. The left panel plots spreads and predictions for bonds with durations less than 4 years, with data for bonds with four to seven year durations and longer-duration bonds in the next two panels on the right. Clearly, the model predicts spreads well for bonds with durations under four years, but increasingly over estimates spreads as duration increases.

The systematic over-prediction of longer dated spreads appears to result from our assumption of a Gaussian evolution of spread volatility. For practical purposes, volatilities are calculated using a maximum of nine months of daily spreads whose contributions decrease exponentially with a three-month half-life. The volatility for each individual bond is adjusted by the square root of its duration T relative to that of the nine-month volatility to scale the spread compensation for bearing the risk premium for longer periods of time. That is, for a bond i of duration T, we compensate for time difference in bearing the risk as:

$$\sigma_{i,T} = \sigma_{i,1} * \sqrt{T} \ , \tag{5}$$

where the subscript 1 is used to denote the nine-month volatility calculation. The problem with the Gaussian volatility assumption is illustrated in the right panel of Figure 8. The dark area illustrates how the spread envelope having a Gaussian volatility process would evolve over time. The lighter area, superimposed on the dark, provides a more realistic picture of the envelope of spread volatility; a process that is bounded absolutely by zero and has an upper bound limited by the bond's recovery value in default. The figure also shows that for short periods of time the Gaussian assumption can be a reasonable approximation and this is supported by the accuracy of spread predictions for short-dated bonds in Figure 8.

Recall that our objective is to estimate default probabilities using spreads and spread volatilities. Because the structure of long-term spread volatility is not well documented, estimation of the volatility correction with time is problematic. Our approach, at least provisionally, is to convert spreads from bonds with durations greater than one year to their one-year equivalent spreads. To do this, we fit the term structure of firms' bond spreads using a Nelson-Siegel (1987) procedure. If no term structure is available for a given firm, an average term structure of spreads is used derived from spreads of firms having similar PDs. The left panel of Figure 9 displays spread curves fit to median bond spreads by maturity and rating category and how the spread from a triple-B bond of 8.5 year maturity is adjusted downward to its one-year equivalent.

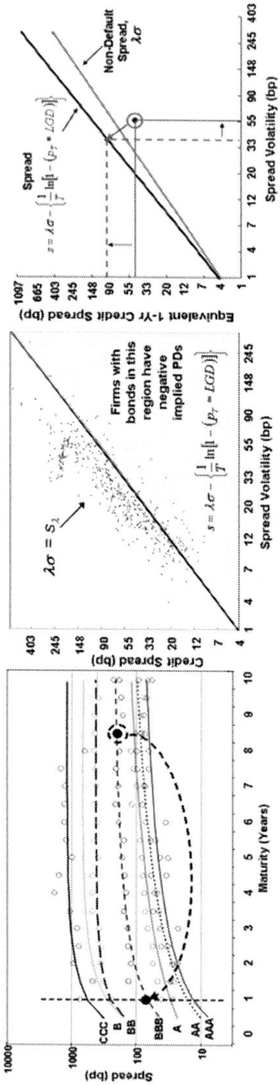

Figure 9. Left: Adjustment of spreads for bonds of matuities greater than one year to their one-year equivalent spreads. Middle: Applying Equation 4 to raw spreads and volatilities can imply negative PDs. Right: The risk premium versus volatility (gray line) and best-fit relationship between log spread and log volatility (black line). The vector adjustment procedure is also illustrated.

The one-year equivalent spread method eliminated the systematic error in spread predictions by maturity. On any given day, the risk premium is first determined as depicted in the middle panel of Figure 5, but using one-year equivalent spreads for bonds having PDs from the HPD model using $LGD=60\%$ and $T=1$. Then, with spread volatilities and one-year equivalent spreads for the entire sample of bonds, Equation 4 is applied to derive one-year p_1 on all bonds. The middle panel of Figure 9 shows credit spreads and spread volatilities for the bonds in the sample along with the upward sloping line for which $\lambda\sigma$ is a constant. The shaded area below the line encompasses points for which measured credit spreads are less than $\lambda\sigma$. Such points are problematic since, when Equation 4 is applied, they produce negative implied default probabilities, $p_1 < 0$. Given the thousands of bonds analyzed daily it is not surprising that we observe a small fraction of outliers. Still how to handle inconsistencies in pricing and valuation as they affect our measures of inferred default probabilities is a practical problem.

The solution is demonstrated in the right and middle panels of Figure 9. Recall that the non-default spread function is the line of constant λ times σ. The sample point in that panel is below the negative p_T line, but its spread and volatility are adjusted along the vector perpendicular to the best fit spread-versus-volatility line. Those adjustments, shown by the dashed lines in the figure, are used with Equation 4 to solve for that firm's default probability. Similar adjustments are applied to all points above or below the line, even those with PDs from the HPD model, so that adjusted spreads and volatilities fall on the average line. Then, the adjusted spreads and volatilities are input to Equation 4 to solve for firms' default probabilities. This adjustment not only solves the problem of negative PDs, but ensures that all PDs from the model are consistent with the average risk premium as calibrated using the PDs from the HPD model.

5. Calculating and Interpreting Market-Implied PDs

The market-implied PD method can be divided into four main operations as described below.

Step 1: Assign Credit Spreads and Spread Volatilities

Beginning with a set of bond spreads over time, our current method requires three-months of daily spread data from a single bond in order to generate a firm's market-implied PD. Each bond's credit spread is converted to its *one-year equivalent (OYE)*. If a firm has more than one bond, we use a Nelson-Siegel procedure to fit a curve to those bonds. Then, for a bond of maturity *T*, the *OYE* spread is calculated as:

$$s_{OYE} = s - \left(s_T - s_1\right) \,, \tag{6}$$

where s is the original spread of the bond, s_T is the spread on the spread curve at T (which may or may not match s), and s_1 is the spread on the fit curve at $T=1$. For firms with only one bond, the spread curve is assumed to have the shape of the curve fit to median spreads of the nearest credit rating category after which Equation 6 is applied.

Step 2: Determine the Current Credit Risk Premium.

Default probabilities are assigned to all bonds from commercial and industrial firms that have PDs from the HPD model. Given those PDs, bond durations, and an assumed constant recovery value of 40% the spread compensation from default is estimated using Equation 3. Then, the spread value of the credit risk premium s_λ is obtained by subtracting s_d from the credit spread, s_{OYE}. A line is then fit to the points having coordinates (log s_λ, log σ_s), while constraining the slope of that line to equal 1.0.[6] The intercept of the resulting line is the risk premium, λ_t and the line can be described as $\lambda_t \, \sigma_s = s_\lambda$.

Step 3: Adjust Spread and Volatility to Normative Function

An issuer may have multiple bonds outstanding, but cross-default provisions imply that all bonds will have the same PD. Although all bonds from an issuer are used to estimate λ_t, only one s_{OYE} per issuer is assigned by taking the geometric average of the one-year equivalent spreads of all that firm's bonds. Similarly, the volatility for a given issuer is calculated as the geometric average of the one-year volatilities of its bonds. Values of s_{OYE} are plotted against σ_s for all firms (with and without PDs from HPD) as in the right panel of Figure 9 and a line is fit to those points. For each firm, adjusted values of s_{OYE} and σ_s are computed, called s'_{OYE} and σ_s', by moving them via an orthogonal vector onto the best-fit line to the ensemble of spreads.

---

[6] In general, slopes of best fit lines to (log s_λ, log σ_s) are 1.0 on average, but we impose the 1.0 slope constraint to ensure a constant risk premium per unit of volatility regardless of spread magnitude.

Step 4: Assign Market-Implied PD and Rating

Given firms' OYE spreads and spread volatilities, implied PDs for each firm are computed using Equation 4 with λ_t, $T=1$, and $LGD=60\%$ for all firms along with estimates of each firm's s^{t}_{OYE} and σ_s^t. The resulting PDs for our sample firms for February 10 appear in the left panel of Figure 10. The lines in the figure correspond to rating category boundaries defined as the geometric means of median market-implied default probabilities from adjacent rating categories. In addition, these boundaries are lines of constant PDs as shown by the labels in the figure. Note that the iso-PD lines would be straight lines if spread and volatility axes were scaled in equal units. Thus, the left panel of Figure 10 shows how we map market-implied PDs to agency equivalent credit ratings.

6. Generating PDs for Global Sovereign Issuers

Although generating accurate estimates of PDs for sovereigns has proved difficult within existing frameworks, one can estimate sovereign PDs, using the market-implied method. Spreads from bonds of major sovereigns are converted to their one-year equivalents and those spreads and volatilities were plotted in a spread-volatility graph similar to that shown in the right panel of Figure 9. Then, applying our spread and volatility vector adjustment we generated the inputs to Equation 4 and calculated the market-implied PDs for those countries. The resulting PDs for those sovereigns appear in the table and graph in Figure 11 along with the five-year CDS spreads (where available). Not surprisingly, given the recent turmoil in the peripheral European credits, Greece is the riskiest sovereign tested with a 16% implied one-year PD, with PDs for Ireland and Portugal only slightly lower. Also, notice that both Ecuador and Venezuela have implied PDs greater than 10%. Market-implied PDs for these sovereigns were computed assuming that recovery values for all these credits are 40%. It is likely that this is not correct and we are currently enhancing the model to be able to adjust PDs for differences in recovery value. Hence, these PDs must be viewed as preliminary estimates, subject to future refinements.

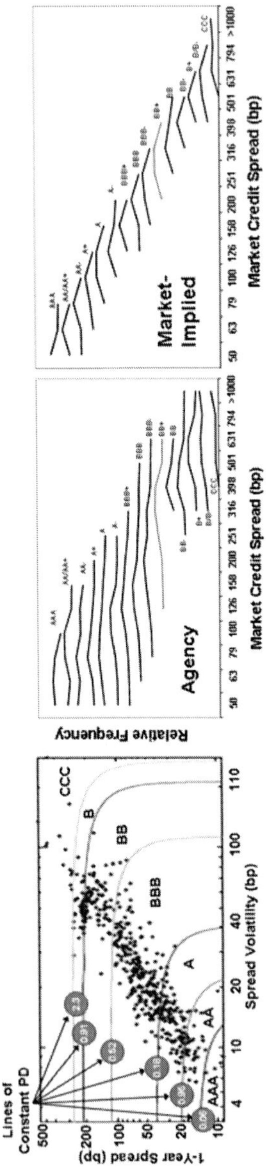

Figure 10. Left: One-year equivalent spreads versus volatility and lines of constant PDs corresponding to major letter rating boundaries. Comparison between distributions of credit spreads by agency rating (middle) and market implied ratings (right).

Country	Markit Implied PD (%)	5-Year CDS Spread (bp)	Country	Markit Implied PD (%)	5-Year CDS Spread (bp)
Greece	16.13	916	Domincan Rep.	0.55	289
Ecuador	11.11		El Salvador	0.48	286
Venezuela	10.93	1002	Latvia	0.44	260
Pakistan	7.92	810	Indonesia	0.34	150
Ireland	5.66	625	Chile	0.30	80
Iceland	4.53	292	Colombia	0.28	112
Ukraine	4.10	443	Russia	0.24	138
Argentina	3.90	542	Morocco	0.23	157
Jamaica	2.84	776	Turkey	0.22	146
Vietnam	2.80	379	Uruguay	0.21	148
Portugal	2.73	447	Peru	0.16	108
Lebanon	2.41	371	Guatemala	0.16	162
Macedonia	2.15		Panama	0.14	101
Sri Lanka	1.45	295	Philippines	0.13	135
Romania	1.20	293	Brazil	0.13	111
Kazakistan	0.97	162	China	0.11	74
Jordan	0.88	287	Mexico	0.10	113
Costa Rica	0.79	150	Poland	0.08	150
India	0.72		Israel	0.07	114
Malaysia	0.66	78	Sovenia	0.06	86
Hungary	0.61	366	South Africa	0.06	125
Spain	0.60	265	Slovakia	0.03	88
Lithuania	0.55	262	Luxembourg	0.01	

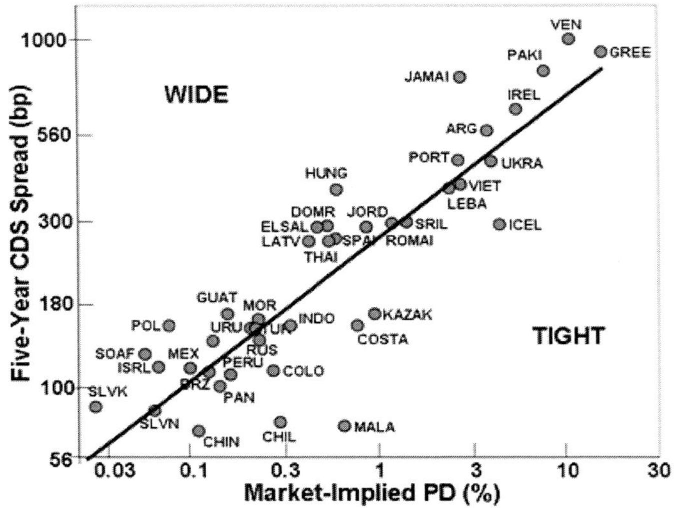

Figure 11. Table (left) and graph (right) of market-implied PDs and 5-Year CDS spreads for Sovereigns, 26-Jan-11.

References

Altman, E. I. (1968). Financial Ratios, Discriminant Analysis and the Prediction of Corporate Bankruptcy, *Journal of Finance Vol. XXIII (4)*, September.

Bohn, J. (2000). A Survey of Contingent-Claims Approaches to Risky Debt Valuation, *Journal of Risk Finance*, pp. 53-70.

Choudhry, M. (2006). *The Credit Default Swap Basis*, Bloomberg Press, New York.

Citigroup Index (2011). Citigroup Global Fixed-Income Index Catalog – 2011 Edition, fi.index@citi.com.

Keenan, S., Sobehart, J. and Benzschawel, T. (2003). The Debt and Equity Linkage and the Valuation of Credit Derivatives, In *Credit Derivatives: The Definitive Guide*, J. Gregory (Ed.), Risk Books, London, pp. 67-90.

Moody's Investors Service (2010). Corporate Default and Recovery Rates: 1920-2009, February.

Nelson, C. R. & Siegel, A. F. (1987). Parsimonious Modeling of Yield Curves, *Journal of Business 60 (4)*, pages 473-89;

Sharpe, W. (2000). *Portfolio Theory & Capital Markets*, McGraw-Hill, New York.

Sobehart, J. and Keenan, S. (2002). Hybrid Contingent Claims Models: A Practical Approach to Modeling Default Risk, *Credit Ratings: Methodology, Rationale and Default Risk*, M. Ong (ed.), Risk Books.

U.S. Treasury (2007). *Advanced Capital Adequacy Framework – Basel II,* Federal Register, No. 235, December 7, pp. 69287-69445.

CHAPTER FIFTEEN

DEVELOPING A PRACTICAL CREDIT RISK MODEL FOR BANKERS IN THE CASE OF MORTGAGE LOANS PORTFOLIO IN MAURITIUS

INDRANARAIN RAMLALL[1]

Abstract

This paper develops a credit risk model that focuses on the repayment capacity of household borrowers in Mauritius. The research is innovative and distinguishes itself from previous credit risk models as it shifts away from modeling the default of borrower to modeling their repayment capacity, as captured by the Debt Service Coverage Ratio (DSCR). The main advent of such a modeling approach is that it is not only more practical but also more proactive as the lender usually directly knows the underlying forces that induce or deter DSCR. Continuous (Ordinary Least Squares), binary (Probit & Logit) and a 'discretisized' (Ordered logit) metric for DSCR are employed in the study. Interaction variables have also been incorporated in the model to obtain richer results. Results show that margin cover and loan tenor exert positive effects on the DSCR while cost of the loan and dummy variables, representing loan for construction and borrowers from the public sector, all negatively impact on DSCR.

---

[1] The author is from University of Mauritius, Réduit, Mauritius. Address: Department of Economics and Statistics, University of Mauritius, Réduit, Mauritius. Tel: (230) 4037948. Email address: i.ramlall@uom.ac.mu or ramindra0001@yahoo.co.uk The model used in this paper has originally been devised by the author himself while he was working at a major international bank in Mauritius. The author sincerely thanks Mr Naim Maudabokus for the data and comments from participants at the First International Conference on Credit Analysis and Risk Management, held in Rochester, Michigan, USA in July 2011.

There is also some evidence as to the interaction between town dummy and margin cover impacting on DSCR. However, no evidence is found as to age (low economic significance), arrears and for the town dummy variable impacting on borrower's repayment capacity. Overall, findings suggest that bankers should be highly cautious when gauging on the level of margin cover to use as it constitutes the single most important risk-mitigating device when it comes to dealing with the moral hazard problem, a latent problem in any loan.

Introduction

What factors influence the repayment capacity of borrowers who contract mortgage loans? In this paper, I investigate the relationship between the repayment capacity[2] of borrowers with their attributes along with other control factors for an upper-income developing country. Indeed, most credit risk models have been motivated mainly on theoretical background like the structural and reduced-form credit risk models, with stress being laid on default. This is where my paper contributes to the banking and finance literature. First, this paper innovates from all previous models by proposing a credit risk model which directly befits the banker/lender by catering for the practical forces that underlie the repayment capacity of a borrower. The main blessing of such a model relative to previously well-established default prediction models is that it induces a higher level of proactiveness in credit risk management as the credit officers and risk management personnel directly know the positive and negative factors that thwart on the repayment capacity of their clients. Second, apart from its practical flavour, the model proposed is deemed universal as it can be adopted for any type of country as long as the focus is on mortgage loans.

This paper is organized as follows. In the next section, I briefly discuss the related literature pertaining to credit risk modeling. In section 3, I describe the dataset and the variables used in this study along with the econometric model. In section 4, I present the empirical results. Finally, I conclude in Section 6.

[2] Throughout the rest of the paper, repayment capacity and DSCR will be used interchangeably.

Related Literature

Risk is now a concept that cuts across diverse fields such as health and safety and software engineering. In finance, risk[3] is usually considered as the identification and measurement of probability of a certain event that triggers loss. One of the most important features in finance has been the constant development accomplished in the area of credit risk modeling. Now viewed as a classical structural credit risk model, the Merton (1973, 1974) model, inspired by Black and Scholes (1973) option pricing theory which focuses on default risk measurement became widely accepted among both practitioners and academicians. Under the Merton model, it is posited that a company is unlikely to default as long as the value of its liabilities is less than the market value of the company's assets[4].

With time, the literature on credit risk modeling has been extended to cater for the shortcomings of the structural model, namely nil information asymmetry between the lender and the borrower, default prevailing only at the maturity date, zero coupon bond and flat term structure of interest rates. The reduced-form models resort towards a different information set compared to that of the structural form model. Black and Cox (1976) propose a model whereby default can manifest at any time. Geske (1977, 1979) extends the model to cater for a coupon bond in lieu of the zero coupon bond. In the same vein, Nielsen et al. (1993) and Longstaff and Schwartz (1995) incorporate stochastic interest rates, in particular a vasicek (after Vasicek, 1977) process for interest rate in lieu of the flat term structure of interest rates. Finally, the third generation models, comprise of KMV and CreditMetrics. The KMV model is a variant of Merton model with the difference that it tilts towards the probability of default instead of debt valuation. On the other hand, the CreditMetrics model is a portfolio model, developed by JP Morgan and geared towards credit risk evaluation.

The credit risk models discussed have mainly been applied for corporate loans and hence are not much useful for mortgage loans. The rationale is that a company has limited liability and a person has less incentives to default even if the value of his/her housing loan exceeds the

---

[3] Risk refers to downside risk in this case.

[4] The value of the firm is tantamount to the sum of its liabilities and equity value. Should liabilities exceed the firm's value, then, equity value becomes negative so that it is better for the company to default, bearing in mind the limited liability feature of a company. In contrast, when market value exceeds liabilities, this increases the residual payoff of the shareholders so that default is unlikely to manifest.

market value of all his/her assets as it is personal ownership which is at stake. Bearing in mind these caveats, the current study resorts towards a different and more pragmatic approach to credit risk modeling using a unique database for a Mauritian financial institution which is involved in the housing loan business.

Econometric Methodology and Hypothetical relationship for Variables

This study resorts towards a unique database on 15,600 borrowers who contracted housing loans from a financial institution in Mauritius. All data points collected pertain to the period ending October 2010. The data set comprised of different attributes of borrowers along with information relating to the loan amount granted. Consequently, information such as the date as to when the loan was disbursed, the applied interest rate thereon, the time period over which the loan repayment has been scheduled, the value of security offered, purpose of the loan, the borrowers' monthly income and the sector in which the borrower is employed, and his/her place of residence. To assess such repayment capacity, recourse is made towards the DSCR, computed as the monthly gross income of the borrower over its Equal Monthly Instalment (EMI). Technically speaking, the DSCR should be at least equal to 1.0 but, it transpired that in some cases, the DSCR are even less than one, reflecting co-borrowed loans. To remove such bias in the sample, estimation is done comprising only of DSCR above 1.0 with that model serving as the base model for all the variations undertaken in econometric methodology. The econometric model is specified below.

$$DSCR_i = \beta_0\, Tenor_i + \beta_1\, MarginCover_i + \beta_2\, Age_i + \beta_3\, Cost_i + \beta_4 Arrears_i + \beta_5 TownDum_i + \beta_6\, PublicDum_i + \beta_7 ConstructionDum_i + \beta_8 MarginCover_i{*}TownDum_i + \beta_9\, Cost_{i*}PublicDum_i + \beta_{10} Tenor_i{*}ConstructionDum_i + \beta_{11} TownDum_i{*}ConstructionDum + \varepsilon_i \qquad (1)$$[5]

[5] Alternative versions of tenor, age, cost and margin cover, all squared have also been tried but none is found to entail strong economic significance compared to when their values are employed without squaring them. Ironically, when they are employed in the analysis, the subsequent Variance Inflation Factors become exceedingly high, symptomatic with the presence of multicollinearity in the estimation process.

Where

DSCR:	Debt Service Coverage Ratio
Tenor:	Loan Maturity
Margin Cover:	Security Margin Cover
Age:	Age of borrower
Cost:	Interest cost of the loan
Arrears:	Loan arrears
TownDum:	Locational dummy variable for the borrower
PublicDum:	Public employment dummy variable for the borrower
ConstructionDum:	Dummy variable where purpose of loan is for construction

The above model is run with all variables defined in table 1 in the appendix section. Different metrics for DSCR are employed. Under the continuous metric, DSCR is computed as monthly income over EMI with OLS estimation technique being employed for the analysis. The benefit of using the continuous measure is that it directly conveys information pertaining to the real extent of repayment capacity[6]. Three different models will be considered. Model (1) considers all values for DSCR while model (2) exclusively focuses on DSCR higher than one. Finally, under the same continuous metric, natural logarithm is used for the dependent variable, tenor, margin cover, age and cost of the loan to sieve out the elasticities coefficients in model(3). Results are shown in table 4.

Thereafter, a binary metric for DSCR is employed whereby DSCR is constrained to zero for values ranging between 1 and 15 and one for values stretching beyond 15 (ranging between 15 and 31). Such analysis is reinvigorated if the banker would like to gain more insight as to how the abovementioned factors that drive repayment capacity differ for borrowers imbued with robust repayment capacity ($15 \leq$ DSCR < 31) relative to those found in lower range ($1 \leq$ DSCR < 15). In a nutshell, this exercise is synonymous to sieving out the forces that influence borrowers that are found in the robust repayment capacity range. In that case, logit and probit estimation models are employed. Finally, the Ologit model is used whereby the values of DSCR are "discreticised" as follows: 1 in case $1 \leq$ DSCR< 5, 2 in case $6 \leq$ DSCR< 10, 3 in case $11 \leq$ DSCR< 15, 4 in case $16 \leq$ DSCR< 20, 5 in case $21 \leq$ DSCR< 25 and 6 in case $26 \leq$ DSCR< 31. The purpose for including the Ologit model is basically geared towards

[6] The best analogy that can be taken pertains to the hedging literature whereby binary or continuous metrics have been employed.

assessing the forces at different discrete values of DSCR and is considered to be in-between OLS and probit/logit models. Consequently, the use of these three modeling approaches is expected to yield better results and insights on the abovementioned credit risk model. The hypotheses are laid out as below.

(a) Tenor (+)

A priori, the longer the maturity or tenor of a loan, the lower the amount that the borrower needs to pay and this indirectly enshrines his/her repayment capacity. A positive relationship is thereby expected to subsist between the tenor of the loan and DSCR.

(b) Margin Cover (+)

The aim for taking ample margin cover is to ensure that there prevails no moral hazard post granting the loan in that there are lesser chances that the borrower defaults. For a banker who already grants a loan, the concern will be more on moral hazard meaning that certain borrowers who pass the screening stage of the credit processing mechanism may latter deliberately default once they avail of the loan amount. Consequently, bankers have devised an important mechanism to alleviate such a malicious act from the part of the borrowers. How? Well, bankers take a higher security value in their favour under security purview, well in excess of the loan amount taken so that the borrower knows that default would be synonymous with losing more than the loan amount taken. A positive relationship is thereby anticipated to prevail between margin cover and DSCR.

(c) Age of the borrower(+)

As the borrower's age increases, this enhances his repayment capacity in the form of annual salary increments, additional qualifications gained usually resulting into more increments, and also following promotions as the borrower moves up the rung of the ladder in his/her organisation. All these factors converge towards a positive relationship between DSCR and the age of the borrower.

(d) Cost of the loan(-)

The cost of the loan is captured by the interest rate and the higher the interest rate, the larger will be the EMI so that the lower will be the DSCR.

However, it is expected that the impact of such a factor is likely to lower than that of margin cover since interest rate resetting at any financial institution emanates from gradual changes in the main stance of monetary policy in that country.

(e) Loan arrears(-)

Loan arrears signify the inability of the borrower to make good for the periodical payments as scheduled by the lender. The higher the number of unpaid scheduled payments, the larger will be the value for the arrears and the larger will be the readjusted EMI based on the same loan tenor. In that respect, a negative relationship is thereby expected to prevail between loan arrears and DSCR.

(f) Dummy variables: TownDum(+); PublicDum(-) & ConstructionDum(-)

A locational dummy has been used to categorise borrowers than reside in the district of Port-Louis and Plaine Wilhems, which represents the city and comprise all the towns present in Mauritius. It is hypothesized that people who live in the city or towns are likely to be wealthier and better off in terms of their repayment capacity compared to those found in the villages. It is expected that people who work in the public sector are expected to have poorer repayment capacity since the private sector offers the best salary packages in view of luring the most efficient and performing human capital. Finally, a last dummy variable has been incorporated to cater for the specificity of the loan. As a matter of fact, housing loan includes loan for construction, renovation and extension as well. To consider construction loans only, a dummy variable has been used for same and it is anticipated that such a loan type will exert downward pressure on repayment capacity as the loan amount is usually higher.

(g) Interaction dummies/variables

However, the above model could be misspecified in case there are important interactions. For instance, it could be that margin cover is higher for borrowers found in the town so that the use of both variables could cater for such a state of affairs. Indeed, the value of land in Mauritius tends to be very high in towns relative to non-town places so that the use of MarginCover*TownDum is expected to significantly improve on the

DSCR of the borrower. Similarly, since the loan value for construction loans tends to be higher than those for non-construction purposes, this is anticipated to generate higher loan maturity levels. Consequently, recourse is made towards Tenor*ConstructionDum as another independent variable in the credit risk model. Since borrowers working in the public sector are likely to avail of higher credibility that would most likely translate into lower borrowing costs, it becomes interesting to also analyse the impact of an interaction dummy variable that incorporates Cost*PublicDum simultaneously as one variable. Finally, the last interaction variable constitutes an interaction dummy which is a composition of TownDum* Construction Dum. However, while analysing the correlation coefficients, it appears that Cost*PublicDum and Tenor*ConstructionDum exhibited significant correlations with PublicDum and ConstructionDum, respectively, rendering them ineligible for the analysis. Consequently, only MarginCover*TownDum and TownDum*ConstructionDum variables have been retained for the analysis.

Empirical Results

The summary statistics for all variables are depicted in the appendix section in table 2. The minimum period for the housing house revolves around two years while the highest around 19 years which befits the current norms in Mauritius. As per the correlation coefficients in table 2, it appears that multicollinearity is not an issue of concern. Prior to implementing the regression analysis, each variable is analysed for potential outlier effects and post removing all outliers, the final sample comprised of 13,724 borrowers. Later, as the focus is more towards DSCR higher than one, this led to total observations of 13,636.

Within each model considered, whether OLS or any of the limited dependent variable model, margin cover systematically occasions a positive effect and that at the 1% significance level with the strongest statistical significance and second highest economic significance, independent of whether the focus is on the continuous or on the binary metric. In the case of the elasticity coefficient under the log-linear[7] model, margin cover has the highest economic significance in terms of the elasticity coefficient of 0.28%, i.e., DSCR changes by 0.28% following a 1% change in margin cover. Otherwise, under the OLS model, a 1% change in margin cover occasions around 61% change in DSCR. Under the logit and probit models, the marginal effects are also the highest ones

[7] These models are also referred to as log-log or double-log models.

and revolve around 0.60% and 0.48%, respectively, endorsing the fact that robust DSCR are positively affected by higher margin cover. Similarly, under the Ologit model, strong marginal impact is obtained and which stands around 0.23%. Hence, irrespective of the model under consideration, there is general convergence as to margin cover entailing the highest impact on DSCR. Such a finding bodes well with the fact that bankers should use margin cover as their main weapon in alleviating any latent moral hazard effects that may prevail post the granting of a loan.

Under OLS approach for model (1) and model (2), a 1% change in the age of the borrower causes about 1% change in DSCR. However, in the case of the log-linear model age is found to be statistically insignificant. Similarly, under the logit, probit and Ologit models, the marginal effects are found to have low economic significance.

Under the OLS approach, a 1% change in tenor triggers around 22% change in DSCR. The elasticity of tenor with respect to DSCR is also positive and stands around 0.18%, i.e., DSCR changes by 0.18% ensuing a 1% change in tenor. Under the probit and logit models, a 1% change in tenor trails behind a 0.46% and 0.15% change, respectively, in the probability that DSCR lies in the range of 15 to 31. Under the Ologit model, it transpires that a 1% change in tenor has a positive effect of 7.74% on DSCR. Overall, the tenor of the loan or loan maturity period triggers a positive impact on DSCR. This can be explained by the fact that the longer the loan maturity, the lower the repayments the borrower needs to make under his/her Equal Monthly Loan Instalment.

The cost of loan as captured by the interest rate on the loan exerts a negative effect on the repayment capacity of the borrower. While the effect is around -6% and -16% under the OLS and elasticity models, under the limited dependent variable model, the impact seems to be statistically insignificant under the probit and logit models but not under the Ologit model where the effect stands around -3%. The statistical insignificance under the probit and logit model points out that interest rate does not matter when DSCR is assessed in terms of binary level. Such a finding clearly underscores the need for a continuous DSCR to best sieve out the effect of interest rate. Indeed, as aforesaid, any central bank in the world would not like to recklessly adjust its interest rate so that the process of changes is a smooth one and hence its effect is best captured when the dependent variable is also a continuous measurement.

Despite the fact that the arrears variable posts the anticipated negative sign, nonetheless, it is found to be impotent in terms of statistical significance, independent of the model under consideration in table 5, except for Ologit approach. Subsequently, this implies that arrears do not really strain hard on DSCR. This could reflect that the institution is already adhering to very sound credit policy schemes in view of shunning arrears problems.

In the case of the categorical independent variable that represents a borrower coming from the public sector, a negative effect is noted meaning that borrowers who work in the public sector possess a rather subdued repayment capacity. Under OLS, a 1% change for borrowers in the public sector entails around 32% fall in DSCR with an impact of -0.04% in the case of the elasticity model. Again, as expected the effect is higher under the Ologit model (-13.50%) compared to probit/logit model (-0.46%). This could signify that borrowers from the private sector are likely to avail of higher salaries as the private employers vigorously attempt to lure the best and most efficient human capital in order to maximise efficiency and thereby optimise on profits. Moreover, it also bears testimony to the fact that the promotional exercise in the public sector is geared mainly towards level of seniority accomplished compared to the private sector where it is chiefly based on the experience gained, productivity and intelligence of the staff. The locational factor of the borrower, as captured by the town dummy, is not found to be influencing DSCR because, is almost all of the models under scrutiny.

Table 4: Econometric Results under OLS approach

	Model(1) OLS: DSCR <1	Model(2) OLS: DSCR ≥1	Model(3) OLS-Natural Logarithm
Tenor	0.2212	0.2263	0.1845
	(9.76)***	(9.92)***	(7.66)***
Margin Cover	0.6206	0.6184	0.2488
	(70.55)***	(70.22)***	(60.68)***
Age of borrower	0.0094	0.0121	0.0218
	(2.57)**	(3.26)***	(0.98)
Interest cost	-0.0661	-0.0621	-0.1557
	(-3.85)***	(-3.61)***	(-6.84)***
Arrears on loan	-0.3566	-0.3293	-0.0777
	(-2.04)*	(-1.87)*	(-3.01)***
Borrower-Town	0.0799	0.0879	-0.1276
	(0.88)	(0.96)	(-10.02)***
Borrower-Public	-0.3278	-0.3265	-0.0492
	(-3.96)***	(-3.93)***	(3.71)***
Loan-Construction	-1.7155	-1.7230	-0.4405
	(-21.42)***	(-21.45)***	(-38.28)***
MarginCoverTown	-0.0158	-0.0165	0.0278
	(-1.24)	(-1.30)	(17.26)***
TownDumConstructionDum	-0.0406	-0.0438	0.0668
	(-0.32)	(-0.34)	(3.56)***
Intercept	2.3839	2.2642	1.3809
	(6.17)***	(5.19)***	(9.47)***
Adj R-squared	0.4528	0.4530	0.4089
F(10, 13713)	1136.45	570.70	1152.98
Prob > F	0.0000	0.0000	0.0000
Observations	13724	13636	13636
Root MSE	3.3132	3.3126	0.4908

Note: The table presents the multivariate analysis of the impact of different factors on the DSCR for borrowers who contracted mortgage loans. The table reports point estimates of the coefficients followed by their t-values in parentheses. The definitions and constructions of the variables are in the Appendix. * , ** and *** denotes statistical significance at the 10%, 5% and 1% level, respectively. Model (1) considers values of DSCR even less than one while model (2) is estimated based on DSCR values exceeding one and subsequently all models are based on the same observations[8]. Finally, model(3) considers the natural logarithm[9] of DSCR, tenor, margin cover, age of borrower and interest cost, respectively to compute the elasticity coefficients in the case that DSCR is above one.

---

[8] The rationale is that there were only few observations less than one under DSCR and also that, DSCR should technically be above one for a lender to enter into a transaction with the borrower.

[9] Natural logarithms could not be applied to variables having zero values and in these cases, the coefficients collapse into semi-elasticities coefficients for Loan construction dummy, town dummy, public dummy and arrears on loan.

Table 5: Econometric Results for Limited Dependent Models

	Model (4) **Probit**[10]	Model (5) **Logit**	Model (6) **Ologit**
Tenor	0.0046	0.0015	0.0774
	(5.58)***	(6.54)***	(6.33)***
Margin Cover	0.0060	0.0048	0.2292
	(21.91)***	(24.27) ***	(40.64)***
Age of borrower	0.0004	0.0004	0.0067
	(3.51)***	(3.56)***	(3.40)***
Interest cost	-0.0002	-5.9e-05	-0.0268
	(-0.44)	(-0.11)	(-3.00)***
Arrears on loan	-0.0064	-0.0046	-0.1813
	(-1.01)	(-0.79)	(-1.82)*
Borrower-Town	0.0021	0.0046	0.0101
	(0.95)	(0.80)	(0.32)
Borrower-Public	-0.0046	-0.0046	-0.1350
	(-2.08)**	(-1.60)	(-3.07) ***
Loan-Construction	-0.0365	-0.0365	-1.2990
	(-8.66)***	(-8.17)***	(-30.20)***
Intercept	-0.1635	-0.1362	Na
	(-11.38)***	(-11.07)***	
Pseudo R2	0.3147	0.3073	0.2251
Wald chi2(8)	743.94	834.73	3058.63
Prob > chi2	0.0000	0.0000	0.0000
Observations	13636	13636	13636
Log likelihood	-1899.50	-1920.01	-10767.455

Note: The table presents the multivariate analysis of the impact of different factors on the DSCR for borrowers who contracted housing loans. The table reports the derived marginal effects followed by their z-values in parentheses. The definitions and constructions of the variables are in the Appendix. * , ** and *** denotes statistical significance at the 10%, 5% and 1% level, respectively. Model (4) resorts a probit model whereby DSCR between 1 and 15 is censored to zero and DSCR between 15 and 31 is censored to 1. Model (5) used the same binary method as per model (4) but now under logit estimation approach. Finally, model (6) resorts to a *"discretisized"* limited dependent model à la Ologit philosophy as follows: 1 in case 1 in case $1 \leq$ DSCR< 5, 2 in case $6 \leq$ DSCR< 10, 3 in case $11 \leq$ DSCR< 15, 4 in case $16 \leq$ DSCR< 20, 5 in case $21 \leq$ DSCR< 25 and 6 in case $26 \leq$ DSCR< 31. At first glance, regression coefficients for Ologit model tends to lie in-between those of the OLS and the probit/logit model.

[10] Since the coefficients under the probit, logit and Ologit models are not directly interpretable as under OLS approach, their marginal effects have been computed (See Brooks (2008)) and reported in the table. Under the logit and Ologit model, recourse is made towards the cumulative logistic distribution and in case of probit, the cumulative normal distribution is used.

The last independent dummy variable which represents the purpose of the loan, namely loans which have been contracted solely for construction in lieu of extensions/renovations of houses, is found to be not only statistically significant but also rejoices over robust economic significance. As a matter of fact, a 1% change in loan for construction dummy entails around -172% change in DSCR under OLS approach. Under the probit and logit models, the marginal effects stand around 3.65%. Such a result manifests by virtue of larger funds taken for loans under construction purposes so that they exert considerable pressures on the repayment capacity of the borrower. Finally, none of the interaction variable/dummy is found to be statistically significant in table 4 for model (1) and model (2) and hence they are utterly overlooked in table 5.

Conclusion

Conventional and recent developments in credit risk models have been geared mainly towards modelling the probability of default. This paper contributes to all the previous models by proposing a credit risk model which directly befits the banker/lender by catering for the practical forces that underlie the repayment capacity of a borrower and thus induces a higher degree of proactiveness in credit risk management.

The significance of margin cover as a driver for higher repayment capacity signifies that it effectively serves as a moral hazard mitigation mechanism so that any credit policy should incorporate it as a vital credit risk management tool. The tenor of the loan also positively influences. Based on the adverse effects of the US subprime crisis on the exporting arm of Mauritius, it seems considerate for the lenders/bankers in Mauritius to cling towards a readjustment of their loan maturities to enshrine the repayment capacity of bruised borrowers who are subject to a fall in their income.

The fact that borrowers from the public sector exhibit poor repayment profiles signifies that the credit risk manager should diversify his portfolio by incorporating more private borrowers. The negative relationship between the interest cost and DSCR justified the bearish monetary policy stance in Mauritius following the US Subprime crisis in mitigating financial causalities. However, in case the upward interest rates adjustment is faster than the income growth of the borrowers, then, this would invalidate the whole purpose of the fiscal stimulus packages.

The low economic significance for age implies that borrowers do not usually get fresh increments when they get new qualifications. Or it could be that any yearly increments based on experience or increments pertaining to acquisition of new certificates are not huge enough as to significantly boost their income. Since housing loans meant for construction exerts the highest effect and with a negative sign on DSCR, this implies that bankers need to be very cautious when they are dealing with such type of loans. This also explains as to why in many countries, housing loans for construction are of longer time periods, stretching beyond one decade in most cases.

Finally, no major evidence is found regarding arrears and town dummy impacting on the repayment capacity of the borrowers, suggesting that the institution already avails of solid arrears management and wealth people also stay in villages due to lesser air and noise pollution, let alone the fact that they now possess all amenities like towns.

I believe that I have achieved a certain level of "credit-realization" in my life post developing the abovementioned credit risk model. As nothing but change is the constant feature in life, in that respect, I hope to later refine or enhance the modelling feature of the model to further contribution in the sphere of practical credit risk modelling.

Appendix

Table 1: List of variables

Variable	Definition
DSCR	DSCR defined as monthly income of the borrower divided over his/her Equal Monthly Loan Instalment
Cost	Interest Cost of the loan
Margin Cover	(Security Value - Loan Amount)/ Loan Amount
PublicDum	1 in case borrower works in the public sector, 0 otherwise
TownDum	1 in case borrower resides in a town, 0 otherwise
ConstructionDum	1 in case the purpose of the loan is for construction, 0 otherwise
Outstanding Loan	Outstanding loan amount/Original loan amount
Age of borrower	Age of the borrower
Arrears	Arrears/Oustanding loan amount

Table 2: Summary Statistics

Variable	Mean	St. dev.	Min	Max
Tenor	7.8527	1.8370	1.76	19.11
Margin Cover	3.6980	4.5968	0.02	54.64
Age of borrower	41.1209	8.4288	20.28	86.82
Interest cost of loan	9.9577	2.2090	3.0	14.0
Arrears on loan	0.0724	0.1655	0	3.9585
Borrower-Town	0.3919	0.4882	0	1
Borrower-Public	0.1374	0.3443	0	1
Loan-Construction	0.3214	0.4670	0	1
DSCR	5.5506	4.4774	1.0064	30.9622

Note: The table presents summary statistics for the sample used in the multivariate analysis. Constructions and definitions of the variables are spelt out in the Appendix. The first column shows the mean values while columns (2), (3) and (4) depicts the standard deviation, the minimum value and the maximum value for each variable.

Table 3: Correlation matrix of independent variables used in the model

	DSCR	Tenor	Margin Cover	Age of borrower	Cost of loan	Arrears on loan	Borrower-Town	Borrower-Public	Loan-Construction
DSCR	1.0000	0.1058	0.6440	0.1189	-0.0188	-0.0071	0.0238	-0.0173	-0.3117
Tenor		1.0000	-0.2818	-0.3749	-0.6609	-0.1812	-0.0539	-0.0433	0.2080
Margin Cover			1.0000	0.1933	0.1462	0.0446	0.0361	0.0165	-0.2421
Age of Borrower				1.0000	0.1462	0.1147	0.0805	0.0539	-0.0931
Cost of loan					1.0000	0.1369	0.0491	0.0631	-0.1014
Arrears on loan						1.0000	0.0093	-0.0750	-0.0368
Borrower-Town							1.0000	-0.0250	-0.0262
Borrower-Public								1.0000	-0.0084
Loan-Construction									1.0000

References

Akerlof, G. (1970), "The Market for "Lemons": Quality Uncertainty And The Market Mechanism", *Quarterly Journal of Economics,*Vol 89, 488-500.

Black, F. and M. Scholes. (1973), "The Pricing of Options and Corporate Liabilities", *The Journal of Political Economy*, 81(3), 637-654.

Black, F. and J. C. Cox. (1976), "Valuing Corporate Securities: Some Effects of Bond Indenture Provisions", *Journal of Finance*, 31(2), 351-367.

Brooks, C. (2008), Introductory Econometrics for Finance, Cambridge University Press, 2nd Edition

Duffie, D. and K. J. Singleton. (1999), "Modeling Term Structures of Defaultable Bonds", *Review of Financial Studies,* 12(4), 687–720.

Geske, R. (1977), "The Valuation of Corporate Liabilities as Compound Options", *Journal of Financial and Quantitative Analysis*, 12, 541-552.

—. (1979), "The Valuation of Compound Options", *Journal of Financial Economics*, 7, 63-81.

Jarrow, R., and S. Turnbull. (1992), "Credit Risk: Drawing the Analogy," Risk Magazine, 5(9).

Leland, H. and K. B. Toft. (1996), "Optimal Capital Structure, Endogenous Bankruptcy, and The Term Structure of Credit Spreads", *Journal of Finance* 51(3), 987–1019.

Longstaff, F. A. and E. S. Schwartz. (1995), "A Simple Approach to Valuing Risky Fixed and Floating Rate Debt", *Journal of Finance*, 50(3), 789-819.

Merton, R. C. (1973), "Theory of Rational Option Pricing", Bell *Journal of Economics and Management.*

—. (1974), "On the Pricing of Corporate Debt: The risk structure of interest rates", *Journal of Finance*, 29(2), 449–470.

Nielsen, L. T., J. Saá-Requejo, and P. Santa-Clara. (1993), "Default Risk and Interest Rate Risk: The Term Structure of Default Spreads," Working Paper, INSEAD

Vasicek, O. (1977), "An Equilibrium Characterization of the Term Structure", *Journal of Financial Economics*, 5, 177-188.

CHAPTER SIXTEEN

EXPLORING ALTERNATIVE MEASURES OF CREDIT CONCENTRATION RISK

ADITYA BISEN, SHRUTI AMRUTE AND GOUTAM SANYAL[1]

Concentration Risk refers to the risk arising out of above average exposure to counterparties, including exposure to borrowers or borrower groups (Credit Risk), currencies (Market Risk), suppliers of credit (Liquidity Risk) or business/IT systems (Operational Risk) [1]. This paper focuses on measurement of Concentration Risk arising from banks' corporate portfolio using easily implementable techniques.

Banks take large exposure to certain counterparties. Literature provides conflicting opinion on credit portfolio concentration. On the one hand, academicians point to repeated crises that have also stemmed from the credit risk being concentrated in borrowers with similar characteristics. As a result, a case for portfolio diversification is made. On the other hand, studies such as Winton (1999) claim that excessive diversification only reduces profitability without significantly reducing risk.

Practitioners have always argued in favor of moderate degrees of concentration and claim that the practice of assuming large exposures in the banking book is a conscious part of business strategy. One possible reason for the strategy may be, as argued by Boyd and Nicolo (2003), that better understanding of the customer and informational advantages allow banks to increase profitability while managing risk effectively. Empirical evidence supports the line of thinking. It is also argued that concentrated exposure resulting from better understanding of sectoral risks and returns

[1] The authors work as part of the credit risk management group at ICICI Bank Ltd. The views expressed in the paper are however, personal and not that of the organization. The authors would like to thank Dr. Rajeev Singhal, Associate Professor of Finance at Oakland University, Rochester for providing valuable inputs to the paper.

would allow banks to price products efficiently, resulting in better credit flow. Additionally, it may be argued that any attempt to diversify through exposures to sectors where banks have limited understanding would augment risk instead of mitigating it.

Despite the argument in favour of concentration, caution is required and the need to identify, quantify and benchmark credit concentration risk has emerged.

The Vasicek formula specifies the capital charge against a facility extended to a borrower by accounting for probability of default (PD), loss given default (LGD) and maturity. It forms the basis for capital computation under the methodology prescribed by the Basel Accord (2006). The formula however, makes two important assumptions. Firstly, it assumes that a credit portfolio is infinitely granular. Secondly, it presumes that only one systematic factor affects all firms, an assumption in contrast to real world situations where firm-specific returns may be affected by multiple factors. As a result, the formula may not fully account for concentration risk. The Accord prescribes accounting for the concentration risk as part of the Supervisory Review process, commonly known as Pillar II.

Several measures may be used to quantify concentration risk. The Gini coefficient and HHI provide summary measures for comparison. Both however, fail to provide actionable benchmarks, besides suffering from intuitive deficiencies. Multi-factor models (MFM), based on Monte-Carlo simulations are a more rigorous approach but at the same time computationally challenging and time consuming. Easily implementable, closed form solutions are required if a bank is to integrate concentration risk analysis with the day-to-day risk management process. The paper presents a relatively simple approach to measuring credit concentration risk.

Measuring Credit Concentration Risk

Gini Coefficient & Herfindahl Hirshman Index

The Gini coefficient is generally used to measure income inequality in countries. In case of a bank's credit portfolio, it indexes the amount of the portfolio allocated to different percentages of obligors. In other words, the Gini coefficient calculates the distance of the current portfolio from one that is perfectly granular. A Gini coefficient of zero indicates a portfolio that is equally distributed amongst all borrowers while a value of one means that one borrower accounts for the entire portfolio.

The Herfindahl Hirschman Index (HHI) is a statistical measure incorporating the relative size of all firms. It is traditionally used to measure the level to which an industry is monopolized and is calculated by summing up the squares of market share of each firm in the portfolio. In case of a bank's credit portfolio, the HHI can be similarly applied to arrive at an index that measures concentration of an industry or a single borrower. If the portfolio is highly granular with equal distribution across borrowers, HHI will tend to zero. The upper limit is one, where the portfolio consists of a single borrower.

Both, Gini coefficient and HHI have the advantage of being computationally less demanding. One only needs borrower data to arrive at the value, which could then be compared across banks. Each measure however, has its shortcomings. The Gini coefficient does not consider the size of the portfolio. A portfolio consisting of two borrowers with equal exposures would return the same Gini value as a portfolio of fifty borrowers with equal exposures. The fact that the latter is granular and the former concentrated is not captured. The HHI, on the other hand, depends heavily on the industry classification. Too many industries would artificially drive the index lower, whereas too few would make it higher. Finally, there are no clear ways to arrive at a benchmark for comparison and therefore provide few action points to the managers.

Multifactor Model

The multi-factor model addresses the assumption of a single systemic factor affecting firm returns under the Vasicek model. It captures name and sector concentration accounting for economy wide and industry specific factors.[2] The Monte Carlo simulation framework can then be used to calculate a loss distribution. The 99.9 percentile will be indicative of the VaR. Capital charge as per the VaR model, less expected loss gives the capital requirement (unexpected loss).[3] It is for this reason that the MFM capital charge is assumed to be the 'correct' approximation of concentration risk for purposes of this paper as noted by Duellmann (2006)[4].

Although the multi-factor model provides an accurate measure of the concentration risk, it is expensive to develop and difficult to maintain. Additionally, it is time consuming and hence provides few inputs to real time decision making. As a result, closed form solutions are required to

[2] The BCBS working paper on Credit Concentration Risk acknowledges this point

[3] An LGD = 45 percent is assumed

[4] A number of other papers acknowledge the accuracy of the MFM in estimating concentration risk

approximate the MFM capital charge while retaining the basic tenets involved in its construction.

Granularity Adjustment

To address the 'infinite granularity' assumption of the Vasicek formula, we use Gordy and Lutkebohmert's granularity adjustment (GA) (2007). The authors have modified the original GA developed by Gordy (2004)[5] with significantly reduced computational requirements. Without delving into the specifics, we focus only on applicability of the adjustment for our illustrative portfolio. The authors have arrived at a simplified closed form solution that can easily be applied to any credit portfolio with available data. The model however, only approximates name concentration risk. High exposures to different sectors are not captured, making the GA an incomplete measure of concentration risk.

BET and Infection Model

The BET developed by Moody's was one of the first and is currently the most widely accepted approach to assess credit risk in securitization structures such as CDO and CLO. The key idea behind the model was to map the real portfolio to a hypothetical homogenous portfolio with the same Probability of default (PD) and total exposure. The number of defaults is binomially distributed. The product of average exposure size, loss given default (LGD) and the 99.9% percentile of the binomial loss distribution (with D[6] and weighted average PD) returns the VaR. The unexpected loss is simply the VaR computed above less the expected loss calculated by multiplying the PD, LGD and the total exposure.

The Infection Model extends the Binomial Expansion Technique (BET) to calculate the impact of sectoral concentration. It attempts to supplement the Multi-factor model by requiring fewer data inputs. It is computationally less challenging, making it an attractive alternative.[7] Through various tests, Duellmann shows that the infection model performs better than the BET model in approximating the results of the multi-factor model. It utilizes the basic tenets of the BET but introduces a new type of default dependency.

---

[5] See M, Gordy (2004),*Granularity adjustment* in portfolio credit risk measurement.

[6] Where, D, the diversity score, is the number of uncorrelated obligors in the portfolio. e.g. a diversity score of 25 for a portfolio with 100 borrowers would imply that 100 correlated borrowers effectively equal 25 uncorrelated borrowers.

[7] A number of other models for approximating Pykhtin's model are available. Analysis of all however, is beyond scope of this paper.

Any exposure in the 'hypothetical portfolio' is assumed to either default autonomously with a probability of p or because of *infection* (with a probability of q). In other words, an exposure that is financially sound could still default on account of *infection* from another exposure.

A key contribution of Duellman was in the computation of q, the probability of infectious defaults. The variable was found to be dependent on the sectoral concentration of the portfolio, the weighted average PD and the intra and inter sector asset correlations.

Duellman prescribed the following functional form for computation of q;

$$\ln(q) = \beta_0 + \beta_1 \ln(HHI) + \beta_2 \ln(\bar{p}) + \beta_3 \ln(\bar{\rho}^{intra}) + \beta_4 \ln(\bar{\rho}^{inter}) + \epsilon$$

A loss distribution that accounts for the diversity score, defaults in the hypothetical portfolio, the probability of default and probability of infection is used to arrive at the value at risk. The unexpected loss (capital charge) is then calculated by subtracting the expected loss from the VaR computation above

Portfolio Construction

For illustrative purposes, we setup a 'base' portfolio. A total of 500 borrowers are assumed and a portfolio distribution mirroring real bank portfolios in emerging markets is attempted by referencing data available in the public domain. The illustrative portfolio is concentrated in 'A-' and 'BBB' rating categories. Further, the portfolio of 500 borrowers is segregated into 19 different sectors[8].

A range of PD scenarios have been selected. At the upper end of the scale, CRISIL[9] India long term PDs have been assumed to reflect the probability of default typical of an emerging market. At the lower end, Standard & Poor (S&P) developed market PDs typify lower default probabilities characteristic of advanced economies. In addition, three

---

[8] These include Automobiles & Components, Banks & Diversified Financials, Capital Goods, Chemicals & Fertilizers, Consumer Durables, Consumer Services & Telecom, Consumer Staple, Energy, Infrastructure, Real Estate & Cement, Materials & Industrials, Metals & Mining, Pharmaceuticals & Biotechnology, Retail, Software & Services, Sugar, Tech Hardware & Equipment, Textiles, Transportation and Utilities.

[9] CRISIL is majority owned by Standard & Poor and is largest external rating agency in India

moderate PDs were arrived at by multiplying the CRISIL PDs by different adjustment factors. The five PD scenarios cover a broad range of probabilities of default. [10]

To compute inter and intra sector correlations for the Indian Market, listed companies based on market capitalization and data availability were selected and segregated into the 19 different sectors mentioned earlier. End of day equity prices for these firms were used to compute *inter-firm* correlations spanning a 12 month period. The average correlations between all firms within a sector were assumed to represent intra-sector correlation. Similarly, the average correlation between firms of two different sectors was assumed to reflect inter-sector correlation. Correlations over a 12 month period were computed every quarter for the past three years and scenarios were designed to cover the highest and lowest correlations witnessed. Towards this end, base intra and inter sector correlations (0.28 and 0.23 respectively) were multiplied by adjustment factors ranging from 1.5 to 0.4. An adjustment factor of 0.4 reduced all observed inter and intra sector correlations by 60% (multiplied by 0.4). Similarly, an adjustment factor of 1.5 increased all observed inter and intra sector correlations by 50% (multiplied by 1.5). Adjustment factors of 0.4, 0.8, 1.0, 1.2 and 1.5 were used. Correlations of 0.6 and 0.7 were also included to test for, separately, model behavior in case of very high correlations.

An analysis of the correlations regime used by Duellmann is warranted. Several combinations of inter and intra sector correlation were used by the author in order to test the efficacy of the Infection model over a range of scenarios. Two points emerge, *firstly* the deviation between intra and inter sector correlations is found to be very large in many cases (0.3 for intra and 0.05 for inter in one scenario). However, we were unable to witness such large deviations between the two measures in the Indian scenario and find it unintuitive that the two would vary so much. *Secondly*, we question the use of *both* inter and intra sector correlation when computing the infection probability since one can expect both measures to move in tandem when averaged over a large set of companies. Credence to this hypothesis is lent by correlation between the two measures witnessed when comparing the average correlation for the Indian market over the past few quarters. One finds a high degree of correlation between intra and inter sector correlation. The graph below illustrates this view. A correlation of 0.9986 was observed over the time period.

---

[10] The PD floor for any grade has been fixed at 0.03%, in line with Basel II guidelines. Additionally, rounded values have been used.

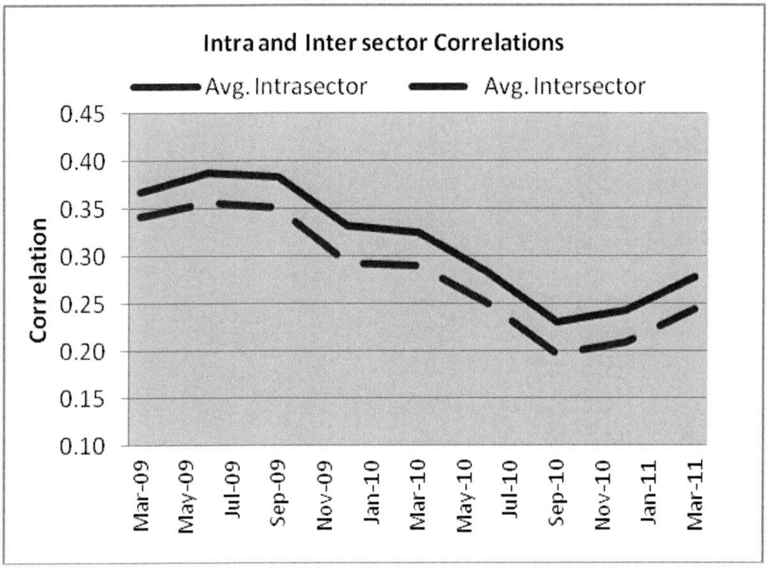

As a result, when recreating the model specification employed by Duellmann, using the scenarios outlined in this section earlier, the coefficients of inter and intra sector correlations had high p-values, indicating insignificance and multi-collinearity.[11] The correlation scenarios used by Duellmann were not related in similar fashion hence returning significant p-values for the coefficients of the two measures.

Finally, 3 portfolios of different concentrations were constructed by changing the Gini coefficient and HHI. The Gini coefficients and HHI for the three portfolios are provided in the table below. As a result, with 3 different portfolios, 5 different PD scenarios and 5 different correlations, 75 scenarios were arrived at for the Model estimation process

Model Estimation

The paper stated two critical assumptions of the Vasicek formula employed by the IRB approach in Basel II – the assumption of infinite granularity and a single systematic factor. The multifactor model addresses both these assumptions. As a result, the *difference* between the multifactor model capital charge and that of the Vasicek formula would give us an

[11] Although a high R^2 was achieved.

estimate of the capital charge attributable to concentration risk. Since the IRB capital charge on the 'base' scenarios is 6.21%, that returned by the MFM is 10.65% and the IM, 9.28%, the concentration risk charge in case of both models would be 4.44% and 3.07% respectively. Since use of either measure doesn't impact our analysis, we will retain the use of the model capital charge for model estimation in place of the *model difference approach.*

In addition to the critique mentioned in the earlier section, the MFM arrives at a more conservative value as opposed to the IM, though it improves on the BET loss estimate on account of infectious defaults. Banks' and regulators would however, require higher accuracy from a closed form solution before adoption.

Table 3: Overall MFM-IM errors

Model	Median Error	Mean	Standard Deviation
Infection Model	18.95%	19.34%	8.67%

An adjustment is proposed. Empirically, it is acknowledged that borrowers with higher ratings (lower PDs) tend to have higher unexpected losses than borrowers with lower ratings. One reason could be the apparent greater room for 'downside risk' (downgrades) available to higher rated obligors as compared to lower rated borrowers.[12] A 'AAA' rated borrower can face more downgrades (higher increments in capital charge to be held against the exposure) before reaching non-performing category as opposed to a 'B' rated borrower. The IRB formula attempts to account for this observation by means of a 'maturity adjustment' which is an inverse function of PD.[13]

---

[12] See BCBS paper, 'An Explanatory Note on Basel II IRB Risk Weight Functions' (2005)

[13] Another intuitive reason may be presented. The expected and unexpected losses are lower for higher rated borrowers within the Basel II capital framework, and higher for lower rated borrowers. Since, the maximum loss on a facility extended to a borrower equals the outstanding exposure for both, borrowers with higher and lower ratings, the losses associated with tail risks can be expected to be higher for higher rated borrowers. Additionally, inter and intra sector correlations are not captured within EL and UL. As a result, we are left with a relationship between PD and correlations, one that is not accounted for in the original calibration of q.

Literature also lends support to this hypothesis. Borrowers with higher ratings, tend to have higher asset correlations. This follows from the intuition that larger firms, who tend to have higher ratings, also have larger systematic risk, and are more closely correlated with the performance of the economy. In contrast, smaller firms with lower ratings have higher default probabilities and lower asset correlations as noted by Zhang, Zhu and Lee (2008)

To account for this relationship, we introduce an interaction term, the product of natural logarithmic of PD and correlations, to Duellmann's infection parameter q and tested the results.

We derived the q values (an input into the IM model) by back calculating the value of *q* for which the capital charge as per the IM equaled that of the MFM. A regression was run with these *q's* as the dependant variable and HHI, and the aforementioned interaction term as independent variables. A regression without the interaction term was also run for comparison. The value of *q* now takes the form[14];

$$\ln(q) = \beta_0 + \beta_1 \ln(HHI) + \beta_2 . \ln(\bar{\rho}^{inter}) + \beta_3 \ln(\bar{p}) . \ln(\bar{\rho}^{intra}) + \epsilon$$

To verify the accuracy of our results, the regression coefficients obtained by including the interaction term were used in place of those prescribed by Duellman. These were compared with the results obtained from the original Duellmann calibration. The median error term fell from 18.95% (original calibration) to 3.15% after inclusion of interaction term. The variability of the error term also came down significantly.

Portfolio Statistics	Duellmann	With Interaction term
R^2	NA	0.9577
Adjusted R^2	NA	0.9559

[14] Alternate model specifications were also attempted. While most returned high R^2 and adjusted R^2, one (or more) variable with high p-values would be present. The chosen 'form' had the lowest p-values for all independent variables, accounted for the interaction between PD and correlations and included the affects of all the variables originally used for calibration by Duellmann. A high R^2 and adjusted R^2 and low variance of errors strengthened its case.

Median Error[1]	18.95%	3.15%
Mean Error[1]	19.34%	3.56%
Standard Deviation	8.67%	3.15%

[1] Error with respect to the Multi-factor capital charge

The paper establishes the following values for the regression equations to be used with the equation given earlier in this section. The coefficients are in line with the intuitive understanding on the behavior of sector concentration, firm probability of default and inter and intra sector correlations and their impact on probability of infection[15];

	β0	β1	β2	β3
Coefficient	2.008267	2.081932	0.668977	-0.123834
Standard error	0.236448	0.107493	0.125546	0.024725
p-value	0.0000	0.0000	0.0000	0.0000

The particular model specification not only address the subject of interaction between PD and correlations but also deals with the issue of correlation between the inter and intra sector correlation highlighted earlier while at the same time retaining all relevant variables.

Evaluation

To test the model specification outlined in the earlier section, we set up out of sample portfolios. Four portfolios of varying granularity were constructed in a manner similar to construction of the 'base' portfolio. Three PD scenarios were adopted - the opposite ends of the PD spectrum highlighted in section 4, i.e. CRISIL India PDs and S&P Developed

[15] An increase in the probability of infection raises the capital charge as per the Infection Model. A positive coefficient for sectoral concentration and inter sector correlation would increase the value of q and the capital charge. Similarly, an increase in the probability of default and intra-sector correlations should also increase the capital requirement. Since the product of the two variables is being used, a negative coefficient is correct.

Market PDs in addition to 'Moderate PD 2'. A correlation regime using adjustment factors of 1.5, 0.8, 0.4 were used. Correlations of 0.6 and 0.7 were also included to test for, separately, model behavior in case of very high correlations. As a result, a total of 48 out-of-sample scenarios (4x3x4) are used to test performance of the model. Tables below present the results of this exercise.

Table 6: Overall Test Portfolio results

Model	Median Error	Mean	Standard Deviation
Adjusted Infection Model	3.24%	4.52%	4.07%

Managing Concentration Risk - A practitioner's perspective

Although Basel II norms require recognition of concentration risk and recommend setting aside economic capital under Pillar 2, few banks were found to be doing so. Limits based on regulatory requirements and internal estimates were the most popular measure used to tackle the risk. While limit setting is a widely appreciated policy tool for portfolio management and could be a useful instrument for keeping credit concentrations in check, it could however, be compromised to pressures or quarter/year-end targets. Careful monitoring is therefore required to ensure the efficacy of the exercise.

In restricting the limit structure to individual borrower, sector or groups, one misses out on a number of sources of concentration risk such as kind of facility, type of collateral and exposures with certain tenors to name a few. To set a limit on every source of concentration would be an enormous exercise. Fortunately, we can summarize a majority of this information in a single figure, i.e. economic Capital, since the Vasicek formula incorporates information on all factors affecting probability of default, loss give default and maturity.

The limits-based structure may now be refined. Individual, sector, group limits may be defined in terms of economic capital, e.g. economic capital contribution of an individual borrower should not exceed 5 percent. The advantage is that the same borrower need not figure in different limits (ratings, tenor, facility etc.). A single figure of economic capital is able to capture a range of obligor/facility characteristics.

A few issues however remain. One such concern is that potential growth in an industry is not captured in the economic capital number. Simple summation of economic capital figures for each exposure would ignore industry effects. Multiplying the economic capital attributed to each exposure by an adjustment factor would address this issue. A high growth industry would see an adjustment factor smaller than 1 indicating a lower *'effective'* capital for exposures in a high growth environment. Similarly, a low growth industry would see an adjustment factor more than 1 indicating a higher *'effective'* capital for exposures falling in a low growth situation. In principle, this would translate into a higher economic capital limit for sectors with a positive outlook and a lower limit for those with a negative outlook.

Summary and Conclusion

Banks in the past have been repeatedly exposed to credit concentration risk. The crises have also stemmed from the credit risk being concentrated in borrowers with similar characteristics. The US Savings and Loans (S&L crisis of the 1980s and 1990s) crisis for example, saw hundreds of financial institutions face bankruptcy due to sectoral concentration.

In order to quantify concentration risk, the Gini coefficient and HHI provide summary measures for comparison. Both however, fail to provide actionable benchmarks. Multi-factor models (MFM), based on Monte-Carlo simulations are a more rigorous approach but are at the same time computationally challenging and time consuming. Easily implementable, closed-form solutions are required if a bank is to integrate concentration risk analysis with the day-to-day risk management process. Gordy's Granularity Adjustment offers an easy closed-form solution, but only accounts for name concentration risk.

The Binomial Expansion Technique (BET) initially developed by credit rating agencies to value credit derivatives offers an alternative to the multi-factor model. It fails however, in producing an accurate estimation of the MFM capital charge in the presence of related defaults. An infection model (IM), in particular the specification developed by Duellmann improves upon the BET. It attempts to mimic the probability of joint default central to the multi-factor models by considering the probability of being infected by another asset in addition to independent defaults. This paper finds that the correlation regime used by Duellmann does not entirely reflect real world scenarios, in particular those seen in India and possibly in other emerging markets. In contrast to the assumptions made by Duellmann, it was empirically observed that inter and intra-sector correlations tend to move together. Additionally, the IM capital charge is found to have significant errors vis-à-vis the more accurate MFM when employing correlation assumptions observed for the Indian market.

This paper attempts a slightly alternative calibration of the infection model. Introduction of a variable that accounts for the interaction between probability of default of a borrower and its correlations with other exposures in the credit portfolio is found to be statistically significant. The errors vis-à-vis the MFM capital charge are found to reduce significantly following this modification.

The adjustment proposed in this paper has produced encouraging results when tested over a range of real world scenarios. It promises, with a few refinements, to offer a viable alternative to multi-factor models in estimation of concentration risk in credit portfolios.

References

Concentration Risk in Credit Portfolios (June 2006), *Deutsche Bundesbank*

Basel Committee on Banking Supervision (November 2005), International Convergence of Capital Measurement and Capital Standards, a revised framework, *Bank for International Settlements*

A Winton (1999), Don't Put All Your Eggs in One Basket? Diversification and Specialization in Lending, Working Paper No 00-16, *University of Minnesota.*

Boyd, H John and de Gianni Nicolo (2003), Bank risk taking and competition revisited, Working Paper, *International Monetary Fund*

Gordy, Michael B. and Eva Lütkebohmert (2007), Granularity adjustment for Basel II, Discussion Paper No. 01/2007, *Deustche Bundesbank*

Zhang, Jing, Fanlin Zhu and Joseph Lee (2008), Asset correlation, realized default correlation, and portfolio credit risk, *Moody's K.M.V*

Lentino, James V. (July 2005), Establishing exposure limits for a credit Portfolio, *the RMA journal*

Bonollo, Michele, Paola Mosconi and Fabio Mercurio (January 2009), Basel II Second Pillar: an Analytical VaR with Contagion and Sectorial Risks

Basel Committee on Banking Supervision (April 2004), Bank Failures in Mature Economies, Working Paper No. 13, *Bank for International Settlements*

—. (April 2008), Cross-sectoral review of group-wide identification and management of risk concentrations, The Joint Forum, *Bank for International Settlements*

—. (November 2006), Studies on credit concentration risk, Working Paper No. 15, *Bank for International Settlements*

Davis, Mark H.A. and Violet Lo (April 2001), Infectious Defaults, Quantitative Finance, Vol. 1, No. 4, pp. 382-387.

Duellmann, Klaus (2006), Measuring business sector concentration by an infection model, Discussion Paper No. 03/2006, *Deustche Bundesbank*

Egloff, Daniel, Markus Leippold and Paolo Vanini (2005), A Simple Model of Credit Contagion, *University of Zurich*

Hayden, Evelyn, Daniel Porath and Natalja von Westernhagen (2006), Does diversification improve the performance of German banks? Evidence from individual bank loan portfolios, Discussion Paper No. 05/2006, *Deutsche Bundesbank*

Lopez, Jose A (2002), The empirical relationship between average asset correlation, firm probability of default and asset size, *Federal Reserve Bank of San Fransisco,* Working Paper no. 2002-05

Master circular on exposure norms and statutory/other restrictions (June 2008), *Reserve Bank of India*

Morris, Joanne (December 2001), Risk diversification in the credit portfolio: An overview of country practices, Working Paper, *International Monetary Fund*

Pykhtin, M (2004), Multi-factor adjustment, Portfolio Credit Risk, *Risk Magazine*, pp 85-90

RBI guidelines on securitization of Assets, RBI No. 2005-06/294 (February 2006), *Reserve Bank of India*

V Acharya, I Hasan and A Saunders (2006), Should Banks Be Diversified? Evidence from Individual Bank Loan Portfolios, *Journal of Business*, Vol 79, No 3, pp 1355-1412.

CHAPTER SEVENTEEN

FRAMEWORK FOR CONSUMER CREDIT RISK ANALYTICS

SENTHIL RAMANATH[1]

Introduction

Because much of credit research is directed toward analyzing government or corporate debts, there is a paucity of investigations into consumer credit. This research attempts to fill in this gap by examining the consumer default risk that must be assessed by lending organizations to make a decision on whether or not to extend credit for an individual. The best practice in assessing this consumer credit risk is the focus of this paper.

Lending and borrowing began thousands of years ago when the trading began, but not until 1950's did we started to score a consumer's likelihood of paying back on their obligation. Experian, Equifax, and TransUnion started to offer formal FICO scores. Consumer Credit Risk has loosely evolved from FICO score, to internal scoring model, to strategic risk cut, to combinations thereof.

There are a variety of modeling approaches. The common ones are logistic models, linear regression, survival analytics, and decision tree. While the mathematical rigor in modeling is getting higher and higher, the process has stayed the same for the last couple of decades.

Credit risk analytics is used for a number of different purposes such as loan origination, account management, collections, credit loss forecasting, and marketing. Each function usually builds a separate model, Origination model, Account Management- Credit Limit model, Collections Recovery model, Credit Loss Forecasting model for booking allowances, and finally Lead Scoring model for marketing. The assumptions used are across these models are usually not consistent and not easily translatable due to differing modeling frameworks employed. For instance if Loss Foresting model predicted higher losses there is no quantitative method to adjust the

[1] Head of Credit Risk Analytics, ACE Cash Express.

Loan Origination model except judgmentally tightening it due to the disparate modeling methodology.

This paper will point out the shortcomings of current state of consumer credit risk management practices and provide the reader with an alternative holistic approach; a unified framework which cuts across the spectrum of corporate needs and enables decision makers to create and fine-tune risk analytics with confidence.

Standard (not best) Practices

Credit scoring process

Scoring starts with historical performance data. First, the modeler defines what a bad loan is. This may be same as accounting charge off definition or arbitrary 60 or 90 day past due loans. Once 'bad' flag is determined, the modeler will select attributes that may indicate customer's credit worthiness and perform a logistic regression with the variables to obtain the probability of default, which is scaled to a score range.

Score cutoff determination process

Score cutoff has been a cyclic process. Figure 1 explains this iterative process. Each company depending on their customer pool and the products they are offering will tend to identify an optimal approval rate over a period of time. This is an evolutionary process- as the executives identify the link between operational measures and accounting P&L, they start to form the intuition. Based on this 'business knowledge', approval rate and hence the approval score is determined. As the external environment change, the company may tweak the approval score and monitor the operational metrics to ensure the change was a good one. In addition to the score, companies may add strategic risk cuts – these may be a result of an ad-hoc univariate analysis that certain segment of customers is not profitable. Over period, the initial scoring model loses its steam and does not work as well and the company refits the model parameters using the latest data or builds a new model including the variables used in the strategic risk cut. Once the new model is built, there is a task of determining what the cutoff score is. Usual approach is to hinge on the historical approval rate and make minor tweaks from there.

Figure 1 - Score cutoff determination process

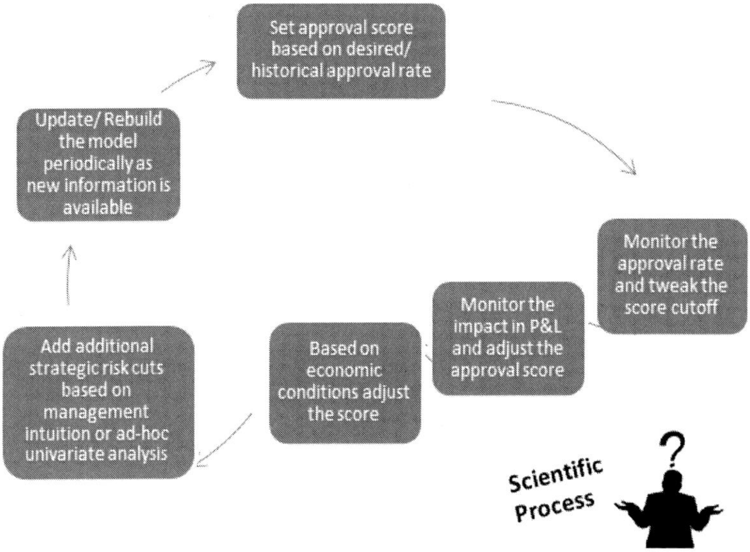

The process described above is rather cumbersome, has too much wiggle room, and has no direct connection to profitability. Accounting P&L measurement is lagged measurement since the losses are only trued up after the charge off and until then accounting would use a provisional (estimated) loss. Due to the lag in visibility of the impact of score change on profitability, uncertainty sets in. Within this period, external environment might have changed or the company may have altered other origination and account management policies.

Credit limit setting process

This is important quantitative element of the risk management is often considered as an art and does not get enough mathematical rigor. The figure 2 below has the various classes of attributes and some common variables. Typically, one ratio from the left box and one or more attributes from the 3 boxes on the right are used set the credit limit. For example, a credit card company may use customer's tenure (attribute) with them to decide on a credit limit to income ratio. A mortgage company may use customer's credit score to come up with Loan-to-Value ratio. This framework is reasonable, but most companies use management estimates (without proper statistical underpinning) to decide on the relationship between the variables such as customer tenure and credit limit to income ratio.

Moreover, these rules are often set at the inception of a product and rarely optimized later. Credit limit setting is a challenging problem to solve. Customer's default probability may change depending on what credit limit policy is in place. Instead of picking few attributes to set credit limit a comprehensive model created to maximize value would give a significant boost to the bottom line.

Problems with traditional credit risk management approaches

Wrong target- good/bad indicator is not good enough. Are all the goods the same? Are all the bads equally bad? How about partially collected loans? Where do you draw the line? Is the account that cured on the 60th day past day good and the one that cured on the 61st day bad?

The answer is – you don't have to draw a line. Luckily, we have cash associated with loans. The following is an excerpt from bankinganalyticsblog.fico.com – explaining performance of a model. [http://bankinganalyticsblog.fico.com/2011/04/predicting-strategic-default.html]

- The model was precise in identifying strategic defaulters among a 30-to-180-day delinquent population (not yet written off).
- It found 76% of the strategic defaulters in the 30% of the population receiving the most risky scores.
- The analytic separation is sharp—the most risky decile of borrowers are 200-times more likely to strategically default than the least risky decile of borrowers.

Looking at the lowest scored x% of the population identifying y% of the high risk customers is a very standard way of comparing model scores. There needs to be an involved secondary calculation to make any sense out of these results and make it actionable.

Figure 2 - Credit Limit Setting

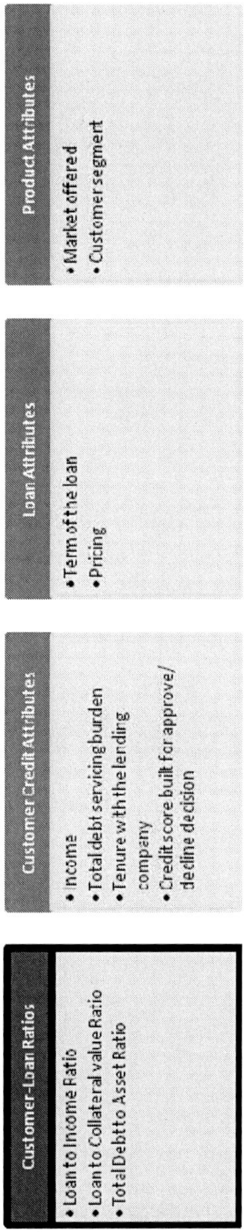

Proposed Framework for Consumer Credit Risk Analytics

Start with Customer Lifetime Value (LTV)

'Customer lifetime value' estimation is not just marketing Holy Grail; it is also an essential part of credit risk management. Calculate the marginal value from all the loans and then cumulate it by customer to identify remaining customer value for each loan.

Vintage-age Customer Value (VAV)

In order to keep the relevancy and work with the limited historical data, it is practical to limit the customer value to a specific period. For instance in credit card industry, identify the first 1 year, 2 year, 4 year and 8 year values obtained per customer in a segment. Based on these values extrapolate the customer LTV. For analytical purposes, select a vintage age customer value (VAV) as a proxy for customer lifetime value (LTV).

Vintage-age customer value (VAV) is defined as the cumulative *remaining marginal transaction value* for the next *x* years for a given customer, including the current transaction.

Selecting a vintage age (x number of years) for the VAV computation has the following tradeoffs:

- Longer the age, it is better proxy for customer LTV
- Shorter the age the more recent origination can be used for analytics (this factor usually dominates the tradeoff decision)

Choose a vintage age and then for each transaction with a customer calculate the VAV. In your scoring models instead of predicting good or bad, now you can use VAV. This would provide you with a significant lift in sloping power. This vintage age value enables you to include repeat business with the same customer and it includes the intensity of default (percent collected).

This is a paradigm shift from simply using ones and zeros and not considering the values in between and higher (repeat customers). For instance, a model may identify the bottom 2% of the customers account for 40% of the default population (0.8% of all population). Unless we know what is the remaining value including the repeat business from the other good customers in the bottom 2% (1.2%) it is not possible to make a business decision.

While customer value or the vintage age value sounds like panacea, it is often involved process to determine that. In the following sections, I will be discussing ways to account for the collection efforts and terminal value (liquidation value) in the calculation.

Framework for including the collections spent in the marginal value

Collection department expenses are generally considered marginal costs due to the large staff and homogeneity of the job. Here is a framework to allocate collection expense down to a specific loan. This way one can arrive at marginal loan value and vintage age value for a specific customer.

The following equation packs collection expenses into a factor called collections daily discount rate:

$$\sum_{i=1}^{h} \frac{Cl_i}{(1+\mathrm{CDD})^i} + \mathrm{CE} = \sum_{i=0}^{h} Cl_i$$

Equation 1 - Collection daily discount

h = number of days in collection before the debt is sold off
Cl_i = actual collection amount on the ith day after an account hits collection
CDD = Collections daily discount rate
CE = Collections expense (actual)

The first term in the equation above is discounted collection recovery amount using a discount rate CDD. The second term is collection department expense. When you add these two terms, discounted collection recovery and department expense, you get right side of the equation (sum of raw collection recovery amount).

Iterate the equation above with varying CDD values until it converges to a stable value. Solve for separate CDD values for different product types. This is a required component to calculate the marginal loan valuation, which then leads to customer value.

Marginal Loan Valuation

The equation 2 below gives the marginal value of a loan. Upon calculating this, we may cumulate all the subsequent business from the same customer for the next x number of years to get vintage-age customer value.

$$MV = -L - O + \sum_{n=1}^{m} \frac{a_n P_n}{(1+MCR)^n} - PP * \sum_{n=1}^{m} a_n + \sum_{i=1}^{h} \frac{(C_i/(1+CDD)^i)}{(1+MCR)^{\left(k+\frac{i}{d}\right)}} + \frac{T}{(1+MCR)^{\left(k+\frac{h}{d}\right)}}$$

Equation 2 – Loan Marginal Value

MV = marginal loan value
L = loan amount
O = marginal origination expense
m = total number of payments
d = number of days in a payment period
a_n = probability of nth payment
P_n = nth payment amount (includes pre-payments)
MCR = marginal capital rate per installment period
PP = marginal processing expense per payment
h = number of days in collection before the debt is sold off
C_i = expected collection amount --'i' days after the account hits collection
CDD = Collections daily discount rate
T = net terminal value from debt/collateral sale
k = number of payments made before the account goes to collections

On the right side of the equation the first two terms are the loan amount and the origination expense. The 3rd term is discounted cash flow based on the probability of the payments and the forth term is marginal payment processing expenses. The fifth term has the cash flow from collections. This is discounted not just by the marginal capital rate but also by the collections daily discount (CDD) rate. The framework for calculating the CDD was provided in the previous section. The last part of the equation is the terminal value received from the sale of the asset. This may be liquidation of the collateral or simply sale of the loan to 3rd party debt collector.

The loan valuation framework provided here can be used for a secured or an unsecured loan. While the economics will be different for each lending product, type the framework can be applied universally with little or no modification.

Conclusion

What you model is much more important than how you model. Score customers based on the vintage age customer value (VAV), instead of simply using good/bad indicator. Using the good/ bad indicator is a bad approach. It not only misses the severity of the losses it also ignores the potential repeat business from customers and will most likely result in conservative underwriting than what is warranted in industries where there are lots of repeat business.

This customer value based measure provides much better insights and transparent impact to the bottom-line. This eliminates arbitrariness from decision making since we do not have to select a loss definition and figure out the lost business from repeat customer business separately.

- Instead of saying:

  The model found 76% of the strategic defaulters in the 30% of the population receiving the most risky scores.

- Now, we could say:

  The model catches $43 MM of the strategic defaulters, while adversely getting rid of $125 MM of good originations ($13 MM in projected customer value). Net benefit is $30 MM/year.

In addition, this framework can be extended for optimizing the credit limit as well. This framework eliminates the need for numerous extra steps needed to quantify the impact of a risk-cut or expansion. This approach provides a concrete way to limit the risk and grow the top-line.

Use the vintage age customer value based framework for all the modeling needs of the company whether it is origination model or credit loss forecasting for accounting or lead scoring model for the marketing. This unified framework will provide a platform for all stakeholders to share their insights with one another and make a change in their strategy with confidence. With any change in strategy, the executives will now have better idea of the resulting impact to customer value and the impact on the P&L.

CHAPTER EIGHTEEN

ARE THERE COUNTERPARTY RISK PREMIA CONTAINED IN CDS SPREADS?

STEFAN MORKOETTER, JOHANNA PLEUS, AND SIMONE WESTERFELD[1]

1. Introduction

During the financial crisis of 2007 and 2009 investors were not only confronted with widening CDS spreads, but also faced unexpected termination of CDS contracts as a result of protection sellers' default. It became manifest that protection buyers are not only exposed to the credit risk of the underlying but also to the default probability of the protection seller. In the weeks prior to the Lehman default it was reported that protection buyers demanded a discount for credit default swaps issued by Lehman Brothers. For the purpose of our research question, we therefore define counterparty risk as the default probability of the protection seller. To capture counterparty risk in the valuation of CDS, financial literature suggested a Merton (1974) style default correlation framework until the crisis of 2007/2008. This approach relies on ex-ante asset correlations by assessing ex-interim default correlation structures between the reference entity and the protection seller. However, in the financial crisis this framework was observed not to fully reflect the counterparty risk dimension of credit default swaps.

---

[1] Dr. Stefan Morkoetter is from Swiss Institute of Banking and Finance, University of St. Gallen, Rosenbergstrasse 52, CH-9000 St. Gallen, phone: +41 71 224 7755, fax: +41 71 224 7088, Stefan.morkoetter@unisg.ch. Johanna Pleus is from Stern Stewart & Co., Salvatorplatz 4, D-80333 Munich, phone: +49 89 242 071343, fax: +49 89 242 07111, jpleus@sternstewart.de. Dr. Simone Westerfeld is from Swiss Institute of Banking and Finance, University of St. Gallen, Rosenbergstrasse 52, CH-9000 St. Gallen, phone: +41 71 224 7039, fax: +41 71 224 7088, simone.westerfeld@unisg.ch.

In this context our contribution is geared towards introducing and explaining three new counterparty risk proxies. By doing so we propose a more short-term focused valuation framework for CDS contracts, which should help to overcome the shortfalls experienced throughout the financial crisis. Besides the well-known determinants of CDS spreads we therefore extend the established pricing model. The first proxy for counterparty risk refers to the credit risk of the largest financial institutions issuing CDS contracts (average contributing banks' CDS spreads). Secondly, these CDS spreads are adjusted for the CDS index level and creating abnormal counterparty returns in excess to corresponding market levels. Obtaining the third measure default correlations between reference entity and protection seller based on asset return correlation structures are modeled (Hull and White, 2000b). By introducing our market-based measures we are able to reflect actual market conditions of counterparties and do not solely rely on long-term ex-ante data. This approach enables to directly reflect changes in market conditions, i.e. increasing credit risk or volatility spikes.

At the end of this chapter we also briefly present empirical proof relating to the practical importance of our new valuation framework with regard to measuring counterparty risk with CDS contracts. Based on a panel regression analysis for CDS spreads trading between 2004 and 2009 in Europe and North America we show that our new counterparty risk measures further enhance the overall prediction of CDS pricing models.

2. CDS Valuation Framework

2.1 Counter Party Risk and Credit Default Swaps

As mentioned this paper aims at introducing three different measures of counterparty risk, reflecting ex-interim market conditions, enhancing the existing CDS pricing framework. Only the third measure incorporates Merton-style (1974) asset correlation structures. Further, these proxies are analyzed in the context of a series of additional control variables having proven to incorporate pricing power for determining CDS spreads.

As default risk has a negative impact on CDS premia (Hull & White, 2000b), the risk of a joint default of the underlying reference entity and the issuing counterparty is to be considered in pricing CDS contracts. Since counterparty specific quotes for single CDS contracts are not available on common CDS platforms (e.g. Markit) provided by Bloomberg, Datastream, or Reuters, the analysis relies on three proxies for aggregate counterparty default risk.

Designing an aggregate measure for credit risk of the dominating counterparties in CDS trading the first proxy cures this lack of data transparency. The Markit platform provides an overview of the banks contributing to the iTraxx and CDX Index. Thus, the first proxy of counterparty default risk (CPDR1) is defined as the arithmetic mean of CDS spreads of all contributing financial institutions to the respective index implying the overall creditworthiness of the counterparties on an actual-actual basis:

$$CPDR1_t = \frac{CDS_{1t} + CDS_{2t} + \ldots + CDS_{Nt}}{N} \tag{1}$$

Reflecting current market conditions of counterparties in our pricing model this measure immediately mirrors changing market conditions like increasing credit risk or volatility spikes. Being derived from observed market prices for credit risk the measure overcomes the rigidity of the pricing models following the approach of Hull and White (2000b) with regard to tightening of credit risk of major counterparty.

Furthermore, the general market sentiment is extracted in order to create our second measure for counterparty risk by subtracting the corresponding quote of the iTraxx Index or CDX Index from the CPDR1 measure at each trading point. Thus, deviations of the relevant CDS counterparties from index returns are reflected giving abnormal counterparty risk returns:

$$CPDR2_t = CPDR1_t - Index_t. \tag{2}$$

Hence, $CPDR2_t$ reflects the pooled default risk of the contributing counterparties less the overall credit risk in the market.

The third proxy for counterparty default risk constructed as the correlation coefficient between the firm's equity returns and the arithmetic mean of the equity returns of the counterparties, being defined as contributing parties to ITRX and CDX indeces quoted on Bloomberg, at the respective trading point in time *t* by applying a regression analysis over a rolling time frame of 24 months prior to time *t*:

$$CPDR3_{it} = DEFCOR_{it}. \tag{3}$$

2.2 Control Determinants

Market-based Determinants

With regard to the **risk-free rate of return**, a negative correlation is expected and may be explained by the existence of lower spot rates during recessionary times, implying a higher number of corporate defaults (Benkert, 2004). Hence, the increased probability of default of the reference entity would result in an enhanced CDS premium. The long-term risk-free rate is approximated by the 10-year Treasury bond yields and the short-term rate by the 2-year Treasury bond yields. From a macro-economic perspective, the impact of the **slope of the term structure** on CDS spreads is ambiguous and may be interpreted both as an indicator the future economic conditions (Estrella & Mishkin, 1996) as well as an inflation indicator (Zhang et al, 2008). On the one hand, a higher slope of the term structure would imply an anticipated improvement of the overall economy resulting in lower default probabilities and therefore decreasing CDS spreads. On the other hand, a higher slope of the term structure would be associated with increasing inflation rates implying restrictive central bank initiatives resulting in a worsening of business conditions and consequently higher CDS premia. In accordance with Ericcson et al. (2009) the slope of the term structure is computed as the difference between the 10-years (long) and the 5-years (short) risk-free interest rates of the respective country of origin.

Increasing **market returns** reflect improving conditions in the overall economy which consequently result in decreasing CDS spreads. Furthermore, inclining **market volatility** signals an increase of uncertainty regarding the economic conditions. Therefore, high market volatility would have a positive effect on CDS premia (Zhang et al., 2008). Moreover, the respective **CDS Index** ($Index_t$) also serves as an indicator for the market development. The index is defined as the equally weighted average of the constituent CDS spreads. Therefore, an increase in the CDS index is expected to be positively correlated to the CDS premium. In order to establish consistency to the drawn sample over time, the European index equals the Markit iTraxx Index Series 1 and the North American index equals the Markit CDX Investment Grade Index Series 3.

Firm-specific Determinants

In this paper the **rating class** is used as a proxy of the underlying firm's credit quality. A good credit rating implies a lower probability of default and hence results in a decreased CDS premium (Daniels and Jensen, 2005). For the underlying firms' credit ratings the Standard &

Poor's long-term issuer credit rating is retrieved where available and in the other cases the Moody's senior debt rating is applied. In line with Cossin & Hricko (2001) the ratings will be either analyzed by introducing dummy variables for each rating class or by assigning numeric values ($Rating_i$) to each rating class ranging from 1 for the highest rating (AAA or Aaa) and 17 for the lowest rating class (C).

A firm defaults if the value of its assets drops below the value of debt (Merton, 1974). By implication, the **leverage ratio** of the reference entity is crucial for determining the distance-to-default as a high leverage would imply a higher probability to cross the default barrier. In other words, an increase in leverage results in an increased probability of default and consequently in an increase of the CDS premia. In line with Ericcson et al. (2009) the leverage ratio of the reference firm is computed as:

$$Leverage_{it} = \frac{Total\ Liabilities_{it} + Preferred\ Equity_{it}}{Market\ Value\ (Equity)_{it} + Total\ Liabilities_{it} + Preferred\ Equity_{it}} \quad (4)$$

whereas total liabilities and preferred equity are book values that are quoted on a quarterly basis. The market value of equity equals the market capitalization defined as the factor of the last equity price and the number of shares outstanding at the end of month *t*. In accordance with the influence of leverage on CDS spreads, positive firm-specific **equity returns** augment the value of equity and hence diminish the leverage of the firm. Accordingly, the CDS spread is supposedly negatively impacted by equity returns (Zhang et al., 2008).

Black and Scholes (1973) define equity as a European call option on the underlying firm's assets, where the level of debt constitutes the strike price. Thus, enhanced **asset volatility** would increase the probability that the asset value falls below the debt level and accordingly leads to an augmented default probability. Following the approach by Cossin & Hricko (2001) first the equity volatility $EQVol_{it}$ is computed by applying the GBM as a scaling measure using the mean return μ_t and standard deviation σ_t over the 24 months prior to time *t*. Second, the historical market volatility $MarketVol_{it}$ is estimated accordingly.

Trade-specific Determinants

In bond markets higher **liquidity** generally results in decreased compensation for liquidity risk and hence in a diminished yield spread (Amihud and Mendelson, 1991). Tang and Yan (2007) document a comparable pattern for CDS markets. In line with their research we use bid-ask spreads of the traded instruments in order to obtain a proxy for the liquidity from a transaction costs perspective. The monthly last bid- and ask-quotes are derived for each CDS contract.

3. Data Sample

The following analysis of the impact of counterparty risk on CDS premia is based on a data sample of 198 different reference entities. The data set includes both European and North American reference entities, which are derived from the Markit iTraxx Index Series 1 for the European market and from the Markit CDX Investment Grade Index Series 3 for the North American market. In order to be able to exclude any potential bias relating to company size or trading volume, the analysis mainly focuses on the most liquid, most frequently traded contracts in terms of transaction volume. The time period of this analysis ranges from September 2004 until December 2009. In terms of maturity structure and underlying securities we follow existing finance literature and use CDS contracts on corporate senior debt with a fixed maturity of five years.

Following the research by Zhang et al. (2008), monthly data is applied in order to minimize the effect of autocorrelation resulting in a mitigation of an estimation bias. As Zhang et al. (2008) suggest high CDS spreads indicate the existence of bilateral agreements on upfront payments, observations with spreads above 15% are removed from the data. We excluded all reference entities which were either not publicly or had CDS spreads quoted for less than 24 months. All data is retrieved from Bloomberg. In total the iTraxx data sample consists of 5053 and the CDX data sample of 5379 observations.

Time-weighted average CDS spreads of the respective index constituents per year for the three rating clusters ranging from AAA to A, BBB, and BB to C ratings. Overall, CDS spreads in lower rating classes exceed the AAA rating classes and CDS spreads increase significantly in 2008 and 2009 in the CDX and iTraxx index.

Table 1: Overview on Yearly Mean CDS spreads Across Rating Categories

	AAA to A		BBB		BB & C		Total	
Year	CDX	iTraxx	CDX	iTraxx	CDX	iTraxx	CDX	iTraxx
2004	29.88	25.68	47.09	53.12	57.74	42.99	41.03	39.57
2005	27.41	26.05	45.47	53.19	86.43	79.39	42.93	44.69
2006	20.61	17.32	34.47	41.33	96.96	66.47	36.36	34.27
2007	21.82	20.77	35.36	42.20	138.16	76.91	42.46	37.99
2008	93.84	94.98	143.78	159.50	483.56	328.88	163.53	154.68
2009	157.68	108.05	241.73	166.48	635.96	454.78	252.68	181.91
Total	46.82	48.56	75.73	85.68	211.97	178.59	80.28	82.06

Table 1 depicts the yearly mean CDS spreads across the different rating categories providing a first confirmation of the negative relationship the quality of rating class (e.g. low default probability) and level of CDS spreads.

4. Empirical Results: Impact of Counterparty Risk

In order to determine the impact of the cross-sectional and time-series variables described in the previous section a panel data analysis is conducted both for a multi-factor model (see Table 2). Obtaining unbiased and efficient results it is tested whether the time series model variables exhibit autocorrelation by the Lagrangian multiplier test (Wooldridge, 2002) and to what extent individual exogenous variables are related to each other due to multicollinearity. In order to adjust for serial autocorrelation of order one as well as for non-stationary attributes, the first differences approach is applied. The differenced samples are further analyzed with regard to multicollinearity. Multicollinear attributes are removed from the selection of pricing determinants: short-term interest rate ($dInterest_{it}^{2}$), slope of the term structure ($dSlope_{it}$), and market volatility ($dEQVol_{it}$). In order to exclude extreme outliers in both samples observations with a differenced CDS spreads exceeding the 10% limit are excluded from the sample. We divide our data sample into a European panel (n=5053) and a North America panel (n=5379). Taking these adjustments into account the general regression model is designed as:

$$dCDSSpread_{it} = \alpha + \beta_1 dInterest_{it}^{10} + \beta_2 dReturn_{it}^{firm} + \beta_3 dReturn_{it}^{Market} + \beta_4 dEQVol_{it} + \beta_5 dLeverage_{it} + \beta_6 dLiquidity_{it} + \beta_7 dCPDR1_t + \beta_8 dCPDR2_{it} + \beta_9 dCPDR3_{it} + u_{it} \quad (5)$$

Table 2: Multiple Panel Data Regression Model

Results of the multi factor panel data regressions applying the fixed effect model with robust error variance matrix to the differenced sample for Europe (n=5053) and North America (n=5379); Overall R-Squared fluctuates between 22.7% and 23.0% (Europe) and between 19.4% and 19.6% (North America); model significance provided by a significant F-statistic. We use monthly changes for both the dependent and independet variables. The analyzed time period covers 2004 till 2009.

Europe

	(1)	(2)	(3)	(4)	(5)
VARIABLES	cds_spread	cds_spread	cds_spread	cds_spread	cds_spread
Liquidity	-55.01**	-55.01**	-55.01**	-55.41**	-55.41**
	(-2.542)	(-2.542)	(-2.542)	(-2.568)	(-2.568)
$Return^{firm}$	-1.686	-1.686	-1.686	-3.907	-3.907
	(-0.104)	(-0.104)	(-0.104)	(-0.251)	(-0.251)
$Return^{market}$	36.59	36.59	36.59	38.90	38.90
	(1.317)	(1.317)	(1.317)	(1.402)	(1.402)
EQVol	-1.069	-1.069	-1.069	-1.996*	-1.996*
	(-1.644)	(-1.644)	(-1.644)	(-1.710)	(-1.710)
Leverage	16.67**	16.67**	16.67**	16.82**	16.82**
	(2.376)	(2.376)	(2.376)	(2.368)	(2.368)
Index	-0.353	0.0663	-0.775	-0.0771	0.628**
	(-0.557)	(0.157)	(-0.979)	(-0.112)	(2.137)
Interest[10]	-10.68	-10.68	-10.68	-10.66	-10.66
	(-0.967)	(-0.967)	(-0.967)	(-0.964)	(-0.964)
CPDR1		0.198*			0.453*
		(1.935)			(1.806)
CPDR2			-0.847**		-0.513**
			(-2.579)		(-2.084)
CPDR3				10.45*	10.45*
				(1.956)	(1.956)
Constant	-4.141*	-3.188	-4.086*	-3.518	-1.303
	(-1.762)	(-1.436)	(-1.743)	(-1.443)	(-0.575)
Observations	5,379	5,379	5,379	5,379	5,379
R-squared	0.227	0.227	0.227	0.230	0.230
Number of cds_id	91	91	91	91	91

North America

	(1)	(2)	(3)	(4)	(5)
VARIABLES	cds_spread	cds_spread	cds_spread	cds_spread	cds_spread
Liquidity	-34.40	-34.25	-34.01	-33.65	-31.62
	(-1.382)	(-1.378)	(-1.367)	(-1.351)	(-1.275)
$Return^{firm}$	-88.67**	-88.48**	-89.73**	-86.67**	-87.49**
	(-2.520)	(-2.499)	(-2.533)	(-2.484)	(-2.490)
$Return^{market}$	444.6	445.2	161.2	426.3	-188.0
	(0.763)	(0.769)	(0.305)	(0.739)	(-0.412)
EQVol	-0.107	-0.106	-0.106	-0.102	-0.0957
	(-0.417)	(-0.413)	(-0.438)	(-0.380)	(-0.389)
Leverage	97.04	96.94	97.38	99.11	98.92
	(1.422)	(1.422)	(1.429)	(1.457)	(1.459)
Index	-0.0717	-0.128	-0.180	-0.0496	-0.739
	(-0.177)	(-0.239)	(-0.456)	(-0.123)	(-1.113)
Interest[10]	-56.71	-50.17	-43.76	-54.99	25.52
	(-1.156)	(-1.153)	(-0.868)	(-1.124)	(0.631)
CPDR1		0.127			1.018
		(0.254)			(1.462)
CPDR2			-0.992**		-2.168**
			(-2.012)		(-2.537)
CPDR3				-6.002	-5.761
				(-0.831)	(-0.791)
Constant	15.87	16.65	-1.399	15.05	-16.37
	(0.479)	(0.504)	(-0.0468)	(0.459)	(-0.625)
Observations	5053	5053	5053	5053	5053
R-squared	0.194	0.194	0.194	0.195	0.196
Number of cds_id	107	107	107	107	107

Robust t-statistics in parentheses
***** p<0.01, ** p<0.05, * p<0.1**

Based on a Hausman test a fixed-effects model is specified for the analysis of the determinants of CDS spreads for our regression model. Additionally, relying on a joint Wald test the model is adapted so that not only entity- but also time-fixed-effects are taken into account. The main aim of this model (see Table 2) is to test if the inclusion of counterparty measures, CPDR1, CPDR2, and CPDR3 in addition to already well-documented CDS pricing determinants contributes to the understanding of CDS pricing dynamics.

Panel Europe

We observe that all three counterparty risk measures have a significant impact on the CDS spreads with the strongest impact relating to CPDR2. Furthermore, the corresponding credit risk of the main counterparties in terms of CDS trading is positively associated with the spread levels (CPDR1). In other words, if the credit quality of the parties underwriting the CDS contracts declines, the CDS spreads become more expensive for the protection buyer. At first sight, this finding renders surprising, since it is expected that higher default probability of the counterparty results in lower CDS spread levels for the protection buyer. However, one has to take into account that CPDR1 also captures market sentiment as the total average counterparty CDS spreads is analyzed, not only its idiosyncratic component. Against this backdrop, we argue that in case of a decline of the overall creditworthiness the credit worthiness of the counterparties is also following this trend. In order to isolate the idiosyncratic (credit) risk of CPDR1 CPDR2 subtracts the CDS index returns from the CDS counterparty spreads. By doing so, counterparty risk is isolated from general market sentiment. Based on the correlation coefficients for CPDR2, we observe the expected results: the lower the protection seller's credit quality is, the lower the corresponding CDS spread. Therefore, we empirically show a relationship between counterparty risk and the risk of the underlying reference entities. These results also hold for the North American data sample. Finally, on an α-level of 10% also the default correlation between the individual firm equity returns and the arithmetic mean of the equity returns of the counterparties prove to be significant (CPDR3). Based on the observed positive coefficients for CPDR3 we are able to confirm the findings of Hull & White (2000a, 2000b) and agree that a higher correlation between reference entity and counterparty positively impacts the CDS spread levels. With regard to the set of control variables, we also focus on liquidity, equity volatility (EQVol) and on the leverage factor. In addition to the counterparty risk measures these variables are the only components absorbing a statistically significant impact on the CDS spreads within our multi-factor model - even though the empirical significance for equity volatility is rather weak. Thus, we are able to confirm the results of Tang and Yan (2007) with regard to the impact of liquidity and Ericcson et al. (2009) against the background of debt leverage. We show that higher debt leverage leads to higher CDS spreads, whereas liquid CDS markets lead to lower CDS spreads. Based on our results, equity volatility in turn negatively impacts CDS spreads, which is rather surprising against the risk attributes of asset volatility: high levels of asset volatility are often viewed as a risk factor and should therefore be positively correlated with CDS spreads. However, it is noteworthy, that in case of equity volatility only modest empirical results are confirmed.

Panel North America

As documented for Europe, CPDR2 also has a significant, negative impact on the CDS pricing levels for the North American panel. However, in contrast to Europe, only CPDR2 incorporates pricing power, whereas for the European panel CPDR3 bears new empirical insight. With regard to the control variables we also detect significant different patterns as observed for Europe: Not liquidity and leverage, but individual firm equity returns mainly drives the CDS spreads in addition to CPDR2. In the North American model, $return^{firm}$ exhibits a strongly negative coefficient, statistically significant at the 5%-level and in line with the theoretically expected impact. The coefficients of the CDX $Index_t$ in the multiple panel regressions of the North American sample have a negative sign albeit at statistically insignificant level. Therefore, the CDX index does not serve as a reliable market-based determinant in the North American case for the time span considered within the scope of this analysis (this finding also holds for European sample).

A series of robustness checks is conducted in order to control if the presented results are biased due to specific events or certain impact factors. We do not disclose the detailed results in this chapter, but will opine on our findings upon request. First, we found that counterparty risk (CPDR2) has been reflected in the CDS spreads for North American reference entities already prior to the financial crisis, whereas for European reference entities the pricing impact only intensified with the outbreak of the financial crisis in September 2008. Second, the results of counterparty default risk measures CPDR1 and CPDR2 are robust for the European data sample across the different rating categories. Only for the third measure we find a negative coefficient for the rating class with the highest credit quality. It is not surprising, however, that in the case of a very good reference entity rating a high default correlation leads to decreasing counterparty risk, since implying that the counterparty holds a high rating, which by definition indicates lower CDS spreads. From an economic perspective, this observation makes perfectly sense as protection buyers do not buy protection from a counterparty carrying a rating below the rating of the reference entity.

5. Conclusion

From the angle of analyzing counterparty risk in CDS trading activities we propose three different measures in order to better capture the default risk of CDS protection seller. The first two measures are market-based and directly refer to the credit risk of the banks trading CDS contracts with CPDR1 still absorbing market movements and CPDR2 focusing on abnormal counterparty CDS returns. Our third measure is developed in line with prior research by Hull and White (2000a, 2000b) and focuses on correlation structures of asset returns between CDS counterparties and reference entities. Based on an analysis for Europe and North America from 2004 until 2009 our main findings are: First, we show that counterparty risk is reflected in the pricing of CDS contracts. Abnormal counterparty CDS returns lead to lower CDS spreads for the protection buyer, whereas the impact of counterparty risk is decreasing with a higher creditworthiness of the underlying reference entity. Second, we find that counterparty risk (CPDR2) has been reflected in the CDS spreads for North American reference entities already prior to the financial crisis, whereas for European reference entities the pricing impact only intensified with the outbreak of the financial crisis in September 2008. Third, market-based counterparty risk measures have a higher impact on the pricing of CDS contracts as compared to measures relying on the correlation structures of asset returns of reference entities and CDS counterparties. We contribute to existing literature by extending the framework of modeling counterparty risk in proposing a short-term market oriented perspective. By introducing our market-based measures we are able to better reflect current market conditions of counterparties and do not have to rely on long-term ex-ante data only. This allows us to immediately mirror changing market conditions like increasing credit risk or volatility spikes.

References

Amihud, Y., & Mendelson, H. (1991). Liquidity, maturity, and the yields on U.S. Treasury securities. *Journal of Finance 46*(4), pp. 1411-1425.

Benkert, C. (2004). Explaining Credit Default Swap Premia. *The Journal of Futures Markets 24*(1), pp. 71-92.

Black, F., & Scholes, M. (1973). The Pricing of Options and Corporate Liabilities. *The Journal of Political Economy 7*, pp. 637-654.

Cossin, D., & Hricko, T. (2001). Exploring for the Determinants of Credit Risk in Credit Default Swap Transaction Data. *Working Paper, HEC University of Lausanne*, pp. 1-65.

Daniels, K. N., & Jensen, M. S. (2005). The Effect of Credit Ratings on Credit Default Swap Spreads and Credit Spreads. *The Journal of Fixed Income*, pp. 16-33.

Ericcson, J., Jacobs, K., & Oviedo, R. (2009). The Determinants of Credit Default Swap Premia. *Journal of Financial and Quantitative Analysis 44*(1), pp. 109-132.

Estrella, A., & Mishkin, F. S. (1996). The Yield Curve as a Predictor of U.S. Recessions. *Current Issues in Economic and Finance 2*(7), pp. 1-6.

Hull, J., & White, A. (2000a). Valuing Credit Default Swaps I: No Counterparty Default Risk. *Journal of Derivatives 8*, pp. 29-40.

Hull, J., & White, A. (2000b). Valuing Credit Default Swaps II: Modeling Default Correlations. *Journal of Derivatives 8*, pp. 12-22.

Merton, R. C. (1974). On the Pricing of Corporate Debt: The Risk Structure of Interest Rates. *The Journal of Finance 29*(2), pp. 449-470.

Tang, D. Y., & Yan, H. (2007). Liquidity and Credit Default Swap Spreads. *University of Hong Kong Working Paper*, pp. 1-42.

Wooldridge, J. M. (2002). *Econometric analysis of cross section and panel data*. Cambridge, MA: The MIT Press.

Zhang, B. Y., Zhou, H., & Zhu, H. (2008). Explaining Credit Default Swap Spreads with Equity Volatility and Jump Risks of Individual Firms. *BIS Working Paper 181*, pp. 1-41.

CHAPTER NINETEEN

ARE NEW CORPORATE BONDS OVERPRICED?

IGOR KOZHANOV, JOSEPH P. OGDEN
AND FARINDOKHT VAGHEFI[1]

Introduction

The question we address in this article is whether new corporate bonds issued in the United States in recent years are fairly priced after accounting for risk and terms in the bond contract. This question is important for two reasons. First, new corporate bonds are a significant source of external financing for U.S. firms. Generally the aggregate volume of new corporate bonds (roughly $100 bn. in a typical recent year) dwarfs the volumes of both initial public offerings and seasoned offerings of stock. Second, investors are keenly interested to know whether new corporate bonds are fairly priced, and therefore will provide price performance, similar to otherwise comparable seasoned corporate bonds.

We examine a sample of 965 corporate bonds issued during the years 2005-09. We choose this sample period because it allows us to use the TRACE (Trade Reporting and Compliance Engine) database, which was fully implemented in January 2005, to calculate post-issuance (secondary market) price performance as part of our pricing analysis. We find that, on average, the discrepancy between yield on a new corporate bond, Y, and the contemporaneous yield on a benchmark index matched on credit rating, maturity, and callability, Yb, (Y-Yb), is *negative*. This result is fairly robust to subsample scrutiny by firm size, issuer frequency, trading

---

[1] Igor Kozhanov is Assistant Professor of Finance at the University at Buffalo-SUNY. Joseph P. Ogden is Professor of Finance at the University at Buffalo-SUNY. Farindokht Vaghefi is a doctoral student of finance at CUNY-Baruch. The authors are grateful for data support provided by personnel at Citi's Yield Book division. All errors are the authors' alone. This article is based on a working paper by the same authors, titled "The Pricing and Performance of New Corporate Bonds: TRACE-Era Evidence."

behavior on TRACE, and credit rating. We also find that, on average, long-term benchmark-adjusted returns on new bonds are *negative*, and that this result is fairly robust. The evidence therefore indicates that new corporate bonds are generally *overpriced.*

Literature Review

Existing evidence on the pricing of new corporate bonds is mixed. Early studies by Sorensen (1982), Ederington (1974), and Lindvall (1977) find that the yields on new corporate bonds are *higher* than comparable seasoned bonds, indicating that new corporate bonds are *underpriced.* However, Fung and Rudd (1986) find that when better quality bond price data is used, such underpricing disappears. Several studies address the issue by examining *initial returns* on new corporate bonds. Lindvall (1977), Weinstein (1978), Datta et al. (1997), Cai, Helwege, and Warga (2007), and Goldstein and Hotchkiss (2007) all find that new corporate bonds have high initial benchmark-adjusted returns, also suggesting that new corporate bonds are underpriced.

However, two related types of studies raise doubt about whether new corporate bonds are underpriced. First, Spiess and Affleck-Graves (1999), Clarke, Dunbar, and Kahle (2001), Bradshaw, Richardson, and Sloan (2006), and Cohen and Lys (2006) all document evidence that debt-issuing firms are generally overpriced, as their stocks generally have high (low) pre- (post-) issuance abnormal returns. This evidence indirectly suggests that new corporate bonds would be overpriced, rather than underpriced.

Second, the use of initial post-issuance returns to assess initial pricing status is open to question. In the stock IPO literature, studies have found that IPOs have very large first-day returns but very poor long-term performance thereafter (e.g., Ritter 1991; Loughran and Ritter,1995; Hanley, 1993; Krigman, Shaw, and Womack, 1999). These results have led some researchers to question the basic conclusion that IPOs are underpriced at the offering. Purnanandam and Swaminathan (2004) compare valuations of IPO firms (based on the offer price) to valuations of industry peer firms. They find that the median IPO was significantly *overpriced* at the offer price relative to peers. Moreover, they find that the more highly overpriced IPOs have especially high first-day returns and especially low long-term returns. In addition, Krigman, Shaw, and Womack (1999) document evidence that large, supposedly informed, traders flip "hot" IPOs that are destined to perform worst in the future. That is, informed traders take advantage of the immediate post-issuance increase in price, which is driven by uninformed investors, by selling to them. (See also Aggarwal (2003).) This 'flipping potential' hypothesis explains the return reversal evidence observed in the IPO market, and suggests that high initial post-issuance returns indicate overpricing rather than underpricing.

The flipping potential hypothesis may also apply to the market for new corporate bonds. Specifically, "hot" new corporate bonds may actually be overpriced at issuance, and yet will exhibit high initial returns because of high demand by uninformed retail investors, which further drives up their price. However, these issues are then even more overpriced, and so will have poor long-term performance after an initial trading period. Moreover, flipping potential may be greater with the advent of TRACE, which has substantially enhanced the ability of both informed (institutional) and uninformed (retail) investors to trade corporate bonds (Bessembinder et al., 2006; Bessembinder and Maxwell, 2008). Indeed, Goldstein and Hotchkiss (2007) document indirect evidence of flipping in the market for new corporate bonds.

Data and Methodology

Data

We used the Securities Data Corporation (SDC) database, the FINRA (Financial Industry Regulatory Authority) database, Citi's Yield Book database, and the TRACE database to identify and screen new corporate bonds issued in the U.S. by publicly-traded U.S.-incorporated firms between January 2005 and August 2009. We initially identified 3,682 new corporate bonds issued by U.S. firms in the U.S. during this period. From this total we eliminated 1,249 issues of retail notes (which are small-volume bonds issued frequently and directly to retail investors), 124 bonds that had non-standard characteristics (puttable, STEP, zero-to-full (ZTF) issues, and 144A bonds), 298 bonds that were not rated by any of the three major credit rating agencies, and 548 issues that were not traded on TRACE within 180 days of issuance. The large number of eliminations on the basis of non-trading attest to the thinness of trading in corporate bonds, even in the TRACE era. These eliminations resulted in a preliminary sample of 1,463 bonds. Finally, we eliminated 498 bonds that were issued by either privately-held firms or firms whose equity traded publicly for less than 18 months prior to the bond offering. Our final sample then consists of 965 new corporate bonds.

We use Yield Book to collect information about bond issues, bond indicative data, and rating histories from three major rating agencies

(Standard and Poor's, Moody's and Fitch), while other indicative data is obtained from FINRA. We also use Yield Book for yields and returns on benchmark indexes. Yield Book's corporate indexes are more detailed than those that can be obtained from Lehman, including breakdowns by credit rating, maturity, and callability. TRACE is our source of all secondary-market bond prices.

Roughly half of our sample bonds (480 in total) were issued by firms that had not issued another bond within 18 months before or after the focal bond. Issuer frequency is an important variable because bonds issued by frequent issuers may be less likely to be mispriced. Both Spiess and Affleck-Graves (1999) and Butler and Wan (2010) restrict their samples of new corporate bonds to issuers that did not have another bond offering within five years. We do not restrict our sample in terms of firm-level issue frequency because we want to investigate the effects of issue frequency on bond pricing and performance. We do so by splitting the sample by issue frequency, as defined.

A total of 790 (175) of the bonds in our sample traded (did not trade) within 7 days of the offering. Unfortunately, bonds that did not trade within 7 days of issuance also have more spotty trading activity thereafter, so we do not, and practically cannot, assess the post-issuance performance of bonds that do not trade soon after issuance. Nevertheless, given the general thinness of trading in corporate bonds, it is important to at least examine the characteristic and *initial* pricing of thinly-traded bonds, which we do.

The bond issuers in our sample generally are very large and mature. At year-end before the offering, 71.1% of the firms are in the largest size decile (decile 10) in terms of market equity value relative to all NYSE, AMEX and NASDAQ firms, and 81.7% of the issuers have been publicly traded for more than 10 years. However, the infrequent issuers, and the firms that issued bonds with late trading commencement on TRACE, are somewhat smaller and younger. Bonds of infrequent issuers and those with late trading commencement also tend to have lower credit ratings. Maturities range widely, but bond maturities of more than 20 years are unusual. Regarding callability, the industry standard is the *make whole* call provision, accounting for 78.8% of all bonds in the sample. Finally, offering dates are fairly evenly distributed across the sample years. This is important because the sample period includes a credit crisis in late 2008 to early 2009. Relatively few bonds in our sample were issued during the crisis.

Methodology

We calculate yield discrepancy, (Y-Yb), as the difference between yield on a new corporate bond, Y, and the contemporaneous yield on a benchmark index matched on credit rating, maturity, and callability, Yb. Y, Yb, and (Y-Yb) are expressed in percent throughout the article.

All bond returns are benchmark-adjusted holding-period returns, and are calculated as follows. Denoting the offer price as P_0 and a subsequent trade-weighted price at date t as P_t, the holding-period return on the bond is

$$R_{0,t} = (P_t - P_0 + AccInt)/P_0, \quad (1)$$

where AccInt is the accrued interest on the bond over the period (0, t). Denoting as $Rb_{0,t}$ the analogous return on the benchmark index, the bond's benchmark-adjusted return, $Rba_{0,t}$, is

$$Rba_{0,t} = R_{0,t} - Rb_{0,t} \quad (2)$$

Benchmark-adjusted returns from the offer price to 1, 2, 6, and 18 months after the offering are denoted as $Rba_{0,1}$, $Rba_{0,2}$, $Rba_{0,6}$, and $Rba_{0,18}$, respectively. Benchmark returns from the end of the first month to the end of 2, 6, and 18 months after issuance are denoted as $Rba_{1,2}$, $Rba_{1,6}$, and $Rba_{1,18}$, respectively. All Rba's are expressed in percent and are not annualized.

Evidence

Yield Discrepancy

Mean values of our yield discrepancy measure (Y-Yb) are shown in Table 1 for the full sample and various subsamples. For the full sample, the mean is -0.583%, and is highly significant (t-value=17.80). Moreover, the mean value of (Y-Yb) is reliably negative for all subsamples in the table. Mean (Y-Yb) it is noticeably smaller in magnitude for small-cap issuers vs. large-cap issuers, and for lower-rated bonds vs. higher-rated bonds. Mean (Y-Yb) is very similar for (i) frequent vs. infrequent issuers, and (ii) bonds that are initially traded early vs. later on TRACE. The overall evidence attests to the ubiquity of the *overpricing* of new corporate bonds in the TRACE era, and is in contrast to much of the evidence on yield discrepancy found in earlier studies, discussed earlier.

Benchmark-Adjusted Returns

Table 2 shows mean benchmark-adjusted holding period returns for various periods and subsamples. Note that we exclude bonds that did not trade early on TRACE from this analysis. Panel A shows mean benchmark-adjusted returns from the offer price to 1, 2, 6, and 18 months after issuance, for the full sample and various subsamples, while Panel B shows benchmark-adjusted returns from 1 month after issuance through 2, 6, and 18 months after issuance, again for the full sample and various subsamples.

For the full sample, mean $Rba_{0,1}$ is reliably positive for the full sample as well as every subsample. These results are consistent with prior literature, as discussed earlier. However, mean benchmark-adjusted holding period returns tend to fall after the first month, so that for the full sample $Rba_{0,18}$ is negative, though insignificant. Thus, initial positive benchmark-adjusted returns tend to be reversed in the long-term. Indeed, for the full sample the mean benchmark-adjusted return from month 1 through month 18, $Rba_{1,18}$, is reliably *negative*, and shown in Panel B. This return-reversal evidence is consistent with the flipping potential hypothesis, and therefore suggests that new corporate bonds are actually *overpriced* despite their initial positive benchmark-adjusted returns.

An Illustration of the Price Behavior of New Corporate Bonds

To illustrate the price performance of new corporate bonds, we focus on the subsample of BBB-rated bonds. We develop a representative bond for this subsample by calculating the average coupon rate and maturity. We then calculate the fair value of this representative bond by applying the average benchmark yield, Yb. The resulting fair value is $96.50 per $100 of par value. This fair value is assumed constant for 18 months after 'issuance.' In contrast, the offer price of the representative bond is $100, and its post-offering price behavior over time is dictated by average benchmark-adjusted returns of the BBB-rated bonds displayed in Table 2. The actual price initially rises from $100 at issuance to a peak relative price of $100.79 after 1 month, and then falls to a final price of $97.54 18 months after issuance. Thus, the initial overpricing is 3.63% (=100/96.50), the overpricing peaks at 4.45% (=100.79/96.50) after 1 month, and the overpricing after 18 months is only 1.08% (=97.54/96.50).

The Economic Importance of Bond Overpricing

The economic importance of the overpricing of new corporate bonds can be measured by the excess market value of a given entire issue. Using the values calculated above for the BBB subsample and the median issue size for BBB bonds in our sample, $450 mn, our estimate of the economic value of the overpricing of the typical BBB-rated bond is $16.32 mn (=3.63% of $450 mn). By comparison, average amount of money left on the table due to underpricing of equity IPOs in 1980–2001 is $17 million per IPO (2001 dollars; see Ritter and Welch (2002, Table I)). Moreover, given that U.S. firms issue several hundred bonds in a typical year, the economic importance of bond overpricing is measured in $ billions annually.

Summary

This paper provides new evidence on the pricing and performance of new corporate bonds issued in the U.S. by seasoned publicly traded U.S firms during the TRACE era (i.e., 2005-09). In contrast to evidence from previous studies, we find that new corporate bonds are generally overpriced based on yield discrepancy (Y-Yb). For the typical BBB-rated bond issue of $450 mn., our estimate of the excess market value at issuance is $16.32 mn. New corporate bonds have reliably *positive* benchmark-adjusted returns over the first month after issuance. However, these initial returns are reversed by 18 months after issuance. This return-reversal behavior is consistent with flipping activity in the early secondary market, whereby informed investors purchase overpriced bonds at the offering and then sell them at a yet higher price to uninformed investors in the initial secondary market.

References

Aggarwal, Reena, 2003. Allocation of Initial Public Offerings and Flipping Activity, Journal of Financial Economics 68, 111–135.

Bessembinder, Hendrik, and William F. Maxwell, 2008. Transparency and the Corporate Bond Market. Journal of Economic Perspectives 22, 217–234.

Bessembinder, Hendrik, William F. Maxwell, and Kumar Venkataraman, 2006, Market Transparency, Liquidity Externalities, and Institutional Trading Costs in Corporate Bonds, Journal of Financial Economics 82, 251–288.

Bradshaw, Mark T., Scott A. Richardson, and Richard G. Sloan, 2006, The Relation between Corporate Financing Activities, Analysts' Forecasts and Stock Returns, Journal of Accounting and Economics 42, 53–85.

Butler, A.W., H. Wan, 2010. Stock Market Liquidity and the Long-run Stock Performance of Debt Issuers. Review of Financial Studies 23, 3966-3995.

Cai, Nianyun (Kelly), Jean Helwege, and Arthur Warga, 2007, Underpricing in the Corporate Bond Market, Review of Financial Studies 20, 2021–2046.

Clarke, Jonathan, Craig Dunbar, and Kathleen M. Kahle, 2001, Long-Run Performance and Insider Trading in Completed and Canceled Seasoned Equity Offerings, Journal of Financial and Quantitative Analysis 36, 415–430.

Cohen, Daniel A., and Thomas Z. Lys, 2006, Weighing the Evidence on the Relation between External Corporate Financing Activities, Accruals and Stock Returns, Journal of Accounting and Economics 42, 87–105.

Datta, Sudip, Mai Iskandar-Datta, and Ajay Patel, 1997, The Pricing of Initial Public Offers of Corporate Straight Debt, Journal of Finance 52, 379–396.

Ederington, Louis H., 1974, The Yield Spread on New Issues of Corporate Bonds, Journal of Finance 29, 1531–1543.

Fung, W. K. H., and Andrew Rudd, 1986, Pricing New Corporate Bond Issues: An Analysis of Issue Cost and Seasoning Effects, Journal of Finance 41, 633–643.

Goldstein, M. and E. Hotchkiss, 2007. Dealer Behavior and the Trading of Newly Issued Corporate Bonds, Working paper, Boston College and Babson College.

Hanley, Kathleen Weiss, 1993. The Underpricing of Initial Public Offerings and the Partial Adjustment Phenomenon, Journal of Financial Economics 34, 231–250.

Krigman, Laurie, Wayne H. Shaw, and Kent L. Womack, 1999, The Persistence of IPO Mispricing and the Predictive Power of Flipping, Journal of Finance 54, 1015–1044.

Lindvall, John R., 1977, New Issue Corporate Bonds, Seasoned Market Efficiency and Yield Spreads, Journal of Finance 32, 1057–1067.

Loughran, Tim, and Jay R. Ritter, 1995, The New Issues Puzzle, Journal of Finance 50, 23–51.

Purnanandam, Amiyatosh K., and Bhaskaran Swaminathan, 2004, Are IPOs Really Underpriced?, Review of Financial Studies 17, 811–848.

Ritter, Jay R., 1991, The Long-Run Performance of Initial Public Offerings, Journal of Finance 46, 3–27.

Sorensen, Eric H., 1982, On the Seasoning Process of New Bonds: Some Are More Seasoned Than Others, Journal of Financial and Quantitative Analysis 17, 195–208.

Spiess, D. Katherine, and John Affleck-Graves, 1999, The Long-Run Performance of Stock Returns Following Debt Offerings, Journal of Financial Economics 54, 45–73.

Weinstein, Mark I., 1978, The Seasoning Process of New Corporate Bond Issues, Journal of Finance 33, 1343–1354.

Table 1
New-Issue Yield Vs. Benchmark (Y-Yb, %)

Sample	N	Mean	t-value
Full Sample	965	-0.583	-17.80 ***
By Firm Size:			
Small & Medium	279	-0.358	-4.95 ***
Large	686	-0.674	-19.34 ***
Difference		*-0.316*	*4.42* ***
By Issuer Frequency:			
Frequent	485	-0.625	-14.04 ***
Infrequent	480	-0.540	-11.25 ***
Difference		*0.085*	*-1.31*
By Traded Early on TRACE:			
Yes	790	-0.582	-16.45 ***
No	175	-0.584	-6.95 ***
Difference		*-0.002*	*-0.02*
By Rating Class			
Class 1: AAA, AA, A	332	-0.783	-15.46 ***
Class 2: BBB	392	-0.488	-10.82 ***
Class 3: BB, B, CCC	241	-0.461	-5.67 ***
Difference: Class 1 vs. 2		*-0.295*	*4.35* ***
Difference: Class 1 vs. 3		*-0.321*	*3.52* ***
Difference: Class 2 vs. 3		*-0.026*	*0.31*

Significance indicators: ***(1%); **(5%); and *(10%).

Table 2

Mean Benchmark-Adjusted Holding-Period Returns (Rba, %)

Panel A: From offer price to:				Panel B: From 1 month to:		
1 month ($Rba_{0,1}$)	2 months ($Rba_{0,2}$)	6 months ($Rba_{0,6}$)	18 months ($Rba_{0,18}$)	2 months ($Rba_{1,2}$)	6 months ($Rba_{1,6}$)	18 months ($Rba_{1,18}$)
All issues that traded early on TRACE (N=790)						
1.162	1.153	0.639	-0.252	-0.009	-0.523	-1.413
(13.34)***	(9.83)***	(3.38)***	(-0.79)	(-0.14)	(-3.06)***	(-4.64)***
Frequent Issuers (N=422)						
1.381	1.584	1.231	0.540	0.203	-0.151	-0.841
(12.23)***	(10.90)***	(5.32)***	(1.32)	(2.39)**	(-0.69)	(-2.10)**
Infrequent Issuers N=368)						
0.910	0.658	-0.041	-1.160	-0.252	-0.950	-2.070
(6.80)***	(3.54)***	(-0.13)	(-2.37)**	(-2.43)**	(-3.58)***	(-4.47)***
Rating class 1 (AAA, AA, and A; N=319)						
1.470	1.590	1.431	1.394	0.120	-0.039	-0.075
(10.68)***	(8.76)***	(5.11)***	(2.93)***	(1.14)	(-0.15)	(-0.16)
Rating class 2 (BBB; N=355)						
0.792	0.738	0.049	-1.656	-0.054	-0.743	-2.448
(6.62)***	(4.77)***	(0.19)	(-3.76)***	(-0.62)	(-3.00)***	(-5.57)***
Rating class 3 (BB, B, and CCC; N=116)						
1.447	1.220	0.264	-0.480	-0.227	-1.183	-1.927
(5.49)***	(3.07)***	(0.4)	(-0.47)	(-0.97)	(-2.18)**	(-2.11)**

T-values are shown in parentheses. Significance indicators: ***(1%); **(5%); and *(10%).

CHAPTER TWENTY

THE DISTRESSED CORPORATE DEBT CYCLE FROM A HEDGE FUND INVESTOR'S PERSPECTIVE[1]

PING CHEN, JOSÉ F. GONZÁLEZ-HERES AND STEVEN S. SHIN[2]

This article describes the corporate distressed debt cycle from the perspective of a hedge fund investor by dissecting the cycle into uniquely different states that evolve, and switch, over time based on macroeconomic and market factors. It shows evidence that the distressed cycle consists of three states—Deteriorating Credit State, Improving Credit State, and Static Credit State—each with unique characteristics that have implications on expected returns for the strategy. It also presents evidence that these states are path dependent and exhibit an element of memory, which enhances the effectiveness of the proposed state-specific models. The cycle follows a sequential and circular process that begins with the Deteriorating Credit State, is followed by the Improving Credit State, and ends in the Static Credit State, with the cycle subsequently repeating. We use PCA analysis as a discovery process to search for the most important factors in predicting distressed hedge fund returns over the different states in the cycle. We find the Distressed Ratio to be the most effective factor

---

[2] Ping Chen, Ph.D. is a research analyst for the Fund of Hedge Funds portfolios at Morgan Stanley Alternative Investment Partners in West Conshohocken, PA. p.chen@morganstanley.com José F. González-Heres is a portfolio manager for the Fund of Hedge Funds portfolios at Morgan Stanley Alternative Investment Partners and a member of its Investment Committee in West Conshohocken, PA. jose.gonzalez-heres@morganstanley.com Steven S. Shin, CPA, CFA is a research analyst for the Fund of Hedge Funds portfolios for Morgan Stanley Alternative Investment Partners in West Conshohocken, PA. steven.shin@morganstanley.com

throughout the cycle, followed by an equity factor that applies only to the Static Credit State. We define the Distressed Return Model as a three-state regression model and use it to predict HFRI Distressed Securities Index returns. Given the importance of the Distressed Ratio factor, we also propose a regression model that can be used throughout the cycle (state independent) to forecast the Distressed Ratio using macroeconomic and market leading indicators. We also find that the models are efficacious in estimating their respective dependent variables. We observe that although, on average, distressed hedge fund managers have generated attractive risk-adjusted returns, successful investing during certain states is more dependent on bottom-up (manager picking) skills than on top-down decisions relating to the strategy. In the Deteriorating Credit State, investors need to rely on strong manager selection skills to help avoid losses. Whereas during the Improving Credit State, good manager selection skills should generate excess positive returns. During the Static Credit State, the investor is less dependent on manager selection skills since most managers are expected to earn near the average return of the strategy. Finally, we introduce the Distressed Regime Switching Model as an unbiased check on the qualitatively determined states used by the Distressed Return Model. We believe that the Distressed Regime Switching Model is effective and can be used as an "early-warning" indicator in identifying state inflection (trigger) points. Taken together, the suite of estimation models allows investors to make more informed decisions.

In conclusion, the models discussed in this article capture the key characteristics of each credit state in the corporate distressed cycle. By effectively detecting state transitions, the models can assist the asset allocation process from a top-down perspective. Our models indicate that we entered a new cycle in the fourth quarter of 2007. This is the third such cycle since the inception of the high-yield bond market in the late 1980s. Although the last two cycles have an overwhelming set of similarities, there are subtle differences that models cannot capture. These differences can have a material impact on individual manager selection and strategy allocation decisions, and as such, we recommend that quantitative methods be used in conjunction with a strong understanding of the underlying investment strategy.

CHAPTER TWENTY ONE

DEBT GOVERNANCE, RISK TAKING AND COST OF DEBT

TOKE HJORTSHØJ AND CHENYANG WEI

1. Introduction

Corporate governance essentially touches on the design of governance mechanisms by which various capital suppliers protect their investments and ensure themselves a fair rate of return. In U.S., discussions on corporate governance have been largely centered on how different aspects of corporate governance should be structured to incentivize shareholder value maximization. As residual claimholders under limited liability, shareholders are entitled to all the upward potential of pursuing various risky strategies (after the fixed debt payments are fulfilled) while only exposed to limited downside risk. This payoff structure essentially makes equity investments a call option on the firm's assets.

As a result, outside situations of financial distress, any attempt to increase (1) the asset value, or (2) the asset risk tend to increase the value of this "asset" call option. The focus of this chapter is on the second aspect which is related to a company's risk-taking behavior. Of particular interest here is how creditors control firms' risk taking via the governance mechanisms chosen by them – the debt covenants. In the sections to follow, we first briefly discuss the rationale for having a corporate governance structure to control the unavoidable conflicts between shareholder and creditors; secondly, we summarize recent research findings that strong debt governance (1) reduces risk taking, (2) mitigates managerial risk-taking incentives as shaped by CEO compensation, and (3) alters the negative effect of CEO's risk-taking incentives on bond pricing.

2. Agency Cost of Debt, Managerial Incentives and Debt Governance

Extensive academic research has shown that conflicts exist between different classes of claimholders who pursue separate yet connected income streams of a company. Specifically, as owners of the firm, shareholders always have incentives for pursuing policies that do not necessarily benefit other claimholders. As two academics pointed out in their seminal work in 1976, besides selecting positive NPV projects that at least do no harm to anyone, a shareholder-aligned CEO could adopt strategies that increase stock price at the expense of creditors. The costs associated with these expropriations are termed "Agency Costs of Debt", which would ultimately have to be borne by shareholders because rational creditors charge higher interest rates for the money lent to firms where agency costs of debt are more likely. Situations involving agency costs of debt include excessive risk taking, assets sales, dividend payout, share repurchase, or simply adding more debt with higher seniority than the current ones, just to name a few. The economic impact appears to be real. For example, debt market generally reacts negatively to announcements of dividend increase or share repurchase. Of particular relevance to this chapter, firms implementing different risk-taking incentives for the CEO are found to operate with different risk profiles. In their published study, Coles, Daniel and Naveen report that higher risk-taking incentives, as measured by the sensitivity of the CEO's stock and option value to the firm's stock volatility, lead to riskier policies including higher leverage, more R&D investment, and a more concentrated operation in fewer business lines. Creditors appear to react to the risk-taking incentives in a consistent manner - firms giving more risk-taking incentives to their CEOs have to pay higher premium for financing through the debt market. Overall, existing evidence seems to suggest a solid link between managerial incentives and firm risk, and the existence of such strong incentives appears to be received negatively by creditors.

In response to managers' shareholder friendly incentives, creditors use covenants as the governance mechanism to protect their investments. Two prominent finance academics, Clifford Smith and Jerold Warner, were the first to provide a comprehensive description and a qualitative analysis of the roles played by different types of bond covenants in disciplining managerial behavior (see, Smith and Warner (1979)). For example, in debt indentures creditors can either impose direct restrictions on adoption of certain type of risky investment projects or use various ratio tests (such as fixed charge coverage ratio or leverage ratio) to indirectly reduce the firm's flexibility in funding risky projects through further borrowings (see Box 1 for a classification).

Despite extensive research on debt agency conflicts, very little empirical evidence exists on how debt governance affects firms' risk taking behavior. Moreover, if compensation schemes carrying higher incentives for risk taking indeed leads to higher asset risk, does debt governance help mitigate such effect to the extent that it protects creditors' investment? The research summarized in this chapter presents the first attempt at addressing these questions.

3. Measuring Risk Taking, Debt Governance and Managerial Incentives

An empirical investigation of the link between risk taking and two prominent governance mechanisms (managerial incentives and debt governance) is a challenging task. To start with, neither academics nor practitioners have reached any agreement on what is the best way for measuring excessive risk taking and debt governance. For example, there is no consensus on what determines the "optimal" level of risk taking, and therefore researchers lack of an objective benchmark for detecting whether certain level of risk taking is excessive or inadequate. Likewise, different types of debt covenants discipline distinct dimensions of a firm's operation, e.g., financing, investment, payout, just to name a few. And it is very difficult to have a quantitative measure which could reflect the overall strength of a package of covenant indentures. As a result, researchers ask a less ambitious question – is the cross-sectional relationship between risk taking and covenant intensity consistent with the notion that strong debt governance constrains firms' scope for risk taking.

Risk taking

To measure risk taking, we first estimate firm asset risk using the market-based approach developed by Moody's KMV (Crosbie & Bohn (2003)). We then define an industry-adjusted asset risk adjustment ratio (IRAR) to capture the year-to-year dynamics of risk taking. Moody's KMV model equity as a Merton (1974) European call option on the firm's asset value. The approach is parsimonious enough to allow researchers to derive a small number of inputs required for the Black-Scholes option pricing model, while capturing the key "residual claim" feature of shareholders' payoff structure.

In order to examine the ex post unanticipated risk taking, we follow Skinner (1989) and Brown, Harlow, and Starks (1996) to calculate a risk adjustment ratio (next year's asset risk divided by the current asset risk). And to filter out industry-wide factors we follow Fang & Zhong (2004) to calculate and industry-adjusted risk adjustment ratio (IRAR).

Debt Governance

When measuring debt governance, we construct two firm-level measures which are motivated by earlier research by Billet, King & Mauer (2007) and Smith and Warner (1979), respectively.

We focus on nonconvertible bonds issued in the post-1990 period using Mergent's Fixed Income Securities Database (FISD). FISD is a comprehensive database with more than 550 data fields on over 140,000 corporate bonds, corporate medium-term notes, supranational, U.S. agency, and U.S. Treasury debt securities. Not only provides the database detailed information on the bonds' characteristics such as time-to-maturity, coupon type/rate, offering amount, maturity, callable and putable features. It also provides a comprehensive coverage on more than forty types of covenants disclosed in the bond's prospectus.

The first debt governance measure is very similar to the proxy developed in Billet, King & Mauer (2007). On the contract level, covenant density is defined as the total number of covenant provisions included in the debt indenture. On the firm level, a covenant index is then defined as the weighted average covenant intensity of the firm's outstanding bonds, with the weight being each bond issue's outstanding amount. The second debt governance measure is developed from a different perspective. Based on a classification of bond covenants (see Box 1 for a description) which groups covenants into categories reflecting distinct aspects of firm operation, the number of categories addressed by the debt indenture is used to capture the scope of protection a covenant package provides. A firm-level weighted average measure is then computed following the weighting scheme of the first measure to reach the second debt governance proxy.

Managerial risk taking incentives

We follow recent methodology used in Coles, Daniel & Naveen (2006) to measure managerial risk-taking incentives embedded in CEO compensation. In particular, option Vega based on the Black-Scholes model is computed for each CEO's total option holdings. Vega measures the change in the dollar value of an executive's wealth for a change of 1 percentage point in the annualized standard deviation of stock returns.

4. Empirical Findings

Risk Taking and Debt Governance

We use a standard regression framework to first examine the impact of debt governance on firms' risk taking behavior. The advantage of a regression analysis is that it allows researchers to control the impact of many other firm characteristics which could affect the firm's risk taking choice. The key variable to be analyzed is the annual risk taking measure IRAR, and the key explanatory variable is the firm's debt governance measure.

After filtering out the possible impact of factors such as surplus cash, tangibility, market-to-book ratio, book leverage, firm size, and asset risk in the previous period, we uncover a negative relation between annual changes of asset risk and the strength of debt governance. Our empirical model estimates that increasing the debt governance proxies from the minimum to the maximum level is associated with a reduction in the firm's industry-adjusted asset risk adjustment ratio (IRAR) of up to 25 percent from the previous period.

The evidence is, however, consistent with at least two competing explanations. Financial contracting theories predict a causal relationship where strong debt governance (through restrictive covenants) prohibit the manager from selecting risky but negative-NPV projects that transfer wealth from senior claimholders to shareholders. An alternative view, however, suggests that risk level and contracting are both endogenous variables driven by unobserved factors.

Agency theories suggest increased risk taking incentives among firms close to default. Recent work by Fang & Zhong (2004) and Larsen (2006) support the predictions by documenting risk-shifting (measured by IRAR) behavior is most prominent among firms with high default probabilities. Therefore, if stronger debt governance leads to lower risk taking, the effect would be stronger among firms more likely to default. This hypothesis presents an opportunity to shed lights on relative validity of a causal relationship between debt governance and risk taking.

We use two proxies for closeness to financial distress: a model-implied default probability[1] (DP) and a firm's credit rating. Since firms close to financial distress are more likely to engage in risk-shifting, we expect strong debt governance to play a more significant role when default probability is high. Indeed, regression analysis employing either proxy for default risk confirms that, for a "high default probability" firm, stronger debt governance is associated with an extra 25 percent reduction in risk-taking measures by IRAR, as compared to either default-prone firms with weak debt governance or firms that are default-remote.

Overall, debt governance appears to be an economically important mechanism in reducing asset risk. And the effects appear to be stronger when firms are incentivized to shift risk under financial distress, when agency conflicts are expected to be most severe.

Managerial Incentives and Debt Governance

To further shed lights on the mechanism underlying the risk-mitigating effect of debt governance, we next focus on the impact of debt governance on the managerial incentives behind risk taking. According to recent findings by academics (see, e.g., Coles, Daniel & Naveen (2006)), CEOs whose compensation portfolio is more sensitive to volatility of the company stock (higher option Vega) indeed implement riskier policies including more borrowing, higher R&D investment, and more focused operations in less business lines. This incentive effect seems to be recognized in the bond market, as there appears to be a non-trivial spread premium charged on bonds issued by companies giving their CEOs high risk-taking incentives. If debt governance is effective in controlling debt agency conflicts, we expect the impact of Vega on risk taking and bond pricing to be mitigated in the presence of strong debt governance.

Our analysis shows that strong debt governance significantly mitigates the impact of Vega on risk taking. Without strong debt governance, high Vega (above the sample median) is associated with an annual increase of 7

---

[1] Based on the Merton (1974) model, the default probability (DP) is the probability that the market value of assets, V, falls below the strike price X, defined as the current liabilities plus half the long-term debt maturing in one year. $DP_t = N\left(-\frac{\ln(V_t/X_t) + \left(\mu_V - \frac{1}{2}\sigma_V^2 - \delta_V\right)T}{\sigma_V}\right)$, where μ_V is the continuously compounded expected annual return on assets, δ_V is the average historical payout rate, and T is the one-year default horizon.

percentage points in IRAR, relative to low-Vega firms. With strong debt governance, the difference in IRAR due to Vega is reduced to 1 percentage point.

In terms of cost of debt, our analysis shows that the impact of risk-taking incentives on credit spread is not monotonic, but rather depends on the strength of debt governance in place. With weak debt governance, our regression results confirm existing research that indeed high Vega is not received favorably by bond investors and a positive premium results. With strong debt governance, however, the spread-Vega relationship appears to be reversed – a one-million-dollar increase in Vega is associated with a drop in spread of as much as 266 basis points. With strong protection, bond investors seem to no longer worry about the potential appropriation by excessive risk taking.

5. Contributions to Existing Research

To the best of our knowledge, this chapter presents the first large-sample evidence that strong debt governance reduces risk taking, and weakens the managerial incentives for risk taking. It contributes to the literature on debt contracting in two ways. First, a large body of the literature has been centered on the ex ante efficiency of the covenant choice, namely the "costly contracting hypothesis" (Smith and Warner (1979)). In particular, recent findings seem to suggest that higher covenant intensity is indeed compensated by lower offering yield. Our findings show that firms with strong debt governance appear to be more constrained in risk taking ex post, offer one potential explanation for pricing impact of strong debt governance. Second, by focusing on the role of covenant protection in shaping corporate risk-taking policy, we complement a number of recent studies which find that creditor control rights have first-order ex post impact on corporate investment policy (Chava and Roberts (2008) and Nini, Smith, and Sufi (2009a)), capital structure decision (Roberts and Sufi (2009)), and on corporate governance and firm value (Nini, Smith, and Sufi(2009b)).

6. Implications for Investing

The structure of the bond indenture is one important aspect of limiting the downside risk when investing in corporate bonds. The degree of restrictions depends on the company issuing the bond – is it a mature cash flow positive company or a growth company with high initial investments where the future tells the profitability of today's decisions. Therefore investors need to weight risk relative to return, in balancing sufficient flexibility granted to companies with the proper degree of control. This chapter shows that as the investor sees higher risk for the company to end in a distressed situation, the investor needs to demand more restrictive covenants. As the company gets near to the default boundary shareholder-aligned managers could have stronger incentives to go with low-probability yet high-potential-return projects, essentially making shareholders better off with a small-chance super return with creditors bearing the majority of the downside risk. Restrictive covenants, in situations like this, appear to be particularly important for creditors to mitigate the excessive risk taking and protect their investments.

Investments into corporate bonds with very high credit risk are exactly the philosophy for distressed bond investors. Those investors are not seeking to avoid entering distress ultimately but instead taking advantage of an overreaction of the investors less willing to hold distressed bonds. This chapter suggests that the balance between debt governance and CEO risk incentives might be something crucial for distressed bond investors to bear in mind. Having strong debt governance in place allows distressed bond investors to better monitor and control managers' risk decision.

Equity investors and analysts need to account for debt governance when making recommendations. For investors seeking a control, the restrictiveness of the bond indenture potentially restrict managers' decision making and subsequently the expected future company enterprise value. There are many channels for the constraints to take effect, e.g., restrictions on investment decision, asset sales, and on mergers, etc. Furthermore, often in existence are certain limitations on dividend payouts, share buy-backs and limits on additional debt which clearly have a valuation impact. The chapter shows that equity investors need to build in bondholder governance in their estimate of the enterprise value and make the future strategy in accordance with the existing bond documentation.

7. Conclusion

One of the crucial continuing tasks of the board of directors is to align the executives with the long-term interest of shareholders through properly designed incentivizes. It is not an easy task – while the positive side with a carrot driving the CEO for shareholder value maximization has long been the center of the discussions, extreme cases do exist where too risky decisions with low probability to succeed were driven by an incentive pay not in line with the long-term credit healthiness of the company.

Research summarized in the chapter suggests an interesting interaction effect between managerial incentive and debt governance. Although the context here is the firm's risk take and the cost of debt financing, the implications seem far broader given that the exact channels of these effects remain to be discovered. Also left out of the research so far is the valuation effect of debt governance on equity, which arguably could be far more complex. Nevertheless, the interaction of governance mechanisms serving different classes of capital suppliers appears an under researched area, and the evidence so far seems to suggest it is a factor with important implications for corporate policies, valuation and risk management.

References

Billett, M.T., King, T.H.D., Mauer, D.C., 2007. Growth opportunities and the choice of leverage, debt maturity, and covenants. Journal of Finance 62, 697-730

Black, F., Scholes, M., 1973. The pricing of options and corporate liabilities. Journal of Political Economy 81, 637-659

Brown, K.C., Harlow, W.V., Starks, L.T., 1996. Of tournaments and temptations: An analysis of managerial incentives in the mutual fund industry. Journal of Finance 51, 85-110

Chava, S., Roberts, M.R., 2008. How does financing impact investment? The role of debt covenants. Journal of Finance 63, 2085-2121

Coles, J.L., Daniel, N.D., Naveen, L., 2006. Managerial incentives and risk-taking. Journal of Financial Economics 79, 431-468

Core, J., Guay, W., 2002. Estimating the value of employee stock option portfolios and their sensitivities to price and volatility. Journal of Accounting Research 40, 613-630

Crabbe, L., 1991. Event risk – An analysis of losses to bondholders and super poison put bond covenants. Journal of Finance 46, 689-706

Crosbie, P., Bohn, J., 2003. Modeling default risk. Moody's KMV

Fang, M., Zhong, R., 2004. Default risk, firm's characteristics, and risk shifting. Yale ICF Working paper (04-21)

Jensen, M., Meckling, W., 1976. Theory of the firm: Managerial behavior, agency costs. Journal of Financial Economics 3, 305-360

Larsen, P.T., 2006. Default risk, debt maturity and levered equity's risk shifting incentives. Working paper, University of Aarhus

Merton, R.C., 1974. On the pricing of corporate debt: The risk structure of interest rates. Journal of Finance 29, 449-470

Nash, R.C., Netter, J.M., Poulsen, A.B., 2003. Determinants of contractual relations between shareholders and bondholders: investment opportunities and restrictive covenants. Journal of Corporate Finance 9, 201-232

Nini, G., Smith, D., Sufi, A., 2009a. Creditor control rights and firm investment policy. Journal of Financial Economics (forthcoming)

Nini, G., Smith, D., Sufi, A., 2009b. Creditor control rights, corporate governance and firm value. SSRN eLibrary

Roberts, M., Sufi, A., 2009. Control rights and capital structure. Journal of Finance 64, 1657-1695

Skinner, D.J., 1989. Options markets and stock return volatility. Journal of Financial Economics 23, 61-78

Smith, C.W., Warner, J.B., 1979. On financial contracting: An analysis of bond covenants. Journal of Financial Economics 7, 117-161

Appendix

Bond Covenant Classification

Extending the covenant classification proposed in Smith and Warner (1979), we group each bond's covenant provisions into six categories, with each representing a unique dimension of a firm's operating policies, along which agency costs of debt could result from overly shareholder-friendly policies.

1) Production/Investment Covenants: Possible direct restrictions of the firm's production/investment decision include restrictions on investment, the sale of assets and on mergers. In addition, creditors can require the contract to be secured by certain assets, or require the firm to take certain actions for the maintenance of the assets.

2) Dividend Covenants: Debt covenants frequently restrict not only the payment of cash dividends, other forms of distributions such as repurchase. Myers (1977) points out that dividend covenants help solve the underinvestment problem.

3) Financing Covenants: To prevent claim dilution, purchasers of the current bond issue can require restrictions that limit either any future debt issuance or the seniority of the debt to be issued in the future. For example, the Negative Pledge Covenant prohibits the firm from issuing secured debt unless the current issue is secured on a pari passu basis.

4) Default-related Covenants: These covenants protect the holders of certain issue from the potential value loss due to an event of default in any other debt issue of the same company. For example, Cross Default Covenant activates an event of default in the issue when an event of default has occurred to any other debt of the issuer.

5) Event-related Covenants: In the 80.s, the leveraged buyouts (LBOs) caused significant losses to bondholders. In 1986, "poison put" covenant was introduced to allow investors to sell their holdings back to the issuer at par in the event of a hostile takeover. Later on, another type of covenant, "super poison put", was introduced, which allows sell-back if two designated events are triggered: (1) a major capital structure change, and (2) a rating downgrade from investment to speculate grades.

6) Bonding Covenants: Bonding activities are "expenditures made by the firm which control the bondholder-stockholder conflict" (Smith and Warner (1979)).

CHAPTER TWENTY TWO

RELEVANCE OF CDO RATING DOWNGRADES ON THE BANK'S SHARE PRICE

ANIT DEB, FRANK LEHRBASS AND DIRK SCHIERECK[1]

Abstract

Rating grades are supposed to express the financial soundness of a bank or a particular product to the market. We examine the impact of single product rating announcements on the originating bank's share price by considering collateralized debt obligations (CDO). We infer equity price reaction from rating announcements applying standard event study methodology. Our results reveal a strong negative link between equity and CDO rating announcements at announcement day but no long term abnormal returns.

1. Introduction

Rating downgrades have been widely researched with most studies concentrating on the bank-wide risk assessment. In this study we intend to evaluate rating implications from single product rating announcements. As such, we use rating announcements from collateralized debt obligations (CDO). While securitized products benefited from high rating grades and

---

[1] Dipl. Wirtschaftsing. Anit Deb, Department of Law and Economics, Darmstadt University of Technology / Germany, deb@bwl.tu-darmstadt.de. Dr. Frank Lehrbass, Schlossmannstrasse 39, 40225 Dusseldorf / Germany, frank.lehrbass@gmx.de. Frank works for a large European corporation in the commodity business in a front office role. Dr. Dirk Schiereck, Department of Law and Economics, Darmstadt University of Technology / Germany, schiereck@bwl.tu-darmstadt.de.

solid performance just before the crisis, it became apparent that the poor underlying assets of the CDO resulted in investor mistrust.

In theory, risk associated with CDO deals is transferred to a special purpose vehicle (SPV) that issues bonds to investors in different tranches that range from senior tranches to the equity tranche that is mostly held by the originating bank. With this process, risk should be transferred from the originator to the investor via the bankruptcy remote SPV. As a result losses from CDO deals should hardly affect the originating bank above the equity tranche. But the worsening CDO quality should lead to impairments on the bank's asset position and impact the profit and loss of the bank.

The reality of the CDO market showed that there is much more complexity. If the first loss piece is already written down, there is no need for impairments. Other forms of CDO can be constructed in a way that the originating bank is a broker - rather than an originator - with no first loss piece at all in the CDO. These single tranche CDO have no feedback channel to the brokering bank. But still, rating downgrades could affect the bank's reputation.

Even though the CDO business may be considered as a secondary one, the bank's reputation can still be impacted. An aspect that is widely underestimated is linked to lawsuits. Banks or prosecutors sued originators or brokers on grounds of having consciously sold low quality assets to investors. These lawsuits shed a bad light on the reputation of the bank. So concerns arising from so called secondary businesses can indeed impact the bank.

A characteristic of synthetic CDO deals was that banks held not only the first loss piece but as well the super senior tranches that ranked higher than the senior tranches and were considered as almost riskless. The super senior tranches were big in size and rating downgrades of subordinated tranches were followed by downgrades of the super senior tranches. Due to their size the impairments were considerably high and created a severe threat to the involved bank.

The hypotheses examined in this study are:

- Rating announcements for CDO are, in general, of material impact to the originating bank's equity value since impairments impact the profit and loss of the bank.
- During times of economic stress, the market expects downgrades and reacts indifferently to rating announcements.

We apply standard event study methodology with short term and long term equity price effects. The short term event study includes equity price reaction of up to 20 days before and 20 days after the actual announcement day. In the long term event study we analyze the interdependence between equity and debt quality with a three months anticipation and post announcement observation. The stock-listed banks considered in this sample are headquartered in Europe and the USA with a strong activity in CDO origination. We summarize our results with the following findings:

- Equity price response from rating announcements on CDO is quickly absorbed by the market. At announcement day, highly negative equity price response is noticed.
- During times of economic stress and expectations about upcoming rating downgrades, equity prices still respond negatively to CDO rating announcements.
- In certain cases, like CDO from US banks, the market expects downgrades and reacts indifferently.

Summarizing, we deliver proof that CDO rating announcements can have a material impact on the bank's share price due to the above mentioned feedback channels. We conduct with section 2 summarizing the relevant literature, section 3 proposes the applied methodology and data, section 4 presents the results and section 5 finally concludes the research.

2. Literature review

Rating grades are an important instrument and became even more important with the Basel II framework by determining the regulatory capital requirement based on external ratings. Generally, rating grades shall express the credit quality of an entity or a financial product. Given the high relevance of rating grades, we expect market response from rating announcements. In terms of market efficiency it is questionable whether the market already incorporates rating announcements in advance due to publicly available information or responds significantly at the event caused by new or unexpected information.

Implications of rating announcements have been researched in various ways. Past research concentrated on stock prices, bond prices or both. Over the last years, research was extended to examine derivative products like credit default swaps (CDS) as well. A good overview of rating implications exists (Norden and Weber 2004; Trutwein and Schiereck 2011). Some notable studies found anticipated rating announcements (Grier and Katz 1976; Weinstein 1977; Pinches and Singleton 1978; Glascock, Davidson Iii et al. 1987; Steiner and Heinke 2001), whereas other studies found no evidence of anticipated market response prior to the rating event (Griffin and Sanvicente 1982; Wansley, Glascock et al. 1992).

As we investigate implications of rating announcements on CDO, we consider the relevant literature referring to securitization (Higgins, Mason et al. 2009). The paper documents that rating downgrades of asset backed securities (ABS) induce significant negative share price reactions and future securitization issuing is affected.

3. Data and methodology

3.1 Data

We extract data from several sources. For equity market prices we use Thomson Reuters and for rating announcements Bloomberg. We select the total return prices that take stock splits and dividend payments into account. In order to select data for CDO as the proxy to represent the debt quality, we narrow the search for rating announcements by selecting CDO as issue type. In terms of linking the issuer of the CDO deal to the originator, we first need to identify the SPV in relation to the bank.

In contrary to the bank's issuer rating that assesses the bank's financial strength, rating agencies are obliged to evaluate each tranche of a CDO deal independently. In common practice, rating agencies publish rating announcements of tranches belonging to the same CDO deal simultaneously. As long as rating announcements occur for the same CDO deal in the largest event window [-20; 20], we consider the first announcement as our event date. This seems justified because the downgrade of a CDO tranche implies the downgrade of the subordinated tranches due to the loss allocation inherent in CDO deals. We rather consider confounding events when there are rating announcements on more than one CDO deal done by the same bank in our largest event window [-20; 20]. With this approach we try to relate only the rating announcement as the indicator of abnormal returns in our observation and considerably reduce our sample size.

The sample consists of CDO rating announcements from banks headquartered in Europe and the USA. We select all downgrade announcements in the period from 1999 until June 2010. From 6002 rating announcements of US banks and 2007 rating announcements of European banks, we consolidate the list by filtering CDO from stock-listed banks. This leaves us with 1227 rating announcements for US banks and 1743 rating announcements for European banks. After that we select banks with a considerable activity in CDO. This leaves us with 513 rating announcements for US banks and 765 rating announcements for European banks. We consolidate rating announcements of CDO tranches belonging to the same CDO deal as one event. The remaining events consist of 83 events from US banks and 176 events from European banks. After that we identify confounding events by disallowing major events that are disclosed during the event window [-20; 20] in order to diminish bias.[2] Our final sample size of 238 events consists of 72 events from US banks and 166 events from European banks.

CDO started to receive investor attention in the past decade. We take this into account and limit our time horizon from January 1999 until June 2010.

3.2 Methodology

We measure stock price reactions implicated by rating announcements. For that purpose we apply a standard event-study approach that is designed to quantify abnormal returns within a specified event period. We measure abnormal returns considering stock market effects with the adjusted market model approach (MacKinlay 1997).
We consider market-model adjustments to calculate the cumulative average abnormal return (CAAR):

$$CAAR_{n,i,[t_0-\tau,t_0+\tau]} = \sum_{n=1}^{N} \sum_{t=t_o-\tau}^{t=t_0+\tau} (R_{i,t} - \hat{\alpha}_i - \hat{\beta}_i R_{m,t})$$

Where $R_{i,t}$ is the return of the bank at time t, $R_{m,t}$ is the security's market return at time t, N is the number of observations, $\hat{\alpha}_i$ and $\hat{\beta}_i$ are parameters derived from the ordinary least square regression with the estimation period beginning 200 days before the event and a lag time of 30 days in order to avoid leakage effects. The largest event window in our observation is set equal to 41 days, starting 20 business days before and ending 20 business days after a rating announcement. We subdivide our analysis in 9 time intervals and repeat them for all subsamples. We use adjusted stock returns that take relevant changes such as dividend payments or stock splits into account. In addition to standard t-test statistics we test for event induced increases in variance (Boehmer,

[2] Here we selected corporate news published in journals such as the Financial Times and Wall Street Journal

Musumeci et al. 1991). Non-parametric tests are conducted by applying the Wilcoxon signed-rank test.

In order to control for anticipation and post announcement effects we calculate the buy-and-hold abnormal returns (BHAR) with monthly returns:

$$BHAR_{i,t} = BHR_{i,t} - BHR_{m,t}$$

Where $BHR_{i,t}$ is the stock's return at time t and $BHR_{m,t}$ is the market's return at time t. In addition to that, we conduct a multivariate regression analysis and control for heteroskedasticity (White 1980).

Table 1 Sample characterization, CDO rating announcements

	Events per year												
Country	**1999**	**2000**	**2001**	**2002**	**2003**	**2004**	**2005**	**2006**	**2007**	**2008**	**2009**	**2010**	**Total**
France			2	3			1			2	1	1	10
Germany		1	1	6	8	8	13	21	27	20	12		117
Netherlands							2	2		2	1		7
Spain								3		1			4
Switzerland								4	4	2	1	4	15
UK							1	3	4		2	3	13
USA	1						42	4		5	7	13	72
Total	**1**	**1**	**3**	**9**	**8**	**8**	**59**	**37**	**35**	**32**	**24**	**21**	**238**

4. Results

4.1 Cross-link equity and debt quality with CDO rating announcement

We raised the question whether rating agencies still preserve their power on the financial markets. In order to do so, we relate rating announcements of credit market products to the stock market. In light of the financial crisis, negative rating announcements were widely expected. From our literature review we researched that rating announcements mostly deal with information that is publicly available. In this context, information about the bank is publicly available whereas information on CDO is scarce. With this in mind, we expect that market response caused by rating announcements for the bank's issuer rating is stronger than for CDO rating announcements. We differentiate our findings between short term and long term observation.

Short term equity price reaction to CDO rating announcements

In a first analysis referring to CDO rating announcements we investigate whether the market considers rating announcements of CDO deals independently from the originating bank. The null hypothesis is that there are no abnormal returns caused by rating announcements. The results in the overall 238 event sample indicate highly significant abnormal returns with CAAR= -0.96% (t-value=-2.604) right on the event day [0;+0]. The results suggest that CDO rating announcements serve as a proxy for the debt quality and its impact on the bank's equity value is material. The impact of CDO rating announcements is not lagged because equity value response is absorbed very quickly by the market. In the event windows [-1;+2], [-1;+1] and [0;+2] we get significantly negative abnormal returns at the 5% confidence level. In the introductory part we raised the question if the implicit recourse, a characteristic of CDO deals, does not fully transfer the risk from the bank to the bankruptcy remote SPV. The results highlight that the market assesses that risk still resides with the bank. With this in mind, the true sale assumption, meaning an effective risk transfer, is questioned. On a longer period of event windows we get different results. Once the rating announcements are absorbed, there are no abnormal returns noticed in larger event windows [-5;+5] or [-10;+10]. Interestingly, the mean and median of the largest event window [-20;+20] deliver positive values. With a total sample of 238 events it appears that investors interested in the banks doing CDO business do not consider CDO rating announcements to be a prime driver in their investment decision related to bank's share.

We mentioned that the growing importance of rating agencies could force investors to blindly rely on rating grades as a means of quality measurement. The results outline that rating announcements on CDO are still a decisive event but generally quickly incorporated.

Anticipation and post-announcement effect of CDO rating announcements

We mentioned in our literature review that some empirical studies found evidence that rating announcements were anticipated by market participants. Significantly negative abnormal returns were found for bonds 90 days prior to a rating downgrade or negative watch listings (Steiner and Heinke 2001). The anticipation assumption is supported with negative rating downgrades preceded by rising CDS spreads (Hull, Predescu et al. 2004). Contrary results were found with no abnormal performance 6 months before and after the event (Weinstein 1977).

In order to observe lead and lag effects we provide a long term event study with monthly BHAR calculation (Loughran and Ritter 1995). We account for anticipation effects by limiting the pre-event period to 3 months prior to the event. We select the market index as the reference index in our analysis.

If rating downgrades were expected and already priced, we would expect significantly abnormal returns to take place before the actual event. The long term effect of CDO rating announcements is slightly different. The long term BHAR emphasizes that the cross-link between the equity and debt quality is limited to the event day.

Table 2 Equity price response to CDO rating announcements, total sample

	Cumulative Abnormal Return		t-Test	Boehmer Test	Wilcoxon signed rank test	
Event window	Mean	Median	t-value	z-score	z-score	Nobs
[-10;+1]	-1.33%	-0.39%	-1.279	-1.436	-0.940	238
[-5;+1]	-1.17%	-0.33%	-1.228	-1.304	-1.036	238
[-1;+1]	-1.18%	-0.22%	-2.281**	-2.087**	-3.181***	238
[-5;+5]	-0.48%	-0.22%	-0.903	-0.997	-1.169	238
[-10;+10]	-0.66%	-0.15%	-0.905	-1.030	-0.575	238
[-20;+20]	0.30%	0.02%	-0.260	0.361	-0.064	238
[0;–0]	-0.96%	-0.25%	-2.604***	-2.351**	-4.646***	238
[-1;+2]	-1.13%	-0.44%	-2.193**	-2.036**	-2.929***	238
[0;+2]	-1.01%	-0.29%	-2.080**	-1.976**	-2.756***	238

***, **, and * indicate statistical significance at the 1%, 5%, and 10% levels, respectively.

Table 3 BHAR with CDO rating announcements, total sample

	BHAR		t-Test	Johnson Test	Wilcoxon signed rank test	
Holding Period (in months)	Mean	Median	t-value	J-value	z-score	Nobs
[-3;-2]	-0.22%	0.59%	-0.256	-0.256	-0.114	238
[-3;-1]	0.27%	-0.13%	0.261	0.262	-0.061	238
[-3;0]	0.21%	-0.17%	0.163	0.165	-0.471	238
[0;1]	-0.34%	-0.25%	-0.391	-0.389	-0.700	238
[0;2]	-0.09%	0.06%	-0.079	-0.077	-0.236	238
[0;3]	0.68%	-0.51%	0.482	0.483	-0.174	238

***, **, and * indicate statistical significance at the 1%, 5%, and 10% levels, respectively.

4.2 Multivariate regression analysis

This section reports regression analysis of the bank's return on explanatory variables designed to identify the drivers of abnormal returns. The dependent variable is the cumulative abnormal return (CAR) derived from the event window [0;0]. We use bank characteristics, risk categories and binary variables for regional and time dependencies. The bank characteristics are the market value (log market value) and the market to book ratio. The time dummy separates events that took place before 2006 and after 2007. The regional dummy differentiates between CDO from European and US banks. We include the systematic risk increase as an independent variable to take the elevated volatility during the financial crisis into account. Here, we separate the time period from 2007-2009 and subtract the systematic risk from the time period 2004-2006. Another important dummy variable is whether the originating bank received a downgrade on the bank's issuer rating three months prior to the event day. Literature suggests that the issuer downgrade is essential in terms of explaining abnormal returns for securitized products (Higgins, Mason et al. 2009).

The t-statistics of the coefficient estimates are based on White's heteroskedasticity-consistent standard errors (White 1980). All our models outline that there is a highly significant negative impact with the intercept in model 1 = -0.027 (t-value= -2.715). Size characteristics do not support the negative abnormal returns. In model 1 the log market size is positive = 0.005 (t-value=1.957). This fits to intuition that people might think that a bank is too big to fail. In line with the corresponding literature, the bank's issuer downgrade prior to the event is of core importance with a strong impact of -0.011 (t-value= -2.066) in model 1. Interestingly, prior to the outbreak of the financial crisis the results indicate that investors showed no nervousness related to CDO rating announcements. All the models indicate a suitable regression model with an adjusted r-squared greater than 0.1. The systematic risk increase apparently does not play a decisive role. Overall, the strong link of the equity and debt quality with rating announcements is highlighted in our analysis.

Table 4 Multivariate regression for CDO rating announcements

Model	**1**	**2**	**3**
Intercept	-0.027	-0.032	-0.026
t-value	*-2.715****	*-2.762****	*-2.597****
Bank characteristics			
Log Market Size	0.005	0.005	0.005
t-value	*1.957**	*1.999***	*1.999***
Market to Book Ratio	0.002	0.002	0.002
t-value	*1.775**	*1.725**	*1.725**
Region			
Europe (Dummy=1)		0.003	
t-value		*0.924*	
US (Dummy=1)			-0.003
t-value			*-0.924*
Time			
before 2006 (Dummy=1)		0.004	
t-value		*1.806**	
after 2007 (Dummy=1)			-0.004
t-value			*-1.806**
Risk characteristics			
Downgrade issuer rating (Dummy=1)	-0.011	-0.010	-0.010
t-value	*-2.066***	*-1.830**	*-1.830**
Systematic risk increase	0.000	0.000	0.000
t-value	*-1.316*	*-1.147*	*-1.147*
Model parameters			
adjusted r-squared	0.116	0.120	0.120
F-statistics	8.770***	5.562***	5.570***
N	238	238	238

5. Conclusion

The recent financial crisis has shown that reputation is a key asset for bank managers. Usually, the debt quality of a bank as expressed in rating grades provides insight into the bank's financial situation. In this paper we intend to examine which rating announcements do impact the value of a bank.

We obtain significant equity price effects at announcement day when considering CDO rating announcements. Even though CDO activity has gained attention over the last years, rating agencies recognized that providing rating grades for structured credit products like CDO became a considerable profit contributor. Nonetheless, neither the rating agencies nor the market participants were cautious enough to assess the risk CDO were bearing. Beginning with the subprime credit crisis, the high rating grades were questioned by the market. In the wake of the financial crisis, CDO were blamed to bear incalculable risk. As this became a concern of investors and rating agencies, a downgrade wave of CDO deals resulted in general mistrust. Our results indicate that rating downgrades of CDO had no material impact to the bank on a long term basis. Furthermore, our results reveal that expectations about rating downgrades were existent especially for CDO done by US banks, although we did not make this explicit.

Overall, bank managers should concern about the overall bank's financial stability as this is the decisive factor from the investor's perspective.

References

Boehmer, E., J. Musumeci and A. B. Poulsen (1991). "Event-study methodology under conditions of event-induced variance." *Journal of Financial Economics* **30**(2): 253-272.

Glascock, J. L., W. N. Davidson Iii and G. V. Henderson Jr (1987). "Announcement effects of Moody's bond rating changes of equity returns." *Quarterly Journal of Business & Economics* **26**(3): 67.

Grier, P. and S. Katz (1976). "The Differential Effects of Bond Rating Changes Among Industrial and Public Utility Bonds by Maturity." *The Journal of Business* **49**(2): 226-239.

Griffin, P. A. and A. Z. Sanvicente (1982). "Common Stock Returns and Rating Changes: A Methodological Comparison." *The Journal of Finance* **37**(1): 103-119.

Higgins, E. J., J. R. Mason and A. Mordel (2009). "The Information Content of Asset-Backed Securities Downgrades, and the Motivation behind Them." *Working Paper*.

Hull, J., M. Predescu and A. White (2004). "The relationship between credit default swap spreads, bond yields, and credit rating announcements." *Journal of Banking & Finance* **28**(11): 2789-2811.

Loughran, T. and J. R. Ritter (1995). "The New Issues Puzzle." *The Journal of Finance* **50**(1): 23-51.

MacKinlay, A. C. (1997). "Event studies in economics and finance." *Journal of Economic Literature* **35**(1): 13-39.

Norden, L. and M. Weber (2004). "Informational efficiency of credit default swap and stock markets: The impact of credit rating announcements." *Journal of Banking & Finance* **28**(11): 2813-2843.

Pinches, G. E. and J. C. Singleton (1978). "The Adjustment of Stock Prices to Bond Rating Changes." *The Journal of Finance* **33**(1): 29-44.

Steiner, M. and V. G. Heinke (2001). "Event study concerning international bond price effects of credit rating actions." *International Journal of Finance & Economics* **6**(2): 139-157.

Trutwein, P. and D. Schiereck (2011). "The fast and the furious--Stock returns and CDS of financial institutions under stress." *Journal of International Financial Markets, Institutions and Money* **21**(2): 157-175.

Wansley, J. W., J. L. Glascock and T. M. Clauretie (1992). "Institutional bond pricing and information arrival: the case of bond rating changes." *Journal of Business Finance & Accounting* **19**(5): 733-750.

Weinstein, M. I. (1977). "Effect of a rating change announcement on bond price." *Journal of Financial Economics* **5**(3): 329-350.

White, H. (1980). "A Heteroskedasticity-Consistent Covariance Matrix Estimator and a Direct Test for Heteroskedasticity." *Econometrica* **48**(4): 817-838.

CHAPTER TWENTY THREE

SYSTEMATIC RISK ESTIMATION: OLS V. STATE-SPACE METHODS

JOSEPH CALLAGHAN, LIANG FU
AND JING LIU[1]

In finance, capital asset pricing model (CAPM) is used to determine the relationship between an asset's risk and its required rate of return. The model identifies two types of risks that are associated with an asset: one is systematic risk, which is also called market or non-diversifiable risk; the other one is idiosyncratic risk, which is diversifiable (Sharpe 1964 and Lintner 1965). The CAPM model is mathematically represented as $E(R_i) = R_f + \beta_i[E(R_m) - R_f]$, where $E(R_i)$ is the expected return on the capital asset; R_f is the risk-free rate of interest often surrogated by the interest yield on US government bonds; beta β_i is the sensitivity of the expected excess asset returns to the expected excess market returns; and $E(R_m)$ is the expected return of the market. The key parameter in the above CAPM model is β (beta) coefficient. It measures the part of the asset's statistical variance that cannot be removed by the diversification provided by the portfolio of many risky assets, in other words, β is a measure of an asset's non-diversifiable risk, systematic risk, or market risk. β is not only important in estimating the risk associated with individual stock in the equity market, it is also crucial in determining yield spread of corporate bond in the bond market. Conventionally, the yield spread of corporate bond is explained by expected default loss and tax premium; however, as documented in Elton, Gruber, Agrawal, and Mann (2001), while expected default only accounts for a small fraction and state taxes explain a substantial portion of the yield spread, the remaining portion of the spread is related to the risk premium. The rationale is that since "the

[1] The authors are from Oakland University.

return on corporate bonds is riskier than the return on government bonds, investors should require a premium for the higher risk", thus "a large part of the risk on corporate bonds is systematic rather than diversifiable" (Elton et al. (2001), pp.247).

Conventional adoption of CAPM model assumes the stationary of the risk factor β. This is a rather naïve assumption. Ohlson and Rosenberg (1984) find two kinds of stochastic variation in β: there is an attendency for βs to converge rather slowly towards the stationary mean, and in that sense it is clear that the model of βs requires a "memory"; that is modeled by a stationary first-order, autoregressive process. At the same time, in each period, there is a purely random (serially independent) perturbation in β. We focus on investigating the time-varying property of β by applying a more general form of CAPM mode, namely, the market model. The use of market model is without the loss of generality. The key difference between the CAPM and market model is whether the return of the capital asset and return of the market is adjusted by risk-free asset. In particular, market model is depicted as $R_i = \alpha_i + \beta_i R_m + \epsilon_i$, where R_i is the single asset return, R_m is the return of the market index in which the asset is traded, α_i is an additive constant, β_i is the beta coefficient which indicates the sensitivity of R_i to the changes in R_m and ϵ_i is the error component (a random variable, with mean zero and variance equal to σ_ϵ^2, which assumes independently and identically distributed values). The model assumes that the risk of the portfolio can be divided into two components: the first component can be reduced by the mean of diversification; the second component depends on market risk. The parameter β_i can be interpreted as representing the relationship between the riskiness of the single asset and the market index volatility; as it is given by the covariance between the respective returns over the variance of the index returns.

In order to incorporate the time-varying property of the beta coefficient in the market model, the literature has been utilizing different modeling techniques; among these modeling techniques, Kalman filter method is the mostly commonly adopted. A dynamic system such as the time-varying β can be represented in a general form known as the state space model. The general form of a state space model defines an observation (or measurement) equation and a transition (or state) equation, which together express the structure and dynamics of a system. A state space model can be used to incorporate unobserved variables into, and estimate them along with, the observable model to impose a time-varying structure of the market model β. Additionally, the structure of the time-varying β can be explicitly modeled within the Kalman filter framework to follow any stochastic process. The Kalman filter recursively forecasts conditional βs from an initial set of priors, generating a series of conditional intercepts and β coefficients for the market model (Harvey, 1994).

The Kalman filter method estimates the conditional β, using market model $R_i = \alpha_i + \beta_i R_m + \epsilon_i$. The above market model represents the observation equation of the state space model. However, the form of the transition equation depends on the form of stochastic process that βs are assumed to follow. In other words, the transition equation can be flexible, we assumes that β follows a mean-reverting first-order autoregressive process.

The state-space representation of the dynamics of the market model is then given by the following system of equations

$$R_{it} = \alpha_i + \beta_{it}^{KAR} R_{mt} + \epsilon_{it}$$
$$(\beta_{it}^{KAR} - \bar{\beta}) = \varphi(\beta_{it-1} - \bar{\beta}) + v_{it}$$

We focus on the forecastability of β across alternative models by comparing the forecast errors of β itself rather than its future returns counterpart as most prior literature adopts. Two alternative modeling techniques in estimating and forecasting β are considered: one is simply the ordinary least square (OLS) model by the market model, and the other one is the state-space model using Kalman filter.

Given that β of a security is defined as the covaribility of the security returns with the market returns divided by the variance in market returns; therefore, we derive benchmark β by using "looking-back" return data with market model. More specifically, the benchmark β at any given point in time is calculated by regressing forward-looking individual stock returns against market return. The rationale of this approach is based on the argument that if investors were to have perfect information (foresight) about the future, the covaribility of the individual stock and the market in any given point of time would incorporate all information from this point onward in time. Therefore, by "looking-back", the market model would capture the ideal information environment and the realized β would serve the purpose of benchmark β. This "rational expectations approach to beta estimation" establishes a suitable benchmark from which to compare forecasted betas under different estimation methods. This is the first study in our knowledge to derive benchmark β in such a simple and straightforward way.

We use daily stock returns data for the period 1 January, 1998 to 31 March, 2007 and the data is sourced from the Center for Research in Security Prices (CRSP). We use twenty-five companies in the Dow Jones Industrial Average (DJIA).

We then use non-overlapping daily stock return for any given company in the sample to generate quarterly average forecast of β series. This β forecast is labeled as β_{it}^{OLS}. β_{it}^{OLS} uses quarterly return information; however, the criticism of this process is that it fails to take into consideration the evolution of β itself. As new information comes in every trading day, β, as a risk measure, is updating itself to adjust the risk implication. To address this criticism, we introduce Kalman filter approach to estimate β coefficient to incorporate the time-varying property. To operationalize Kalman filter approach, an initial prior of β coefficient is required. We use daily stock return from 1998 to 1999 to derive the initial estimate of β. With this prior, we use all return data from 1998 to 2000 to derive the first β forecast under Kalman filter algorithm. This β forecast is labeled as β_{it}^{KAL}. Both β_{it}^{OLS} and β_{it}^{KAL} are derived from historical market information; however, the key difference is that β_{it}^{OLS} reflects only the most recent three months market information, while Kalman filter approach allows β_{it}^{KAL} to update continuously based on the whole prior history.

The forecast β series from both models are then compared with the benchmark β, which is labeled as β_{it}^{B}. β_{it}^{B} is derived from the market model based on forward-looking quarterly daily stock and market returns. Specifically, the last quarter in our sample period is the first quarter of 2007, this quarter is treated as the "holdout" period for the derivation of the last benchmark β in the β_{it}^{B} series.

The forecast error of β, is the difference between the benchmark β and the forecast β, the forecast errors from the two models are $\varepsilon_{it}^{OLS} = \beta_{it}^{B} - \beta_{it}^{OLS}$ & $\varepsilon_{it}^{KAL} = \beta_{it}^{B} - \beta_{it}^{KAL}$. A group of measures derived from the forecast error are designed to evaluate forecasts. Mean errors (ME) $ME_i^{OLS} = \frac{1}{n}\sum_{t=1}^{n} \varepsilon_{it}^{OLS}$ & $ME_i^{KAL} = \frac{1}{n}\sum_{t=1}^{n} \varepsilon_{it}^{KAL}$ are used to assess whether the models over or under-forecast β series.

The accuracy of each forecast is measured by a particular loss function. Two popular loss functions are Mean squared error (MSE) and Mean absolute error (MAE): $MSE_i^j = \frac{1}{n}\sum_{t=1}^{n}(\varepsilon_t^2)_j$ & $MAE_i^j = \frac{1}{n}\sum_{t=1}^{n}|\varepsilon_t|_j$, where $j = OLS, KAL$. The lower the forecast error measure, the better the forecasting performance. However, it does not necessarily mean that a lower MSE (MAE) indicates a superior forecasting ability, since the difference between the MSEs (MAEs) across alternative modeling techniques may not be significantly different from zero. Therefore, it is important to check whether any reductions in MSEs (MAEs) are statistically significant.

Diebold and Mariano (1995) develop a test of equal forecast accuracy to test whether two sets of forecasts error have equal mean value. Let $L(\varepsilon_t)_j$, where $j = OLS, KAL$ be the loss function (either MSE or MAE) for two competing models OLS and Kalman filter approach. To determine if one model predicts better than another we test the null hypotheses $H_0{:}E[L(\varepsilon_t)_{OLS}] = E[L(\varepsilon_t)_{KAL}]$ against the alternative $H_1{:}E[L(\varepsilon_t)_{OLS}] \neq E[L(\varepsilon_t)_{KAL}]$. The Diebold-Mariano test is based on the loss differential

$d_t = L(\varepsilon_t)_{OLS} - L(\varepsilon_t)_{KAL}$. The null of equal predictive accuracy is then $H_0{:}E[d_t] = 0$.

The Diebold-Mariano test statistic is $S = \frac{\bar{d}}{(var(\bar{d}))^{\frac{1}{2}}}$, where $\bar{d} = \frac{1}{n}\sum_{t=1}^{n} d_t$ is the mean of the difference between loss functions and $var(\bar{d}) = \gamma_0 + 2\sum_{k=1}^{\infty}\gamma_k$, $\gamma_k = cov(d_t, d_{t-k})$ is the asymptotic variance of $\bar{d}$.

The following table presents the test results of the Diebold-Mariano statistics. The table reports the t-statistics and the p-value of two loss functions. A significant p-value with a positive t-statistics is an indicator that β_{it}^{KAL} performs better than β_{it}^{OLS} in reducing the forecast errors. A significant p-value with a negative t-statistics is, on the other hand, an indicator that β_{it}^{OLS} has superior forecastibility than β_{it}^{KAL} in producing smaller forecast errors.

More than half of the companies have a negative t-statistics regardless of the specification of the loss function. This means that OLS forecast β performs better than its Kalman filter approach counterpart. However, not all these companies show a significant differential between two measurements. For the majority of them, although the t-statistics are negative, p-values are not significant. This indicates the indifference between two models in forecasting β. Two companies in the sample have significant results from Diebold-Mariano statistics. These two companies are Du Pont and Pfizer. Take Pfizer as an example, the t-statistics for mean-squared error and mean-absolute error loss functions are -2.30 and -2.50, they are both significant at 5% level. The negative t-statistics with significant p-value indicate that OLS forecast β for Pfizer performs well in explaining the relationship between the individual stock and the market return as reflected by smaller forecast errors. Incorporating all prior information to allow β to evolve over time does not add more power to the β coefficient. Therefore, conventionally simple market model is sufficient to estimate the risk measure β for this particular company.

We do find a couple of companies in the sample that shows the superiority of Kalman forecast β. One company is Home Depot Inc. In both loss function specifications, the t-statistics are 2.39 and 2.42, with a 5% significant p-value. The other company is IBM. Notice that IBM is quite different from Home Depot, as well as the majority of other companies in the sample. For the majority of the companies in the sample, the test results from two different loss functions are quite consistent. More specifically, either both specifications show significance or they both fail to show such differential significance. Moreover, the sign of the t-statistics tend to be consistent across alternative loss functions. However, IBM has a t-statistics of 15.71, which is highly significant under mean absolute error specification, on the other hand, if mean-squared error function is applied; the t-statistics is only 1.22, which fails to differentiate two models. This means that if we define the loss function to be mean absolute error, Diebold-Mariano test provides the result that the β forecast derived from Kalman filter algorithm outperforms its OLS counterpart in reducing the forecast errors.

The employment of Kalman filter approach is based on the criticism that market model assumes that β is stationary over time, while it in fact is time-varying. Kalman filter algorithm allows β to evolve overtime and takes into consideration of updating new information as time goes by. Even though we did not find significant difference between two modeling techniques in terms of reducing the forecast errors of β directly, our results are consistent with Frees (2004) that more sophisticated engineering approach may not attribute to forecast accuracy of β coefficient in the market model. However, we cannot rule out that a few other reasons may also contribute to the results. For example, the derivation of benchmark β may bias against finding significant difference between two models; or the loss functions weigh positive and negative forecast error equally and fails to consider the market's diverse reaction between different signs of the forecast errors; or the absence of random perturbation in β proposed in Ohlson and Rosenberg (1984). Nonetheless, the importance of fully understanding and correctly estimating β may well exceed its application in the equity market. Equity and debt can be recognized as contingent claims written on the same set of productive assets and hence should share common risk factors. Therefore, if corporate bond returns move systematically with equity in the market, then corporate bond expected returns would require a risk premium to compensate for the nondiversifiability of corporate bond risk, just like equity. As a result, systematic risk compensates for a considerable portion of the yield spreads of the corporate bonds. A better understanding of the time-varying property of β would help determining the systematic risk premium, which is a significant component of yield spreads.

Company	d_t |MSE		d_t |MAE	
	t-statistics	p-value	t-statistics	p-value
3M CO	-0.63	0.5328	-0.16	0.8735
ALCOA INC	-1.53	0.1389	-1.24	0.2269
ALTRIA GROUP INC	-0.44	0.6616	0.36	0.7243
AIG INC	-0.12	0.9071	-0.32	0.7529
AMERICAN EXPRESS CO	-0.76	0.4563	-0.78	-0.4443
BOEING CO	1.97	0.0613	0.86	0.4015
CATERPILLAR INC	-0.40	0.6916	-0.89	0.3807
CITIGROUP INC	0.86	0.4007	1.52	0.1426
COCA COLA CO	-1.58	0.1271	-1.24	0.2288
DISNEY WALT CO	-0.75	0.4596	-0.86	0.3996
DU PONT	-2.97	0.0071	-3.17	0.0044
GENERAL ELECTRIC CO	-0.65	0.5202	-0.30	0.7662
GENERAL MOTORS CORP	1.17	0.2537	1.33	0.1978
HEWLETT PACKARD CO	0.35	0.7275	0.69	0.5001
HOME DEPOT INC	2.39	0.0254	2.42	0.0239
IBM CORP	1.22	0.2352	15.71	<.0001
INTEL CORP	-1.60	0.1224	-2.02	0.0556
JOHNSON & JOHNSON	-1.03	0.3157	-0.98	0.3366
JPMORGAN CHASE & CO	-1.23	0.2317	-1.54	0.1389
MCDONALDS CORP	1.25	0.2235	-0.29	0.7754
MERCK & CO INC	-1.76	0.0915	-1.44	0.1653
MICROSOFT CORP	-1.50	0.1483	-1.58	0.1291
PFIZER INC	-2.30	0.0316	-2.50	0.0205
UNITED TECH CORP	1.38	0.1813	1.29	0.2113
WAL MART STORES INC	-0.31	0.7582	0.43	0.6679

Discussion and comments from 1st Credit Risk Conference (July 21st ~23rd, 2011):

- For the dynamic system equations

$$R_{it} = \alpha_i + \beta_{it}^{KAR} R_{mt} + \epsilon_{it}$$
$$(\beta_{it}^{KAR} - \bar{\beta}) = \varphi(\beta_{it-1} - \bar{\beta}) + v_{it}$$

  - What values are given to φ and $\bar{\beta}$?
  - Sensitivity analysis using different assumptions?
  - What about α?
- Does beta really follow AR(1) process?
- How about using monthly returns to reduce noise and less frequent estimation?
- Is there any regime shift in the sample period? For example, 1999-2000 was the internet bubble period.
- Would the time-series behavior of beta vary with bigger sample? Would Kalman filter approach perform better for stocks with certain characteristics?
- Why not using CAPM, which is more theory based?

References

Elton, E., Gruber, M., Agrawal, D., Mann, C., 2001. Explaining the rate spread on corporate bonds. Journal of Finance 56, no. 1, 247-277.

Diebold, F., Mariano, R., 1995. Comparing predictive accuracy. Journal of Business & Economic Statistics 13, no. 3, 253-263.

Harvey, A., 1994. Forecasting, structural time series models and the Kalman filter. Cambridge University Press, Cambridge.

Lintner, J., 1965. The valuation of risky assets and the selection of risky investments in the portfolios and capital budgets. Review of Economics and Statistics 47, 13-37.

Ohlson, J., Rosenberg, B., 1982. Systematic risk of the CRSP equal-weighted common stock index: A history estimated by stochastic-parameter regression. Journal of Business 55, no. 1, 121-145.

Sharpe, W., 1964. Capital asset prices: a theory of market equilibrium under conditions of risk. Journal of Finance 19, 425-442.

CHAPTER TWENTY FOUR

NEW RISK ANALYSIS TOOLS IN ACCOUNTING (ADJUSTED Z SCORE)

SEONG CHO AND LIANG FU

Examination of Altman's Z Score

Altman's Z score is widely used to measure the bankruptcy probability. Furthermore, it has a variety of applications in industry practice and academia as a representative credit risk measure. Although there are several variant versions of the equation for the Z score, the industry standard form is calculated based on the financial statements and stock prices as follows:

Z Score Bankruptcy Model:

$$Z = 1.2T_1 + 1.4T_2 + 3.3T_3 + 0.6T_4 + .999T_5$$

where,

T_1 = Working Capital / Total Assets
T_2 = Retained Earnings / Total Assets
T_3 = Earnings Before Interest and Taxes / Total Assets
T_4 = Market Value of Equity / Total Liabilities
T_5 = Sales/ Total Assets

As can be noted in the formula, the Z score is constructed to increase when the liquidity improves, and/or earnings (or sales revenue) increase. Thus, a high Z score means a high level of liquidity and earnings leading to the less chance of bankruptcy. On the other hand, a low Z score is translated into a high probability of bankruptcy. Put In accounting terms, an increase in current assets, earnings, additional sales, or gains are all translated into a higher Z score meaning lower probability of bankruptcy than before.

Changes in Accounting Attributes

While financial statements are a major source of credit analysis or risk assessment like Z score, the attributes of financial statements are going through major changes in recent years. Especially, two distinctive events greatly changed the financial reporting environment; 1) Sarbanes Oxley Act of 2002 (SOX), and 2) International Financial Reporting Standards (IFRS).

First, since the enactment SOX, public accounting firms are under great scrutiny with tightened standard in their application of Generally Accepted Accounting Principles (GAAP) to their clients. Due to the increased audit risk, the new enactments induced CPA firms to react very conservatively in their audit procedure, in turn, not allowing their clients much of room for discretionary decisions. On the other hand, it introduced a great information asymmetry. While prior to SOX, the public eye on the quality of the audit was loose that allowed boosting earnings, during the post SOX era firms have tendency to adjust earnings downwards reflecting conservative auditors' positions. Thus, the new regulatory enactment and firms' reaction to the new regulation distorted accounting numbers.

Next, along with these regulatory changes, the worldwide move of globalization is gradually forming towards harmonized accounting standards of IFRS. One aspect of this harmonization of accounting standard is the principle based accounting that involves fair market value or estimation based accounting, which requires professional judgments. However, this new accounting paradigm has the potential of generating several different sets of financial statements for the same business transaction. Furthermore, due to the collapse of the global financial system in recent years, investors are very sensitive to economic indicators that can easily distort the traditional accounting recording principles. After all, using the conventional Z score using financial statements that do not reflect accounting attributes properly may mislead the creditors or investors. With diversified accounting numbers as a result of using a different set of accounting principles, it has become difficult to maintain homogeneous risk measures. Z score is not an exception to this environment changes, and it deserves an attention to make it useful.

Distortion of Z score

As noted before, the Z score relies on accounting numbers that any accounting recording change causes the distortion in Z while most of the firms are likely to prefer to increase Z score for their capital market incentives. Some examples of accounting change that increases Z score (lowering the probability of bankruptcy) are as follows:

- Increase Sales with Credit
  - Current Ratio Increase

- Underestimation of expenses
  - Earnings and Retained earnings increase

- Equity is overstated for the following reasons:
  - Positive Special Items
  - Deferring the recognition of asset impairment
  - Classify Capital lease as Operating Lease

This kind of financial reporting is quite prevailing among US firms, which is documented in accounting and finance literature. After all, Z score is not comparable across firms and years.

Illustration of distortion of Z score.

To illustrate the distortion of Z score via accounting practice, the case of credit sales increase is illustrated in the following example:

Balance Sheet	**Before Distortion**
Current Asset	10000
Noncurrent Asset	100000
Total Assets	**110000**
Current Liability	10000
Noncurrent Liability	70000
Common Capital	1500
Retained Earnings	6800
Net Income	11700
Total Lib & Equity	**100000**

Income Statement	
Sales	100000
COGS (60%)	-60000
Gross Margin	40000
SGA	-20000
Income Before Interest and Taxes	20000
Interest Expense	-2000
Pretax Income	18000
Tax Expense	-6300
Net Income	11700

In addition, the stock price is $5 per share with 5000 shares outstanding. Based on the above example, Z score will be 1.78 which is translated into the probability of bankruptcy as 22% without any distortion. Suppose the earnings are doubled via relaxed credit criteria for sales activities. Then assuming all other operating margins and other things are equal, the new financial statement (distorted) will be as follows:

Balance Sheet	**After distortion**
Current Asset	50000
Noncurrent Asset	100000
Total Assets	**150000**
Current Liability	24000
Noncurrent Liability	70000
Common Capital	1500
Retained Earnings	6800
Net Income	37700
Total Lib & Equity	**140000**

Income Statement	***After Distortion***
Sales	200000
COGS (60%)	-120000
Gross Margin	80000

SGA	-20000
Income Before Interest and Taxes	60000
Interest Expense	-2000
Pretax Income	58000
Tax Expense	-20300
Net Income	37700

As a result of the distortion by credit sales increase, the Z score increases to 3.02. Thus, corresponding bankruptcy probability becomes 2.2%. While the new increased credit sales significantly lowers the bankruptcy probability, the increased receivables account will ultimately make the business more risky due to the increased uncertainty with the receivable collection. Unless there is an adequate adjustment of Z score to reflect the increased business risk, using the unadjusted Z score without reflecting the traits of financial statements will greatly distort the credit risk ratings.

Adjusted Z score

In practice, we don't know exactly which accounts are affected by the earnings management or various estimation methods of accounts in financial reporting. Thus, it will be almost impossible to adjust Z scores to the ones before distortion. However, prior studies on earnings management provide us with tools to estimate the potential distortion amount in earnings, so called earnings management (EM). Thus, we can use this estimated EM to adjust Z score as close as possible before distortion happened. Since the distortion amount mostly affect earnings number and eventually affecting retained earnings and total assets, the new adjusted Z score, the proposed adjusted Z score equation would look as follows to be used in practice:

Adjusted Z Score Bankruptcy Model:

Adjusted Z score = 1.2 × (Working Capital-EM) / (Total Assets - EM)
+ 1.4 × (Retained Earnings - EM)/ Total Assets - EM)
+ 3.3 × (Earnings Before Interest and Taxes - EM)/ Total Assets - EM)
+ 0.6 × Market Value of Equity / Total Liabilities
+ .999 × (Sales - EM)/ Total Assets - EM),
where EM is the estimated distortion amount.

As noted in the formula, considering the fact that most of firms record return on assets less than 100%, it is likely that Z scores are to be reduced when earnings increase portion is adjusted. This means that the firms distorting accounting numbers upwards are likely bias their Z score upwards. As a result, many of potential bankrupt firms are hidden from the sight of creditors or investors by sending wrong information of lower bankruptcy probability than reality. The adjusted Z score model will improve to adjust for this kind of distortions and improve the usefulness of Z score.

Discussion and comments from 1st Credit Risk Conference (July 21st ~23rd, 2011):

- Providing the background for the earnings management would help to assess the risk
- More rigorous investigation of earnings management estimation would increase the usefulness of the new model (e.g. tools for types of accruals, real operations of management)
- After all, Earnings Management is an endogenous behavior, management's choice.
- Managers have enough information about the future. So, it might be difficult to attribute all the distortions
- Some Earnings Management may reflect the reality closer than non managed accounting numbers
- Finally, what is the economic consequence of distorting Z score? Do we really need to adjust? Is it really bad?

CHAPTER TWENTY FIVE

REVISITING THE ALTMAN DEFINITION OF DISTRESSED DEBT AND A NEW MECHANISM FOR MEASURING THE LIQUIDITY PREMIUM OF THE HIGH YIELD MARKET[1]

JOSÉ F. GONZÁLEZ-HERES, PING CHEN AND STEVEN S. SHIN[2]

Twenty years after the Altman definition of distressed debt was first published, we find strong empirical evidence supporting the definition's efficacy over long periods of time. After analyzing 9,838 bond issues on an out-of-sample basis over the period of 1990-2009, we find that constituents of the Merrill Lynch High Yield Master II index trading at risk premiums, over comparable US treasuries, in excess of 1,000bp, experienced a long-term average default rate between 48% and 51% – as postulated by Altman in 1990. Furthermore, we find that the relationship between the two Altman definitional components, risk premium-threshold (1,000bp) and default rate (50%), shows that the incremental default rate for each additional unit of premium-threshold stabilizes at the intersection of the 960-1,140bp premium-threshold and at the long-term average default rate of 48% to 51%. We therefore conclude that the Altman

---

[2] José F. González-Heres is a portfolio manager for the Fund of Hedge Funds portfolios at Morgan Stanley Alternative Investment Partners and a member of its Investment Committee in West Conshohocken, PA. jose.gonzalez-heres@morganstanley.com Ping Chen, Ph.D. is a research analyst for the Fund of Hedge Funds portfolios at Morgan Stanley Alternative Investment Partners in West Conshohocken, PA. p.chen@morganstanley.com Steven S. Shin, CPA, CFA is a research analyst for the Fund of Hedge Funds portfolios for Morgan Stanley Alternative Investment Partners in West Conshohocken, PA. steven.shin@morganstanley.com

definition has been highly effective at characterizing distressed debt over long periods of time.

Additionally, we introduce precision to the time-to-default dimension of the Altman definition, which had been silent on this point. For distressed securities that ultimately default, the median time-to-default is observed to be 14 months, with 90% of the population defaulting within 46 months. We also find that a differentiating factor between distressed securities that eventually defaulted, versus those that did not default, is higher OAS volatility characteristics of the former.

Equally important, we find that the Altman definition does not hold over short periods of time due to the distortive effects of liquidity on default rates. However, we find that this phenomenon can be temporarily adjusted using a bootstrap method that controls for the default rate component of the Altman definition while varying the risk premium-threshold component. The resultant adjustment is defined as the High Yield Liquidity Premium, which is associated with liquidity factors based on cluster analysis. This method provides a practical approach to discern the liquidity premium embedded in the OAS of the high yield market. We have found that there has been ongoing research regarding bond market liquidity since 1959, with varying degrees of scope and applicability. For example, Fisher [1959] argued that the liquidity of corporate bonds is related to their "marketability", which is proportional to the market value of the outstanding bond issue. Fleming [2003] finds that the bid-ask spread of U.S. treasury securities is useful in measuring liquidity because of the high transparency and high trading volume. However, Mahanti et. al. [2008] argue that for illiquid markets (corporate bonds), due to the lack of sufficient transaction information and the frequency thereof, they propose the use of the ownership of securities to discern their accessibility by a dealer, as a proxy for liquidity. Friewald, et. al. [2010] find speculative grade bonds to have lower liquidity and increased sensitivity to changes in liquidity as compared to investment grade bonds.

The High Yield Liquidity Premium exhibits high variability, with negative values corresponding to excess liquidity, and positive values reflecting illiquidity, in the high yield market. Over each of the past two cycles, the average High Yield Liquidity Premium has been near zero (-15bp), indicating that liquidity equilibrium is reached over the course of full cycles despite interim imbalances (+587bp as of December 2009). Because the High Yield Liquidity Premium is only observable after a considerable time lag, due to the time-to-default characteristics of distressed debt, we use cluster analysis techniques to discern an observable market proxy (AAA corporate credit spreads). Finally, we add practicality to the analysis by introducing a Stochastic Beta regression model that adjusts the Altman premium-threshold definitional component for concurrent liquidity conditions.

This finding leads to further decomposition of the high yield Index OAS, beyond the liquidity factor, into an additional credit component (Residual Credit Premium) that is derived from the total high yield OAS, after subtracting the liquidity factor (High Yield Liquidity Premium). Interestingly, the Residual Credit Premium is estimated to be relatively stable, and positive (average of +507bp), over the past 20-year period, which may reflect a consistent perception of the fundamental creditworthiness of high yield bonds by investors and rating agencies when adjusting for contemporaneous liquidity conditions.

Finally, we conclude with the general observation that liquidity appears to be the dominant factor explaining the variability of the OAS for high yield securities. It is also importantly related to the default rate characteristics of distressed securities.

References

Fisher, Lawrence. "Determinants of Risk Premiums on Corporate Bonds", *The Journal of Political Economy,* Vol. 67. (1959), p. 217

Fleming, Michael J. "Measuring Treasury Market Liquidity", *Economic Policy Review,* Vol. 9, No. 3, (2003), pp. 83-108

Mahanti, Sriketan, Amrut Nashikkar, Marti Subrahmanyam, George Chacko, and Gaurav Mallik, "Latent Liquidity: A new measure of liquidity, with an application to corporate bonds", *Journal of Financial Economics,* Vol. 88, No. 2, (May, 2008), pp. 272-298

Friewald, Nils, Rainer Jankowitsch, and Marti G. Subrahmanyam, "Illiquidity or Credit Deterioration: A Study of Liquidity in the US Corporate Bond Market during Financial Crises", *Working Paper, Vienna University of Economics and Business, New York University Stern School of Business*, (2010).

CHAPTER TWENTY SIX

VALUATION OF CORPORATE LOANS UNDER RISK NEUTRAL MEASURE

TERRY BENZSCHAWEL[1]

Abstract

Most loans trade infrequently and methods for discounting loan cash flows typically ignore effects of default and the option for early prepayment. This report presents a model for pricing corporate term loans and revolving credit lines within the risk-neutral framework. Importantly, the model accounts for credit- and market-related term loan prepayments and for drawdown and repayment of revolving credit lines. The method models the credit-spread dependent prepayment option using a lattice of risk-neutral credit transitions determined from historical data and modified to be consistent with market prices of credit default swaps. The model provides estimates of the average lives of loans, average times to default, and generates loan price sensitivities to relevant market movements. Finally, the model values revolving lines of credit using data on historical average usage patterns and their dependence on credit quality.

1. Introduction

Relatively few corporate loans trade frequently in the secondary market and most of these are *leveraged loans* (i.e., from creditors with credit ratings below investment grade). The illiquidity in the secondary loan market makes it difficult to discover meaningful prices for most loans and belies the need for a model that generates prices consistent with the market

[1] The author is from Citi Institutional Clients Group, New York, NY, USA. Email: terry.l.benzschawel@citi.com

values for traded loans. There are thousands of corporate loans outstanding. The left panel of

Figure 1 shows that loans with reported prices have been increasing dramatically over the past few years, rising from about 2,000 per day in 2003 to over 6,000 prices daily in 2008. However, less than several hundred of those loans trade on any given day and, as shown in the middle panel of

Figure 1, quotes on traded loans are usually available from only one dealer. In fact, the right panel of Figure 1 indicates that over half of the prices reported on those loans do not change over any given month and only about 3% (approximately 200 out of 6,000) have more than ten price changes in any given month.

A model for loan valuation is presented below that prices term loans and revolving credit lines. The model generates prices and credit spreads for illiquid loans as implied from bond prices and credit default swap spreads. It also values the credit-state-dependent loan prepayment option and incorporates information from credit dependent pricing grids and usage patterns. The model outputs a variety of risk measures including expected default times, losses due to default, sensitivities to changes in loan prices due to changes in credit risk premiums, and changes in recovery values in default. Finally the model calculates implied changes in portfolio values and expected losses in response to market moves.

The model is currently used for implementation of FAS 159, the "Fair Value Option" on loan portfolios, determining market-implied spreads for new loan origination, and implementation of FAS 107 for quarterly mark-to-market of loan portfolios for publicly traded firms. Other successful applications include calculating margin requirements and risk for counterparty credit exposure, providing pricing and risk measures for a broker/dealer's global portfolio, and proprietary trading of corporate loans.

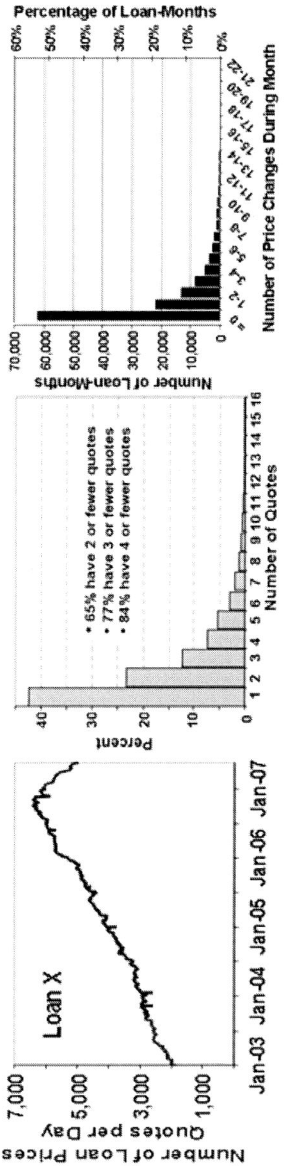

Figure 1. Left: Number of loans with daily price quotes. Middle: Number of dealer quotes on each loan. Right: Number of price changes for loans in any 30-Day period.

2. Credit Spreads for Loans

Like bonds, loans are coupon paying instruments and contain risk of default whereby an obligor may fail to make timely payments of interest and/or principal. However, loans differ from bonds in several important respects. That is, loans are private agreements, not securities; loans are typically floating rate instruments paying quarterly premiums with little interest rate risk, while bonds typically have fixed semi-annual payments; loans are often collateralized or contain restrictive covenants; and loans are prepayable at par.

The loan analogue to the bond spread, called the loan's credit *spread-to-LIBOR* has been used to characterize the riskiness of loans, where the credit spread, s, over LIBOR is calculated as:

$$V = \sum_{i=1}^{4n} \frac{c_t/4}{\left(1+\frac{r_t+s}{4}\right)^i} + \frac{F}{\left(1+\frac{r_{4n}+s}{4}\right)^{4n}} \,, \tag{1}$$

where V is the market value of the loan, c_t is the coupon (LIBOR + contractual spread), r_t is the spot LIBOR rate for maturity t, and F is the face value of the loan to be repaid at maturity. Loan coupons are generally paid quarterly and then reset relative to the prevailing three-month LIBOR rate and this is reflected in Equation 1. Using Equation 1, one can calculate a credit spread for any loan whose market price is known, or conversely, if given a spread, one can derive a price quote.

One problem using Equation 1 for loan valuation is that it fails to account for the fact that loans, unlike the majority of bonds, are typically prepayable at par on any given coupon date. As shown in Figure 2, if a firm's credit improves or the prevailing loan rate over LIBOR decreases, the likelihood of prepayment increases; the borrower can refinance at a lower rate. Conversely, if a borrower's credit deteriorates or lending rates increase, it will not be advantageous for the borrower to refinance. The loan prepayment option increases the uncertainty regarding the expected receipt of cash flows and complicates comparisons of relative value among loans based on their credit spreads. Unfortunately, pricing the prepayment option has proved difficult due to its dependence on the evolution of an obligor's credit state and the changing market costs of borrowing.

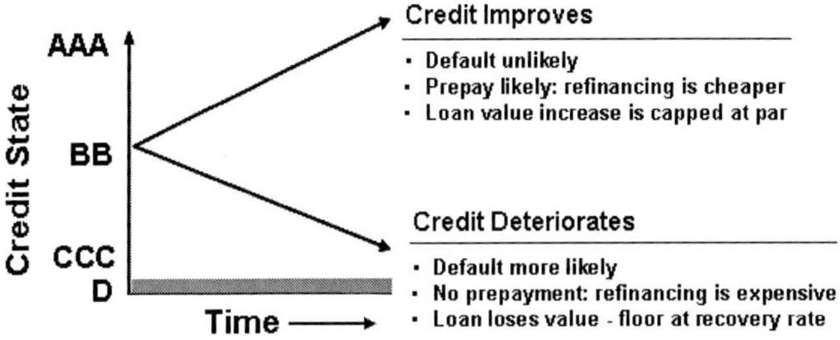

Figure 2. The credit state dependence of the loan prepayment option.

3. Loan Pricing via Backward Induction

To account for the effects of default and the credit-state dependence of loan prepayments and revolving credit line usage, loans are priced by backward induction on a lattice of credit rating versus time as shown in Figure 3. The figure provides an example of a five-year term loan issued to a double-B rated obligor with a coupon of LIBOR+200bp and an assumed recovery value in default of 75%. This example is used to illustrate the construction of the lattice and the pricing of a loan. Although the lattice shown has annual time steps, for actual pricing, the nodes of the lattice are constructed at quarterly time intervals.

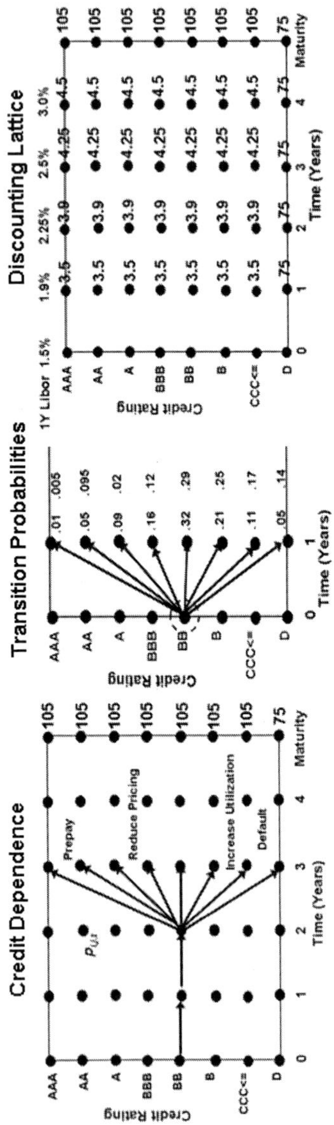

Figure 3. Diagrams of lattices of credit ratings versus time used for pricing loans. Left: Credit-dependence of prepayment decision. Middle: Assignment of physical and risk-neutral default probabilities. Right: Assignment of nominal cash flows to pricing matrix.

3.1 Assign Cash Flows, Transition Probabilities and Discount Rates to the Pricing Lattice

The left panel of Figure 3 illustrates again the influence of credit state on loan prepayment. As credit state increases, the obligor will likely prepay the loan. The middle panel of the figure shows how transition probabilities are assigned when given an obligor's initial credit state, in this case double-B. The left-most set of probabilities are from historical ratings transitions and the right set of probabilities are risk-neutral probabilities derived from daily credit default swap (CDS) premiums.[2] The transformation from physical to risk-neutral default probabilities are calculated from CDS spreads using a method described by Jarrow, Lando and Turnbull (1997). The right portion of Figure 3 demonstrates how nominal cash flows are assigned to the lattice. Forward LIBOR rates appear at the top and at each annual time step in the lattice and when added with the 200bp premium produce the cash flows assigned in the diagram. Notice that in default, an absorbing state in the lattice, the cash flow is the recovery value of 75 and that at maturity, the loan pays the principal plus the coupon.

3.2 Value the Loan Using Backward Induction

The backward induction method described in this section is designed to work with any risk-neutral credit state transition matrix. Recall that the reason for pricing loans using the backward induction method is to account for the obligor's credit-state and risk-premium dependent prepayment option as well as firms' options to draw on credit lines of revolving loans.[3] The methods used to price term loans are a core component of the model for pricing variations on term loans such as revolving credit lines, letters of credit, and amortizing loans. Those structures are considered separately.

---

[2] We use historical ratings transitions from Standard & Poor's (Vazza, Aurora, Kraemer, Kesh, Torres and Erturk, 2007) in our actual pricing lattice. CDS premiums are obtained from market quotes by traders at Citi's Institutional Clients Group and/or form Markit Partners, LTD.

[3] Several versions of the backward induction method have been proposed over the years. (See, for example, Rizk 1993, Bohn (2000), and Wen and Zeng, 2005) The version presented herein embodies elements that are common to most of these methodologies

Figure 4 illustrates pricing the term loan. The pricing lattice illustrates the important features of the model. Risk-neutral ratings (and default) transitions are first propagated forward from the pricing date to loan maturity and the cash flows are propagated backward as sums of state probability-weighted cashflows discounted one period at forward LIBOR. The left portion of the lattice in Figure 4 from *t=0* to *t=2* shows how the obligor's credit state evolves over time. In the lattice, probabilities are assigned reflecting risk-neutral ratings transitions between each node at time *t* to all nodes at *t+1*. Thus, the probability of being at a given node will be conditional upon all the previous transitions. As discussed in detail we use ratings transition probabilities based the Jarrow, Lando and Turnbull (JLT) method applied to historical data from credit rating agencies modified by the credit spreads from the CDS and LDS markets.

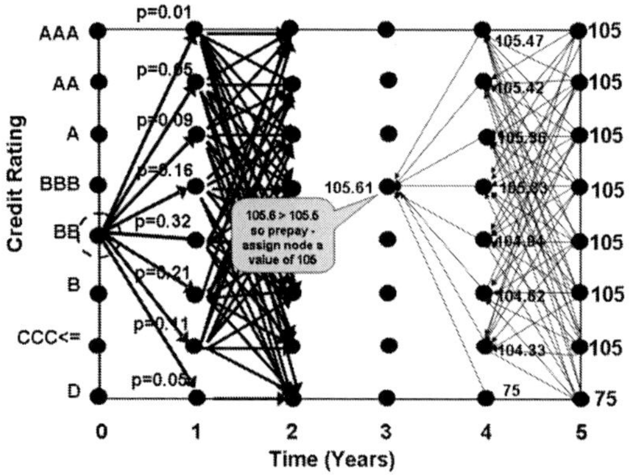

Figure 4. Loan pricing method showing forward propagation of risk-neutral ratings transitions and backward propagation of price values from maturity. The example is for a double-B rated obligor with loan parameters as described in the text. Calculation of node values uses backward induction, whereby values at each non-defaulted node are the coupon value at that node plus the sum of the conditional cashflows from the later date discounted one period at forward LIBOR. A refinancing penalty of 0.5% of the principal is assumed.

In the model, the decision to prepay the loan is evaluated at each node in the lattice, working back from maturity. At each node the discounted value of the future cashflows (i.e., the node value) is compared with the cost of prepayment. If the cost of holding the loan is higher than prepaying, then the principal of the loan is prepaid along with the coupon due at that node. Figure 4 illustrates the prepay decision process in which node values for the sample loan are shown for *T* and *T-1* and a single node at *T-2*. For the loan, the cost of prepayment is the par value of 100 plus the coupon (*L+2%=5%*) plus a 0.5 prepayment penalty.[4] The diagram shows that values for all nodes at *T-1* are less than the 105.5 economic value of prepayment, so there is no refinancing at that time and all node values are unaltered. However, at *T-2* years, the node value for the double-B credit state is 105.61, exceeding the refinance value. In that case, the value of 105.61 at that node is replaced by 105.0 for subsequent discounting back to the pricing date.

3.3 Mathematical Formulation

Having provided the intuition that underlies the loan pricer, a more formal description of the model is provided. Recall that we use obligor credit-state dependent risk-neutral ratings transitions calculated using the JLT method to assign probabilities of transitioning among nodes in the pricing lattice. The backward induction method is then applied as illustrated in Figure 4. At the maturity *T* of the loan, the borrower pays the principal plus coupon, $F + c_i$, or the recovery value in default, $F*R$. Those probability-weighted cashflows are discounted back to each node at the previous period, in this case *T-1* using forward LIBOR at *T-1*. That is, for each node at time $i<T$ and non-default credit state *j* (i.e., *AAA.AA+. … . CCC*) an value, $v_{i,j}$ is calculated as

$$v_{i,j} = \min\left\{\left(\frac{1}{(1+\frac{f_{i+1,i}}{4})}\sum_{k=D}^{AAA}(P_{j,k,i} * v_{i+1,k})\right) + c_i, K_i\right\} , \tag{2}$$

where $P_{i,k,j}$ is the probability of migrating from state *j* to state *k* from *i* to *i+1*, f_i is the forward LIBOR rate from time *i* to *i+1*, K_i is the terminal value of the loan at time *i*, and $v_{T,j} = F+c_T$. Thus, at each node *i,j* we compute the induced value, compare it with the terminal value, K_i and set the value at that node, $v_{i,j}$ to the lesser of the two. That is, if the induced value exceeds the terminal value, the loan is effectively repaid and terminates. Also, if the loan defaults at time step *i* the loan terminates with

[4] The 0.5 point prepayment penalty was suggested by traders on Citi's loan trading desk for loans having no pre-specified penalty, reflecting frictions involved in the prepayment process.

a value $v_{i,D}=F*R$ for all remaining i. Finally, the value of $v_{i,j}$ at time $t=0$ (in this example, at $v_{0,BB}$) is the model price of the loan.

Although Equation 2 is useful for calculating prices of illiquid loans and for estimating the coupon premiums to charge for new loans, it is less useful for evaluating relative value among existing loans. That is, relative value among fixed income instruments is typically better assessed using a credit spread measure. In fact, the credit spread for a loan can be calculated by discounting its expected non-default cashflows by a constant amount over the LIBOR curve such that the discounted value matches its current market price. For all non-default cashflows at a given time, the borrower will either prepay the principal and terminate, or pay a coupon and continue. The prepayment region in the time and-credit-state lattice can be determined using the values of $v_{i,j}$ in Equation 2. The probability of prepaying at period i is the sum of the probabilities of reaching nodes whose values of $v_{i,j}$ equal those capped at the terminal values K_i. Given the probability transition matrix and the set π of all prepayment nodes we can calculate the probability of prepayment at time i conditional on no previous prepayment.

Let the conditional probability of prepayment at time i be denoted q_i. The likelihood of prepayment at time $i=1$ from initial state j is

$$q_1 = \sum_{k \in \pi} P_{j,K,0} \quad , \tag{3}$$

For all times $i>1$ we must add the condition that the loan did not prepay before time i. Thus,

$$q_{\mathrm{i}} = \prod_{m=1}^{i-1} (1 - q_m) * \sum_{k \in \pi, l \notin \pi} P_{l,k,i-1} \quad , \tag{4}$$

Then the value of the discounted cash flows is given by

$$Vj = \sum_{i=1}^{T} D_i * \prod_{j=1}^{i-1} \left(1 - q_j\right) * \left[\left(q_i * K_i\right) + \left(\left(1 - q_i\right) * CF_i\right) \right] \quad , \tag{5}$$

where $CF_i=c/4$ for $i<T$; $CF_i=(c/4 + F)$ for $i=T$, and the discount margin D_i is given by

$$D_i = \prod_{j=0}^{i} \frac{1}{\left(1 + \frac{f_{j,j-1} + \hat{s}}{4}\right)} \quad , \tag{6}$$

The credit spread s is determined by iteratively changing the parameter $\hat{s}$ and recalculating the discounted value of the cashflows, V_j, until V_j converges to P, the market price.

4. Amortizing Loans

Many loan contracts have scheduled payments of principal prior to the maturity of the loan. To accommodate this, let **A** be a vector of amortization values, where each value corresponds to a time step in the lattice pricing. For example, for the term loan in Figure 4, **A** = (0, 0, 0, 0, 1.0), indicating no amortization payments prior to maturity. Consider the amortization schedule for the loan that is scheduled to pay down 10% of the original principal each year and the remainder at its five-year maturity. In this case, **A** = (0.1, 0.1, 0.1, 0.1, 0.6) and the payment at each annual coupon date prior to maturity is 10% plus the nominal coupon. Note that the amount of the coupon as well as the amount recovered in default decreases with decreases in the principal outstanding. The outstanding principal F at any time step t prior to maturity T can be specified by assigning a time dependence to F such that

$$F_t = \sum_{k=t+1}^{T} A_k \quad for\ t < T \quad , \tag{7}$$

and the amount of face value to be added to the coupon at any given scheduled amortization date is F_r - $F_{t-1.}$ As for term loans, the obligor will prepay the entire principal when economically appropriate and this is assessed in the backward induction algorithm as described above.

5. Valuing a Term Loan

The loan pricing processes is demonstrated by using the model to value an actual term loan. Although not identified by name, the actual terms of the loan and the firm's associated market data are real and appear in Figure 5. The loan was rated as single-B and had a five-year LCDS trading at a spread of 780bp. The actual loan had a nominal coupon of L+375bp, 3.2

years remaining until maturity, and a 0.50 point penalty for early repayment of principal. Finally, the recovery value in default assumed for pricing is 70% of face value.

Input Data	
Firm:	XYZ
Rating:	B
Market Price:	96.06
Coupon:	L+375bp
Maturity:	3.2 Yrs
Coupons/Yr:	4
Recovery Rate:	70%
Prepay Cost:	0.50
LCDS 5Y:	780bp

Model Output	
Price:	94.67
No Prepay Price:	94.75
Loan Spread:	534bp
Prepay Value:	0.073
Prepay Spread Value:	2.8bp
Effective Duration:	2.3 Yrs
Effect of Default:	0.5 Yrs
Effect of Prepayment:	0.1 Yrs

Figure 5. Left: Main model inputs and indicative data; and Right: Model summary output.

The risk-neutral ratings transition matrix computed to accommodate the 780bp LCDS spread and the lattice was populated with risk-neutral transition probabilities and expected nominal cash flows for default and non-default states. The backward induction method was then applied and the model price was computed. In addition, the effective duration of the loan, the value of the prepayment option we also calculated and these appear in the right portion of Figure 5. The most fundamental output is the loan price; 94.67 in this example. The pricer also calculates the loan price with no prepayment option. That value is 94.75, just 0.7 above the price with prepayment, demonstrating the small value of the prepay option (only 2.8bp of credit spread) given the large discount of the current loan price to par. Also of interest is the option-adjusted spread to LIBOR of the loan, which is now calculable given the pattern of coupon payments output from the pricing lattice. Even though the sample loan has a coupon of L+375bp, its option adjusted spread is 534bp. The model also outputs the effective duration, in this case 2.8 years, and the shortening effects of prepayment and default on the duration of the loan. Finally, the model generates an expected time to principal (ignoring default), which indicated when the principal is likely to be repaid given the prepayment option. Due to the small value of prepayment for this loan, the expected time of principal repayment is 3.1 years, just slightly shorter than the 3.2 year maturity of the loan.

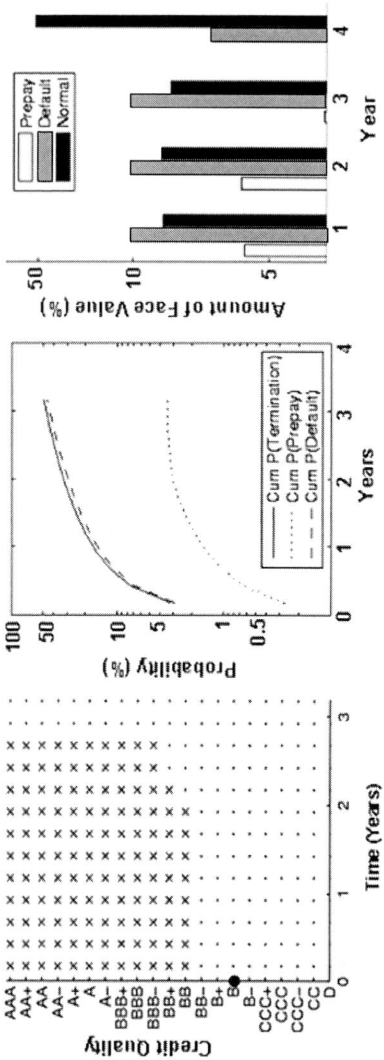

Figure 6. Analysis of cash flows from loan pricing model. Left: "Xs" indicate nodes at which B-rated credit will prepay principal at par; Middle: Probabilities of loan termination by default and prepayment as well as total termination by year; Right: Relative sources of expected cash flows form default, prepayment and nominal flows (coupons and principal).

The model also outputs a detailed analysis of the cash flows from the loan that result from default, prepayment and nominal coupons and principal payments. Examples of those appear in Figure 6. The left panel of the figure displays nodes from the model's pricing grid in which X's on those nodes indicate points at which the model calculated a prepayment of principal and to which the terminal value of the loan (coupon plus principal) is assigned. The middle panel of Figure 6 displays the likelihood of terminations of the loan from the present date to maturity (solid line) and, for termination prior to maturity, contributions from its component factors of prepayment (dashes) or default (dots). The probability axis of the graph is in logarithmic units, enabling display of the relatively small contribution from prepayment to loan termination. The figure demonstrates that most of the termination of the loan prior to maturity is the result of default. The model also outputs an analysis of the fraction of the cash flows from the loan that result from default, prepayment and nominal coupons and principal payments and those appear in the right panel of the figure. That is, each bar in the right panel of Figure 6 is the probability-weighted size of the expected cash flows from default, prepayment or coupons and principal. For example, the likelihood of the loan going to maturity and paying the principal and coupon is roughly 50% of the sum of the expected cash flows from all sources.

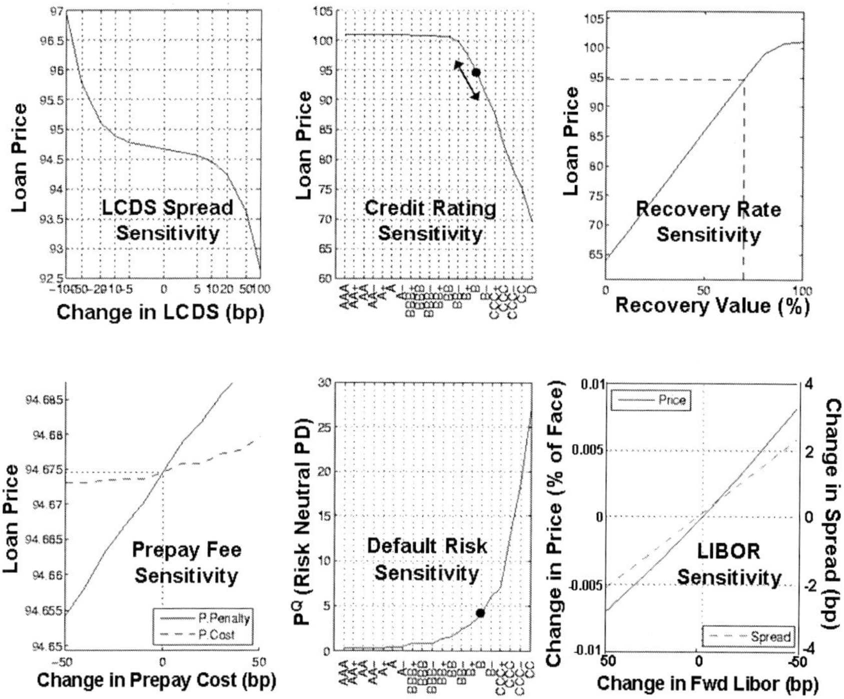

Figure 7. Sensitivity dashboard for various parameters from the loan pricing model.

The model outputs numerical values of loan price sensitivities to changes in various market parameters and some profit and loss related quantities. These include:

- **CS01:** The price sensitivity to a 1bp change in credit risk. This is calculated by bumping the firm's credit curve up and down by 1bp and taking the average difference in price.
- **RV01:** The recovery value sensitivity is the expected change in price due to a 1% change in the assumed recovery rate in default.
- **ETP:** Expected time to prepayment is calculated by comparing the coupon with the credit curve and is the point at which prepayment probability is 50%. This could be longer than the term of the loan.

- **ETD:** The expected time to default is calculated using the issuer's credit curve and is the point at which the cumulative default probability is 50%. This also could be longer than the loan's maturity.
- **Credit Beta:** Measures historical the co-movement in the loan price with respect to moves in the loan CDS index.
- **dV01:** Loan price change for a 1bp change in LIBOR (small for floating rate loans).
- **Daily P/L:** Estimates daily changes in loan P/L based on market moves and their effects on these and other factors.

The model also outputs charts that illustrate those sensitivities, some of which appear in Figure 7. The left hand graph in the top row of shows sensitivity to the calibration parameter, the LCDS spread, on the price of the loan whereas the middle and right panels of the top row show how credit ratings and recovery rate affect loan price. The graphs in the lower row of Figure 7 show how changes in prepayment fee (left panel), initial credit state (middle) and LIBOR (right panel) affect prices from the model for the sample credit.

6. Model Calibration and Pricing Revolving Credit Lines

The model is also able to value revolving credit lines as a combination of a term loan and a commitment. Space limitations prohibit a full description of the model for revolving credit lines, but some features of the approach are described in this section. Issues regarding calibration of the model to market prices and accounting for the influence of the cash versus CDS basis are also discussed.

6.1 Incorporating Loan Funding Costs and Partially Drawn Lines of Credit

The effects of financing costs on cash loans are not accounted for in models using only CDS levels for discounting loan cash flows. Funding costs are reflected in the CDS versus cash basis and these can be large as shown in the left panel of Figure 8**Error! Reference source not found.**. The loan pricer estimates funding costs daily as the median CDS versus cash basis of the investment grade CDS index (CDX.IG.NA) constituents. This financing cost is added to the forward LIBOR rate used to discount the amount of the loan.

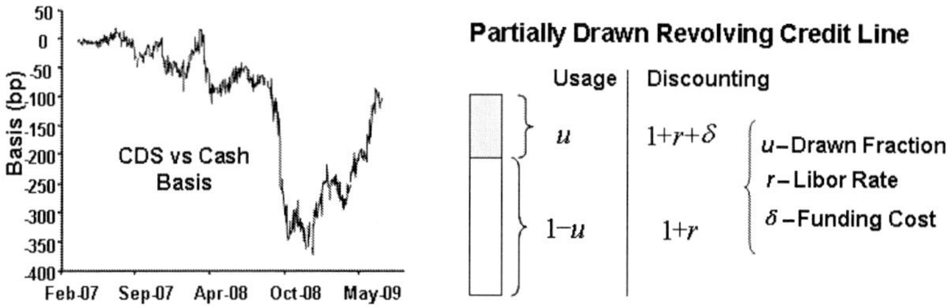

Figure 8. Left: The CDS minus cash credit spread basis. Right: Illustration of a partially drawn credit revolving credit line with discounting differences between drawn and undrawn portions.

Revolving credit lines are unfunded or partially funded commitments by lenders that can be drawn at the discretion of the borrowers. The revolving facility can be likened to a corporate credit card as it can be drawn upon and repaid multiple times during its term. Funding costs also affect differentially drawn and undrawn portions of revolving credit lines. To value revolving loans, the model splits the obligation into two parts: a drawn fraction u and undrawn fraction $1-u$ as shown in the in the right panel of Figure 8. The drawn amount, u, is treated as a fully-funded term loan as described above and is discounted at Libor plus funding cost, whereas the undrawn amount $(1-u)$ is discounted at LIBOR. There are other fees associated with revolving credit lines (not shown) and these are also accounted for within the model.

Like term loans, revolving credit lines have credit dependent features and these have been incorporated into the valuation methodology. These include pricing grids for drawn and undrawn amounts and credit-state-dependent usage of revolving credit lines. For example, the left panel of Figure 9 depicts a typical credit rating dependent fee schedule for the undrawn portion of a revolving loan and a schedule of spreads to LIBOR for the drawn portion of the commitment. Notice that the coupon spread is dependent on the amount drawn, being lower for smaller drawn amounts. The middle panel of Figure 9 depicts a similar schedule, but one in which the fees are determined based on the firm's CDS premium. For CDS spread-based fees, usage is converted to a CDS-implied rating.

Credit Rating	Undrawn Fee (bp)	Drawn Fee (bp)	
		<= 50%	> 50%
AAA	50	100	130
AA	50	120	156
A	50	140	182
BBB	70	170	221
BB	70	200	260
B	70	220	286

CDS Spread (bp)	Fee (bp) Undrawn	Fee (bp) Drawn	Implied Credit Rating
<200	50	200	BB+ and Higher
<400	50	CDS quote	BB- to B+
>=400	50	400	B- and Lower

Mapping of Daily CDS to Rating

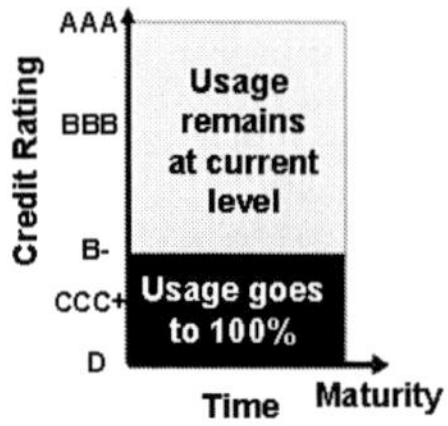

Figure 9. Left: Ratings based schedule of fees for undrawn and drawn portions of revolving loans. Middle: Fee schedule and conversion chart for CDS based fees. Right: Assumed credit dependency for usage of revolving credit lines.

The right panel of Figure 9 depicts an assumed pattern of usage for a revolving loan. That is, for all credit states above triple-C-plus, the usage remain as the current drawn amount, whereas, when credit dips below single-B-minus, it is assumed that the entire amount of the commitment is drawn. In practice, the model is sufficiently flexible that pricing grids and usage parameters can be specified for individual loans.

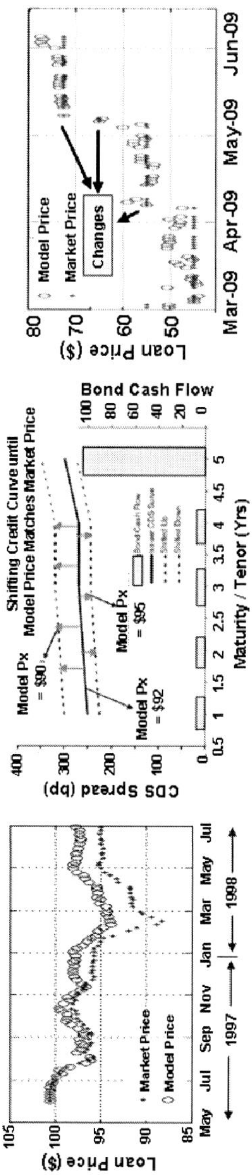

Figure 10. Left: Market prices for a liquid loan and model prices calibrated to the obligor' CDS curve diverge over time. Middle: Adjustment of obligor credit curves to match loan price. Right: Model price extrapolation and re-calibration in response to changes in price quotes.

6.2 Model Calibration

We observed that model and market prices can deviate over time. In addition, despite calibration of loan discount rates to CDS premiums and accounting for the CDS versus cash basis, observed market prices can deviate from model prices. For example, the left panel of Figure 10 shows market prices and model values for a liquidly traded loan. Although congruent for several months, they begin to deviate consistently. Since one objective of the model is to provide loan prices that would be similar to market prices if available, the model is calibrated daily using both the current CDS curves and prices of loans traded that day. The credit curve adjustment for liquid loans is then applied to adjust credit curves of illiquid loans. To do this, the loan prices are calibrated to match the market prices by adjusting credit curves (probability of default) upward or downward to match the traded price as depicted in the middle of Figure 10. Possible interpretations of the need for calibration even after accounting for the CDS versus cash bond basis are funding cost, liquidity premium and model error.

The right panel of Figure 10 shows market prices for an illiquid loan which changes infrequently and the extrapolated prices from the model. At each observed price change the model is recalibrated such that the price matches the quoted price. That calibration factor is maintained as an adjustment until the next change in quoted market price.

6.3 Comparing Risk-Neutral Pricing to Floating Rate Bond Model

Recall that in the yield to maturity (YTM) loan valuation method in Equation 1, a loan is modeled as a risk free floating rate bond. The YTM method is typically used to calculate loan sensitivities to credit rates, whereby the method requires as input a loan price, the expected cash flows of the loan, and a LIBOR curve. The YTM method discounts expected cash flows by solving for the yield spread, *s*, which matches the loan price. The YTM method does not consider default risk level or recovery rate in default. To account for the possibility of prepayment, users of the YTM often decrease the nominal maturity of the loan when pricing and for risk management purposes. A common assumption for a variant of the YTM method is a standard three-year prepayment and this model is designated $\text{YTM}_{3\text{Yr}}$, whereas YTM signifies the calculation with nominal maturity.

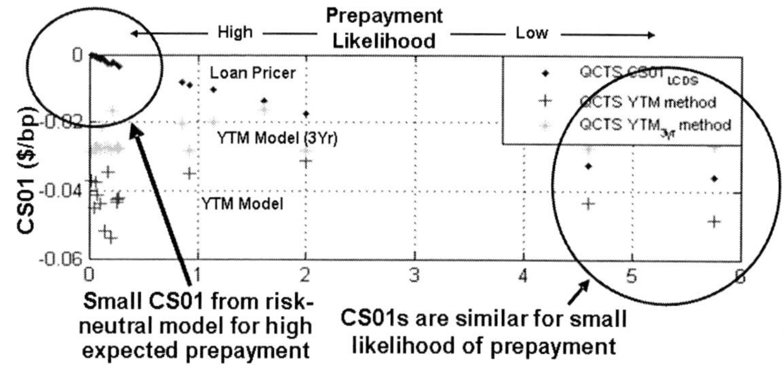

Figure 11. The effect of expected time to prepayment on CS01s from the risk-neutral loan prices and two versions of the YTM model. The symbols at the top are from the risk-neutral loan pricer; those in the middle are from the YTM_{3Yr} model and those at the bottom from the YTM model. The x-axis is

The models were compared with the risk-neutral loan pricer in calculating CS01s for loans as a function of prepayment likelihood. Expected times to 50% prepayment probability were calculated using risk-neutral loan pricer for a set of loans and CS01s were plotted from the that model and the YTM models in Figure 11. The x-axis is the expected time to 50% prepayment from the risk-neutral pricing model. The diamonds are from the risk neutral model and the light crosses from YTM_{3Yr} and dark crosses from the YTM model. The plots demonstrate that a major determinant of CS01 is the loan's effective duration. For the risk-neutral pricing model, the sooner the expected prepayment, the smaller the effect of a 1bp change in the credit curve. Contrary to expectations regarding prepayment and CS01s, CS01s from both versions of the YTM pricer are relatively insensitive to prepayment. However, the fact that CS01s from all models converge as prepayment likelihood decreases is as expected.

References

Bohn, J. (2000). A Survey of Contingent-Claims Approaches to Risky Debt Valuation, *The Journal of Risk Finance,* pp. 53-70, Spring 2000.

Jarrow, R., Lando, D. and Turnbull, S. (1997). A Markov Model for the Term Structure of Credit Spreads, *The Review of Financial Studies, 10 (2),* pp. 481-523.

Rizk, H. (1993). GMPM Valuation Methodology: An Overview, Citi Markets and Banking.

Vazza, D., Aurora, D., Kraemer, N., Kesh, S., Torres, J. and Erturk, E. (2007). Annual 2006 Global Corporate Default Study and Ratings Transitions, Standard and Poor's, January.

Wen, K. and Zeng, B. (2005). CreditMark Valuation Methodology, Moody's Investors' Service, December 24.

CHAPTER TWENTY SEVEN

RECOVERY RATES MODELING

ABDOLREZA NAZEMI,
MARKUS HÖCHSTÖTTER,
AND SVETLOZAR T. RACHEV[1]

Introduction

As of today, we can still feel the impact of the crisis that started in 2007. To grasp its exact taxation of the corporate world, we recommend consulting [30]. The figures are dramatic: the annual numbers of default as well as the average amount of debt outstanding between 2007 and 2011 have almost tripled compared to the period between 1981 and 2006. But the impact has not only been felt across the corporate and sovereign world but also on the consumer side as many employees were laid off by tilting or at least insecure employers. This was exacerbated by an additional lending freeze by commercial banks. The current situation brings into memory the world financial crisis of 1929 and the great depression afterwards. So far, governments and central banks have responded by bailing out large corporations as well as enforcing the rights of individual borrowers, and imposing harsh regulation on the financial industry.

To prevent something of this sort in the future, one has to design devises that could prevent distress in certain areas and industries from arising or at least spreading. The danger of crises has generally grown according to [31]. But in addition to crises alone, the condition has

[1] Abdolreza Nazemi and Markus Höchstötter are from Statistics, Econometrics and Mathematical Finance at the School of Economics and Business Engineering, Karlsruhe Institute of Technology, Germany. Svetlozar T. Rachev is from Department of Applied Mathematics at Stony Brook University in New York and Statistics, Econometrics and Mathematical Finance at the School of Economics and Business Engineering, Karlsruhe Institute of Technology, Germany.

worsened by a breath-taking growth in debt both sovereign as well as corporate or personal which will amplify any arising shock to the financial industry compared to previous periods. For the USA alone, the [9] report that the public sector debt amounts to over 14 trillion dollars while US corporate and privates have both accumulated similarly shocking amounts. [32] states that this tendency is paralleled in Europe, especially in the private sector. The need for the expansion of lending will remain a pressing issue if this trend is not reversed. In the predetermined manner, strong and capable methods have to be introduced and reinforced to direct the lender's attention to the inherent risks of his debt positions. This alone will help to reign in the possible damage that can result from a borrower's default on repaying the debt.

One early step was taken in 1988. Then, the Basel Committee of Banking Supervision under the auspices of the Bank of International Settlement conceived a set of minimal capital requirements in the lending business. This was subsequently amended by what is known as the Basel II accords of 2004 mostly introducing risk assessment methodology.[2] Even a third set of accords, the so called Basel III accords, followed as detailed in [5]. The terminology and definitions given in the Basel II accords are used widely in the context of credit risk even beyond banks, in the narrow sense. That is, the definitions of loss, expected loss, the loss given default conditional of default as well as recovery rate, and related loss thresholds such as the value-at-risk (VaR) have become commonly used terminology. In this chapter, we will concentrate on the definitions of loss related to a credit event. Also, we will emphasize the methodology related to calculation of the recovery rate or, equivalently, the loss-given-default (LGD). Furthermore, we will cover a sufficient amount of literature on defaulted debt to provide a good overview of the current state-of-the-art. It will become obvious that difficulties arise from ambiguous definitions of the recovery rate. To see this, since the time-interval for the related work-out process can be chosen arbitrarily, ultimate recovery, for example, is a very misleading term. Moreover, we will see how the type of debt as well as the collection process influence recovery.

Expected loss parameters

As stated in [32], a financial institution generally offers five types of lending or, in other words, there exist five types of financial debt. Accordingly, financial debt can be coarsely classified as sovereign,

[2] For details, we refer to [4].

corporate, retail such as consumer lending, bank, or equity. As can be found in [4], the Basel accords set regulatory standards for financial institutions in handling the risks inherent in the different types of lending by demanding an adequate capital base. For the quantification of the risks, the Basel II framework introduces parameters related to the default in the lending process and the resulting loss hereafter. It is the objective of this section to present these parameters in the context of their definitions.

Credit Risk and Capital Requirements

The most important parameters determined by the Basel II accords are the exposure at default, the loss-given-default, the probability of default and as parameters of location of the loss distribution, the expected loss as well as the value-at-risk (VaR). [14] provide a good overview. The use of such parameters for the credit risk capital requirements demands knowledge of their values. As mentioned in [6], the Basel II accords allow banks to estimate them according to two approaches. The first is the standard approach and the second is the internal ratings based approach (IRB). In the standard approach, the estimates rely on ratings generated by external agencies. The IRB, on the other hand, permits banks to implement their own internal risk models and estimation methods.

Exposure at Default

Exposure at default is one of the key parameters in the Basel II regulation. There has been done a lot of research about PD estimation but research about EAD and LGD have not been enough. While default itself is not uniquely defined in the International Convergence of Capital Measurement and Capital Standards, the regulation introduced by [4] requires a bank to refer to a reference definition of default constituted for its internal use. For example, [30] set default as taking place "on the first occurrence of a payment default on any financial obligation rated or unrated, other than a financial obligation subject to a bona fide commercial dispute." In general, it can be considered either as the worsening of the borrowers conditions such that he will most likely be unable to meet his obligations or as some sort of delay in the scheduled repayment process beyond some threshold on the account of the borrower.

The exposure at default (EAD) then is the residual of the original debt that is still owed by the borrower. Its calculation can be very much dependent on the type of debt. [1] add that the considered exposure is significantly influenced by financial collateral. Two approaches have to be considered in this context, the simple and the comprehensive one. The simple approach allows the complete acknowledgement of collateral for the reduction of exposure while the comprehensive approach diminishes the reduction on by some haircut.

Probability of Default

In the regulation, the probability of default (PD) is defined as the "likelihood that a loan will not be repaid and fall into default. This PD will be calculated for each company who has a loan." Furthermore, the bank has to consider the credit history of the counterparty. Also, any characteristic of the investment has to be taken into account for the calculation of the PD. General economic conditions will also influence the likelihood of default. It has been found that LGD is positively correlated with PD as stated in, for example, [6]. [20] points out different models for PD estimation and also, while [14] compare predictive accuracy of different classifiers using credit application data.

Parameters of Location of the Loss Distribution

According to the Basel regulation, the expected loss (*EL*) from a default is composed of *PD*, *LGD*, and *EAD* in the following way

$$EL = PD \times LGD \times EAD$$

[6] mentions four risk elements in the computation of EL. One is the uncertainty at the account level. That is the ineptitude of any model to predict default for each individual account. The others are model estimation uncertainty, uncertainty with respect to the distribution of EAD, and the uncertainty arising from ignorance of the exact distribution of LGD exacerbated by its correlation with PD. The key parameters that determine the credit risk of financial assets, i.e., PD, LGD, and EAD yielding the EL have to observe over a one-year horizon.

The value-at-risk (VaR) quantifies a threshold loss that will not be exceeded at a given confidence level defined as 99 percent. So, in calculating the value-at-risk, the Basel accords request the 99th percentile, one-tailed confidence interval of the loss distribution.

An efficient allocation of regulatory and economic capital calls for accurate estimates of these parameters. Moreover, this will also be paramount for the pricing of the credit risk in the context of debt instruments and credit derivatives.

Recovery rate and loss given default

For various purposes, there are different definitions for default that are utilized by different institutions. Before we define LGD, it is vital to have stated a precise definition for default. According to the Basel II accord, we have the following definition:

"A default is considered to have occurred with regard to a particular obligor when one or more of the following events have taken place.
(a) It is determined that the obligor is unlikely to pay its debt obligations (principal, interest, or fees) in full;
(b) A credit loss event associated with any obligation of the obligor, such as charge off, specific provision, or distressed restructuring involving the forgiveness or postponement of principal, interest, or fees;
(c) The obligor is past due more than 90 days on any credit obligation; or
(d) The obligor has filed for bankruptcy or similar protection from creditors."

[1] defined loss-given-default (LGD) as generally the outstanding amount owed after default has been recorded and consequently turns into the credit that is lost by a financial institution when a borrower defaults. The recovery rate (RR) is the complement of the LGD, that means $RR = 1 - LGD$. The calculation of LGD is a complicated process and requires computing with attention to internal recovery cash flows.

The repayment amount includes recovery from facilities or collateral sale. Guarantees, assets from the borrower and restructured or cured exposures can also be considered. The regulation explicitly demands including material direct and indirect costs arising from the handling of defaulted exposure excluding internal costs as stated in [25]. As [25] mention, the LGD has to be based on the economic loss incurred by the entity and should be known. In Basel II, the economic loss is not the same as the accounting loss. In addition to the borrower related characteristics, it needs to reflect macro-economic conditions such as GDP, unemployment rate etc. In the IRB, LGD estimates are acceptable for retail exposure only while in the advanced internal rating based approach (IRBA), estimates can also be used for corporate, sovereign, and bank exposures. The LGD estimation in the IRBA approach is a challenging topic.

There are different ways to calculate LGD that are dependent on the definitions of EAD and different options of recoveries.

Workout LGD: The workout LGD calculates LGD using the proportion of the difference between positive and negative cash flows at time τ after the default relative to EAD:

$$LGD = 1 - \frac{\sum_i NPV(CF_i^+, \tau_i, r_i) - \sum_j NPV(CF_j^-, \tau_i, r_j)}{EAD}$$

where CF^+ and CF^- are positive and negative cash flows and r is the discount rate. Negative LGD can occur, when the penalty fees and penalization interest rate values for the defaulted asset are more than the discounted value because in these cases, the net present amount of recoveries is more than EAD. Negative LGD samples are eliminated from the data and are replaced with zero. In a workout process, there are cash recoveries and non-cash recoveries such as repossessions, restructuring but detection of non-cash flow recoveries is very complicated.
According to Basel II, there are two kinds of negative cash flows: direct and indirect ones. The valuation of indirect costs such as office expense during the recovery process is more demanding than measurement of direct costs. On the other hand, negative cash flows were divided into internal and external costs. External ones are expenses such as legal costs and outsourcing expenses and internal expenses such as staff costs and technologies expenses.

Market LGD: In the Market LGD definition, we calculate LGD based on the market price of the defaulted financial product or residual market values of traded companies early after the default; typically 30 days after the default event. Consequently, this definition is applied only for defaulted bond and loans which trade in the market and it is not applicable to retail portfolios. The sense of market soon after the default has more influence on market price and this price can be very volatile. For this reason, some financial companies prefer to use the mean of the market price in a period after default. In fact, when market LGD is calculated, we suppose that the market is efficient but the actual recovery for defaulted bonds and loans is still unknown. Another disadvantage of market LGD is that we do not assume costs during the recovery process.

Implied Market LGD: Implied Market LGD is another method of LGD measuring, which is estimated by looking at credit spreads on the non-defaulted loans, bonds, or credit default currently traded. The idea is that prices of risky instruments reflect the market's expectation of the loss and may be broken down into PD and LGD. Implied market LGD estimation could be used for mortgage portfolios.

Implied historical LGD: Porto (2011) classified implied historical LGD in two different definitions, ex post and ex ante. Firstly, ex post implied historical LGD is defined and then ex ante implied historical LGD will follow.

Ex post implied historical LGD: We suppose that our portfolio consist of *N* assets and that, at first, *D* assets are defaulted while other assets are not defaulted. EL is defined in the following way according to [26]

$$EL = \sum_{i=1}^{D} [EAD_i - (\sum_{J=1}^{J_i} R_{i,j} - \sum_{K=1}^{K_i} P_{i,k})]$$

where $R_{i,j}$ is cash inflow for asset i in time j and $P_{i,j}$ is cash out flow for asset i in time k. We assume that we can estimate the EAD for all non-defaulted assets and that their EAD amounts are based on possible defaults in the considered time. The EAD amounts for non-defaulted assets should be evaluated at the same time that we estimated LGD. Implied historical LGD (ILGD) is calculated from the following formula

$$ILGD_{t_0} = \frac{\sum_{i=1}^{D}[EAD_i - (\sum_{j=1}^{J_i} R_{i,j} - \sum_{K=1}^{K_i} P_{i,k})]}{\sum_{i=1}^{N} EAD_i(\frac{D}{N})}$$

The numerator of this equation is equal to EL and the denominator of this equation is PD multiplied by EAD, in our portfolio.

[26] points out that the workout LGD will be lower than the implied historical LGD if the average of EAD for non-defaulted assets is more than the average of EAD for defaulted assets and also, when PD is lower, it can be twice the value. On the other hand, only if the average of EAD for non-defaulted assets is equal to the average of EAD for defaulted assets then, the workout LGD and implied historical LGD are identical.

Ex ante implied historical LGD: We suppose that our portfolio has *N* nondefaulted assets then, the loss related to asset *I* is defined

$$L_i = EAD_i \times D_i \times LGD_i \qquad i = 1, \dots, N$$

where D_i is the indicator function of default for asset i. If D_i is independent from $EAD_i \times LGD_i$, then we have

$$E(EAD_i \times LGD_i) = \frac{E(L_i)}{E(D_i)} = \frac{E(L_i)}{P(D_i = 1)}$$

$$E(LGD_i) = \frac{E(L_i)}{E(EAD_i)P(D_i = 1)}$$

Methods

In this section, we present literature using different parametric as well as nonparametric models and methods with applications in modeling LGD or, equivalently, recovery rate for various types of debt. We Endeavour to carry the discussion further into application and evaluation of the methods presented in [29]. For the sake of brevity, we will refrain from explicitly stating any formulae or equations. A more detailed presentation can be found in [22].

Regression models

We begin with the literature on data mining methods related to regression techniques. [2] uses fractional response on homogenous subsamples of the data. The regression data are transformed in a logistic function with parameters from a Bernoulli quasimaximum log-likelihood method. His results are not compelling, however, compared to alternative methods presented in the sequel of this chapter. [7] apply ordinary least squares (OLS) regression for modeling LGD and also decision tree and Tobit regression. Strikingly, it is found that OLS is preferable to the alternatives. Here, PD is a significant covariate as a result of the joint dependence on macro-economic conditions. The data are transformed through logarithmic, beta, and Probit functions.

In [8], LGD is based on OLS using macro variables as covariates. For the transform, fractional, beta, and Probit functions are used, as before. Simple logistic regression for LGD is used by [13]. [16] perform OLS regression including macro variables they transform through logistic regression to obtain a quantity in the LGD scale. This is in agreement with [18]. [27] use fractional response with logistic, inverse Gaussian, and beta transformations to model LGD.

A survey of different data mining techniques for the modeling of LGD is provided by [36]. [23] provide interesting early results. Here, several social, economic and psychological factors related to debt are considered. To discriminate debtors from nondebtors, discriminant function analysis is used. How far people might get into debt and how much of their debts people repay are finally determined by a multiple regression analysis based on these variables.

Distributional approaches

We present here either parametric distributions or related non-parametric approaches for the LGD and the recovery rate. LGD or recovery rates have a density that theoretically should be best described by a beta distribution since the support is limited to the interval [0,1]. This is, for example, mentioned by [19] who apply to the distribution a correction factor, however, to allow for values slightly above 1.0. This is a stylized fact sometimes observed in the context of bonds and also loans.

[12] introduced a beta kernel estimator much of the same spirit as the well-known Gaussian kernel estimator to overcome limitations from the parametric approach. By design, however, it differs from the Gaussian kernel estimator in that it uses the observed sample data as arguments instead of as parameters. This was repeated by [28] and followed by the asymmetric beta kernel by [17]. [10]uses a discrete-continuous hybrid distribution where the continuous part (0,1) is given by a beta mixture with a reparametrized beta distribution to estimate parameters jointly. Finally, [11] introduced an alternative beta kernel estimator for the continuous part of the recovery rate distribution of design of the Gaussian kernel. Here, parameter values are dependent on the observations to encounter the problem of the original beta kernel estimator that failed to represent probability mass one when integrated.

Alternative Methods

Finally, we present a collection of different approaches that have not found widespread use in the context of modeling the LGD or, equivalently, recovery rate. [27] introduce neural networks as a non-linear approach. [3] does the same for the recovery rates. He argues that neural networks in combination with bootstrap display better predictive performance than parametric regression models. This is due to its especially appealing design with several layers of perceptrons transforming input into a weighted functional output. This flexible yet sometimes unintuitive design is particularly apt in separating samples with respect to objective functions such as, for example, zero or full recovery.

[7] use a credit scoring method with macroeconomic variables for LGD in combination with stochastic timing of default. [20] applies various

techniques such as scorecards, a naive Bayes model, and neural networks where the latter partitions the data into good and bad. This is supplemented by nearest-neighbor algorithms.

In [21], the recovery rate is modeled using support vector machines (SVM) whose advantages are stated to be given by the use of key observations only for the sake of speed. The first modeling step consists of a stepwise selection of the most powerful variables for separating the data into homogenous subsets.

[24] apply non-linear techniques such as CART, MARS, LSSVM, and ANN based on their superior performance relatively to linear models. [33] introduces LGD modeling based on a decision tree using a weights-of-evidence (WOE) approach to determine the most significant characteristics for the prediction of high and low LGD. [34] do this, as well, augmenting it by a beta or normal function transformation. [15] emphasize the importance of the respective collection processes for the prediction of LGD. They use text mining methods for detection of elementary parts of the collecting process that are most helpful for increasing the recovery rate.

References

[1] Edward. I Altman, Andrea Resti, and Andrea Sironi. Loss given default; a review of the literature in recovery risk. In E I Altman, A Resti, and A Sironi, editors, Recovery risk: The next challenge in credit risk management, chapter 1, pages 41-59. Risk Books, London, 2005.

[2] João Bastos. Forecasting bank loans loss-given default. Journal of Banking and Finance, Vol. 34(10):2510-2517, 2010.

[3] João Bastos. Predicting bank loan recovery rates with neural networks. Technical report, 2010.

[4] BCBS. International convergence of capital measurement and capital standards. a revised framework, bank for international settlements. http://www.bis.org, 2005.

[5] BCBS. Basel III: A global regulatory framework for more resilient banks and banking systems, bank for international settlements. http://www.bis.org, 2011.

[6] Tony Bellotti. A simulation study of Basel ii expected loss distribution for a portfolio of credit cards. Journal of Financial Services Marketing, Vol. 14:268- 277, 2010.

[7] Tony Bellotti and Jonathan Crook. Credit scoring with macroeconomic variables using survival analysis. Journal of the Operational Research Society, Vol. 60:1699-1707, 2009.

[8] Tony Bellotti and Jonathan Crook. Loss given default models incorporating macroeconomic variables for credit cards. International Journal of Forecasting (forthcoming), 2011.
[9] Board of Governors of the Federal Reserve System. Federal reserve statistical release. http://www.federalreserve.gov, 2011.
[10] Rafaella Calabrese. Regression for recovery rates with both continuous and discrete characteristics, Proceedings of the 45th Scientific Meeting of the Italian Statistical Society (SIS), Italy. 2010.
[11] Rafaella Calabrese and Michele Zenga. Bank loan recovery rates: Measuring and nonparametric density estimation. Journal of Banking and Finance, Vol. 35(5):903-911, 2010.
[12] Song Xi Chen. Beta kernel estimators for density functions. Computational Statistics and Data Analysis, 31:131-145, 1999.
[13] Tsung-Hao Chen and Cheng-Wu Chen. Application of data mining to the spatial heterogeneity of foreclosed mortgages. Expert Systems with Application, Vol. 37(2):993-997, March 2010.
[14] Jonathan Crook, David B. Edelman, and Lyn C. Thomas. Recent developments in consumer credit risk assessment. European Journal of Operations Research, Vol. 183(3):1447-1465, 2007.
[15] Adiel T. de Almeida Filho, Lyn C. Thomas, and Christophe Mues. Optimizing the collection process in consumer credit. Production and Operations Management, Vol. 19(6):698-708, 2010.
[16] Jean M. Dermine and Cristina Neto De Carvalho. Bank Loan Losses-Given- Default: A Case Study. Journal of Banking and Finance, Vol. 30(4):1219-1243, 2006.
[17] Christian Gourieroux and Alain Monfort. (non) consistency of the beta kernel estimator for recovery rate distribution. Technical report, Working Paper, 2006.
[18] Jens Grunert and Martin Weber. Recovery rates of commercial lending: Empirical evidence for German companies. Journal of Banking and Finance, Vol. 33:505-513, 2009.
[19] Greg M. Gupton and Roger M. Stein. Losscalc: Model for predicting loss given default. Moody's, February, 2002.
[20] David Hand. Modeling consumer credit risk. Journal of Management Mathematics, Vol. 12(2):139-155, 2001.
[21] Chen Hao, Ma Yu-Chao, Chen Mu-zi, Tang Yue, Wang Bo, Chen Min, and Yang Xiao-Guang. Recovery discrimination based on optimized -variables support vector machine for nonpeforming loans. Systems Engineering - Theory and Practice, Vol. 29(12):23-30, Dec 2009.

[22] Markus Höchstötter, Abdolreza Nazemi, and Svetlozar T. Rachev. Reflection on Recovery and Loss Given Default. What Is and What Is Amiss. Technical report, Karlsruhe Institute of Technology, 2011.
[23] Sonia M. Livingstone and Peter K. Lunt. Predicting personal debt and debt repayment: Psychological, social and economic determinants. Journal of Economic Psychology, 13:111-134, 1992.
[24] Gert Loterman, Iain Brown, David Martens, Christophe Mues, and Bart Baesens. Benchmarking regression algorithms for loss given default modeling. International Journal of Forecasting (in press), 2011.
[25] Christian Peter. Estimating loss given default: Experience from banking practice. In B Engelmann and R Rauhmeier, editors, The Basel II Risk Parameters, chapter 8, pages 143-174. Springer-Verlag, Heidelberg, 2006.
[26] Rogério F. Porto. A brief note on implied historical lgd. The Journal of Credit Risk, 7(2):73-81, 2011.
[27] M Qi and X Zhao. Comparison of modeling methods for loss given default. Journal of Banking and Finance (in press), 2011.

CHAPTER TWENTY EIGHT

AN EMPIRICAL STUDY OF PROPERTY-CASUALTY INSURERS IMPAIRMENTS

HUONG DANG[1]

Abstract

This study applies a competing risk approach and develops dynamic Cox's hazard models (with time-varying covariates) to investigate endogenous and exogenous factors associated with property-casualty insurers impairments in the U.S. during January 1998-June 2010. The predictive accuracy of the estimated models is assessed using a probability scoring rule. The study finds that (i) the models for impairment events of different outcomes feature different significant risk factors; and (ii) the estimated models are more accurate than a random model and a naive model in forming survival estimates out-of-sample. The results suggest that impairments of different outcomes are distinct phenomenon and should not be treated identical as in previous insurance impairment studies.

1. Introduction

The financial health of an insurer is of vital importance to its regulator and its policyholders. Monitoring the solvency of property-casualty (PC) insurers is particularly challenging due to the random and idiosyncratic nature of the exogenous events they cover. Detecting an impaired PC insurer at an early stage of its financial distress is a concern to any insurance regulator.

In practice, an effective solvency monitoring system has to deal with three aspects of financial impairments: the risk factors associated with the

[1] Lecturer, Department of Economics and Finance, University of Canterbury, Private Bag 4800, Christchurch 8140, New Zealand. Tel: +64 (0)21 0821 2645. Email: huong.dang@canterbury.ac.nz

incidence of an event, the appropriate regulatory actions that should be taken against an impaired insurer, and the appropriate time of regulatory intervention. It is conventional in previous insurance impairment studies to treat all impairment outcomes equivalent. However, an administrative supervision event is likely to have quite different determinants than a liquidation event. Insurance studies have so far focused on understanding the static determinants of a generic impairment event. The literature is rather silent about investigating the dynamic risk factors associated with different types of impairment outcomes and featuring the time structure of probability survival estimates.

This study examines a large sample of PC insurers in the U.S. during January 1998 - June 2010, and aims to answer two questions: (i) Is it reasonable to treat all types of impairment outcomes as equivalent?; and (ii) Are the leading causes for type-specific impairment events the same? This study answers these questions by examining the probable duration of each insurer in the study. How likely is it that by time t (in the set $t = 1$ to T) there will be an impairment event of a type s? It is possible to derive this probability from a survivor function $S(s,t)$ which can be estimated using a Cox's hazard model (Cox, 1972), where $S(s,t) = P(s,T>t)$ and $P(s,T>t)$ is the probability that the impairment outcome s will occur at time T after a time duration of t. The probability estimate is dynamic as t can take on a range of values. This feature is appealing as it may aid regulators in monitoring the survival profiles of insurers and in detecting impaired insurers with sufficient lead time[2].

This study extends the literature in the following way. First, it adopts a survival analysis framework (Allison, 1984) and develops Cox's hazard models with time-varying covariates (Hosmer, Lemeshow, May, 2008, pp. 213-216), which resolve some limitations of the widely used static logit model[3]. The proposed dynamic model accommodates changes in the financial characteristics of insurers and the development of macro-economic environment over time. Second, it applies a competing risk

[2] Whalen (1991, p. 21) found that Cox's hazard model "identified failed and healthy banks with a high degree of accuracy", and "flagged a large proportion of banks that subsequently failed as potential failures in periods prior to their actual demise."

[3] The static logit model uses cross-sectional data and takes into account the value of a variable at an instant of time (LeClere, 1999, p. 10). It fails to accommodate the fact that firms' financial conditions deteriorate as they approach insolvency (BarNiv and McDonald, 1992). In addition, the logit model does not provide a survival forecast as a function of time, and fails to provide early warning of financial distress (LeClere, 1999, p. 38).

approach and treats different impairment outcomes distinct (Allison, 1995, pp. 186-188). Third, the study overcomes computational challenges and features the time structure of probability survival estimates when the proportionality of the Cox's hazard model (Cox, 1972) breaks down. Fourth, the study enriches the literature on the framework for evaluating probability survival estimates by employing the Brier score (Brier, 1950), a popular measure for ex-post evaluation of meteorological forecasts.

The remainder of this Chapter is structured as follows: Section 2 discusses financial impairment outcomes, Section 3 describes the data and variables employed, Section 4 presents the estimation and validation methods, Section 5 summarizes the results, and Section 6 concludes the main findings.

2. Financial impairment

2.1 Impairment outcomes

An insurer can be considered impaired in any of the following scenarios: (i) its ability to conduct normal business is adversely affected; (ii) its financial conditions have deteriorated and triggered regulatory concern; and/or (iii) its capital and surpluses are considered inadequate to meet legal requirements (Best, 2010, p. 8). To classify an insurer as either an impaired or a survived firm, this study follows the approach widely applied in the insurance literature (Browne and Hoyt, 1995; Best, 2009; Best, 2010). A PC insurer is categorized as financially impaired "as of the first official regulatory action taken against it by an insurance department" (Best, 2010, p. 8).

The data employed in this study includes 195 impairments categorized into four outcomes (manners) namely supervision, conservation/ other (involuntary other, confidential order)[4], rehabilitation, and liquidation. A valid question is whether different impairment outcomes should be regarded as identical, as in previous studies on insurance impairment? An overview of the four observed impairment outcomes will provide an insight into this question.

A State regulator may place an insurer under administrative supervision at an early stage of its financial weakness so as to stop it from

---

[4] Due to its low observed frequency, the *other (involuntary other/confidential order)* outcome is combined with *conservation* outcome. This combination makes a conservative assumption that an *other* event should be, at least, treated as a *conservation* event, the least serious of the three event types that involves a State court order.

conducting risky activities or to prevent imminent problems that are detrimental to its policyholders. If the insurer makes no effort to improve its business practices, the regulator can take further enforcement action by making a petition to the relevant State court for an appropriate form of receivership.

Receivership actions include conservation, rehabilitation, and liquidation. Proceedings for receivership actions are generally taken against an impaired insurer in the State where it was incorporated.[5] A regulator may make a petition to the State court for a conservation order with an aim to protect the assets of an insurer. The conservation order provides the regulator the time needed to consider alternative regulatory actions and to choose the optimal resolution that should be commenced against an impaired insurer.

A regulator may also petition a State court for a rehabilitation order so as to remedy an insurer's deteriorated financial conditions, to protect its assets, to run off its liabilities[6], or to prepare it for a smooth transition to liquidation. The order may prohibit the insurer from writing new business, renewing business or limit the amount and type of new business written. The regulator in the insurer's domiciliary State will be appointed the rehabilitator and be authorized to administer the insurer's assets under the court's supervision. The powers of the insurer's directors and managers are generally suspended. The rehabilitator will prepare a rehabilitation plan, and upon approved by the court, effect the transformation means needed (i.e. a re-organization, a consolidation, or a merger) to revitalize the impaired insurer. However, if the rehabilitator determines that any further attempt to rehabilitate the impaired insurer is not feasible and is detrimental to its policyholders and creditors, the rehabilitator can make a petition to the State court for a liquidation order.

Upon the issue of a liquidation order, the regulator will be appointed the liquidator of the insurer, and be authorized to control all aspects of the insurer's business activities under the court's supervision. The rights and the liabilities of the parties involved will be fixed from the date of the liquidation order. Claims from an insolvent insurer's policyholders will be addressed by the State's guaranty fund which is contributed by member (solvent) insurers writing business in that State. "Any claims that the

---

[5] https://i-site.naic.org/help/html/GRID%20FAQs.html#insolvency [access 15 September 2010]

[6] Loss payments under policies do not actually become due until some point in the future (often years). Liquidation of assets at distressed prices usually does not occur in an insurer insolvency nor are immediate payments/settlements to all policyholders made at that time (Weiss, 2010, pp. 7-8)

State's guaranty funds are not able to pay become claims against the estate of the liquidated insurer…" (Best, 2010, p. 20). The owners of the liquidated insurer will receive the residual capital after all obligations and debts are paid.

Overall, from a legal perspective, different impairment resolutions dictate different extents to which a State regulator controls an impaired insurer. From an economic perspective, different regulatory actions bear different costs to the regulator and impose different impacts on the impaired insurer.

2.2 Survival durations

The question next addressed is whether the survival durations of insurers experiencing different impairment outcomes differ. The survival time of an insurer starts from the time it enters the study. The duration ends at the time the firm either exits the study or the observation period terminates.

As shown in Figure 1, the distributions of the survival time of impaired insurers, categorized by impairment outcomes, are positively skewed. It is noticeable that liquidation "candidates" are short-lived whereas rehabilitation "candidates" display a greater tendency to survive. Additional analysis (not reported) indicates that the descriptive statistics of survival time for insurers experiencing different impairment outcomes are statistically different (except rehabilitated and supervised firms). It is thus not reasonable to treat different impairment outcomes identical.

Figure 1: Histogram of survival time to outcome-specific impairment event, 1998-2010

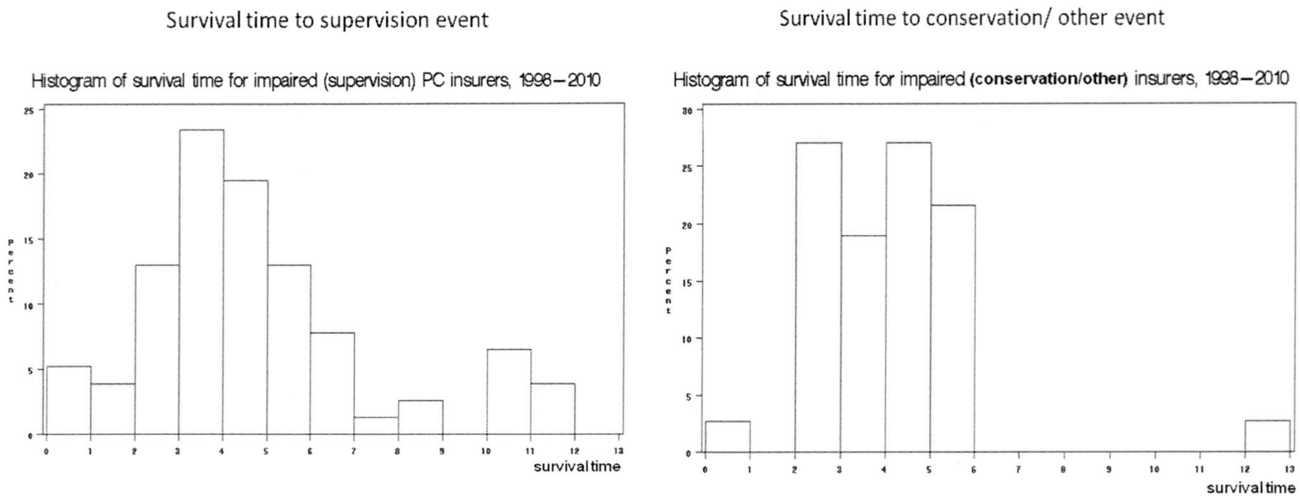

Figure 2: Histogram of survival time to outcome-specific impairment event, 1998-2010 (continued)

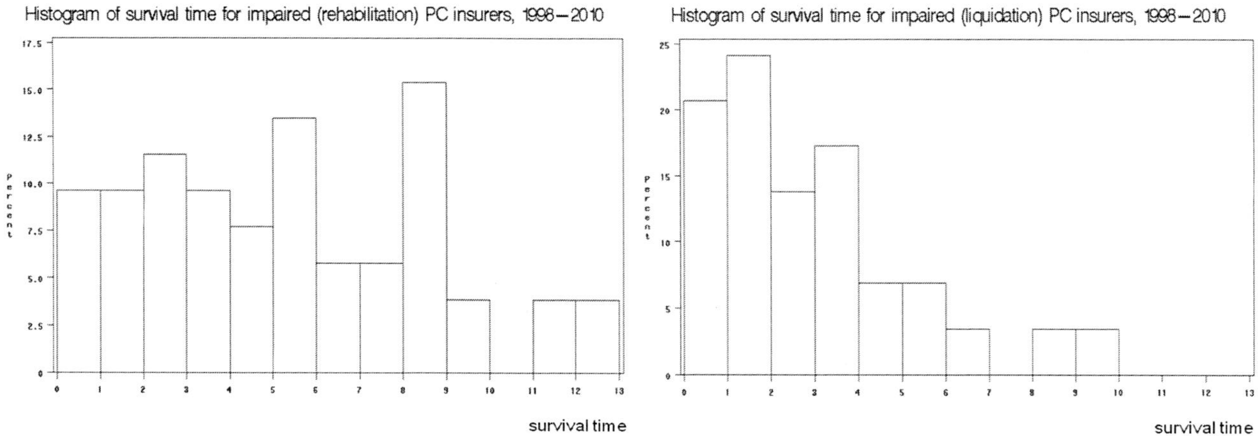

3. Data, samples and variables

3.1 Data and samples

The impairment data were provided by A.M. Best. Firm-specific data were obtained from SNL Financial. Macro-economic data were downloaded from the U.S. Federal Reserve, Bureau of Labour Statistics, and WRDS. The final data set, after filtering process, includes 2098 PC insurers, of which 195 firms (9.3 percent) were impaired and 1903 observations (90.7 percent) were censored (survived).

To construct estimation and holdout samples, this study adopts the random cross-sectional sampling approach applied by Austrian National Bank (Halling and Hayden, 2006, p. 11). The estimation and the holdout samples, respectively, account for 65 percent and 35 percent of observations in the final data set. These samples were randomly constructed except that the total impairment rate in the holdout sample is set equal to the total impairment rate in the estimation sample. Each insurer contributes only one observation to either the estimation or the holdout sample.

3.2 Variables

The endogenous and exogenous factors associated with impairments were identified from previous studies on insurance impairment and financial distress. After checking for multi-collinearity, 40 variables were included in the model, of which 21 are firm-specific qualitative dummies, 14 are firm-specific time-varying, and 5 are macro-economic time-varying. In the interest of a parsimonious model and compact presentation of the results, the backward stepwise estimation procedure is employed. Variables were retained in the models according to the log-likelihood ratio test, at the 10 percent level or better, derived from the maximum likelihood procedure used to estimate the models.

Time-varying variables

Firm-specific and macro-economic variables were constructed as time-varying to accommodate changes in the financial characteristics of insurers and the macro-economic conditions prior to impairments. The firm-specific (macro-economic) values used in the estimation process were updated to the most recent annual (quarterly) value as an impairment event occurred.

Macro-economic variables

Impairment peaks were often triggered or exacerbated by perilous operating environment (Browne and Hoyt, 1995; Best, 2009). It is thus necessary to account for the macro-economic conditions prevailing prior to each impairment event. Moody's *Aaa corporate bond yield* and *S&P500 return* were used to capture the performance of the credit and stock markets respectively. *Yield curve slope,* measured as the spread between 3-month and 10-year Treasury Constant Maturity rates, was included to control for credit conditions and to capture the future prospects of the economy (Estrella and Hardouvelis, 1991). *CPI Inflation rate* and *Unemployment rate* were included to capture the general economic conditions.

As the impairment rate tends to correlate with the lagged effects of macro-economic values (Best, 2009, pp. 11-12), this study applies the approach of Figlewski, Frydman, and Liang (2008), in which each macro-economic variable was computed quarterly as an exponentially weighted average of its lagged observations.

Firm-specific variables

Fourteen variables were employed in the model to capture various financial characteristics such as firm size (*Logarithm of average capital and surplus*), growths in equities (*Capital and surplus growth),* growth in assets *(Admitted asset growth)*, cash flows (*Logarithm of cash from operation)*, financial leverage and liquidity (*Liabilities/Liquid assets*), reserves (*Reserves/Equity*), underwriting performance (*Retention ratio, Operating ratio, Combined ratio, Net premium written growth*), underwriting leverage *(Net premium written/Average capital and surplus),* investment performance (*Return on average equity, Net yield on invested assets, Investment income growth).*

These variables were measured annually during the survival durations of firms in the study. To eliminate outliers, this study applies the approach of Cummins, Harrington, Klein (1995) and Shumway (2001), in which the annual values of a variable were truncated at the 1st and the 99th percentiles of the annual distribution. The *t test* and the *Wilcoxon test* (not reported) indicates that the descriptive statistics of the financial characteristics of firms experiencing different impairment outcomes are statistically different. This suggests that different impairment outcomes were characterized by different endogenous risk factors and have different underlying determinants.

Time-independent variables

Twenty-one time-independent variables were included in the models to control for the organization forms, maturity, business focuses, and domicile regions of firms in the study.

Previous studies found that a stock (a mutual) insurer is more (less) likely to be impaired. Stock companies employ an aggressive underwriting leverage policy, are more active in commercial lines and casualty lines, and expose to volatile underwriting exposures. In contrast, mutual companies adopt a conservative operating philosophy, concentrate more on personal lines and property lines, and enjoy stable performance. In this study, two dummies were created to account for any ownership effects arisen from being a stock or a mutual insurer.

The effects of firm's age since establishment on financial distress are mixed. On the one hand, it can be argued that ageing firms have more debt obligations due in the normal course of business and are more likely to default as time unfolds (Altman, 1998). On the other hand, it may be conjectured that well-established firms have a stable and niche market, a strong business expertise, and are less vulnerable to adverse macro-economic conditions. Matured firms are therefore less likely to be impaired (Kim, Anderson, Amburgey, Hickman, 1995). This study constructed three age dummies to represent the first, the second, and the third quartile of firm age distribution. These dummies capture any non-linear relationships between firm ages and financial impairments (Halling and Hayden, 2006).

The domicile impacts on insurance impairments have received little attention in the literature though the domicile captures important factors such as licensing, regulatory and capital requirements, incorporation law, size of insurance market, competition level, catastrophe frequency. The resources available for solvency monitoring also varies across States (Best, 2010). To capture any domiciliary effects and to keep the number of variables manageable, this study created five domicile dummies, each represents a region designated by SNL Financial. The dummy takes a value of one if the registered business address of an insurer falls in that region, and zero otherwise.

An insurer's spread of risk is commonly proxied by its underwriting exposures in long tail and short tail business lines[7] (Harrington and Nelson, 1986; Lee and Urrutia, 1996). It is suggested that insurers writing business

[7] A long tail (short tail) line implies an insurance coverage that has a lengthy (brief) period between the occurrence of an insured event and the final settlement of a claim (Best, 2009, pp. 45, 46).

in long tail lines are subject to fierce competition (soft market[8]) whereas those in short tail lines have stable performance and are less likely to be impaired. However, as observed in this study period, different short-tail (long-tail) lines exhibit statistically different impairment patterns which require appropriate capital allocations and loss reserves. If an insurer drastically underestimates reserves or does so persistently, this can be detrimental to its financial conditions (Grace and Klein, 2008). It is therefore necessary to account for an insurer's specific business focus line instead of its overall exposures in long tail and short tail business lines. To capture a wide range of business exposures, this study created 11 dummies representing 11 business focus lines[9] designated by SNL Financial.

4. Methods

4.1. Estimation approach

The impairment data includes information on the first regulatory action taken against PC insurers by State regulators in the U.S. Since only the first regulatory action is recorded and examined, each impaired insurer contributes only one impairment event to this study. The occurrence of one type of impairment event removes a financially distressed insurer from the risk of all other impairment events at that time. Impairments of different outcomes can therefore be treated as competing risks.

Insurers that pass the data filtering process will remain in the data set and be incorporated in the estimation process[10]. Four type-specific Cox's hazard models for four observed impairment outcomes were estimated. Additional analysis (not reported) show that the hazards for type-specific

[8] In a soft market, insurers cut price, broaden the terms of coverage or relax the underwriting standards at no additional premium to attract more business or to keep pace with competitors (Grace and Klein, 2008)

[9] The business focus is based on the line of business outlined on the Underwriting and Investment Exhibit Part 1 for PC firms. The lines of business were merged into categories for each filing type. The final focus designation is based on the percentage of net premium written to total net premium written the insurer writes in each of those categories.

[10] Sobehart and Stein (2000, p. 12) suggest that "financial and market information are less likely to be complete or reliable in the time period leading up to default". Missing data may signal impairments. If so, including these insurers in the estimation process when their data are available and treating these observations as censored when their data are incomplete may lead to informative censoring. This violates the underlying assumption of non-informative random censoring in survival analysis (Allison, 1995, pp. 13-14).

events are neither equal nor proportionate. This strengthens the evidence that different impairment outcomes are distinct phenomenon and should be modelled separately.

4.2. Estimation model

The dynamic Cox's hazard models for insurer *m* can be expressed as follow:

$$h_{s,m}(t,Z,Z(t)) = h_{s(0)}(t)\ \exp[Z_{\mathrm{j}}^{\mathrm{m}}\beta_{\mathrm{j}}+Z_{p}^{m}(\mathrm{t})\beta_{\mathrm{p}}\ ] \qquad (1)$$

Where:

$h_{s,m}(t, Z, Z(t))$ is the impairment hazard of an event type *s* at time *t* given insurer *m*'s time-independent covariate vector Z_j^m and insurer *m*'s time-varying covariate vector $Z_p^m(t)$.

$h_{s(0)}(t)$ is the baseline hazard of an event type *s* at time *t*.

β_p is the vector of estimated coefficients for time-varying covariate vector $Z_p^m(t)$.

β_j is the vector of estimated coefficients for time-independent covariate vector Z_j^m.

Taking the product of the likelihood that insurer *m* experiences an event type *s* for all insurers *m* that impaired in manner *s* across all event times observed in the estimation sample gives the partial likelihood. The vectors of the estimated coefficients $\hat{\beta}_p$ and $\hat{\beta}_j$ can be obtained by maximizing the partial likelihood (Hosmer, Lemeshow, May, 2008, pp. 213-216).

In the presence of the time-varying covariates $Z_p^m(t)$, the proportionality assumption of the conventional Cox's hazard model (Cox, 1972) does not hold. It is then not possible to extract the baseline hazard $h_{s(0)}(t)$ from the Cox's regression results. This study takes an approach proposed by Andersen (1992) and Chen, Yen, Wu, Liao, Liou, Kuo, and Chen (2005) to estimate the baseline hazard function at time *t*, $\hat{h}_{s(0)}(t)$.

4.3. Survival estimates and forecast assessments

The estimated hazard of holdout firm q for an event type s at time t can be estimated using firm q's actual covariate vector Z_j^q and $Z_p^q(t)$, the estimated baseline hazard function $\hat{h}_{s(0)}(t)$, and the estimated coefficient vector $\hat{\beta}_p$ and $\hat{\beta}_j$:

$$\hat{h}_{s,q}(t,Z,Z(t)) = \hat{h}_{s(0)}(t) \exp[Z_j^q \hat{\beta}_j + Z_p^q(t) \hat{\beta}_p] \tag{2}$$

The predicted survival function of holdout firm q at time t can be estimated as:

$$\hat{S}_{s,q}(t,Z,Z(t)) = \exp-[\sum \hat{h}_{s,q}(t,Z,Z(t))] \tag{3}$$

The Brier score (Brier, 1950), $B_{t,s}$, is used to assess the predictive accuracy of the hazard model for impairment type s at forecast time t, and is defined as follow:

$$B_{t,s} = \frac{\sum_{q=1}^{N_t} [(\hat{S}_{s,q}(t) - a_{s,q})^2]}{N_t} \tag{4}$$

Where:

$\hat{S}_{s,q}(t)$, obtained from equation (3), is the probability forecast that holdout firm q will survive from the impairment type s at forecast time t.

$a_{s,q}$ is the known outcome survival state of holdout firm q. If holdout firm q survives, $a_{s,q}$ =1, and if holdout firm q experienced the impairment event of type s, $a_{s,q}$ =0.

N_t is the number of observations in the holdout sample and the number of estimates at forecast time t.

5. Estimation and forecast performance results

5.1. Estimation results

The Cox's dynamic hazard models for four observed impairment outcomes were estimated as in equation (1). The estimation results are given in Panel A - Table 1. Panel B – Table 1 summarizes the number of events and censored observations in the estimation and holdout samples. Panel C – Table 1 provides the statistics on the fit of the estimated models.

5.2. Estimated models

As shown in Panel A - Table 1, the hazard of outcome-specific impairment events depends significantly upon a number of factors. The significant variables, however, differ across event types.

It is found that the financial characteristics of an insurer have modest marginal impacts on its impairment risk. Insurers adopting aggressive financial leverage policy (*Liabilities/Liquid assets*) or having a low *Return on average equity* are subject to a higher risk of all types of impairments. Those with a high growth in admitted assets (*Admitted asset growth)* have a lower receivership risk. Those with a large insurance leverage exposure (*Net premium written/Average capital & surplus)* are more likely to be supervised, conserved, or rehabilitated. Business focus indicators have substantial impacts, particularly on the hazards of receivership events. For example, focusing in *Auto* line[11] raises the hazard of a conservation/ other, a rehabilitation, a liquidation event, respectively, by 632 percent, 526 percent, 599 percent. Organizational form factors are not significant in any model. It is possible that the effects of organizational forms were picked up by the effects of business focus variables. While the foregoing provides a general picture of the results, there are marked differences between the models.

Impairments of different types exhibit contrasting financial characteristics. This is evidenced by the coefficient signs of *Retention ratio, Capital & surplus growth,* and *Net premium written growth*, which reverse across models. The *Retention ratio* captures the effect of reinsurance transactions. Insurers actively transfer risks through reinsurance transactions have a lower *Retention ratio*.

---

[11] The primary causes of recent impairments for auto-focused insurers are inadequate pricing, deficient loss reserves, rapid growth and small size (measured by policyholders' surplus) (Best, 2009, p. 19).

While reinsurance exposes ceding companies to counterpart credit risk and makes them more vulnerable to supervision and conservation events, prudent reinsurance transactions make ceding companies less susceptible to liquidation. Insurers with rapid growths in net premiums written (*Net premium written growth)* have a higher risk of being supervised but a lower risk of going through receivership proceedings. Similarly, rapid growths in capital and surplus (*Capital & surplus growth)* makes an insurer more likely to receive a conservation order but less likely to be supervised and rehabilitated.

It is found that different impairment events are characterized by different determinants. Firms with large cash flows from operations (*Logarithm of cash from operations)* yield a lower risk of being placed in supervision. Those setting aside more reserves in relation to their equity have a greater risk of receiving a conservation order (*Reserves/Equity).* Insurers with small sizes (*Logarithm of average capital & surplus),* or having poor underwriting and investment performance *(Combined ratio, Net yield on invested assets)* are more likely to be liquidated.

Ageing insures are more vulnerable to supervision and conservation/ other events. Being in the second and the third age quartile (*Dummy age2, Dummy age3)* raises the conservation/ other risk and the supervision risk by 130.3 percent and 101.4 percent respectively. Being in *Commercial medical malpractice line* and *Reinsurance* makes an insurer, respectively, 501.8 percent and 564.9 percent more likely to be conserved. Focusing in the *Commercial financial line* (*Commercial general liability line)* increases the liquidation (rehabilitation) probability by 426.9 percent (377.5 percent). Being in *Commercial worker compensation line*[12] raises the hazard of a supervision and a conservation/ other event, respectively, by 148.5 percent and 685.2 percent.

[12] The primary causes of recent impairments for insurers focused in *commercial workers' compensation line* are inadequate pricing, deficient loss reserves and rapid growth (Best, 2009, p. 19).

Table 1: Type-specific Cox's dynamic hazard models for impairment events of different outcomes

Panel A: Parameter estimates

Variables	Model-supervision event			Model-conservation/other event		
	Parameter Estimate	Standard Error	Hazard ratio	Parameter Estimate	Standard Error	Hazard ratio
Size and growth						
Logarithm of Average Capital & Surplus						
Capital & Surplus Growth (%)	-0.015**	0.007	0.986	0.015**	0.007	1.015
Admitted Assets Growth (%)				-0.021**	0.009	0.980
Cash flow, liquidity, reserves						
Logarithm of Cash From Operations	-0.065***	0.024	0.937			
Liabilities/ Liquid Assets (%)	0.008***	0.002	1.008	0.016***	0.003	1.016
Reserves/ Equity (%)				0.002*	0.001	1.002
Underwriting performance						
Net Premiums Written (NPW) Growth (%)	0.004***	0.001	1.004	-0.011**	0.005	0.989
Net Premiums Written/ Average Capital & Surplus (%)	0.003	0.002	1.003	0.005***	0.002	1.005
Retention Ratio (NPW/ Gross premium written) (%)	-0.011**	0.005	0.989	-0.021***	0.008	0.979
Operating Ratio (%)						
Combined Ratio (%)						

Panel A: Parameter estimates (Continued)

	Model-rehabilitation event			Model-liquidation event		
Variables	Parameter Estimate	Standard Error	Hazard ratio	Parameter Estimate	Standard Error	Hazard Ratio
Size and growth						
Logarithm of Average Capital & Surplus				-0.691***	0.168	0.501
Capital & Surplus Growth (%)	-0.018	0.011	0.982			
Admitted Assets Growth (%)	-0.022***	0.006	0.978	-0.017**	0.007	0.983
Cash flow, liquidity, reserves						
Logarithm of Cash From Operations						
Liabilities/ Liquid Assets (%)	0.013***	0.003	1.013	0.012***	0.004	1.012
Reserves/ Equity (%)						
Underwriting performance						
Net Premiums Written (NPW) Growth (%)	-0.013**	0.005	0.987	-0.010*	0.006	0.99
Net Premiums Written/ Average Capital & Surplus (%)	0.006***	0.001	1.006			
Retention Ratio (NPW/ Gross premium written) (%)				0.025**	0.01	1.025
Operating Ratio (%)				-0.008***	0.002	0.992
Combined Ratio (%)				0.003**	0.001	1.003

Panel A: Parameter estimates (Continued)

Variables	Model-supervision event			Model-conservation/other event		
	Parameter Estimate	Standard Error	Hazard ratio	Parameter Estimate	Standard Error	Hazard ratio
Investment performance						
Return on Average Capital & Surplus (%)	-0.024***	0.006	0.976	-0.032***	0.007	0.968
Net Yield on Invested Assets (%)						
Investment Income Growth (%)	-0.011	0.007	0.989			
Organization form						
Dummy stock firm						
Dummy mutual firm						
Maturity						
Dummy age1 (1st quartile of age distribution)						
Dummy age2 (2nd quartile of age distribution)				0.834*	0.433	2.303
Dummy age3 (3rd quartile of age distribution)	0.700**	0.332	2.014			
Domicile						
Dummy West						
Dummy Southeast						
Dummy Northeast						
Dummy Midwest						
Dummy Midatlantic				-1.606*	0.851	0.201

Panel A: Parameter estimates (Continued)

Variables	Model-rehabilitation event			Model-liquidation event		
	Parameter Estimate	Standard Error	Hazard ratio	Parameter Estimate	Standard Error	Hazard Ratio
Investment performance						
Return on Average Capital & Surplus (%)	-0.026***	0.006	0.974	-0.033***	0.006	0.968
Net Yield on Invested Assets (%)				-0.306*	0.171	0.736
Investment Income Growth (%)				0.005	0.004	1.005
Organization form						
Dummy stock firm						
Dummy mutual firm						
Maturity						
Dummy age1 (1st quartile of age distribution)						
Dummy age2 (2nd quartile of age distribution)						
Dummy age3 (3rd quartile of age distribution)						
Domicile						
Dummy West				2.499***	0.66	12.17
Dummy Southeast						
Dummy Northeast						
Dummy Midwest	-1.163**	0.57	0.313	1.726***	0.664	5.617
Dummy Midatlantic				1.151**	0.571	3.16

Panel A: Parameter estimates (Continued)

	Model-supervision event			Model-conservation/ other event		
Variables	Parameter Estimate	Standard Error	Hazard ratio	Parameter Estimate	Standard Error	Hazard ratio
Business focus						
Dummy Accident & Health Lines Focus						
Dummy Auto focus				1.991***	0.521	7.321
Dummy Commercial Financial Lines Focus						
Dummy Commercial General Liability Focus						
Dummy Commercial Lines Focus						
DummyCommercial Medical Malpractice Focus				1.795**	0.772	6.018
Dummy Commercial Property Focus	-1.703**	0.750	0.182			
Dummy Commercial Workers Compensation Focus	0.910**	0.440	2.485	2.061***	0.674	7.852
Dummy Reinsurance Focus				1.894*	1.019	6.649
Dummy P&C Minimum Net Premium Witten	-1.506***	0.479	0.222			
Dummy Personal Lines Focus	-2.046***	0.645	0.129			
Macro-economic environment						
Yield curve slope (%)						
CPI inflation rate (%)						
S&P500 return (%)						
AAA corporate bond yield (%)						
Unemployment rate (%)						

Panel A: Parameter estimates (Continued)

Variables	Model-rehabilitation event			Model-liquidation event		
	Parameter Estimate	Standard Error	Hazard Ratio	Parameter Estimate	Standard Error	Hazard Ratio
Business focus						
Dummy Accident & Health Lines Focus						
Dummy Auto focus	1.835***	0.475	6.264	1.945***	0.522	6.995
Dummy Commercial Financial Lines Focus				1.662***	0.485	5.269
Dummy Commercial General Liability Focus	1.563**	0.614	4.775			
Dummy Commercial Lines Focus						
DummyCommercial Medical Malpractice Focus						
Dummy Commercial Property Focus						
Dummy Commercial Workers Compensation Focus						
Dummy Reinsurance Focus						
Dummy P&C Minimum Net Premium Witten				-1.775*	0.926	0.169
Dummy Personal Lines Focus						
Macro-economic environment						
Yield curve slope (%)	-1.642	0.542	0.194			
CPI inflation rate (%)	-0.918**	0.408	0.399			
S&P500 return (%)						
AAA corporate bond yield (%)	-1.606	0.561	0.201			
Unemployment rate (%)	1.023**	0.432	2.780			

Panel B: Summary of the Number of Event and Censored Values

	Supervision est. Sample		Conservation/ other est. Sample		Rehabilitation est. Sample		Liquidation est. sample	
	1362	100%	1362	100%	1362	100%	1362	100%
Event (Type-specific impairment)	47	3.45%	26	1.91%	35	2.57%	18	1.32%
Censored observations	1315	96.55%	1336	98.09%	1327	97.43%	1344	98.68%
Holdout samples								
	736	100%	736	100%	736	100%	736	100%
Event (Type-specific impairment)	30	4.08%	11	1.49%	17	2.31%	11	1.49%
Censored observations	706	95.92%	725	98.51%	719	97.69%	725	98.51%

Panel C: Model goodness of fit

	Model-supervision event	Model-conservation/ other event	Model-rehabilitation event	Model-liquidation event
-2 Log Likelihood (without covariates)	657.967	358.944	491.356	439.024
-2 Log Likelihood (with covariates)	466.804	224.684	288.748	267.547
Likelihood ratio Chi-square	191.163	134.26	202.608	171.47
Degrees of freedom	13	14	13	16
Pr > ChiSq	<.0001	<.0001	<.0001	<.0001

Of particular interest, the impacts of domicile factors vary substantially across models. Being incorporated in the *mid-West* area makes an insurer 68.7 percent less likely to be rehabilitated but 461.7 percent more likely to be liquidated. Registering in the *mid-Atlantic* area reduces the probability of a conservation/ other event by 80 percent but increases the hazard of a liquidation event by 216 percent. Residing in the *West* region raises the probability of being liquidated by over 1000 percent. Three factors contribute to a particularly high liquidation risk in these areas. First, all three regions, especially the *West* states, are highly vulnerable to natural disasters such as tornadoes, hurricanes and tsunamis. California and Alaska make up part of the Pacific Ring of Fire, an area of heavy volcano activities and earthquakes. Second, insurers based in New York and neighboring states were hard hit by the terrorist attack in September 2011. Third, states such as California have been more transparent in reporting impairments, which inflated its impairment incidences relative to other states (Best, 2010, p. 32). It could be that, triggered by weather-related and man-made catastrophe losses, insurers in the *mid-West, West*, and *mid-Atlantic* regions experience deteriorated financial conditions so dramatically and so rapidly that any attempt to linger their life would be detrimental to their policyholders. The optimal regulatory action may therefore be to place them into the liquidation process outright.

Another striking feature is that macro-economic factors are not significant in determining the hazards of impairment events other than rehabilitation. This is not surprising for two reasons. First, fluctuations in economic activities impact on insurers' underwriting and investment performances. Insurers have to review and adjust their leverage, liquidity and reserves policies along the business cycle. The effects of macro-economic conditions on impairment risks are therefore embedded in the effects of firm-specific financial characteristics. Second, regulators' decisions regarding the time an impaired insurer is placed in rehabilitation and the rehabilitation plan needed to revitalize the impaired insurer are generally the functions of the prevailing macro-economic climate. Perilous macro-economic environment can therefore exacerbate the vulnerability of impaired insurers and trigger the occurrence of a rehabilitation event outright.

Overall, the significant factors underlying different impairment outcomes differ. The next question is whether the estimated models exhibit predictive accuracy in forming time-varying survival forecasts out-of-sample?

5.2. Predictive performance assessment

The Brier scores of probability survival estimates generated by the four models at yearly intervals over five year forecast horizon were calculated as in equation (4) and presented in Table 2. The Brier scores of a random model and of a naïve model are used as benchmarks to assess the predictive accuracy of the estimated models. The random model produces random forecasts of 0.5 and has a Brier score of 0.25. The naïve model treats impairments of different outcomes identical, and forms forecasts by setting the survival probability beyond *t* equal to the proportion of insurers that survived beyond a period of length *t* in the generic estimation sample.

Brier scores vary from 0 to 1. A lower Brier score implies better forecast ability. A Brier score of zero indicates perfect prediction ability and a Brier score of one indicates the worst possible predictive accuracy. As shown in Table 2, all estimated models exhibits better predictive accuracy than the benchmark models. Furthermore, the overall discrepancy between probability survival estimates and survival outcomes of holdout firms narrow as the forecast horizon extends. In other words, the forecast performance of the estimated models improves as time unfolds.

Table 2: Brier score of survival probability estimates generated by estimated models

Forecast time (years)	1	2	3	4	5
Number of forecasts (Number of holdout observations)	736	730	716	698	680
Benchmark - Random forecasts	25%	25%	25%	25%	25%
Benchmark - Naive forecasts	8.50%	7.89%	7.23%	5.99%	4.69%
Dynamic hazard model for supervision events	4.05%	3.60%	3.52%	3.09%	2.04%
Dynamic hazard model for conservation/ other events	1.49%	1.51%	1.56%	1.10%	0.73%
Dynamic hazard model for rehabilitation events	4.29%	4.19%	4.03%	3.68%	3.87%
Dynamic hazard model for liquidation events	1.45%	1.27%	0.68%	0.57%	0.46%

6. Conclusion

This study applies a competing risk approach and a survival analysis framework to examine the outcome-specific impairment hazards of property-casualty insurers in the U.S. during January 1998-June 2010. The impairment data include four impairment outcomes namely supervision, conservation/other, rehabilitation, and liquidation. It is found that impairments of different outcomes are distinct phenomenon. Insurers, categorized by impairment outcomes, exhibit statistically different survival duration profiles. To mitigate the consequences of insurer impairments and to minimize the burden placed on State guaranty funds, it is necessary to investigate the risk factors associated with the occurrence and the timing of each impairment type.

This study finds that different impairment outcomes are characterized by different underlying factors. A large capital and surplus base decreases the liquidation probability whereas it does not affect the entries to other impairment resolutions. Ageing insurers are more likely to be placed under regulatory supervision or to receive a conservation order. Perilous macro-economic conditions trigger the occurrence of a rehabilitation event outright but are not significant in determining the hazards of other impairment types. Qualitative factors such as business focus and domicile indicators have strong impacts; however, the magnitudes vary substantially across models. In contrast to previous studies, this study finds that the organizational form of an insurer is not significant in any estimated model and its dynamic financial characteristics generally have small marginal impacts on its impairment risk.

The validation results show that within five-year forecast horizon the estimated models for type-specific impairment events are more accurate than a random model and a naive model in forming time-varying probability survival estimates out-of-sample. The implication is that regulators should run each hazard model separately for each insurer. The time-varying estimates generated by the models help regulators monitor the survival profile of each insurer and provide early warnings of financial impairments. For a specific forecast horizon, the type-specific model generating the estimate with the lowest survival probability is most useful. It suggests the appropriate action that should be commenced against an (impaired) insurer. The proposed approach therefore provide important signals in regards to three aspects of financial impairments: (i) whether an insurer will be impaired; (ii) how it should be impaired; and (iii) when the impairment will likely to occur.

A natural extension of this study is to examine the gap times from non-liquidation regulatory actions to liquidation or forced merger. An insurer can experience multiple impairments before being liquidated or merged by a healthy insurer. The occurrence and the timing of a supervision, a conservation/ other, and a rehabilitation event provide important signals in regards to the severity of "illness" of impaired firms. Non-liquidation regulatory actions can be treated as diagnostic events whereas liquidation and forced merger can be treated as "death" and "reincarnation" event respectively. The study could also be extended by considering impairment events an "illness" process and modeling them as mutual exclusive phenomena.

Future work could also be directed to examine the regulatory environment through time. Each State regulates its insurers under their statues and the common law. The impairment resolution might not be just a function of the conditions of an insurer and of the general economic environment, but also of the dynamic regulatory environment of each State. In other words, impairment is generic, but regulatory actions are conditional on how adept regulators are in discovering the impairment. The study partly accounts for this aspect by including domicile variables in the model. Future work could examine in depth whether there are uniform regulatory statues in the U.S.

Acknowledgements

This study belongs to a project funded by LMUexcellent program at Ludwig-Maximilians-Universität München (LMU). Many thanks to Andreas Richter, Susanne Weber, Institute for Risk and Insurance Management, Center for Advanced Studies at LMU for supporting this project. Thanks are also due to Glenn Boyle, Joseph Callaghan, Austin Murphy, Graham Partington, and to the participants of the following conferences for helpful comments: European Working Group on Financial Modeling Conference, Prague, 2010; New Zealand Finance Colloquium, Christchurch, 2011; Finance and Corporate Governance Conference, Melbourne, 2011; The 5th Annual Risk Management Conference, Singapore, 2011; International Conference on Credit Analysis and Risk Management, Rochester, 2011; Asia-Pacific Risk and Insurance Association Conference, Tokyo, 2011.

References

Allison, P. D. 1984. *Event history analysis: Regression for longitudinal event data.* Sage Publications. Beverly Hills.

—. (ed.). 1995. *Survival analysis using SAS: A practical guide.* SAS Institute Inc., Cary, North Carolina.

Altman, E. 1998. "The importance and subtlety of credit rating migration." *Journal of Banking and Finance* 22: 1231-1247.

Andersen, P. K. 1992. "Repeated assessment of risk factors in survival analysis." *Statistical Methods in Medical Research* 1: 297-315.

A. M. Best Company, I. 2009. 1969-2008 *Impairment Review: Real Estate's Title Insurers Lead 2008 P/C Financial Impairments*. Best's Special Report. Oldwick: NJ.

—. 2010. *Best's Impairment Rate and Rating Transition Study-1977 to 2009*. Oldwick: NJ.

BarNiv, R., and McDonald, J. 1992. "Identifying Financial Distress in the Insurance Industry: A Synthesis of Methodological and Empirical Issues." Journal of Risk and Insurance 59: 543-573.

BarNiv, R., and Hathorn, J. 1997. "The Merger or Insolvency Alternative in the Insurance Industry." *Journal of Risk and Insurance* 64(1): 89-113.

Browne, M., and Hoyt, R. 1995. "Economic and Market Predictors of Insolvencies in the Property-Liability Insurance Industry." Journal of Risk and Insurance 62: 309-327.

Brier, G. 1950. "Verification of forecasts expressed in terms of probability." *Monthly Weather Review* 78(1): 1-3.

Chen, L., Yen, M., Wu, H., Liao, C., Liou, D., Kuo, H. and Chen, T. H. 2005. "Predictive survival model with time-dependent prognostic factors: development of computer-aided SAS Macro program." *Journal of Evaluation in Clinical Practice* 11(2): 181-193.

Cox, D. 1972. "Regression models and life tables." *Journal of Royal Statistical Society Series B (Methodological)* 34: 187-220.

Cummins, J. D., Harrington, S. E., and Klein, R. 1995. "Insolvency Experience, Risk based Capital, and Prompt Corrective Action in Property-Liability Insurance." *Journal of Banking and Finance* 19: 511-527.

Estrella, A., and Hardouvelis, G. 1991. "The term structure as a predictor of real economic activities." *Journal of Finance* 46: 555-576

Figlewski, S., Frydman, H., Liang, W. 2008. "Modelling the effects of macroeconomic factors on corporate default and credit rating transitions." Working paper.

http://pages.stern.nyu.edu/~sfiglews/RecentWP.htm [access 30 March 2010]

Grace, M., and Klein, R. 2008. "Understanding property-casualty insurance profits: The importance of financial strength."

Halling, M., and Hayden, E. 2006. "Bank failure prediction: A two-step survival time approach." Working paper. http://ssrn.com/abstract=904255 [access 30 March 2010].

Harrington, S. E., and Nelson, J. M. 1986. "A Regression-based Methodology for Solvency Surveillance in the Property-Liability Insurance Industry." *Journal of Risk and Insurance* 53: 583-605.

Hosmer, D., Lemeshow, S., and May, S. 2008. *Applied survival analysis: Regression modelling of time-to-event data.* (2nd Ed.) Wiley Series in Probability and Statistics.

Kim, Y., Anderson, D. R., Amburgey, T. L., and Hickman, J. C. 1995. "The Use of Event History Analysis to Examine Insurer Insolvencies." *Journal of Risk and Insurance* 62(94-110).

LeClere, M. J. 1999. "The Occurrence and Timing of Events: The Application of Event History Models in Accounting and Finance Research." http://ssrn.com/abstract=181553 [access 30 March 2010]

Lee, S. H., and Urrutia, J. L. 1996. "Analysis and Prediction of Insolvency in the Property-Liability Insurance Industry: A Comparison of Logit and Hazard Models." *Journal of Risk and Insurance* 63: 121-130.

Sobehart, J., and Stein, R. 2000. "Moody's public firm risk model: A hybrid approach to modeling short-term default risk." *Moody's Rating Methodology*

Shumway, T. 2001. "Forecasting bankruptcy more accurately: A simple hazard model." *The Journal of Business* 74: 101-124.

Weiss, M. 2010. "Systemic Risk and the US Insurance Sector."

Whalen, G. 1991. "A proportional hazard model of bank failure: An examination of its usefulness as an early warning tool." *Economic Review*, Federal Reserve Bank of Cleveland 27(1): 21-31.

CHAPTER TWENTY-NINE

THE EFFECT OF ALLOWING UNREGULATED CREDIT DEFAULT SWAPS

AUSTIN MURPHY

This session involved a presentation of slides summarizing a paper that had recently been accepted for publication in the *International Review of Applied Financial Issues and Policy*. The slides are presented in the Appendix to this chapter.

After explaining how the deregulation of credit default swaps had largely caused the credit bubble that led up to the financial crisis of 2008, there was discussion of some of the various methods of regulating credit default swaps to inhibit another major crisis of this type. Full disclosure of all positions in the credit default swap market was agreed to be an absolute necessity. Requiring capital and reserves to cover potential future payoffs on credit default swaps, like with any insurance policy, was also highly suggested. Although some conference participants felt that the collateral requirements backing those credit guarantees might provide sufficient backing, it is unclear why government regulators should allow unlimited risk-increasing activities in the CDS market any more than they do for leveraged commodity futures speculation.

The Effect of Allowing Unregulated Credit Default Swaps*

by Austin Murphy

[Or How the $60 Trillion CDS Pyramid Scheme Worked!]

*Accepted for publication in the *International Review of Applied Financial Issues and Policy*

Summary of the Largest Pyramid Scheme of All Time

- Lobby the federal government to allow unlimited selling of insurance on debts without any capital requirements or reserves (Mission Accomplished in 2000 when CDSs were classified to be unregulated)
- Sell as much insurance as possible (over $60 trillion by 2008) to generate large bonuses and profits from the cheap insurance premiums short-term (even though the premiums are too low to cover future losses)
- When there isn't enough new premiums to cover losses, get federal government to do big bailout (can pay off "elected" representative some more with profits and bonuses available via the bailout money)

Simple Math of CDS Pyramid Scam

- *Big Profits for all CDS Sellers (via Placing Liability of Large Payoffs to Gov't)*
- *InsPremCDS = PremMkt - LossUncov + extraprof* (1)
- *PremMkt > XcostMkt* (2)
- *InsPremCDS > xcostCDS* (3)
- *NetArb = LossUncov – extraprof – counterloss* (4)
- *LossUncov > counterloss + extraprof* (5)
- *GuarCost = LossUnCov – counterloss* (6)
- *LossUncov* > LossUncov* (7)
- *extraprof* = InsPremCDS – PremMkt + LossUncov** > extraprof (8)

- Lower Cost of Debt with Competing Pyramid Scammers (but hasten collapse)
- *extraprof* = 0* (9)
- *InsPremCDS* = PremMkt - LossUncov*.* (10)
- *XcostCDS* < XcostMkt.* (11)
- *LossUncov* < PremMkt* (12)
- *LossUncov* > counterloss** (13)
- *counterloss* < PremMkt* (14)

Explanation of Pyramid Math

- Institutions can increase profits by selling ever more debt insurance because any future large payouts for defaults on debts insured by CDSs are absorbed by the institutions' liabilityholders when an institution fails (i.e., the government for institutions whose liabilities are implicitly or explicitly insured by the government)
- Since the profits can be increased even when the sale of CDSs for credit premiums less than normally required in debt markets, huge amounts of insurance can be sold (that lower credit premiums in the loan and bond markets due to profitable arbitrage)

Why the Credit Bubble was Concentrated in Home Mortgages?

- Securitized home mortgages can be insured via CDSs with virtually no credit analysis as the debts can be refinanced with rising equity values caused by further mortgages offered to any borrowers (including NINJAs, loans above appraised values, etc.) that are then insured by further CDSs that generate more profits to the institutions issuing the CDS insurance, until real estate prices stop rising and the credit bubble bursts
- Lack of disclosure makes it impossible for the market to determine if any CDS insurer is unable to make contingent payments. Aaa ratings for the CDS insurers (along with government implied guarantees of large institutions) doubt) cause investors to assume CDS insurance to be iron-clad, and so they buy the packaged mortgages backed by CDS insurance
- Loan originators can issue mortgages they know are questionable because they can sell them to investors in packages that will be guaranteed by CDSs

Lots of "Goodies" for Everyone!

- Big profits for the shareholders of the institutional sellers of CDS insurance
- Big bonuses for the employee participants (especially in the form of compensation to loan sellers with limited paperwork)
- Home ownership for those who can't afford it
- Easy cash for existing home owners borrowing on rising home values
- Economy booms via the easy money

The Effect of Competition

- Competition among pyramid scammers drives the price of CDS insurance toward the cost of evaluating credit, and so institutions have the incentive to further reduce the quality of credit analysis as the sellers of CDS insurance computerize their own analysis while mortgage originators just send in the numbers without doing any checking or "soft" analysis
- Result: no doc loans, loans without any viable appraisal, etc.

Conclusions for Regulators

- Need to require full disclosure of all CDS positions at all times so that investors can discipline pyramid scammers
- Government needs to require capital and reserves for CDS contingent liabilities, just as it does for all insurance contracts
- End all business lobbying and political campaign donations to inhibit development of new scams

Suggestions for New Accounting Rules

- Because losses on new loans are lower in their early years after origination, reported profits from CDSs are larger in the early stages of the CDS contracts (just as they are for making and holding new loans)
- This phenomenon encourages excess CDS issuance (and excess loan originations) as the larger profits early provide short-term incentives to pay out larger bonuses, etc. for issuance without regard to long-term credit quality
- A reserve for the increasing losses on CDSs (and loans) should be required in the early years of a CDS (or loan)

Suggestions for Securitization

- Have each loan officer provide a ranking for the credit quality of a loan (that could be adjusted statistically for any illegal systematic discriminatory biases that may unconsciously exist in the loan officer).
- Have that parameter included with the other information on the loan
- Have the loan officer compensated with a long-term bonus that is set as a function of the accuracy of the evaluation of the credit quality of the loan (based on their future defaults), with that bonus being a large portion of the officer's variable compensation

Education of New Lending Officers

- Institutions that can't afford an in-house training program for new loan officers could have new officers be required to show competence in the evaluation of credit through earning a certificate in credit analysis.
- The information provided about a loan packaged in an asset-backed pool could include not only the loan officer's credit ranking of the loan but also whether the officer had earned a certificate in credit analysis

Without Change in Government Policy...

- A potentially even bigger collapse in the future requiring a bailout in excess of the $17 trillion in debt guarantees and purchases provided in 2008 (not to mention the $trillions in cheap loans to financial institutions)
- Hedge funds like Magnetar will continue to be able to profit no matter what (such as by taking a long position in insured debts and then using the income in the early stages of the loans to buy excess CDS insurance on those same debts at the prices that are lower than normal market premiums, so that hedge funds can profit big time when the bubble collapses as well as generate good income until then)
- **Suggestion for new scam by government insured institutions**: Why not try <u>*selling fire insurance on all the buildings in America for a very cheap price*</u> if the government removes all capital and loss reserve requirements for such insurance, doesn't require disclosure of how big the insurance liabilities are for each insurer, and is virtually assured to bail the insurers out when payouts for fire losses exceed the insurance premiums that are brought in? A few million dollars can buy the President and Congress, so it seems as possible as having CDSs issued without capital, loss reserves, or disclosure (and politically palatable, since it would lower home owner costs, reduce business costs, and pump up the economy temporarily)

CHAPTER THIRTY

SPECIAL REPORT ON DEFAULTS AND RETURNS IN THE HIGH-YIELD BOND MARKET: FIRST-HALF 2011 REVIEW

EDWARD I. ALTMAN AND BRENDA J. KUEHNE[1]

Executive Summary

Defaults in the second quarter of 2011 were $1.18 billion, resulting in a quarterly default rate of 0.09%, slightly larger than the quarterly default rate one year prior, but the lowest rate of the past four quarters. This continues a trend of extremely low defaults, during which the quarterly default rates were below 0.50%, that has now lasted for six quarters. The trailing 12-month default rate decreased to 1.08%, down from 1.09% as of the end of the first quarter 2011.

The S&P/LSTA 12-month, dollar-denominated default rate on leveraged loans decreased from 1.11% at first-quarter end to 0.91%, while the issuer default rate decreased from 1.62% to 1.51%. As has been evidenced since the first-quarter 2010, the issuer loan default rate exceeded the dollar denominated rate, which is quite typical for loans and bonds during benign credit cycles.

---

[1] Dr. Altman is the Max L. Heine Professor of Finance and Director of the Credit and Debt Markets Research Program at the NYU Salomon Center, Leonard N. Stern School of Business and a member of the Advisory Board of Paulson & Co. Brenda Kuehne is a Credit and Debt Markets Research Specialist at the NYU Salomon Center. We appreciate the assistance of Alex Dai of the NYU Salomon Center and the several market makers who provided us with price quotations. We offer a special thanks to the various rating agencies, Daniel Sweeney of Credit Suisse, Steven Miller of S&P LCD, Kerry Mastroianni of New Generation Research, and Ty Wallach and Sheru Chowdhry of Paulson & Co.

The recovery rate on defaulted bond issues for the six months ended June 30, 2011 was 59.9%, well above the historical average of 44.8%, and a mere basis point higher than the first-quarter recovery rate. Recoveries on the two debt exchanges thus far in 2011 were 76.7%, while for the remaining defaulting issues it was 54.9%. Default losses for the first six months of the year were 10bp, comparable to the 9bp loss for the same period one year ago.

Returns on high-yield bonds for the six months ended June 30 were 4.98%. The excess return compared to 10-yr US Treasury bonds was 1.88%, tightening by 257bp since the end of the first quarter. Spreads for high-yield bonds over the same 10-yr Treasury benchmark (on a yield-to-maturity basis) were 4.48% as of the end of June, widening 55bp from the first-quarter end.

US high-yield bond issuance in the second quarter was $82.3 billion, notably greater than the same period last year ($33.7 billion), and the highest ever amount of quarterly new issuance on record. Leveraged loan issuance decreased in the second quarter to $116.4 billion, compared to approximately $141.2 billion during the prior quarter, but was still significantly higher than the $66.9 billion issued during the second quarter of 2010. The proportion of high-yield bonds issued at B- or lower was slightly higher than the 29% average of the last five years, with 33.2% issued in these rating categories so far this year, the highest proportion since 2007.

The distress ratio of high-yield bonds yielding more than 1,000bp over 10-yr Treasuries increased from 5.0% at the end of first-quarter 2011 to 7.1% in the second quarter. This is the first quarterly increase in the distress ratio since the second-quarter 2010.

We estimate that the face value of the defaulted and distressed debt market increased to about $1.01 trillion as of June 30, 2011, up from $930.75 billion at the end of the first quarter. The primary reason for this small increase was the rise in the distress ratio. Our market value estimate increased to $562.4 billion (from $523.6 billion one quarter earlier).

Finally, the return on a portfolio of *defaulted* bonds and bank loans for the first six months of the year was 5.13%, with defaulted bonds outperforming defaulted loans—7.18% versus 3.50%.

Defaults and Default Rates

High-yield bond defaults decreased in the second quarter, dropping from $1.73 billion of new defaults in the prior quarter to $1.18 billion. The resulting year-to-date default rate was 0.23% (Figure 1). The second quarter rate (0.09%) was the lowest quarterly measure of the past four quarters, and our eighth lowest quarterly rate since our time series started in 1989 (Appendix A). The second quarter's default rate marks the sixth consecutive quarter of rates less than 0.5%. Since 1989, there have been two longer, consecutive quarterly periods of default rates also below 0.5% -- seven from Q4 2003 to Q2 2005 and nine from Q1 2006 to Q1 2008. The US and Canadian dollar-denominated default rate for the last 12 months fell to 1.08% from 1.09% at the end of the first-quarter 2011, and was lower than the 12-month issuer-denominated default rates calculated by both Moody's (2.6%) and S&P (2.3%). Fitch's dollar-denominated default rate for the last 12 months was 1.1%, with a 0.2% year-to-date default rate, while Moody's last 12-month dollar denominated default rate was 1.4%.

As we have indicated in past reports, when the credit markets are in a strong benign state, dollar-denominated default rates fall to lower levels than do issuer rates. The reverse happens in highly stressed conditions when the dollar rate usually exceeds issuer rates.[2] Hence, dollar default rates are more volatile, less easily modeled, but still quite relevant.

Three high-yield issuers defaulted in the second quarter compared to six in the first quarter, and five in the period one year prior (Appendix B). No large defaults occurred in the second quarter of 2011, resulting in only seven individual defaulting issues from the three issuers. Angiotech Pharmaceuticals, Inc., with $575 million in total bond defaults, was the only issuer to default on more than $500 million in outstanding bonds within the first half of 2011 (Nebraska Book Company was close).

In our default statistics, we include those bonds from distressed exchanges actually tendered. Thus far in 2011, there have been two distressed exchanges, comprising $574.5 million of defaults (19.7% of the total). See Appendix C for the list of 2011 bond distressed exchanges.

The default rate for the last 12 months in the US leveraged loan market was 1.51% based on issuers, and 0.91% weighted by issuance, according to S&P/LCD calculations. These rates represent a decrease versus the first-quarter 2011 (1.62% and 1.11%, respectively). There were three leveraged loan defaults (by issuer) in the first half of 2011 (Appendix D).

According to our comparison of high-yield bond defaults (Appendix B) and leveraged loan defaults (Appendix D), in the first six months of the year, one firm, Sbarro, Inc., defaulted on both bonds and institutional leveraged loans.

---

[2] *High Yield Bonds: Default and Loss Rate Comparison – Mid-Cap versus Large-Cap Issuers*, M. Verde, P. Mancuso and E. Altman November 11, 2005, Fitch.

Figure 2 shows the quarterly and four-quarter moving average default rate since 1989. The spike in default rates experienced during the most recent recession has subsided over the past year and returned to much below-average levels.

Our forecast for the next 12 months ending June 30, 2012 is for a default rate of 3.14%. If the present extremely liquid markets persist and the proportion of low-rated companies that are able to tap both the debt and equity markets for refinancing continues, our forecast will likely be on the high-side. There are several important risks on the horizon (see discussion later) that have increased the required yield on high-yield bonds beyond what the miniscule recent default rates imply.

Figure 1. Historical Default Rates — Straight Bonds Only, Not Including Defaulted Issues From Par Value Outstanding, 1971–2Q 2011 (Dollars in Millions)

Year	Par Value Outstanding[a] ($)	Defaults ($)	Default Rates (%)
2011 (2Q)	1,277,841	2,916	0.228
2010	1,221,569	13,809	1.130
2009	1,152,952	123,824	10.766
2008	1,091,000	50,763	4.653
2007	1,075,400	5,473	0.509
2006	993,600	7,559	0.761
2005	1,073,000	36,209	3.375
2004	933,100	11,657	1.249
2003	825,000	38,451	4.661
2002	757,000	96,858	12.795
2001	649,000	63,609	9.801
2000	597,200	30,295	5.073
1999	567,400	23,532	4.147
1998	465,500	7,464	1.603
1997	335,400	4,200	1.252
1996	271,000	3,336	1.231
1995	240,000	4,551	1.896
1994	235,000	3,418	1.454
1993	206,907	2,287	1.105
1992	163,000	5,545	3.402
1991	183,600	18,862	10.273
1990	181,000	18,354	10.140
1989	189,258	8,110	4.285
1988	148,187	3,944	2.662
1987	129,557	7,486	5.778

1986	90,243	3,156	3.497	
1985	58,088	992	1.708	
1984	40,939	344	0.840	
1983	27,492	301	1.095	
1982	18,109	577	3.186	
1981	17,115	27	0.158	
1980	14,935	224	1.500	
1979	10,356	20	0.193	
1978	8,946	119	1.330	
1977	8,157	381	4.671	
1976	7,735	30	0.388	
1975	7,471	204	2.731	
1974	10,894	123	1.129	
1973	7,824	49	0.626	
1972	6,928	193	2.786	
1971	6,602	82	1.242	
				Standard Deviation (%)
Arithmetic Average Default Rate		1971 to 2010	3.277	3.204
		1978 to 2010	3.561	3.399
		1985 to 2010	4.200	3.535
Weighted Average Default Rate[b]		1971 to 2010	4.254	
		1978 to 2010	4.264	
		1985 to 2010	4.294	
Median Annual Default Rate		1971 to 2010	1.802	

[a] As of midyear. [b] Weighted by par value of amount outstanding for each year.
Source: NYU Salomon Center.

Figure 2. Quarterly Default Rate and the Four-Quarter Moving Average, 1989–2Q 2011

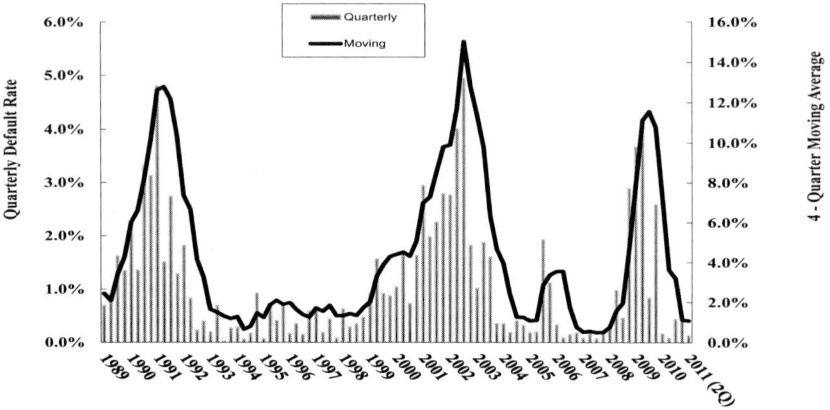

Source: NYU Salomon Center.

Bankruptcies

The total liabilities for Chapter 11 bankruptcies decreased to $15.0 billion in the first half of 2011 from $23.9 billion for the same period one year prior. Figure 3 shows there were 39 filings in the first six months where liabilities were greater than $100 million (with two more than $1 billion), compared with 60 one year earlier, and 114 for all of 2010. MSR Resort & Golf Course, LLC was the largest bankruptcy filing in the first half of 2011, with $1.90 billion in liabilities. Borders, Inc. was the only other billion-dollar bankruptcy. Appendix E lists this year's large Chapter 11 bankruptcies.

Figure 3. Total Filings and Liabilities[a] of Companies Filing for Chapter 11 Bankruptcy, 1989–2Q 2011

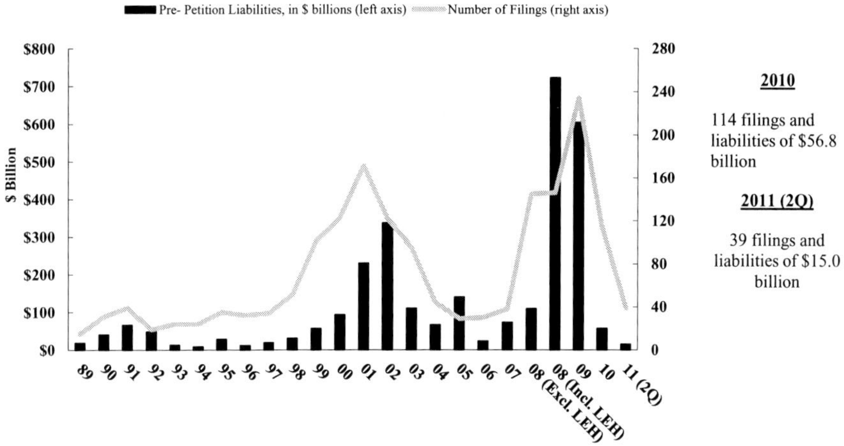

[a] Minimum $100 million in liabilities.
Sources: Appendix E from the NYU Salomon Center Bankruptcy Filings Database.

Industry Defaults

Five of the defaulting issuers were retailing companies, while the remaining four issuers to default within the first-half 2011 were spread equally over the auto/motor carrier, healthcare, miscellaneous, and communications and media industries (Figure 4). Appendix F presents a more detailed breakdown of all nine defaulting issuers. Figure 5 shows the dollar amount of defaulted issues by industry from 1990 to the present. The media and communications industry dominates these historical totals, primarily the result of the telecom meltdown during 2000-02, followed by financial services. However, historically the largest number of defaulting issuers, by far, is in the general manufacturing sector.

Figure 4. Corporate Bond Defaults by Industry (Number of Companies)

Industry	1970 -89	90	91	92	93	94	95	96	97	98	99	2000	01	02	03	04	05	06	07	08	09	10	2Q 11	Total
Auto/Motor Carrier	6	3					1				1			1			4	3		8	9		1	**37**
Conglomerates	5	1	3	3								1			1	1								**15**
Energy	35		4	2	3		1			1	13	1		8	9		1		1	4	8	1		**92**
Financial Services	21	7	14	3	2	1	2	1	2	6	1	6	4	5	6	2	3	2		5	7	7		**107**
Leisure/	9	8	2	4	3	4	3	1	5	5	8	9	6	5	6			3		10	12	3		
Entertainment																								**106**
General Manufacturing	26	5	8	8	7	3	8	6	7	6	16	23	43	22	13	17	12	6	7	10	36	4		**293**
Health Care	4	2	1	1	1		2			2	8	6	3	4	3		2		1	1		2	1	**44**
Miscellaneous	16	4	4	3	1	1	1		3	3	16	34	38	25	16	6	1	4	3	4	5	3	1	
Industries																								**192**
RealEstate/	14	7	5	1			2	1	2	1	4	6	4	3		2	1			6	11	5		
Construction																								**75**
REIT	12			1										1										**14**
Retailing	10	6	15	6	4	5	6	3	6	6	12	7	12	5	5	3	2	2	3	5	5	3	5	**136**
Comm. & Media	17	3	4	1	1	3	2	2	1	6	11	8	39	26	21	6	3	2	4	10	20	6	1	**197**
Transportation	9	1	2			2			2	1	8	5	7	7	6	2	5	1			7			
(Non Auto)																								**65**
Utilities	2			1				1	1			1		0	0									**6**
Total	**186**	**47**	**62**	**34**	**22**	**19**	**28**	**15**	**29**	**37**	**98**	**107**	**156**	**112**	**86**	**39**	**34**	**23**	**19**	**63**	**120**	**34**	**9**	**1,379**

Source: NYU Salomon Center.

Figure 5. Corporate Bond Defaults by Industry (Dollars in Millions)

Industry	**1990**	**1991**	**1992**	**93-94**	**1995**	**1996**	**1997**	**1998**	**1999**	**2000**	**2001**
Auto/Motor Carrier	468	90			215		300	100	430	120	3,737
Conglomerates											
Energy		60	103	600	75	100			3,812	217	4,200
Financial Services	928	696	536	78	687	700	66	689	375	1,968	5,062
Leisure/ Entertainment	498	1,191	159	138	435	293		245	1,100	2,891	3,437
General Manufacturing	2,675	3,695	488	118	616	641	123	247	2,092	2,507	3,138
Health Care	18	1,120			75			125	2,214	1,715	692
Miscellaneous Industries	1,968	4,911	1,378	1,373	1,286	832	461	1,290	7,615	8,352	9,715
Real Estate/ Construction	2,605	417	113	124	190		258	383	385	252	1,110
Retailing	4,443	2,937	1,489	2,832	395	164	2,504	1,241	2,052	3,081	1,586
Communications & Media						460	286	1,549	2,980	5,983	34,827
Transportation (Non Auto)	1,028	1,452		301	562			1,125	310	2,890	1,430
Utilities		1,452	617	85		275	202		75		
Total	**14,631**	**18,021**	**4,883**	**5,649**	**4,536**	**3,465**	**4,200**	**6,994**	**23,440**	**29,976**	**68,934**

Figure 5. Corporate Bond Defaults by Industry (Dollars in Millions) (Continued)

Industry	2002	2003	2004	2005	2006	2007	2008	2009	2010	2011 (2Q)	Total
Auto/Motor Carrier	285		280	3,573	2,692		1,382	16,872		173	**30,717**
Conglomerates	100	690	275								**1,065**
Energy	4,085	11,857		8,895		50	1,511	1,993	3,594		**41,152**
Financial Services	3,803	1,079	110	541	156		26,973	29,274	2,429		**76,150**
Leisure/ Entertainment	21,242	633	1,286	6,861	715		6,022	10,395	1,805		**59,346**
General Manufacturing	2,455	2,108	225	1,396	1,486	2,379	3,747	26,072	850		**57,059**
Health Care	115	3,843		360		520	150		495	575	**12,016**
Miscellaneous Industries	5,594	4,494	1,977	569	409	1,396	1,505	1,787	373	237	**57,522**
Real Estate/ Construction	1,088	77	1,783	174			2,158	4,803	952		**16,873**
Retailing	4,092	877	749	1,059	332	363	1,412	1,015	525	1,495	**34,643**
Communications & Media	47,953	7,603	2,551	150	1,496	765	5,310	30,954	2,787	436	**146,684**
Transportation (Non Auto)	4,711	2,086	2,421	12,376	272			964			**31,928**
Utilities	1,150	1,417									**5,273**
Total	**96,673**	**36,764**	**11,657**	**35,954**	**7,559**	**5,473**	**50,763**	**124,130**	**13,809**	**1,734**	**570,427**

Source: NYU Salomon Center.

Fallen Angel Defaults

As in the prior quarter, none of the defaulted issues thus far in 2011 were from issuers who were originally rated investment grade at issuance. Figure 6 shows the fallen angel proportion of defaults from 1977 to the present based upon number of issues. The average from 1977 to the present is approximately 27%.

Figure 6. Fallen Angel Defaulted Issues by Original Rating (1977–2Q 2011)

Year	Total No. Defaulted Issues[a]	Originally Rated Investment Grade (%)
2011 (2Q)	15	0
2010	55	15
2009	405	32
2008	154	31
2007	35	11
2006	52	13
2005	184	49
2004	79	19
2003	203	33
2002	322	39
2001	258	14
2000	142	16
1999	87	13
1998	39	31
1997	20	0
1996	24	13
1995	29	10
1994	16	0
1993	24	0
1992	59	25
1991	163	27
1990	117	16
1989	66	18
1988	64	42
1987	31	39
1986	55	15
1985	26	4
1984	14	21
1983	7	43
1982	20	55
1981	1	0
1980	4	25
1979	1	0
1978	1	100
1977	2	100
Total	**2,774**	**27%**

[a] Where we could find an original rating from either S&P or Moody's. Sources: Moody's, NYU Salomon Center, and S&P.

Default Losses and Recoveries

Figure 7. Second-Quarter 2011 Default Loss Rate (In Percent)

	Unadjusted for Fallen Angels	Only Fallen Angels	All Except Fallen Angels	Price Adjusted for Fallen Angels
Background Data				
Average Default Rate	0.228	0.000	0.228	0.228
Average Price at Default[a]	59.892	0.000	59.892	59.892
Average Price at Downgrade[b]		0.000		
Average Recovery	59.892	0.000	59.892	59.892
Average Loss of Principal	40.108	0.000	40.108	40.108
Average Coupon Payment	9.566	0.000	9.566	9.566
Default Loss Computation				
Default Rate	0.228	0.000	0.228	0.228
X Loss of Principal	40.108	0.000	40.108	40.108
Default Loss of Principal	0.092	0.000	0.092	0.092
Default Rate	0.228	0.000	0.228	0.228
X Loss of 1/2 Coupon	4.783	0.000	4.783	4.783
Default Loss of Coupon	0.011	0.000	0.011	0.011
Default Loss of Principal and Coupon	0.102	0.000	0.102	0.102

[a] If default date price is not available, end-of-month price is used, when available.
[b] Downgrade to non-investment grade.
Sources: NYU Salomon Center and various dealer quotes.

The weighted-average recovery rate on defaulting issues so far in 2011 has increased slightly since the first quarter. The recovery rate was 59.9% for the first half of 2011 (Figure 7), well above the historical average of 44.8% (Figure 8), and a mere basis point higher than the first-quarter recovery rate. Te resultant default loss was just 10.2bp. This loss includes the foregone coupon of 1.1bp and is for all high-yield company defaults. These relatively high default recoveries during low default periods are consistent with our now accepted thesis that recoveries and defaults are significantly negatively correlated (see our Annual Report for details)[3].

Figure 8 shows loss statistics since 1978, with an arithmetic average annual loss rate of 2.39% (2.88% on a weighted-average basis), significantly higher than the losses experienced in 2010 and thus far in 2011.

Figure 9 lists the average recovery by seniority for 1978–2011. Thus far in 2011, three of the defaulting issues were senior secured, with a recovery rate of 65.8%, compared to a historical average of 57.6%. Eight were senior unsecured, with a recovery rate of 59.4%, compared to a historical average of 38.0%. The large discrepancy in the recovery rate on this seniority, versus the historical average, was partially attributable to the fact that one of the eight defaults, the largest single default by dollar amount thus far in 2011, occurred as part of a distressed exchange (see below). One was senior subordinated, with an average recovery of 48.0%, compared to a historical average of 30.6 %. There were no priced defaults in the first-quarter 2011 in either the subordinated or discount and zero coupon categories. The historical average recoveries on these two classes were 30.7% and 25.4%, respectively. Three issues could not be priced.

[3] E. Altman & B. Kuehne "Defaults and Returns in the High-Yield Bond and Distressed Debt Market: The Year 2010 in Review and Outlook", *Paulson & Co.,* February 04, 2011.

Figure 8. Default Rates and Losses, 1978–2Q 2011 (Dollars in Millions)

Year	Par Value Outstanding [a] ($)	Par Value of Default ($)	Default Rate (%)	Weighted Price After Default ($)	Weighted Coupon (%)	Default Loss (%) [b]
2011(2Q)	1,277,841	2,916	0.23	59.9	9.57	0.10
2010	1,221,569	13,809	1.13	46.6	10.59	0.66
2009	1,152,952	124,130	10.77	36.1	8.16	7.30
2008	1,091,000	50,763	4.65	42.5	8.23	2.83
2007	1,075,400	5,473	0.51	66.6	9.64	0.19
2006	993,600	7,559	0.76	65.3	9.33	0.30
2005	1,073,000	36,209	3.37	61.1	8.61	1.46
2004	933,100	11,657	1.25	57.7	10.30	0.59
2003	825,000	38,451	4.66	45.5	9.55	2.76
2002	757,000	96,858	12.79	25.3	9.37	10.15
2001	649,000	63,609	9.80	25.5	9.18	7.76
2000	597,200	30,295	5.07	26.4	8.54	3.95
1999	567,400	23,532	4.15	27.9	10.55	3.21
1998	465,500	7,464	1.60	35.9	9.46	1.10
1997	335,400	4,200	1.25	54.2	11.87	0.65
1996	271,000	3,336	1.23	51.9	8.92	0.65
1995	240,000	4,551	1.90	40.6	11.83	1.24
1994	235,000	3,418	1.45	39.4	10.25	0.96
1993	206,907	2,287	1.11	56.6	12.98	0.56
1992	163,000	5,545	3.40	50.1	12.32	1.91
1991	183,600	18,862	10.27	36.0	11.59	7.16
1990	181,000	18,354	10.14	23.4	12.94	8.42
1989	189,258	8,110	4.29	38.3	13.40	2.93
1988	148,187	3,944	2.66	43.6	11.91	1.66
1987	129,557	7,486	5.78	75.9	12.07	1.74
1986	90,243	3,156	3.50	34.5	10.61	2.48
1985	58,088	992	1.71	45.9	13.69	1.04
1984	40,939	344	0.84	48.6	12.23	0.48
1983	27,492	301	1.09	55.7	10.11	0.54
1982	18,109	577	3.19	38.6	9.61	2.11
1981	17,115	27	0.16	72.0	15.75	0.15
1980	14,935	224	1.50	21.1	8.43	1.25
1979	10,356	20	0.19	31.0	10.63	0.14
1978	8,946	119	1.33	60.0	8.38	0.59
Arithmetic Average 1978-2010			**3.56**	**44.84**	**10.64**	**2.39**
Weighted Average 1978-2010			**4.26**			**2.88**

[a] Excludes defaulted issues. [b] Default loss rate adjusted for fallen angels was 9.3% in 2002, 1.82% in 2003, 0.59% in 2004, 1.56% in 2005, 0.039% in 2006, 0.20% in 2007, 3.42% in 2008, 7.38% in 2009, 0.66% in 2010, and 0.11% in the second-quarter 2011. Source: NYU Salomon Center.

Figure 9. Weighted Average (by Issue) Recovery Rates on Defaulted Bonds by Seniority Per $100 Face Amount, 1978–2Q 2011

Default	Senior Secured			Senior Unsecured			Senior Subordinated			Subordinated			Discount and Zero Coupon			All Seniorities	
Year	No.	%	$	No.	%	$	No.	%	$	No.	%	$	No.	%	$	No.	$
2011 (2Q)	3	25	65.80	8	67	59.41	1	8	48.00	0	0	0.00	0	0	0.00	12	59.89
2010	6	24	39.46	12	48	57.86	5	20	30.64	2	8	12.67	0	0	0.00	25	46.62
2009	29	10	43.70	226	76	37.22	31	10	24.06	4	1	12.57	7	2	16.84	297	36.13
2008	18	14	30.52	79	63	49.56	23	18	30.25	4	3	21.09	1	1	2.71	125	42.52
2007	10	36	87.24	10	36	47.70	6	21	63.98	2	7	46.53	0	0	0.00	28	66.65
2006	9	18	90.60	26	52	60.90	8	16	50.24	1	2	60.33	6	12	78.31	50	65.32
2005	67	54	76.50	44	36	45.88	7	6	32.67	0	0	0.00	5	4	74.21	123	61.10
2004	27	39	63.67	33	48	56.77	2	3	37.44	0	0	0.00	7	10	43.06	69	57.72
2003	57	28	53.51	108	53	45.40	29	14	35.98	1	0	38.00	8	4	32.27	203	45.58
2002	37	11	52.81	254	75	21.82	21	6	32.79	0	0	0.00	28	8	26.47	340	25.30
2001	9	3	40.95	187	67	28.84	48	17	18.37	0	0	0.00	37	13	15.05	281	25.62
2000	13	8	39.58	47	29	25.40	61	37	25.96	26	16	26.62	17	10	23.61	164	26.74
1999	14	11	26.90	60	47	42.54	40	31	23.56	2	2	13.88	11	9	17.30	127	27.90
1998	6	18	70.38	21	62	39.57	6	18	17.54	0	0	0.00	1	3	17.00	34	40.46
1997	4	16	74.90	12	48	70.94	6	24	31.89	1	4	60.00	2	8	19.00	25	57.61
1996	4	17	59.08	4	17	50.11	9	38	48.99	4	17	44.23	3	13	11.99	24	45.44
1995	5	15	44.64	9	27	50.50	17	52	39.01	1	3	20.00	1	3	17.50	33	41.77
1994	5	23	48.66	8	36	51.14	5	23	19.81	3	14	37.04	1	5	5.00	22	39.44
1993	2	6	55.75	7	22	33.38	10	31	51.50	9	28	28.38	4	13	31.75	32	38.83
1992	15	22	59.85	8	12	35.61	17	25	58.20	22	33	49.13	5	7	19.82	67	50.03
1991	4	3	44.12	69	44	55.84	37	24	31.91	38	24	24.30	9	6	27.89	157	40.67
1990	12	10	32.18	31	27	29.02	38	33	25.01	24	21	18.83	11	9	15.63	116	24.66

Figure 9. Weighted Average (by Issue) Recovery Rates on Defaulted Bonds by Seniority Per $100 Face Amount, 1978–2Q 2011 (Continued)

	Senior Secured			Senior Unsecured			Senior Subordinated			Subordinated			Discount and Zero Coupon			All Seniorities	
Default Year	No.	%	$	No.	%	$	No.	%	$	No.	%	$	No.	%	$	No.	$
1989	9	12	82.69	16	21	53.70	21	28	19.60	30	39	23.95				76	35.97
1988	13	21	67.96	19	31	41.99	10	16	30.70	20	32	35.27				62	43.45
1987	4	13	90.68	17	55	72.02	6	19	56.24	4	13	35.25				31	66.63
1986	8	14	48.32	11	20	37.72	7	13	35.20	30	54	33.39				56	36.60
1985	2	7	74.25	3	11	34.81	7	26	36.18	15	56	41.45				27	41.78
1984	4	29	53.42	1	7	50.50	2	14	65.88	7	50	44.68				14	50.62
1983	1	13	71.00	3	38	67.72				4	50	41.79				8	55.17
1982				16	80	39.31				4	20	32.91				20	38.03
1981	1	100	72.00													1	72.00
1980				2	50	26.71				2	50	16.63				4	21.67
1979										1	100	31.00				1	31.00
1978				1	100	60.00										1	60.00
Total/Avg	398	15	57.60	1,352	51	38.04	480	18	30.61	261	10	30.71	164	6	25.45	2,655	37.80
Median			57.42			46.79			32.73			27.50			17.40		42.15
Standard Dev[a]			17.98			13.31			13.86			17.77			20.70		13.74

[a] Standard deviations are calculated based on the yearly averages.

Sources: NYU Salomon Center and various dealer quotes.

Distressed Exchanges in 2011

Distressed exchanges (DEs) in the first six months of 2011 accounted for about 22.2% of the defaulted issuers (2 out of 9), and 19.7% of the defaulted dollar amount. From 1984 through the second quarter of 2011, DEs accounted for about 11.0% of all defaulting issuers and 12.6% of all defaulted dollar amounts (Figure 10).

Figure 10 indicates the "popular" re-emergence of DEs in 2008–2011 as compared to the last 27 years. Indeed, during this slightly more than three-year period, more than 54% (69 of 126) of all DEs took place. As we have compiled in a recent study, about 46% of all DEs up to 2007 resulted in a subsequent Chapter 11 or 7 bankruptcy filing and 30% of the DE firms were acquired. The data would appear to indicate a DE is oftentimes just a short-term fix.[4] However, the pace at which DEs were being sought as a restructuring alternative slowed considerably, at least in absolute terms, in the second-half of 2009 and into 2010, as other avenues of refinancing became available. Still, 22% so far in 2011 is a relatively high proportion of total defaulting issuers, albeit based on a small total number of defaults.

[4] *The Re-emergence of Distressed Exchanges in Corporate Restructurings*, E. Altman and B. Karlin, NYU Salomon Center Working Paper, 2009 (see E. Altman's website) and published in *The Journal of Credit Risk*, Summer 2009. It is too early to do a longitudinal analysis on the DE classes of 2008- 2010, though we are getting close to adding the "class of 2008" to our analysis.

Figure 10. High-Yield Bond Distressed Exchange Default and Recovery Statistics, 1984–2Q 2011

Year	D/E Defaults ($)	Total Defaults ($)	D/E Defaults (%) to Total $	D/E Defaults (No. of Issuers)	Total Defaults (No. of Issuers)	D/E Defaults (%) to Total No. of Issuers	D/E Recovery Rate[a]	All Default Recovery Rate[a]	Difference Between D/E & All Default Recovery Rate
2011 (2Q)	574.46	2,915.66	19.7	2	9	22.2	76.67	59.89	16.78
2010	4,971.48	13,808.63	36.0	7	34	20.6	65.60	46.62	18.98
2009	23,212.60	124.130.49	18.7	46	120	38.3	42.68	36.13	6.55
2008	30,329.42	50,763.26	59.7	14	64	21.9	52.41	42.50	9.91
2007	146.83	5,473.00	2.7	1	19	5.3	85.17	66.65	18.52
2006	0.00	7,559.00	0.0	0	0	0	NA	NA	NA
2005	0.00	36,209.00	0.0	0	0	0	NA	NA	NA
2004	537.88	11,657.00	4.6	5	39	12.8	58.05	57.72	0.33
2003	1,034.94	38,451.00	2.7	7	86	8.1	78.52	45.58	32.94
2002	764.80	96,858.00	0.8	3	112	2.7	61.22	25.30	35.92
2001	1,267.60	63,609.00	2.0	5	156	3.2	33.12	25.62	7.50
2000	50.00	30,295.00	0.2	1	107	0.9	77.00	26.74	50.26
1999	2,118.40	23,532.00	9.0	6	98	6.1	65.39	27.90	37.49
1998	461.10	7,464.00	6.2	2	37	5.4	17.34	40.46	(23.12)
1997	0.00	4,200.00	0.0	0	0	0.0	NA	NA	NA
1996	0.00	3,336.00	0.0	0	0	0.0	NA	NA	NA
1995	0.00	4,551.00	0.0	0	0	0.0	NA	NA	NA
1994	0.00	3,418.00	0.0	0	0	0.0	NA	NA	NA
1993	0.00	2,287.00	0.0	0	0	0.0	NA	NA	NA
1992	0.00	5,545.00	0.0	0	0	0.0	NA	NA	NA
1991	76.00	18,862.00	0.4	1	62	1.6	31.30	40.67	(9.37)
1990	1,044.00	18,354.00	5.7	7	47	14.9	43.15	24.66	18.49

Figure 10. High-Yield Bond Distressed Exchange Default and Recovery Statistics, 1984–2Q 2011 (Continued)

Year	D/E Defaults ($)	Total Defaults ($)	D/E Defaults (%) to Total $	D/E Defaults (No. of Issuers)	Total Defaults (No. of Issuers)	D/E Defaults (%) to Total No. of Issuers	D/E Recovery Rate[a]	All Default Recovery Rate[a]	Difference Between D/E & All Default Recovery Rate
1989	548.90	8,110.00	6.8	7	26	26.9	44.53	35.97	8.56
1988	390.30	3,944.00	9.9	3	24	12.5	28.40	43.45	(15.05)
1987	33.60	7,486.00	0.4	2	15	13.3	40.70	66.63	(25.93)
1986	114.80	3,156.00	3.6	4	23	17.4	47.68	36.60	11.08
1985	323.30	992.00	32.6	2	19	10.5	55.04	41.78	13.26
1984	100.10	344.00	29.1	1	12	8.3	44.12	50.62	(6.50)
Totals/Averages	$75,006.6 8	$597,310.05	12.6%	126	1,143	11.0%	53.65[b]	43.07[b]	10.58

NA: Not Applicable. [a] Weighted average recovery rates for each year. [b] Arithmetic average of the weighted average

Recovery Rates on Distressed Exchanges

Because DEs are not as dramatic a reflection of a firm's distressed status as a bankruptcy or nonpayment of cash interest on debt, one might expect the recovery rate on DE defaults to be higher than other, more serious distressed situations. Of course, one reason for the larger recoveries in DEs is that lenders need to be offered a "premium" in order to be persuaded to participate in the exchange.

Figure 10 shows the arithmetic average recovery rate on all DE defaults was 53.7% for 1984–2011 (first six months), compared to 43.1% for all defaults, and 36.7% for all non-DE defaults (not shown). Compared to year-end 2010, the first-half 2011 recovery rate on DEs equaled 76.7% versus 65.6%, and 54.9% versus 29.9% on non-DE defaults. 2011's calculations are based on a relatively smaller number of observations which have significantly higher than average recovery rates.

Age of Defaults

Figure 11 summarizes the distribution of defaults after original issuance from 1991 through the first half of 2011. The defaults thus far in 2011 have not, for the most part, closely followed the normal pattern of low defaults in the first year after issuance, followed by high relative default rates in years two through five. In fact, only 27% of the defaults occurred within four years after issuance, while the remaining 73% took place within five to eight years after issuance. Of note, however, is the fact that the number of observations (15 year-to-date) is extremely limited. Figure 12 shows the long-term historical pattern, highlighting the most vulnerable years as two through five.

Figure 11. Distribution of Years to Default from Original Issuance Date (By Years of Default), 1991–2Q 11

	1991		1992		1993/1994		1995		1996/1997		1998		1999	
Years to Default	No. of Issues	% of Total	No. of Issues	% of Total	No. of Issues	% of Total	No. of Issues	% of Total	No. of Issues	% of Total	No. of Issues	% of Total	No. of Issues	% of Total
1	0	0	0	0	3	8	1	3	7	14	2	6	32	26
2	18	13	0	0	6	16	9	28	7	14	5	15	37	30
3	26	19	7	13	5	14	7	22	7	14	10	30	15	12
4	29	21	10	19	2	5	3	9	17	36	3	9	14	11
5	35	26	8	15	4	11	1	3	4	8	10	30	7	6
6	10	7	12	22	8	22	2	6	5	10	2	6	8	6
7	4	3	5	9	7	19	2	6	0	0	1	3	10	8
8	10	7	4	7	0	0	2	6	0	0	0	0	2	2
9	3	2	0	0	0	0	4	13	0	0	0	0	0	0
10+	2	1	8	15	2	5	1	3	2	4	0	0	0	0
Total	**137**	**100**	**54**	**100**	**37**	**100**	**32**	**100**	**49**	**100**	**33**	**100**	**125**	**100**

Figure 11. Distribution of Years to Default from Original Issuance Date (By Years of Default), 1991–2Q 11 (Continued)

	2000		2001		2002		2003		2004		2005		2006/2007	
Years to Default	No. of Issues	% of Total	No. of Issues	% of Total	No. of Issues	% of Total	No. of Issues	% of Total	No. of Issues	% of Total	No. of Issues	% of Total	No. of Issues	% of Total
1	19	10	40	12	29	8	18	9	8	10	16	9	3	3
2	51	28	69	21	51	15	30	15	7	9	13	7	5	6
3	56	31	87	26	61	18	26	13	8	10	9	6	12	14
4	14	8	65	19	56	16	23	11	6	8	22	12	14	16
5	13	7	27	8	45	13	40	20	10	13	14	8	7	8
6	5	3	14	4	21	6	20	10	16	21	17	9	13	15
7	12	7	21	6	8	2	25	12	9	12	13	7	8	9
8	4	2	5	1	7	2	3	1	6	8	11	6	12	14
9	3	2	4	1	12	3	5	2	1	1	5	3	7	8
10+	6	3	3	1	54	16	13	6	6	8	64	34	6	7
Total	**183**	**100**	**335**	**100**	**344**	**100**	**203**	**100**	**77**	**100**	**184**	**100**	**87**	**100**

Figure 11. Distribution of Years to Default from Original Issuance Date (By Years of Default), 1991–2Q 11 (Continued)

	2008		2009		2010		2011 (2Q)		1991-2011 (2Q)	
Years to Default	**No. of Issues**	% of **Total**	**No. of Issues**	**% of Total**	**No. of Issues**	**% of Total**	**No. of Issues**	**% of Total**	**No. of Issues**	**% of Total**
1	9	6	20	5	1	2	0	0	208	8
2	18	12	39	10	6	11	1	7	372	15
3	34	22	66	16	12	22	2	13	450	18
4	30	19	61	15	9	16	1	7	379	15
5	20	13	51	13	6	11	4	27	306	12
6	10	6	58	14	5	9	3	20	229	9
7	9	6	15	4	9	16	2	13	160	6
8	6	4	18	4	2	4	2	13	94	4
9	7	5	16	5	2	4	0	0	69	3
10+	11	7	62	15	3	5	0	0	243	10
Total	**154**	**100**	**406**	**100**	**55**	**100**	**15**	**100**	**2,510**	**100**

Source: NYU Salomon Center.

Figure 12. Distribution of Years to Default From Original Issuance Date: Summary Chart, 1991–2Q 11

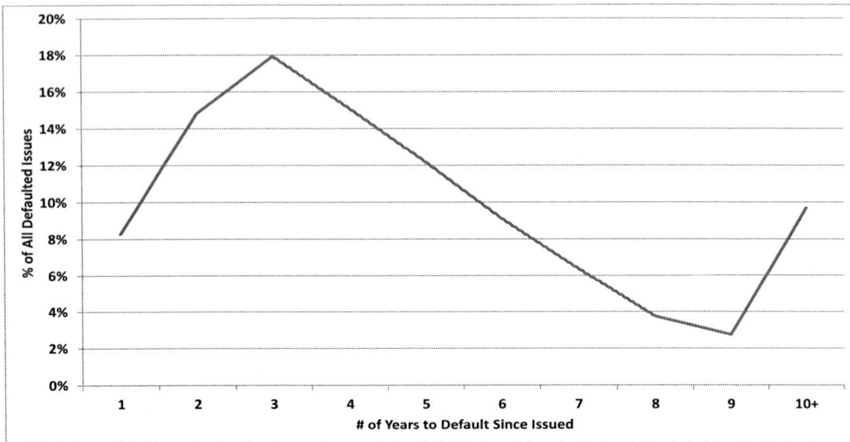

Source: NYU Salomon Center.

Returns, Yields, and Spreads

Figure 13 shows the return on high-yield bonds through the first six months of 2011 was 4.98%. The excess return to 10-yr US Treasury bonds was 1.88%, 257bp less than last quarter-end, and 346bp lower than one year earlier.

Figure 13. Annual Returns, Yields, and Spreads on 10-Yr Treasury and High-Yield Bonds,[a] 1978–2Q 2011

	Return (%)			Yield To Maturity (%)		
Year	**HY**	**Treasury**	**Excess**	**HY**	**Treasury**	**Spread**
2011 (6/30)	4.98	3.10	1.88	7.64	3.16	4.48
2010	14.32	8.10	6.22	7.87	3.29	4.58
2009	55.19	(9.92)	65.11	8.97	3.84	5.13
2008	(25.91)	20.30	(46.21)	19.53	2.22	17.31
2007	1.83	9.77	(7.95)	9.69	4.03	5.66
2006	11.85	1.37	10.47	7.82	4.70	3.11
2005	2.08	2.04	0.04	8.44	4.39	4.05
2004	10.79	4.87	5.92	7.35	4.21	3.14
2003	30.62	1.25	29.37	8.00	4.26	3.74
2002	(1.53)	14.66	(16.19)	12.38	3.82	8.56
2001	5.44	4.01	1.43	12.31	5.04	7.27

Figure 13. (Continued)

	Return (%)			Yield To Maturity (%)		
Year	HY	Treasury	Excess	HY	Treasury	Spread
2000	(5.68)	14.45	(20.13)	14.56	5.12	9.44
1999	1.73	(8.41)	10.14	11.41	6.44	4.97
1998	4.04	12.77	(8.73)	10.04	4.65	5.39
1997	14.27	11.16	3.11	9.20	5.75	3.45
1996	11.24	0.04	11.20	9.58	6.42	3.16
1995	22.40	23.58	(1.18)	9.76	5.58	4.18
1994	(2.55)	(8.29)	5.74	11.50	7.83	3.67
1993	18.33	12.08	6.25	9.08	5.80	3.28
1992	18.29	6.50	11.79	10.44	6.69	3.75
1991	43.23	17.18	26.05	12.56	6.70	5.86
1990	(8.46)	6.88	(15.34)	18.57	8.07	10.50
1989	1.98	16.72	(14.74)	15.17	7.93	7.24
1988	15.25	6.34	8.91	13.70	9.15	4.55
1987	4.57	(2.67)	7.24	13.89	8.83	5.06
1986	16.50	24.08	(7.58)	12.67	7.21	5.46
1985	26.08	31.54	(5.46)	13.50	8.99	4.51
1984	8.50	14.82	(6.32)	14.97	11.87	3.10
1983	21.80	2.23	19.57	15.74	10.70	5.04
1982	32.45	42.08	(9.63)	17.84	13.86	3.98
1981	7.56	0.48	7.08	15.97	12.08	3.89
1980	(1.00)	(2.96)	1.96	13.46	10.23	3.23
1979	3.69	(0.86)	4.55	12.07	9.13	2.94
1978	7.57	(1.11)	8.68	10.92	8.11	2.81
Arithmetic Annual Average						
1978-2010	11.11	8.34	2.77	12.09	6.88	5.21
Standard Deviation	15.34	11.55	18.06	3.24	2.81	2.88
Compound Annual Average						
1978-2010	10.10	7.76	2.34			

[a] End-of-year yields. Source: Citi Yieldbook and authors' compilations.

Spreads for high-yield bonds over the same 10-yr Treasury benchmark (on a yield-to-maturity basis) were 4.48% as of the end of June, widening 55bp from the end of the first-quarter 2011[5]. This yield-spread gradually increased during the quarter, reaching its highest level of the year on June 24th (4.85%), before declining slightly to end the month at a lower level (Figure 14).

[5] Please note that we have always used the yield-to-maturity spread, not the now more commonly cited option-adjusted-spread (OAS). The latter is usually about 100 basis points higher than our measure.

Figure 14. Spread Between High-Yield Bonds YTM and 10-Yr Treasury Notes, Jun 2007 – Jun 2011

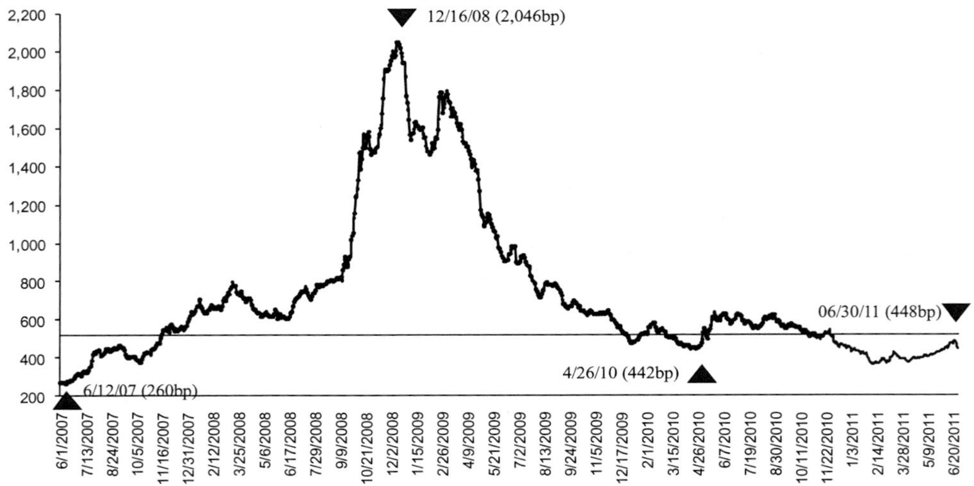

Source: Citi Yieldbook Index Data.

A Continuing Investment Dilemma

Normally, in a credit environment of extremely low default risk, both in terms of recent and near-term future estimates, yield spreads should be below average and the outlook for risky debt markets fairly bullish. The yield spread at the end of the second-quarter 2011 (Figure 14) is below average at 448bp (vs. 521bp average), but only slightly so. However, we feel that there is still a great deal of risk and uncertainty about the future due to concerns about the sluggish growth in the U.S. economy, European sovereign and banking default risk, interest rate increases, the refinancing needs of the federal and municipal government sectors in the U.S., and the deteriorating credit quality of new-issue bond and loan financings, especially high-yield and leveraged loans (Figure 15). These risks would seem to justify at least an average required return, risk premium situation. Indeed, if anything, yield spreads appear to us slightly below average for the risks going forward, especially the European debt crisis (see below).

Figure 15. Major Risks Going Forward (For 2011)

- Real Economy – Primarily U.S. (Double Dip?): Impact on Default Rates, Credit Availability & Credit Quality
- Sovereign Debt Crisis-Europe
    - Looming Corporate Defaults
- Contagion Between Markets – Debt and Equity
- Maturity Schedule on Private and Public Debt
- Lowering of Credit Quality of Newly Issued High-Yield Bonds
- U.S. Municipal Bond & Federal Government Default Risk
- Uncertainties (non-quantifiable)

Source: E. Altman, NYU Salomon Center.

The stock market looks undervalued, with P/E ratios relatively low, excellent growth in many corporate profits, albeit mainly from cost-cutting, and interest rates still at extremely low levels. With all of the above in mind, one could be fairly bullish about the stock market's prospects, yet bearish, or at least not very optimistic about bond markets, especially high-yield. Considering investment choices between various capital markets, it is instructive to observe historical correlations with particular scrutiny of the most recent past.

Figure 16 shows the correlation between the S&P 500 stock index monthly returns vs. both high-yield and defaulted debt indexes. The latter are based on our Altman NYU-Salomon Center Defaulted Bond and the

Combined Defaulted Bond and Bank Loan Indexes. The periods covered are the last three stressed credit cycles: 1990/1991, 2001/2002, and the most recent 2008/2009 (through March). We also observe the correlations for the recovery period since April 2009, and other past recoveries (not shown here), as well as the entire sample period 1987-2011 (June). The results are quite startling.

Typically during stressed credit cycles (and also the subsequent recovery), correlations between the stock market and risky debt markets are quite low - - 12% in 1990/1991, 23% in 2001/2002, and, not shown, -16% and 43% in their subsequent recoveries. Over the entire sample period since we have been tracking defaulted debt as an asset class (1987–present), the correlation between the S&P 500 and defaulted bond returns is only 40%, and a moderate 58% for the high-yield market and stock market returns. However, in the most recent economic and financial collapse of 2008–early 2009, the latter's correlation spiked enormously to 73% and it has continued in the subsequent recovery at 68%. In the most recent cycle (April 2010 – June 2011), the correlation between defaulted bonds and bank loans and the S&P 500 Stock Index was 73% and 80% between the S&P 500 and Citi's High-Yield Bond Index! On any given day, it is likely that if there is bad news about financial or default related uncertainties, both risky bond and stock markets decline, with a flight to quality, and the opposite is true if the news is positive.

Our dilemma, much as it has been for the past year, is that if we are to be bearish about risky debt in the near future, how can we be bullish about the stock market? A more positive spin on the correlation pattern is that the optimistic stock market outlook will dominate bond market uncertainties and both will prosper in the near-term future.

Figure 16. Total Monthly Return Correlations on Various Asset Class Indexes during Stressed and Recovery Credit Cycles

		Citi HY Index	S&P 500 Stock Index
Stressed Cycle I[a] 01/1990 – 12/1991 (24 obs.)	Defaulted Bond Index	68%	12%
	S&P 500 Stock Index	48%	
Stressed Cycle II[b] 01/2001 – 12/2002 (24 obs.)	Defaulted Bond and Bank Loan Index	76%	23%
	S&P 500 Stock Index	54%	
Stressed Cycle III 01/2008 – 03/2009 (15 obs.)	Defaulted Bond and Bank Loan Index	80%	73%
	S&P 500 Stock Index	73%	
Recovery Cycle 04/2009 – 06/2011 (27 obs.)	Defaulted Bond and Bank Loan Index	72%	66%
	S&P 500 Stock Index	68%	
Full Sample Period 01/1987 – 06/2011 (294 obs.)	Defaulted Bond and Bank Loan Index	65%	40%
	S&P 500 Stock Index	58%	
Most Recent Cycle 04/2010 – 06/2011 (15 obs.)	Defaulted Bond and Bank Loan Index	81%	73%
	S&P 500 Stock Index	80%	

[a] Correlation between Defaulted Bond Index and S&P 500 during recovery cycle was -16%.

[b] Correlation between Defaulted Bond and Bank Loan Index and S&P 500 during recovery cycle was 43%, and the Defaulted Bond Index and the S&P was 49%.
Source: E. Altman, NYU Salomon Center.

European Sovereign Debt Crisis

For some time now, we have emphasized that the European sovereign debt crisis was looming as the most critical area for credit markets, with likely implications for global real economic growth. There is now no doubt about this and the European authorities have finally, and quite reluctantly, accepted the reality of a Greek default and have enhanced the safeguards against a further contagion to other minor, and even major, Euro economies. The proclamations in the week of July 18, 2011 that private sector banks and other lenders would share in the burden of "propping-up" Greece by "accepting" a haircut on their Greek government investments of approximately 21% were greeted quite positively by the markets, and spreads and interest rates, as well as the CDS market, rallied. While the Greek debt restructuring, probably to be completed in the early fall, will trigger a "Selective Default" (S&P), it has already triggered a "Restricted Default" (Fitch), and has resulted in a downgrade to one notch above default (Ca) (Moody's); these labels will last for only a very short period. Once an exchange of new bonds for the old obligations occurs, the new bonds will likely trade again as a CCC (Caa) credit. ISDA will not treat this "consensual" arrangement as a CDS default event. Therefore, the pressure is off, at least temporarily, in regards to the European debt crisis and the question of the Euro's survival.

We emphasize several cautions with getting too euphoric about the arrangements for the first "developed" country default in a very long time (over half a century). The reduction of near-term stress in regards to the debt of Greece, Portugal, Ireland, and even Spain and Italy is apparent, although the market's perception of default likelihood amongst the PIIGS countries is still considerable. Figure 17 shows the five-year implied probability of default (PD) derived from CDS market spreads from January 2009 through July 22, 2011 (just after the latest round of rescue and distressed exchanges) amongst the "big-five" vulnerable countries (smaller entities, like Cyprus, are not included). Notice the hierarchy of PDs for all countries going from the 10-20% range in early 2009 to as high as 88.22% for Greece just before the latest rescue plan (dropping to 74.52% after the announcement), to Portugal and Ireland's (64%), with Spain's pinnacle reaching 27.5% and Italy as high as 23.7%[6]. So, will the contagion spread to countries outside of Greece, and what are the implications of the crisis to other than the Euro-Sovereign markets?

We still feel that there is a considerable chance that the crisis will continue to spread to other than Greece, the only country stated to be covered directly by the latest round of rescue policies. Additionally, what is also clear is that the recent near collapse of the Italian bond market in value helped to move Euro officials to act decisively. Indeed, as we have written, the ultimate battle to preserve the Euro may very well take place on the picturesque shores of Italy ("Final Battle for the Euro Will be Fought on Italy's Shores", *Financial Times*, June 21, 2011). If this crisis does spread to Italy, even more than the minor-crisis of July, we believe the results favor Italy because of its fundamental strengths compared to the

[6] After the latest rescue announcement, the remaining countries noted in Figure 17 also enjoyed a rally in their costs of financing and CDS spreads. Note that in the latter, our PDs assume a 40% recovery rate (60% loss).

other four PIIGS countries. However, the result is far from certain, and spreads will widen, in our opinion.

Fundamental Issues and Bottom-Up Approach to Sovereign Risk

Which brings us to the underlying problems in Europe; the fact that several nations in the Euro-block have chronic, fundamental, competitive infirmities that financial bailouts will ultimately find very difficult to forestall a full-scale default. Such large problems will not, in this case, be rectified by traditional means – massive write-offs of debt and currency devaluation, unless the vulnerable countries exit the Euro-block and creditors sustain mark-to-market losses. At least for the moment, these risks have been blunted and the hope is that significant austerity programs, debt forgiveness, buy-backs, and improving Euro-growth in the peripheral countries will solve the chronic malaise.

We are not all convinced that fundamental, non-competitive conditions can be easily reversed. The problems in Europe, combined with a stubbornly relatively strong Euro, will add to the already considerable stress on the private financial and non-financial sectors of these countries. The likely result will be considerable corporate stress and an increase in defaults and bankruptcies in the private sector, which will put a strain on each nation's creditors and bankruptcy judicial systems.

Figure 17. Five-Year Implied Probabilities of Default (PD)[a] from Capital Market CDS Spreads, Jan 2009 - Jul 22, 2011[b]

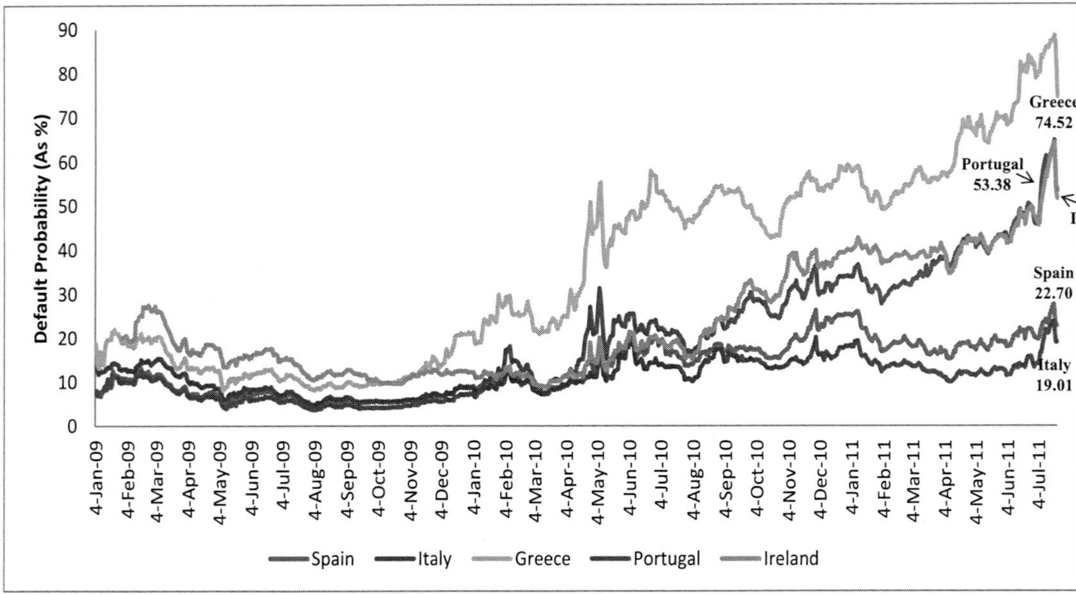

[a] Assumes 40% Recovery Rate. PD computed as $1\text{-}e^{(-5*s/(1-R))}$. [b] On July 19, 2011, PDs for all countries peaked as follows: Greece 88.22, Portugal 64.74, Ireland 64.23, Spain 27.54, and Italy 23.74.
Sources: Bloomberg and NYU Salomon Center.

In order to assess the health of the sovereign, we have proposed a type of "bottom-up" approach that measures and monitors the health of the private sector. As described[7], we developed an index of private sector health by calculating a type of median "Z-Score" (actually Z-Metrics) 5-year, Sovereign PD and compared the results amongst 11 European countries and the U.S. A unique default probability model is used, each for non-financial and for banks. The results are shown in Figure 18. Note that as of year-end 2010, Greece's median, non-financial firm 5-Year PD was the highest (worst) of all 12 sovereign nations (15.28%), as was its weighted average of non-financial and financial PD (16.45% ranked last, 12th). Greece was followed by Portugal (11), Ireland (10), Italy (9) and Spain (8). The top (best) two countries were the Netherlands and Sweden. These results are essentially consistent with the ranks of implied PDs from the CDS market (except for the rank of Belgium), although the median PD is much lower than the CDS implied PD for all PIIGS countries, excluding Italy where they were similar. Admittedly, our *PD,* private sector estimates are based on listed firms only. We hope that many of the world's Central Banks or Ministries of Finance will monitor the health of the private, non-listed company population.

Our PD measure was also a salient, early warning metric at the end of 2008, when all of these countries were investment grade and the implied PDs from financial markets e.g. CDS market) were not that concerned with the Euro situation. We expect that with the newly legislated austerity programs across the board in Europe, particularly Greece, Portugal, Ireland, and Italy, our measure of sovereign risk will deteriorate further. We will update our results for year-end 2011.

---

[7] E. Altman & H. Rijken (2011) "Toward a Bottom-Up Approach to Assessing Sovereign Default Risk" *Journal of Applied Corporate Finance*, winter.

Figure 18. Weighted Average Median Five-Year (PD) for Listed Non-Financial[a] and Banking Firms[b] (Europe and U.S.), 2010

	Non-Financial Firms		Banking Firms					
Country	PD (%)	Weight	PD (%)	Weight	Weighted Average (%)	Rank	CDS Spread PD (%)[c]	Rank
Netherlands	3.56	0.977	11.1	0.023	3.73	1	2.03	1
Sweden	3.71	0.984	17.3	0.016	3.93	2	2.25	2
Belgium	3.85	0.972	12.4	0.028	4.21	3	11.12	8
France	4.36	0.986	14.0	0.014	4.49	4	4.51	5
U.K.	4.28	0.977	15.5	0.023	4.54	5	4.73	6
Germany	4.63	0.983	13.1	0.017	4.77	6	2.50	3
U.S.A.	3.65	0.837	13.8	0.163	5.30	7	3.79	4
Spain	7.39	0.948	10.9	0.052	7.57	8	14.80	9
Italy	7.29	0.906	20.0	0.094	8.48	9	9.16	7
Ireland	3.72	0.906	77.6	0.094	10.65	10	41.44	11
Portugal	10.67	0.971	12.1	0.029	10.71	11	41.00	10
Greece	15.28	0.921	30.1	0.079	16.45	12	70.66	12

[a] Based on the Z-Metrics Probability Model. [b] Based on Altman-Rijken Model (Preliminary). [c] PD based on the CDS Spread as of 4/26/11.

The other risks, itemized in Figure 15, are related to the U.S. economy, including the nation's sluggish growth in 2011, contagion between equity and risky debt ,markets (Figure 16), maturity schedules (see discussion below), lowering of credit quality of newly issued High-Yield bonds (see Figure 23, below), Municipal Bond Market risks and the Federal Government's debt ceiling impasse. The latter will most likely be settled, at least temporarily, before the August 2nd (or is it August 10th?) debt-ceiling deadline, but our nation's debt/GDP ratio is likely to rise considerably over the next two decades unless above average growth can be sustained.

All things considered, there are many factors which cause spreads to be higher than near-term and the next one year's forecasted default rates (see below) would normally imply. Spreads will move in either direction going forward based on whether these risks manifest into realities and/or just increase, or become lessened through aggressive and/or enlightened Government intervention.

New Issues and Other Changes in the High-Yield Market

US high-yield bond issuance in the second quarter was $82.3 billion, notably greater than in the same period last year ($33.7 billion), and the highest ever amount of quarterly new issuance on record. There was, however, a noticeable dip in the last month (June) compared to the first two months of the quarter. In contrast, however, leveraged loan issuance decreased in the second quarter to $116.4 billion, compared to approximately $141.2 billion during the prior quarter, but was still significantly higher than the $66.9 billion issued during the second quarter of 2010. Though both the bond and loan markets had significant amounts of new issuance through the first-half 2011, the loan market appeared to be the primary vehicle used by high-yield, risky debt issuers. This has been a very gradual switch from the source of risky debt issuance in 2009; banks seem intent on catching up to bond markets, especially in the refinancing of near-term maturing leveraged loans.

The size of the high-yield bond market, adjusting for fallen angels, rising stars, defaults, and other changes, was approximately $1.35 trillion at the end of June 2011, according to our calculations. This represents an increase from three months earlier of approximately $48 billion, primarily attributable to the dollar amount of newly issued debt greatly exceeding defaults and other exits from the market. The amount of upgrades exceeded downgrades indicating a continuing perceived improvement in credit fundamentals.

Figure 19. Market Changes and Size of the High-Yield Bond Market, 2Q 11 (Dollars in Billions)

	YTD ($)	
Size of Market (as of December 2010)	1,277.8	
New Issues	161.7	
Fallen Angels	16.7	a
Rising Stars	(13.2)	b
Defaults	(2.9)	
Calls	(40.1)	
Repurchases/Tenders	(42.1)	
Maturities	(17.7)	
Exchanges	14.4	
Size of Market (as of June 2011)	**1,354.6**	

[a] First downgrade to non-investment grade by either Moody's or S&P. [b] Must be investment grade with both Moody's and S&P.
Sources: Credit Suisse and NYU Salomon Center.

The Leveraging of Corporate America

Over the past 27 months, we have witnessed an enormous amount of new issuance in both the investment grade and high-yield bond markets as well as the awakening of the leveraged loans market. Indeed, new issuance of high-yield bonds in 2010 broke the previous record set a year earlier, and if the first six months of 2011 are any indication, a new record will be set again this year. These developments are all the more astounding given the fact that the default rate in 2009 was the second highest ever (see Figure 1) and we just recently went through the most challenging credit cycle since the great depression. What accounts for this impressive recovery in issuer appetite for leverage and also investor optimism in absorbing this huge new issuance?

We can identify at least four reasons to explain the substantial leveraging of corporate America (or releveraging as some analysts point out that the U.S. economy leveraged up dramatically prior to the credit meltdown in 2007 - 2008). These four include:

1. Refinancing needs of existing high-yield bonds and leveraged loans,
2. Unprecedented low interest rates,
3. Attempts to sustain and enhance return-on-equity gains in recent quarters, and
4. Maintaining a cash hoard to participate in M&A activity in the near future.

Refinancing

Estimates of the use of new high-yield bond issues in 2009, 2010, and so far in 2011, show the enormous receptivity for investors in both high-yield bonds and leveraged loans to accept new, longer maturity bonds to replace those debts that were set to mature in 2010–2012. Thus far, new refinancings seem to have been successful in moving maturities out to a further point. Indeed, in just the period from April to September 2010, the LSTA reports that the *reduction* in leveraged loans maturing in 2009–2013 was about $17 billion, $20 billion, $43 billion, $72 billion and $11 billion, respectively, with the largest increase in loan maturities moved to 2015. Similar reductions in near-term maturity are observable for high-yield bonds.

A recent maturity schedule of high-yield bonds and leveraged loans shows the enormous influence of current liquidity conditions and the reduction of near-term maturities and default risk. According to JP Morgan (as of May 31, 2011), over $500 billion of maturing leveraged debt ($103 billion of HY bonds and $409 billion of leveraged loans) originally scheduled to mature in 2012-2014 has been refinanced and extended beyond 2015. While most defaults do not actually occur when a bond issue is scheduled to mature, reduction in near-term maturity risk is still a positive factor.

Critics of these developments point out that short-term adjustment in maturities merely “kick the can down the road” and add to later year uncertainties. Proponents point out that refinancing successes illustrate that many firms’ credit profiles are improving and now is the time to take advantage of the low interest rate “window of opportunity.” The trick is, in our own opinion, not to overdo a good thing. Of course, if firms merely replace existing higher interest debt with lower cost issues, and extend maturities at the same time, then bankruptcy risk, especially in the short-term, will be reduced and expected default rates will be reduced compared to what models based on longer-term dynamics would indicate.

Interest Rates

With the FED available to provide enormous liquidity and with investor appetite for risky debt and higher yielding assets substantial, interest rates have remained low. Figure 13 shows that the yield on 10-year U.S. Treasuries fell from 3.84% at the end of 2009 to 3.29% by year-end 2010, and even further to 3.16% as of the end of June 2011, amongst the lowest levels in our entire 33 years of data. The daily yields during the first half of 2011 have generally remained within this range, though falling as low as 2.87% on June 24th. Only the 2.22% yield at the end of 2008, during the peak of the credit meltdown, was lower. Additionally, the high-yield bond yield-to-maturity level (7.64%) is close to 4.5% below historical averages and is the lowest level since 2004. In fact, in only one year-end instance out of 33 (2004) were yields lower. So, despite record demand for high-yield bonds, interest rates are absolutely and relatively low.

Average yields have dropped despite the increasing risk profile of high-yield bonds. Figure 20 shows the proportion of new issues rated B- or lower by S&P for the first six months of 2011 and annually for 1993–2010. As can be seen, the percentage of new high-yield issuance with ratings B- or lower has moved up from 17.5% in 2008 to 33.2% as of the end of the first-half 2011. This is larger than both the proportion of 25.75% from a year earlier and 26.99% for all of last year, and above the average of 29.47% for the last five years. The current percentage is now above both the historical average and median year-end levels, and similar to what it was in 2005/2006.

Figure 20. Percentage of New High-Yield Issuance Rated B- or Below, 1993–2Q 2011 (Based on the Amount of Issuance)

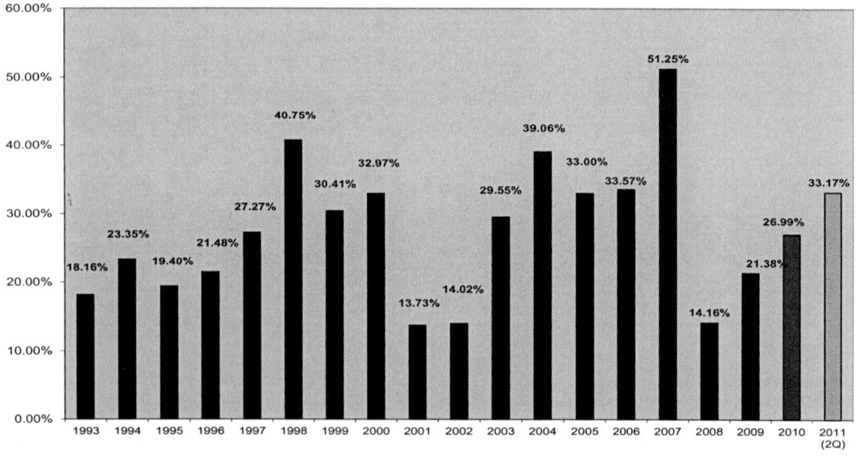

Source: Standard and Poor's Global Fixed Income Research.

ROE Enhancement

One of the promising aspects of the current high-yield and equity environment is the increase in earnings and interest coverage levels of U.S. companies. Despite rising leverage levels, near-term default risk seems to be lessening in tandem with actual falling default levels. Since there is little new investment taking place beyond inventory replacement and also with lackluster consumer demand, earnings increases in 2009 and 2010 are more than likely a function of cost cuts and rising leverage levels. With cost-cutting likely to now be fully exhausted, any continued earnings enhancements are likely to come from (1) what is known as "trading on the equity," i.e. earnings before interest and after taxes that are higher than the cost of new debt and (2) M&A activity (our next factor). Again, skeptics of the strategy point out the double-edged sword of leverage – increased potential returns but higher default risk if earnings levels fall below the cost of debt.

M&A Activity

Our final motivation for corporate America's appetite for higher leverage is cheap financing for M&A activity. Not only is debt financing relatively cheap today, but also it is non-dilutive for the potential acquirers' equity. There are already signs of a pickup in M&A activity and in private equity funds acquisitions, especially in the middle-market arena. We continue to expect this merger trend to accelerate as firms seek ways to sustain and enhance ROE performance.

Proportion and Size of Defaulted and Distressed Public and Private Debt

The defaulted and distressed debt segment of the high-yield and defaulted debt market in the United States was about 21.2% at the end of the first half of 2011, higher than the proportion of 21.0% three months earlier, but well below the combined percentage (30.0%) of one year earlier (Figure 21). The primary reason for the steady decrease since December 31, 2008 had been the drop in the distress ratio of issues trading at least 1,000bp over the 10-yr US Treasury bond. This ratio dropped from 6.3% at the end of 2010 to 4.2% at the end of the first quarter of 2011, but, as happened during the same period one year earlier, "rebounded" to 6.0% during the second quarter. This 6.0% level is based on the combined high-yield and defaulted bond population. The distress ratio for just the high-yield market was 7.1%.[8]

The defaulted bond total is calculated by adding the new defaults of 2011 ($2.92 billion) to the existing defaulted bonds as of year-end 2010, subtracting the bonds of firms whose reorganization plans were deemed effective and who have emerged from Chapter 11 ($16.19 billion — see Appendix G) and, finally, by deducting the value of bonds that defaulted as part of a distressed exchange (DE) ($0.57 billion). In the first half of 2011, the defaulted bond proportion decreased slightly to 15.1%, as the amount of emergences greatly exceeded new, non DE defaults.

Figure 21. Defaulted and Distressed[a] Debt as a Percentage of Total High-Yield Plus Defaulted Debt Market,[b] 1990–2Q 2011[c]

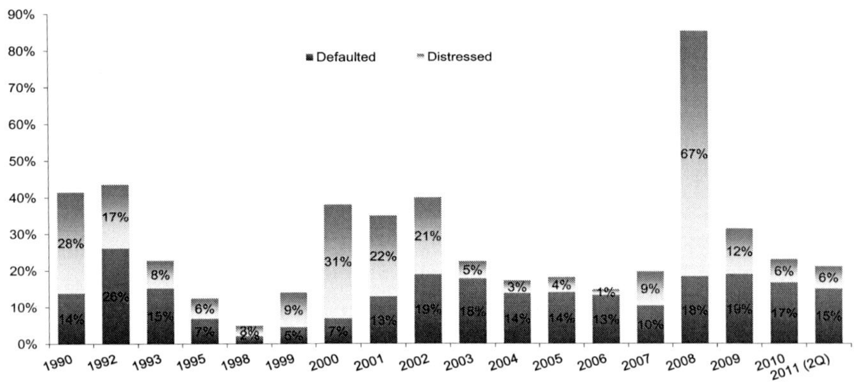

[a] Defined as the option-adjusted spread greater than or equal to 1,000bp over comparable-duration Treasuries.
[b] $1.596 trillion as of June 30, 2011. c Some years not available as no estimates were attempted.
Source: NYU Salomon Center and Banc of America Securities.

Figure 22 shows our estimate of the size of the defaulted and distressed debt markets for both public and privately issued debt. At $241.4 billion as

[8] A study by J. Gonzalez-Heres, P. Chen and S. Shin, "Revisiting the Altman Definition of Distressed Debt and a New Mechanism for Measuring the Liquidity Premium of the High Yield Market", *Journal of Fixed Income*, Fall 2010, shows that about 50% of all distress rated firms default within about four years. The paper also discusses and analyzes the importance of market liquidity in explaining the volatility in the distressed ratio.

of June 30, 2011, the face value amount of public defaulted bonds was $13.8 billion less than at year-end 2010 ($255.3 billion).

The distressed proportion of the total high-yield bond market increased in the second quarter as spreads widened. The estimated face value amount of distressed public debt is $96.5 billion, up by 47% in the quarter from a first quarter total of $65.7 billion, but down 47% from one year (June 2010) earlier ($183.2 billion).

Our private debt estimate is based on a 2.0:1 ratio of private-to-public debt among troubled companies. Applying this ratio to our public debt totals, we estimate that the face value of private defaulted and distressed debt is $675.9 billion (Figure 22). The total face value of the combined public and private defaulted and distressed debt amounted to $1.0 trillion as of June 30, 2011, up $83.1 billion in one quarter, but down by a staggering $547.0 billion from one year earlier.

Our market value estimates are based on current market conditions for public and private bond and loan markets, and our Altman-Kuehne indexes for these securities. Consistent with our observations of both newly defaulted and existing defaulted loan issues in our index, we have chosen to decrease our market-value ratio on defaulted private debt from the first-quarter 2011, but have left the other ratios unchanged. When applied, the average price of our public bonds and private loans indexes results in a market value estimate of defaulted and distressed debt of about $562.4 billion — again, up slightly from the prior quarter, but down considerably from twelve months earlier.

Figure 23 shows our estimates for the total face and market values of defaulted and distressed debt from 1990–2011. The current volumes are lower in size to those observed at the end of 2010, but are still larger than any other year in our data series prior to 2008. The dollars under management that comprise the demand for these securities and other distressed assets has increased considerably over the past two years, however, mainly due to positive returns since 2009 and increased flows into distressed funds.

Figure 22. Estimated Face and Market Values of Defaulted and Distressed Debt, 2009–2Q 2011, (Dollars in Billions)

	Face Value ($)			Market Value ($)			
	31 Dec 09	**31 Dec 10**	**30 Jun 11**	**31 Dec 09**	**31 Dec 10**	**30 Jun 11**	**Market/ Face Ratio[d]**
Public Debt							
Defaulted	279.87	255.27	241.42 a	97.95	102.11	84.50	0.35
Distressed	180.95	97.32	96.55 b	135.71	68.12	67.58	0.70
Total Public	460.82	352.59	337.96	233.67	170.23	152.08	
Private Debt							
Defaulted	699.67	510.54	482.83 c	419.80	280.79	265.56 c	0.55
Distressed	452.38	194.64	193.09 c	361.90	145.98	144.82 c	0.75
Total Private	**1,152.05**	**705.17**	**675.92**	**781.70**	**426.77**	**410.38**	
Total Public and Private	**1,612.86**	**1,057.76**	**1,013.88**	**1,015.37**	**597.00**	**562.45**	

[a] Calculated using: (2010 defaulted population) + (2011 Defaults) - (2011 Emergences) - (2011 Distressed Exchanges).
[b] Based on 7.13% of the high-yield bond market ($1.355 trillion) as of 30 Jun 11. [c] Based on a private/public ratio of 2.0.
Source: NYU Salomon Center and estimates by Professor Edward I. Altman.

Figure 23. Size of the US Defaulted and Distressed Debt Market, 1990–2Q 2011 (Dollars in Billions)

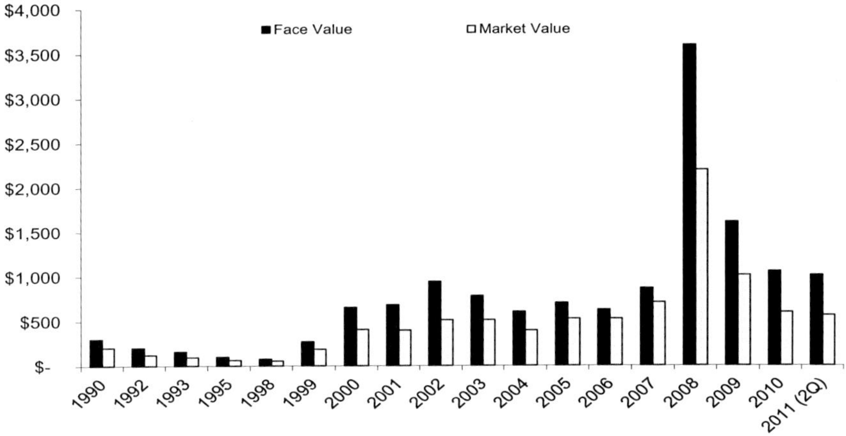

Source: Professor Edward I. Altman estimates and NYU Salomon Center.

Recent Performance of Defaulted Debt

Through the first six months of 2011, the Altman-NYU Salomon Center Defaulted Bond Index was up 7.18%. Defaulted bank loans also provided year-to-date gains of 3.50%. Our combined, long-only index of defaulted bonds and bank loans was up 5.13% for the first six months[9]. Despite a majority of positive monthly returns in the Combined Index for over two years now, the average market/face value ratios for both defaulted bonds and loans remain below historical average levels, indicating upside potential.

Forecasting Default Rates and Recoveries

Forecasting aggregate default and recovery rates is a tricky exercise that can be based on a "bottom-up" approach on individual issues and issuers or a macro, "top-down" approach – or both. For practical and

[9] This compares to an average return for the first-half of 2011 from four Distressed Debt Hedge Fund indexes (Dow Jones/Credit Suisse, Hennessee, HFR, and Van Hedge) of 3.70%. This Hedge Fund index average is based on "net" hedge fund returns, while our Combined Index is "gross" returns.

track-record reasons, we have chosen the top-down approach using both aggregate amounts of new issuance over the last decade stratified by the major ratings categories (mortality statistics) and also point-in-time proportions of issuers by the major non-investment grade, high-yield bond categories. The latter technique is specific only to recessionary results (scenario analysis). Finally, we also analyze the information content of market-based measures, such as yield spreads and distressed ratios, to forecast the near-term default performance of the market. These four techniques, or three in the case of non-recessionary expectations, are then averaged to arrive at our single default rate estimate, although the range of probable outcomes can be observed as well. Our default rate estimates are then used as inputs to form the basis for estimates of aggregate recovery rates on corporate high-yield bond defaults.

Using our standard mortality rate forecasting method for 2008, our forecast of 4.64% for the high-yield bond default rate was remarkably close to the actual 2008 rate, which came in at 4.65% (Figure 24). We then had expected our 2009 default rate forecast would be on the low side, using the same mortality rate methodology. After all, mortality rate incidences of the past had been based on six recession periods covering only about six-and-a-half years of the 39 in our sample period (1971–2009). Therefore, a nonrecessionary, macroeconomic climate dominates our statistics, and with a severe recession in place coming into 2009, we expected the mortality rate methodology to underestimate the actual default results. Indeed, the actual default rate was 10.77% in 2009 compared to our forecast of 7.98%, a respectable under-estimate. Since the mortality method is an actuarial smoothing technique, we know that it will not be sensitive to extreme yearly, abnormal conditions. In 2010, our estimate was considerably higher than the actual default rate as the high-yield bond market was buoyed by exceptional levels of liquidity. For these reasons, we also, when appropriate, consider recession scenario analyses and market-based statistics to provide useful estimates of future results.

Mortality Rate-Based Forecast

Utilizing the updated mortality rate statistics (see our 2010 annual report)[10], and inputting new issuance statistics per rating class over the past ten years, the 2011 default rate estimate was 3.90%, with a recovery rate of about 38% (Figure 24). Our forecast also utilized an estimated expected size of the high-yield bond market for 2011. We update our

---

[10] E. Altman & B. Kuehne "Defaults and Returns in the High-Yield Bond and Distressed Debt Market: The Year 2010 In Review and Outlook", *Paulson & Co.*, February 04, 2011.

mortality statistics annually, so our mid-2012 forecast is the same as the forecast for year-end 2011.

Figure 24. Mortality Rate-Based Forecasts of Default and Recovery Rates in the High-Yield Bond Market, 2008–11

Year	Default Rate	Default Amount ($ Billion)	Recovery Rate
2008 (Forecast)	4.64%	$53.1	39.6%[a]
2008 (Actual)	4.65%	$50.2	42.5%
2009 (Forecast)	7.98%	$92.0	30.0%[a]
2009 (Actual)	10.77%	$124.1	36.1%
2010 (Forecast)	5.06%	$62.5	34.9%
2010 (Actual)	1.13%	$13.8	46.6%
2011 (Forecast)	**3.90%**	**$54.8**	**37.6%**

[a] Based on the log-linear and linear default/recovery rate regressions (see 2010 Annual Report).
Sources: Mortality Rates and Authors' Estimates of Market Size in 2011.

Market-Based Methods for Forecasting Defaults

In 2008, we introduced two alternative methods for forecasting default rates. The first relies on the market's spread on high-yield bonds compared to 10-yr US Treasuries. The second utilizes the proportion of high-yield bonds selling at 1,000bp over 10-yr US Treasuries (distress ratio). In both cases, we regress the market-based measure in period (t) on the subsequent one-year default rate in period (t+1).

Based on the yield-spread regression on December 31, 2007, this method predicted a 4.62% 2008 default rate, essentially a perfect forecast, and as of the end of 2008, it predicted an astounding 20.81% default rate. With an update of the regression model to include 2009's data, we recalculated our originally reported estimated default rate for the 12 months ending December 2010 to be 3.61% (originally 3.89%). As of December 31, 2010, inputting the year-end spread of 4.58% into our updated regression model resulted in a one-year default forecast as of December 2011 of 3.10%. Inputting the second quarter-end spread of 4.48% into our updated regression model as of June 30, 2011 results in a one-year default rate forecast as of June 30, 2012 of 3.01%, lower than the mortality rate forecast.

A second market-based method utilizes the distressed ratio, that is, the proportion of the high-yield bond market trading at least 1,000bp over Treasuries. Inserting the distressed ratio of 7.13% as of June 30, 2011 into our updated regression model reveals an expected 2.52% default rate for the end of the second-quarter 2012.

Figure 25. 2011 and One-Year Default and Recovery Forecasts: Summary of Forecast Models

Model	2011 Default Rate Forecast as of 12/31/2010		Jun. 2012 Default Rate Forecast as of 06/30/2011
Mortality Rate	3.90%		3.90%
Recession Scenarios	n/r		n/r
Yield-Spread	3.10%	b	3.01%
Distressed Ratio	2.59%	c	2.52%
Average of Models	3.20%		3.14%
Recovery Rates[a]	39.8%		40.0%

[a]Based on the log-linear regression, see our Annual Report, February 04, 2011. [b]Based on 12/31/2010 yield-spread of 458.0bp. [c]Based on 12/31/2010 Distressed Ratio of 7.62%. [c]Based on 6/30/2011 yield-spread of 448.3bp. [d]Based on 6/30/2011 Distressed Ratio of 7.13%.
Source: NYU Salomon Center, Citi Yieldbook and Bank of America Merrill Lynch.

Default and Recovery Conclusions

Considering the various forecasting methods, we observe that the forecast is in a relatively narrow range between 2.52% (distressed ratio) and 3.90% (mortality rate). There is no obvious way to reach a consensus from the different techniques, so we simply took an average of the three to obtain our forecasted default rate for the next 12 months (as of June 2012), of 3.14% (Figure 25). Note that we do not utilize a recession scenario technique since most economists estimate now that the probability of a renewed recession over the next 12 months is small, although higher than three or six months ago.

If the default rate turns out to be in the 3% region then, based on past regression results, the recovery rate should average about 40%. However, if the current first half's very low default rate continues for the rest of the year, recoveries will likely stay close to current levels, possibly reaching 60%.

Appendix A

Quarterly Default Rate Comparison: Altman/NYU-Salomon Center (SC) and Moody's U.S. High-Yield Bond Market, 1989–2Q 2011

Quarter	Par Value Bonds Outstandin g ($Bn)	Bonds Defaulted by Quarter ($Bn)	Quarterly Default Rates (%)	Altman/NYU-SC Dollar Based 12-Month Moving Average (%)	Moody's 12-Month U.S. Issuer Based Moving Average (%)
1989					
1Q	165.00	1.15	0.70	2.45	3.25
2Q	172.00	1.40	0.81	2.11	2.70
3Q	189.26	3.07	1.62	3.47	4.39
4Q	185.00	2.49	1.35	4.29	5.93
Total		**8.11**			
1990					
1Q	185.00	4.16	2.25	6.01	7.02
2Q	185.00	2.51	1.36	6.61	8.71
3Q	181.00	6.01	3.32	8.20	9.80
4Q	181.00	5.67	3.13	10.14	10.92
Total		**18.35**			
1991					
1Q	182.00	8.74	4.80	12.67	13.24
2Q	182.00	2.75	1.51	12.73	13.99
3Q	183.00	5.01	2.74	12.18	13.03
4Q	183.00	2.36	1.29	10.31	10.97
Total		**18.86**			
1992					
1Q	183.20	3.33	1.82	7.35	8.33
2Q	151.10	1.26	0.83	6.52	6.54
3Q	163.00	0.37	0.23	4.84	5.84
4Q	151.89	0.59	0.39	3.40	5.73
Total		**5.55**			
1993					
1Q	193.23	0.38	0.20	1.71	5.34
2Q	193.23	1.33	0.69	1.39	4.93
3Q	206.91	0.05	0.03	1.22	4.52
4Q	190.42	0.52	0.27	1.10	3.79
Total		**2.29**			
1994					
1Q	232.60	0.67	0.29	1.35	3.06
2Q	230.00	0.16	0.07	0.60	1.90
3Q	235.00	0.41	0.17	0.76	2.37
4Q	235.00	2.18	0.93	1.45	2.11
Total		**3.42**			

Quarterly Default Rate Comparison: Altman/NYU-Salomon Center (SC) and Moody's U.S. High-Yield Bond Market, 1989–2Q 2011 (Continued)

Quarter	Par Value Bonds Outstanding ($Bn)	Bonds Defaulted by Quarter ($Bn)	Quarterly Default Rates (%)	Altman/NYU-SC Dollar Based 12-Month Moving Average (%)	Moody's 12-Month U.S. Issuer Based Moving Average (%)
1995					
1Q	240.00	0.17	0.07	1.24	1.42
2Q	240.00	1.68	0.70	1.85	2.41
3Q	240.00	0.98	0.41	2.09	2.60
4Q	240.00	1.72	0.72	1.90	3.56
Total		**4.55**			
1996					
1Q	255.00	0.44	0.17	2.01	3.71
2Q	255.00	0.89	0.35	1.58	3.00
3Q	271.00	0.41	0.15	1.36	2.20
4Q	271.00	1.59	0.59	1.23	1.95
Total		**3.34**			
1997					
1Q	296.00	1.85	0.63	1.75	1.87
2Q	318.40	0.60	0.19	1.51	1.92
3Q	335.40	1.48	0.44	1.74	2.33
4Q	335.40	0.27	0.08	1.25	2.20
Total		**4.20**			
1998					
1Q	379.00	2.37	0.63	1.41	2.69
2Q	425.70	1.22	0.29	1.41	3.12
3Q	465.50	1.62	0.35	1.29	2.96
4Q	481.60	2.26	0.47	1.60	3.83
Total		**7.46**			
1999					
1Q	515.00	4.76	0.92	2.05	3.88
2Q	537.20	8.42	1.57	3.31	5.08
3Q	567.40	5.24	0.92	3.85	5.87
4Q	580.00	5.11	0.88	4.15	5.80
Total		**23.53**			
2000					
1Q	584.00	6.06	1.04	4.28	6.36
2Q	595.60	9.97	1.67	4.52	6.61
3Q	597.50	4.32	0.72	4.27	6.64
4Q	608.15	9.95	1.64	5.07	7.03
Total		**30.29**			
2001					
1Q	613.20	18.07	2.95	6.96	7.61
2Q	648.60	12.82	1.98	7.37	7.88
3Q	649.00	14.65	2.26	8.56	9.64
4Q	647.70	18.07	2.79	9.80	10.60
Total		**63.61**			

Quarterly Default Rate Comparison: Altman/NYU-Salomon Center (SC) and Moody's U.S. High-Yield Bond Market, 1989–2Q 2011 (Continued)

Quarter	Par Value Bonds Outstanding ($Bn)	Bonds Defaulted by Quarter ($Bn)	Quarterly Default Rates (%)	Altman/NYU-SC Dollar Based 12-Month Moving Average (%)	Moody's 12-Month U.S. Issuer Based Moving Average (%)
2002					
1Q	669.00	18.54	2.77	9.89	11.00
2Q	674.00	27.07	4.02	11.71	10.03
3Q	757.00	37.48	4.95	15.01	8.63
4Q	756.30	13.77	1.82	12.80	6.96
Total		**96.86**			
2003					
1Q	750.00	7.62	1.02	11.36	5.57
2Q	774.50	14.54	1.88	9.79	5.80
3Q	825.00	13.25	1.61	6.56	5.77
4Q	856.00	3.04	0.36	4.66	5.48
Total		**38.45**			
2004					
1Q	886.00	3.07	0.35	3.96	4.73
2Q	919.60	1.75	0.19	2.38	4.01
3Q	933.10	3.80	0.41	1.27	3.11
4Q	948.50	3.04	0.32	1.25	3.01
Total		**11.66**			
2005					
1Q	939.30	1.68	0.18	1.08	3.02
2Q	952.00	1.87	0.20	1.11	2.42
3Q	1,073.00	20.71	1.93	2.87	2.62
4Q	1,066.10	11.95	1.12	3.37	2.54
Total		**36.21**			
2006					
1Q	1,039.00	3.39	0.33	3.56	2.43
2Q	1,022.35	0.96	0.09	3.47	2.65
3Q	993.60	1.47	0.15	1.71	2.46
4Q	970.40	1.74	0.18	0.76	2.08
Total		**7.56**			
2007					
1Q	1,053.90	0.87	0.08	0.52	1.80
2Q	1,066.80	1.82	0.17	0.56	1.92
3Q	1,075.40	0.88	0.08	0.50	1.67
4Q	1,069.90	1.91	0.18	0.51	0.90
Total		**5.47**			

Quarterly Default Rate Comparison: Altman/NYU-Salomon Center (SC) and Moody's U.S. High-Yield Bond Market, 1989–2Q 2011 (Continued)

Quarter	Par Value Bonds Outstanding ($Bn)	Bonds Defaulted by Quarter ($Bn)	Quarterly Default Rates (%)	Altman/NYU-SC Dollar Based 12-Month Moving Average (%)	Moody's 12-Month U.S. Issuer Based Moving Average (%)
2008					
1Q	1,089.9	3.57	0.33	0.76	1.74
2Q	1,083.4	10.68	0.99	1.56	2.43
3Q	1,091.0	5.02	0.46	1.95	3.40
4Q	1,086.8	31.49	2.90	4.65	4.43
Total		**50.76**			
2009					
1Q	1,083.6	39.86	3.68	8.01	8.12
2Q	1,082.6	44.16	4.08	11.12	11.60
3Q	1,153.0	9.60	0.83	11.56	13.41
4Q	1,177.4	30.51	2.59	10.77	13.22
Total		**124.13**			
2010					
1Q	1,183.0	1.85	0.16	7.31	10.98
2Q	1,210.3	1.03	0.09	3.63	6.29
3Q	1,221.57	5.35	0.44	3.20	3.99
4Q	1,257.78	5.58	0.44	1.13	3.32
Total		**13.81**			
2011					
1Q	**1,277.84**	**1.73**	**0.14**	**1.09**	**2.88**
2Q	**1,306.19**	**1.18**	**0.09**	**1.08**	**2.60**
Total		**2.92**			

Sources: Moody's and NYU Salomon Center (1989–2011).

Appendix B

Defaulted Corporate Straight Bond Issues, 2Q 2011

Company	Bond Issue	Coupon (%)	Maturity Date	Outstanding Amount ($MM)	Default Date
Angiotech Pharmaceuticals, Inc.	Senior sub.	7.75	4/1/2014	250.00	1/30/2011
Angiotech Pharmaceuticals, Inc.[a]	Senior unsecured	4.05	12/1/2013	325.00	1/30/2011
Guitar Center Holdings, Inc.	Senior unsecured	14.09	4/15/2016	401.76	2/24/2011
Sbarro, Inc.	Senior unsecured	10.38	2/1/2015	150.00	3/1/2011
Ahern Rentals, Inc.	Senior secured	9.25	8/15/2013	236.67	3/15/2011
Harry & David Holdings, Inc.[a]	Senior unsecured	5.31	3/1/2012	58.17	3/28/2011
Harry & David Holdings, Inc.	Senior unsecured	9.00	3/1/2013	140.19	3/28/2011
Keystone Automotive Operations, Inc.	Senior unsecured	9.75	11/1/2013	172.70	3/28/2011
Satelites Mexicanos, S.A. de C.V.a	Secured	9.56	11/30/2011	238.24	4/6/2011
Satelites Mexicanos, S.A. de C.V.	Secured	10.13	11/30/2013	197.87	4/6/2011
Perkins & Marie Callender's, Inc.	Senior unsecured	10.00	10/1/2013	190.00	5/1/2011
Perkins & Marie Callender's, Inc.	Secured	14.00	5/31/2013	103.06	6/13/2011
Nebraska Book Company, Inc.	Secured	10.00	12/1/2011	200.00	6/27/2011
Nebraska Book Company, Inc.	Senior unsecured	8.63	3/15/2012	175.00	6/27/2011
Nebraska Book Company, Inc.	Senior disc. notes	11.00	3/15/2013	77.00	6/27/2011
Total				**2,916**	
Total Number of Issues				**15**	
Total Number of Companies				**9**	

[a] FRN.

Source: NYU Salomon Center.

Appendix C

Distressed Exchanges, 2Q 2011

Issuer Name	Distressed Exchange Date	Amount Exchanged ($ Millions)
Guitar Center Holdings, Inc.	2/24/2011	401.76
Keystone Automotive Operations, Inc.	3/28/2011	172.70
Total $ Amount of Distressed Exchanges		**$574.46**
Total Number of Issuers		**2**

Source: NYU Salomon Center.

Appendix D

Leveraged Loan Defaults, 2Q 2011

Company	Default Date
Summit Business Media Holding Co.	26-Jan-11
Sbarro, Inc.	1-Feb-11
Caribe Media, Inc.	4-May-11
Total Number of Companies	**3**

Source: S&P LCD.

Appendix E

2Q 2011 Chapter 11 Filings by Liability Size — Liabilities Greater Than $100 Million (Dollars in Millions)

Company	Date of Filing	Liabilities ($)
MSR Resort & Golf Course, LLC	Feb-11	1,900.00
Borders Group, Inc.	Feb-11	1,293.11
[a]Appleseed's Intermediate	Jan-11	750.00
[a]New Stream Secured Capital, Inc.	Mar-11	750.00
Nebraska Book Company, Inc.	Jun-11	563.97
Satelites Mexicanos, S.A. de	Apr-11	531.64
Terrestar Corp.	Feb-11	494.51
Sbarro, Inc.	Apr-11	486.56
Barnes Bay Development Ltd.	Mar-11	462.00
Jackson Hewitt Tax Service, Inc.	May-11	444.85
Perkins & Marie Callender's,	Jun-11	440.82
Majestic Capital Ltd.	Apr-11	421.76
Constar International, Inc.	Jan-11	414.00
Harry & David Holdings, Inc.	Mar-11	360.83
Hingham Campus, LLC	Jun-11	330.16
DSI Holdings, Inc. (Deb Shops,	Jun-11	271.10
[b]FRE Real Estate, Inc.	Jan-11	250.00
[b]Summit Business Media Holding	Jan-11	250.00
[b]Ultimate Acquisition Partners,	Jan-11	250.00
[b]AES Thames, LLC	Feb-11	250.00
[b]Miramar Real Estate Management,	Mar-11	250.00
[b]Indianapolis Downs, LLC	Apr-11	250.00
[b]KMC Real Estate Investors, LLC	Apr-11	250.00
[b]Waterscape Resort, LLC	Apr-11	250.00
[b]Boewe Bell & Howell Co.	Apr-11	250.00
[b]Scovill Fasteners, Inc.	Apr-11	250.00
[b]Peregrine I, LLC	Apr-11	250.00
[b]Caribe Media, Inc.	May-11	250.00
[b]Wolf Mountain Resorts, LC	May-11	250.00
[b]Hawaii Medical Center	Jun-11	250.00
[b]Los Angeles Dodgers, LLC	Jun-11	250.00
[b]Stellar GT TIC, LLC	Jun-11	250.00
[b]VFF TIC, LLC	Jun-11	250.00
Berkline/Benchcraft Holdings,	May-11	167.50
Southwest Georgia Ethanol, LLC	Feb-11	134.10
GP West, Inc.	Jun-11	132.83
Swiss Chalet, Inc.	May-11	132.74
Seahawk Drilling, Inc.	Feb-11	124.47
Raser Technologies, Inc.	Apr-11	107.80
Total Liabilities		**14,964.75**

[a] Liabilities between $500 million and $1 billion according to petition. Midpoint of range used as estimate.[b] Liabilities of $100-500 million, according to petition. Midpoint of range used as estimate.
Sources: NYU Salomon Center and New Generation Research.

Appendix F

Defaults by Industry, 2Q 2011

Company	Industry
Ahern Rentals, Inc.	Equipment Rental & Leasing - NEC
Angiotech Pharmaceuticals, Inc.	Surgical & Medical Instruments & Apparatus
Guitar Center Holdings, Inc.	Musical Instruments Stores
Harry & David Holdings, Inc.	Retail Stores - NEC
Keystone Automotive Operations, Inc.	Motor Vehicle Supples & New Parts
Nebraska Book Company, Inc.	Book Stores
Perkins & Marie Callender's, Inc.	Retail - Eating Places
Satelites Mexicanos, S.A. de C.V.a	Radiotelephone Communications
Sbarro, Inc.	Retail - Eating Places

Source: NYU Salomon Center

Appendix G

2011 Emergences from Bankruptcy (Dollars in Millions)

	Restructured Bonds ($)
First Quarter	
Advanta Corp.	100
Fairpoint Communications, Inc.	531
General Motors Corp.	10,459
InSight Health Services Holdings Corp.	296
Loehmann's Holdings, Inc.	110
Tronox, Inc.	350
Total First Quarter	**$11,846**
Second Quarter	
Colonial Bancgroup, Inc.	887
Constar International, Inc.	395
Molecular Insight Pharmaceuticals, Inc.	199
Satelites Mexicanos S.A. de C.V.	436
Station Casinos, Inc.	2,300
Wolverine Tube, Inc.	131
Colonial Bancgroup, Inc.	887
Total Second Quarter	**4,348**
Total	**$16,194**

CONCLUSION

The First International Conference on Credit Analysis and Risk Management was an outstanding success in bringing together credit market experts from all over the world to share their knowledge with each other. The wisdom of the individuals was thereby synergized. The focus on the evaluation of individual debts made it a truly unique experience, and it is hoped that this book will further advance research and teaching of credit analysis.

A second conference is being planned for January 3-5, 2013 in Basel, Switzerland, where even more insights into debt markets may be obtained. For updated information on that second conference, please visit the website at http://www.oakland.edu/internationalcreditconference